D0203922

THE EQUAL RIGHTS AMENDMENT

The Equal Rights Amendment Project was created in 1974 by a grant given to the California Commission on the Status of Women by the Rockefeller Foundation. Its purpose is to study the societal impact of the conformance of laws to the ERA, and it has evolved into a national resource center on the equal rights issue. Further information can be obtained from the Project, located at 926 J Street, Suite 1014, Sacramento, California 95814; telephone: (916) 444-9196.

THE EQUAL RIGHTS AMENDMENT

A BIBLIOGRAPHIC STUDY

**COMPILED BY THE EQUAL RIGHTS
AMENDMENT PROJECT**

ANITA MILLER, PROJECT DIRECTOR
HAZEL GREENBERG, EDITOR AND COMPILER

GREENWOOD PRESS
Westport, Connecticut
London, England

Library of Congress Cataloging in Publication Data

Equal Rights Amendment Project.
   The equal rights amendment.

   Includes indexes.
   1. Sex discrimination against women—Law and legislation—United States—
Bibliography. 2. Women—Legal status, laws, etc.—United States—Bibliography.
3. Sex discrimination—Law and legislation—United States—Bibliography. I. Miller,
Anita, 1928- II. Greenberg, Hazel. III. Title.
KF4758.A1E6   016.342'73'087   76-24999
ISBN 0-8371-9058-4

Library of Congress Catalog Card Number: 76-24999

ISBN: 0-8371-9058-4

First published in 1976
Second printing 1977

Greenwood Press, Inc.
51 Riverside Avenue, Westport, Connecticut 06880

Printed in the United States of America

10 9 8 7 6 5 4 3

Contents

Preface

In 1974, the California Commission on the Status of Women received funding from the Rockefeller Foundation to make a national study of the societal impact of conformance of laws to the Equal Rights Amendment, with the goal of promoting public understanding of the issues involved. Several assumptions underlay the formulation of this Project: (1) widespread discrimination on the basis of sex exists in all aspects of our national life and is reinforced by a network of legal protections; (2) the ERA will set forth with unequivocal clarity the principle that equality of rights under the law shall not be denied or abridged on account of sex and will mandate legal change at every governmental level; (3) the resultant legal changes will have broad societal impact, with the major institutions, such as marriage, family, government, education, and commerce, undergoing substantial change as a direct result of requirements to bring federal, state, and local laws into conformance with the ERA; and (4) the process of social change may be facilitated by a wide public knowledge of the issues involved and the alternatives which exist. Assuming, then, the existence of legal backing for sex discrimination, the approaching ratification of the ERA, the far-reaching effects of its implementation, and the possibility of orderly social change, the Commission developed a project to assist in the process of change.

The Project has had two dimensions. The first has included code reviews and the development of guidelines for model codes, to be used as models for conformance in all states, in the areas of family, employment, education, and criminal justice. But the pinpointing of areas of necessary legal change is in itself a preface to the examination of the impact of such change on selected key societal institutions. This second dimension has attempted to generate an understanding of the interaction of social and legal change. Such an understanding will aid in the development of models for legal change which will not only provide required conformance to the ERA, but also make adequate provision for orderly institutional change and give due recognition to human needs.

Fundamental change of the proportion implied here need not be accompanied by chaos if systematic and well-thought-out approaches, rather than hasty and simplistic ones, are used. The Equal Rights Amendment Project has sought to move beyond the inadequacies of a piecemeal approach by addressing the totality of the problem.

All across the country, some of America's finest minds have contributed

their time and knowledge to the ongoing development of the Project, a necessarily broad-based effort requiring a comprehensive sense of society's interactions
as well as specific focus on individual factors. It is with very real pleasure that
we acknowledge and thank those individuals and institutions that have given so
unstintingly to our Project.

Major recognition must be given to Peter Wood, Professor of History, Duke
University, and Marjorie Fine Knowles, Associate Professor, University of
Alabama School of Law, for their special understanding, encouragement, and support. They were there at the beginning and, sharing our vision of society's horizons, never faltered in the journey with us.

For their expertise in specific fields, which lent invaluable assistance in focus-
ing the implications of the ERA on present societal institutions, we wish to thank
a number of women. They include Barbara Allen Babcock, Associate Professor of
Law, Stanford University; Barbara A. Brown and Ann E. Freedman of the Women's
Law Project, Philadelphia; Mary Dunlap and Wendy Webster Williams of Equal
Rights Advocates, San Francisco; Herma Hill Kay, Professor of Law, University
of California at Berkeley; Dale Rogers Marshall, Associate Professor of Political
Science, University of California, Davis; Bernice Sandler, Executive Associate,
Association of American Colleges; and Lenore Weitzman, Assistant Professor of
Sociology, University of California, Davis.

We are also indebted to the members of an advisory symposium in San Francisco whose interdisciplinary focus pointed us in the direction of our book *Impact
ERA: Limitations and Possibilities* (Les Femmes Publishing, 1976): Jessie Bernard,
writer and sociologist; Ruth Glick, Director, National Study of Women's Correc-
tional Programs; Helen Kelley, President, Immaculate Heart College; Marjorie
Knowles; Jessie Kobayashi, Board of Directors, Institute for Educational Leadership; James O. Lewis, Human Relations Executive, California Teachers' Association; Madeline Mixer, Director, Western Regional Office of Women's Bureau,
U.S. Department of Labor; Robert Seidenberg, psychiatrist; Alice J. Vandermeulen,
Economics Department, U.C.L.A.; John Vasconcellos, Assemblyperson, 24th District, California; Lenore Weitzman; Joan Hoff Wilson, History Department, California State University, Sacramento; and Peter Wood.

We are indeed grateful to the attorneys whose learned discussions have displayed
an understanding of the legal whole as well as of the interrelationship of its parts.
An important consequence of these discussions was the Project's cosponsorship of
the Women and the Law Conference at Stanford University School of Law in
March 1975. We wish to thank Diane Blank, Janice Goodman, and Jemera Rone
of Bellamy, Blank, Goodman, Kelly, and Stanley, New York; Rhonda Copelon,
Liz Schneider, and Nancy Stearns of The Center for Constitutional Rights, New
York; Nancy L. Davis and Joan Messing Graff of Equal Rights Advocates, San
Francisco; Ellen B. Ewing, Kentucky Commission on Human Rights; Brenda
Feigen Fasteau, Fasteau and Feigen, New York; Margaret Gates, Co-Director,
Center for Women's Policy Studies; Nancy Gertner, Silvergate, Shapiro and Gert-
ner, Boston; Ruth Bader Ginsburg, Professor of Law, Columbia University;
Isabella Grant, Chairwoman, Committee on Equal Rights, California Bar Associa-

tion; Cynthia Holcomb Hall, judge, U.S. Tax Court; Sarah T. Hughes, judge, Federal District Court. Dallas; Gladys Kessler, Berlin, Roisman and Kessler, Washington, D.C.; Jean L. King, Ann Arbor, Michigan; Sybil H. Landan, Hofstra Law School, Long Island; Sylvia Law, New York University School of Law; Judith Lonnquist, Jacobs, Fore, Burns and Sugarman; Carlyn McCaffrey, Assistant Professor, New York University School of Law; Judy Mears, American Civil Liberties Union, New York; Virginia B. Nordby, University of Michigan School of Law; Kathleen Peratis, Women's Rights Project, American Civil Liberties Union, New York; Elizabeth Rindskoph, Executive Director, New Haven Legal Assistance Association; Sheribel Rothenberg, Assistant Regional Attorney, U.S. Equal Employment Opportunity Commission, Chicago; Barbara Shack, New York Civil Liberties Union; Paula Smith, Salmanson and Smith, Austin, Texas; Nadine Taub, Rutger's Law School; Sarah Weddington, member, Texas House of Representatives; Ruth Weigand, Associate General Counsel, International Union of Electrical Radio and Machine Workers, AFL-CIO; and Mary Wenig, Professor of law, St. John's University Law School and Chairperson of the Equal Rights Committee, American Bar Association, Section of Real Property, Probate and Trust Law.

During the course of the Project, now severed from the Commission and acting independently, the tasks of research and public information have come to fruition in a number of ways. In addition to the aforementioned study on the ERA's societal impact, several specifically legal inquiries were developed and have been realized in print. The first phase was completed with the publication of *ERA Conformance: An Analysis of the California State Codes* (1975). The second legal phase was initially informed by a conference held in Palo Alto in March 1975 on ERA implementation. Participants at this meeting included contributors to *Impact ERA* and prominent Women and the Law conferees. Two significant outgrowths of this meeting were a general analysis of the nationwide legal picture on the ERA, *A Commentary on the Effect of the Equal Rights Amendment on State Laws and Institutions* (1975), and the formation of a national task force to continue the effort toward conformance in each of the fifty states.

Finally, a public information clearinghouse was created, and a nationally circulated magazine, *The Equal Rights Monitor,* has served to collect, collate, and channel information from each state to all the others. This bibliography is another culmination of our efforts to discover a need and then attempt to fill it.

It is our pleasure to acknowledge individuals who are connected specifically to this effort. Particular thanks and affection go to Leah Freeman, Assistant Librarian of Social Sciences at California State University, Sacramento. Not only did her broad knowledge of library resources in general and women's materials in particular make her an invaluable contributor to this work but also her special brand of good cheer, patience, and ever-ready willingness to go out of her way to help solve the myriad problems of collecting and collating this material. She evidenced concern and humor far beyond the call of duty and made a rather dry and difficult task a lot easier and, indeed, more comprehensive than it would have been without her advice.

To Pat Gray, who helped plough through the seemingly infinite set of microfilms and check the never-ending shelves of periodicals, and whose perhaps most
important role was as a rather calm and steady sounding board for the endless
set of difficulties involved in collecting and organizing, we owe more than appreciation but consolation that at long last the task is completed—and sooner and
better because of her help.

Hattie Shepler, who typed and retyped the manuscript, cannot be compensated
adequately for the excellence of the job she has done and the good-natured way
she has done it. Appreciation must often remain in our hearts, incompletely spoken.

Anita Miller, Director
Equal Rights Amendment Project

Introduction

The history of the Equal Rights Amendment has not yet been written. It exists in the often obscure pages of books, magazines, and newspapers, in the archives of women's organizations that have been embroiled in the now fifty-five-year-old controversy, and in the minds of those who personally fought the ideological battle. It is our hope that this bibliography, by providing the entrance to the first and most accessible resource, will also encourage the pursuit of the others, so that the ERA's history may finally be written and understood.

A brief review of the factual highlights of the ERA struggle and the arguments which compose its intellectual saga, with some attempt to guide the researcher through a bibliography whose substance is impossible to categorize by single subjects, will help give organization and perspective to the whole. Specific information on the use of the bibliography and its methodology follow this discussion.

The struggle for the Suffrage Amendment evidenced both a tremendous unity among women in their ideological and active commitment to it and the political efficacy of that unity. The absence of such unity is what has, more than anything else, contributed to the length and difficulty of the fight for the Equal Rights Amendment in both its Congressional passage and its ratification. In fact, the unity in the advocacy of suffrage effectively hid the disagreements about more comprehensive equal rights. But they soon became violently apparent.

The National Woman's Party (NWP), one of the women's organizations which took a leading part in the suffrage movement, called a convention in 1921 to determine whether it would disband or reconstitute and work to eliminate other areas of discrimination. The outcome was the adoption of the goal of complete equality between men and women. This equality was to be accomplished by means of amendments to specific federal and state laws, blanket equality bills in all states, and an amendment to the federal Constitution guaranteeing equal rights. A number of factors seemed to suggest that the time was right for the ERA, among them the Wisconsin constitutional amendment of 1922, equal rights measures in other countries, especially England's Sex Disqualification Act, and many failures in efforts to achieve equality through specific legislation in the states.[1]

At that time, the principle of equality of the sexes remained unquestioned among the women's groups; rather, it was the method of attaining that goal that created dissension—so it was maintained at any rate. All groups execpt the NWP preferred the state-by-state, statute-by-statute approach to equality and opposed all "blanket" legislation. The NWP was considered terribly radical, and for this reason its influence and membership declined drastically in the 1920s. In fact, from 1920 to 1923 its membership decreased from 50,000 to 8,000. It limited itself to legal equality and did nothing for blacks, poor women, or working women; it was very middle class, attracting mostly professional and leisured women, and today would be considered among the most conservative of women's organizations. But at the time the NWP's creation of the ERA was indeed radical. The party even occasionally resorted to violent tactics, as illustrated by its disruption of a 1926 conference sponsored by the Women's Bureau, which opposed the ERA, in order to win time for debate on the Amendment.

Opposition cannot be properly understood, even from the historical point of view, without mention of the major objection outside the NWP had to the ERA. Generally their objection lay in the methodological difference already mentioned, but specifically, one's choice of method depended upon one's position on the protective labor legislation issue, or the legal protection of women generally. And this position in turn ultimately depended on one's view of women, as we will see. Working women in particular felt that the ERA would destroy all legislation designed to protect women in industry from abuse. During the first two decades of the twentieth century, men successfully formed unions and thereby improved their working conditions but women were unable to do so; and at the same time their participation in the work force was increasing. Instead, protective legislation became a means of preventing unfairness to women and of bettering their lot; such legislation had only been deemed constitutional, as being consistent with the state's right to protect the general welfare, in the early 1920s. In contrast, the Supreme Court had ruled against the constitutionality of such legislation for men, since it would interfere with their right to contract their labor and would conflict with the due process clause of the Fifth and Fourteenth Amendments. Thus, working women saw the ERA as a threat to their progress in protecting themselves, and they considered such progress more important than equality. Moreover, they felt that sex was indeed a significant factor in industrial labor and that *true* equality must take account of the biological differences between the sexes, that is, women needed certain protections that men did not need.

Between 1921 and 1923, the position of even the NWP changed on this issue. At first, the NWP argued that the ERA would not endanger these laws, or, that if it did affect them, it would cause them to be extended to men rather than eliminated. Selfishly, the women in opposition believed the progress achieved so far and the possibility of further legislation would be slowed or endangered if protections were to be secured by men as well. Thus, they did not even consider the extension argument a point in the ERA's favor. But by 1923, the NWP perceived protective laws to be a form of reverse discrimination that should indeed be struck down, arguing that they constituted class legislation and discrimination against both men and upwardly mobile and nonindustrial women, that if the laws were worth anything they should apply equally to women and men, and that many protective

laws effectively hindered women's opportunities in employment rather than protecting them. Thus, the NWP changed its attitude of attempting to reconcile the
ERA with the goals of other women's groups to outright opposition to the goal of
preserving protective legislation. It was on just this basis that business and professional women began to shift their attitude in the 1920s and came to side with the
NWP against such laws, which they increasingly came to see as encroachments
upon their freedom, especially as particularly threatening laws and evidence of
discrimination were glaringly publicized. This was the only group of women to
side with the NWP for many years, further evidence of the NWP's rather narrow
constituency and limited representation, since these women were for the most
part not directly affected by the areas in which industrial women felt they needed
protection. Thus, according to one writer, "the equal rights amendment was the
hallmark of impatience in the 1920's, and it was an issue which helped fragment
the women's movement and weaken the progressive impulse."[2] Hence the great
irony inherent in ERA's history.

Evidence of discussion about such an amendment occurs as early as 1914.
However, the NWP formally suggested the Amendment in 1923 at the seventy-
fifth anniversary of the Seneca Falls Convention, and in December of that year
two Republicans from Kansas, Senator Charles Curtis and Representative Daniel
Anthony, introduced it into Congress. The first (unrecorded) hearings were held
by a Senate Subcommittee on February 7, 1924,[3] and by the House in 1925.
Primarily due to NWP pressure, the Amendment was continually introduced in
every session of Congress in both the House and Senate after that time. After
1944, it was included in both party platforms, except in 1964 and 1968. A number of Senate hearings over the years reported it out of committee favorably.

Its popularity grew by the mid-1940s, primarily due to a number of factors
which weakened the major opposition of those favoring protective legislation.
The Fair Labor Standards Act of 1938, as supported by the Supreme Court in
1941, for the first time allowed protective laws for men. Thus, fuel was added to
the NWP's fire and made the basis for opposition to the ERA less reasonable, for
it made the possibility of extending rather than eliminating protective laws more
realistic. In addition, during World War II, protective laws had been nullified—
discrimination was against national policy, and equal pay for protective legislation.
Of course, the one thing that has characterized the opposition consistently, even
to the present day, is the retention of arguments long after their factual and reasonable basis has vanished.

While the depression of the 1930s had militated against considering advances
in the rights of any special group, the war of the 1940s did even more than affect
the protective labor issue. It changed the moral climate as well. The fight for democracy in general and the United Nations Charter, which called for equal rights between men and women, in particular increased the weight of the moral imperative
for giving women equal rights in the United States. Moreover, the NWP's image
had changed over the years because of its work on other widely accepted progressive issues. Then, too, the wording of the Amendment was changed in 1943 to con-

form to other constitutional amendments, especially suffrage and the Fourteenth, and to allow flexibility in state legislation.[4] By the 1940s, over thirty national organizations, including the Democratic and Republican parties, supported the NWP. A favorable committee report was sent to the Senate floor in 1939, and the Republican party endorsed it in 1940 on the ground of this report. So what happened in view of this flurry of support? Despite several of these "ups" in the ERA's history, there were corresponding and obviously overriding "downs."

A strong antifeminist movement developed in the 1940s, and the very goal of equality came to be challenged. The argument took either the form that women should not have equality because of their biological, social, and legal nature or the basically contradictory form that women not only already had equality but indeed were specially privileged. To reconcile this inconsistency, the antifeminists incorporated these "privileges" into their concept of "equality" and separated that concept from the concept of "identity." The ERA was seen as requiring identity of rights and not equality of rights because it ignored sexual distinctions entirely. The Equal Status Bill of 1947, which embodied this sentiment, contributed to the death of the ERA in a period of growing support. It incorporated the principle of equality without identity, supposedly giving women the best of both worlds—rights *and* protection. It enabled ERA opponents to retain the appearance of dedication to equality during a time when the idea was popular. What this bill did was to allow distinctions based on sex if they "are reasonably justified by the differences in physical structure, biological, or social function."[5] In other words, it totally killed the intent or effectiveness of the ERA. Over the years the opposition used debate on this substitute measure and other such measures as a major tactic to delay action on the ERA itself. It is ironic that this antifeminist sentiment was accompanied during the 1950s by the reinstatement of protective legislation (which had only been dropped for the duration of the war) and a return to second class citizenship. Thus after 1950, the moral imperative popular during the 1940s lost its grip, and the ERA struggle had to be connected to the practical and specific effort to obtain equal pay until the Equal Pay Act was passed in 1963.[6]

Another tactic that opponents used to circumvent growing support for the idea of equality was to amend the ERA itself. In 1950, 1953, and 1960, the Senate passed the ERA, but with the Hayden rider attached. This was a floor amendment proposed by Senator Carl Hayden (D., Ariz.) which preserved state protective legislation and killed the intent of the ERA to nullify these laws. Another roadblock was the refusal of Representative Emanuel Celler (D., N.Y.), chairperson of the House Judiciary Committee, to hold hearings between 1948 and 1971. He never even let the ERA get out of committee to the House floor. Such tactical manipulation of the political and Congressional processes contributed greatly to the ERA's long dormancy period despite its increasing popularity.

In 1948 and 1961, Celler introduced a proposal to create a Commission on the Legal Status of Women, whose purpose, it is generally acknowledged, was to kill the ERA. In fact, formal party support in the platforms of 1964 and 1968 is thought to have been withdrawn precisely because Kennedy's Commission on the Status of Women opposed it in 1961, still on the basis of protective laws. Significant groups such as the AFL-CIO, United Auto Workers, League of Women Voters, and the Women's Bureau continued their opposition.

The civil rights movement of the 1960s, both with its tactical militancy and its moral endorsement of equal opportunity and the rights of minorities to equal protection, created the atmosphere for the resurgence of feminism in the late 1960s. This resurgence included a revival of interest in the ERA and the gradual turning of the tide in its favor. In the early 1970s, of course, the concepts of women's liberation were introduced in far more radical areas of life, and the ERA was even relegated to merely one of a great many desired changes. The time was thus definitely riper for a renewed consideration of the Amendment. The National Organization for Women (NOW), formed in 1965, after an internal struggle, voiced its support first. In 1967, President Johnson announced his approval; in 1968, Nixon supported the Amendment in his campaign, although he did little about it after his election. Both his Task Force on the Status of Women and the Citizens' Advisory Council on the Status of Women favored the ERA, however, and their support led the way to a long line of position reversals. The former's report in December 1969 (released June 1970) and the latter's in March 1970 apparently carried great weight. Part of the reason for the change in government sanction was that many state protective laws were voided as a result of Title VII of the Civil Rights Act of 1964. This made it easier for some groups to change their position accordingly, as did the United Auto Workers in 1970, a statewide AFL-CIO women's conference in Wisconsin, and the Women's Bureau, persuaded by Elizabeth Duncan Koontz, in 1970.

As a result of pressure from NOW, the Subcommittee on Constitutional Amendments of the Senate Judiciary Committee held hearings in May 1970 for the first time since 1956. The ERA was reported favorably to the full committee on June 28, 1970. Meanwhile, to circumvent Celler's refusal to hold hearings or issue a report, Martha Griffiths resorted to the rarely used parliamentary device of the discharge petition to get the ERA out of the House Judiciary Committee. She filed the petition on June 11 and by July 20 had the required 218 signatures. On August 10, 1970, the House passed the ERA by 352 to 15 votes; this was the first action by a full House on the ERA since 1923. The Amendment's passage made it glaringly apparent that women's groups had finally united enough to make opposition politically dangerous and their pressure politically potent.

Passage by the House left the burden of final approval on the Senate, where Senator Sam J. Ervin, Jr. (D., N.C.) took the lead in opposing it. On August 17, he offered a substitute amendment which retained all state protective legislation and prevented women from being drafted, adding: "This article shall not impair the validity of any law . . . which is reasonably designed to promote the health, safety, privacy, education, or economic welfare of women, or to enable them to perform their duties as homemakers or mothers."[7] He held Judiciary Committee hearings on this new amendment in September 1970, in which, unlike the May hearings, opponents of the original ERA predominated. On October 7, the debate went to the Senate floor, where irrelevant riders on public school jurisdiction and nondenominational prayer were added to increase the controversy. These crippled the ERA effectively, and no further action was taken.

The ironic position of the Senate of the 91st Congress had been noted. Eighty Senators signed as sponsors of the ERA at a time when no one in the Senate thought it would even get through the House. In 1970, for first time in history, the Senate was in a position to veto the ERA, and each Senator had to consider his or her vote from the standpoint of its political ramifications.[8]

The ERA was again introduced in both the House and the Senate in the 92nd Congress in January 1971, and hearings were finally held by a subcommittee of the House Judiciary Committee in March. For the first time in ten years the Administration supported the ERA, and it was reported favorably out of the subcommittee in April. On June 22, 1971, the full House Judiciary Committee reported it out by a 32 to 2 vote over Celler's opposition, but the Committee added the Wiggins Amendment, which allowed Congress to exempt women from the draft and either Congress or the states to enact laws allowing differential labor standards for men and women. This crippled version was defeated on the floor by 265 to 87. On October 12, 1971, the House passed the ERA by 354 to 23 without amendments.

The Senate Judiciary Committee reported the ERA out on March 14, 1972, without amendments and with only Ervin voting against it. He was still the major opposition on the floor, continually offering nullifying amendments, exempting women from the draft and combat service, retaining protective laws, securing sexual privacy, etc. Any one of these would have doomed the ERA once more, but it was passed without change on March 22, 1972, by 84 to 8. The unified lobbying efforts of women's groups and their adoption of more militant tactics in the manipulation of the political process were responsible.

Immediately those Lobbying efforts were turned toward the ratification fight. By the end of 1972, twenty-two states had ratified; by 1973, the total was up to thirty. Three states ratified in 1974 and one in 1975, leaving four for the necessary thirty-eight by 1979. The greatest opposition has come from the South, with only two Confederate states ratifying, Texas and Tennessee. In October 1973, the AFL-CIO, which had provided major opposition early in the ratification fight, reversed its position and endorsed the ERA. Its reversal may be due partly to Title VII and partly to the company it kept in its opposition, as its association with the very verbal extreme right and left groups may have made it uncomfortable. The major far right opposition comes from the John Birch Society, the National States' Rights Party, the White Citizens Council, Young Americans for Freedom, the Ku Klux Klan, and the Christian Crusade. The leftists in opposition are primarily the Communist Party and the Socialist Workers, their objection being due to the protective labor issue. Independent socialist feminists are divided, though the majority demand extension of protective laws to men. It is important to note, however, that opposition and support cannot be easily stereotyped or confined to political "extremes": opposition ranges from conservative groups and politicians to radical feminist groups involved in new left politics, while support ranges from conservative Republican women generally opposed to "feminism" to the most radical feminists.

The ERA itself, once a radical method of obtaining equality, has become, even among its supporters, almost a symbolic gesture toward that goal. Perhaps the NWP was ahead of its time; perhaps the legal and social climates have changed over half a century; but feminists now consider the radical weapon of the NWP the *minimum* requisite for national commitment to sexual equality.

At least one great irony has come out of the ERA debate: women themselves have been responsible for its continual failure, not male opposition. Only when female unity was reached, at least to some extent, did effective lobbying of the male governmental power center result in success. And now, in the ratification process, it is female opposition epitomized by Phyllis Schlafly's Stop ERA group that is deterring passage. We must, therefore, look more closely at the arguments for and against the ERA beyond the protective laws controversy, though that controversy has played a major role in determining the ERA's fate.

In this brief overview of the history of the ERA, the arguments were used to illustrate the role of external social factors in determining its fate; that is, while the substance of the arguments for and against the ERA remained fairly constant over the years, factors other than the merits of the arguments were responsible for the nature of its slow progress and final passage. The discussion from the historical point of view may obscure the nature and facets of the controversy itself.

The protective labor issue actually involved two questions: Does such legislation really help women? Do women really need that help if men do not? The second of these is at the heart of one's attitude toward women, whether one views them as helpless dependents in need of special care or as independent human beings able to take care of themselves as well as men can with similar advantages. Opponents of the ERA believed that women needed protection biologically, that equality did not imply identity of treatment. The "leisure by statute" approach argued that the nation's very health was involved in protecting women. Today the biological differences argument has come under scientific disrepute; such physical differences have been shown to have little if any bearing on the social and occupational roles which the sexes are required to play. Special protections for one sex only are no longer seen as necessary, especially with industrial technology advanced as far as it is.

Moreover, the NWP believed that protective laws did *not* help women but rather restricted their opportunities in the competitive job market. Ironically and illogically, the opposition countered that job competition did not exist precisely because of occupational sex segregation. Today the absurdity of an argument which uses as a rationale the very situation women are trying to escape would be seen. Opponents continued to emphasize the need for flexiblity in order to have their cake and eat it too. They wanted specific laws which were discriminatory and disadvantageous to women changed while retaining privileges and advantages to women in the law. Thus, to achieve equality, they advocated other means than blanket amendments which offered total and sweeping changes.

The wind was alternately taken out of and put back into their sails with the fluctuations in the need for and status of protective legislation, and the issue was effectively invalidated by Title VII. But the protective labor law controversy is really only a part of the larger controversy of women's privileges, which involves the same underlying questions of whether women are indeed privileged and, if they are, whether they should be. One's attitude toward women is once more at the core of the issue. Special labor protections are only one of a host of privileges which ERA opponents believed women had, deserved, and would lose as a result of the ERA. The husband's obligation to support his family, mother's pensions, exemption from the draft, special welfare and hygiene laws for women and children, lower insurance rates, lower age of majority, and separate bathroom and sleeping facilities were only a few of these. The NWP argued, as it did regarding the protective labor issue, that some of these privileges should be extended to men; moreover, some, the Party said, would really be unaffected by the ERA, since they dealt with a special group of women, such as mothers, just as some laws were for special groups of men, such as soldiers. In general, however, the NWP did not consider women privileged at all but severely handicapped by a network of legal discriminations that restricted them rather than giving them advantages. The opposition emphasized the role of women as mothers, wives, and widows and their need for special treatment by the law, while proponents cited many states in which such laws applied equally to men and women without terrible consequences. The draft became a very large issue in the latter part of the controversy, and women's groups were confused as to how to treat it. Defenses of the ERA on that issue ran from exempting the draft from the jurisdiction of the Amendment to an outright belief that women should be drafted on the same basis as men, a stand taken by the NWP in 1924 in fact, with varying positions in between. The winding down of the Viet Nam conflict and the probility of a volunteer Army did much to quiet the controversy and secure passage without amendment[9]—another external factor thus contributing to the progress of the ERA. The image of women also underwent a change, and the justification of privilege came increasingly to be seen as selfish and the possibility of identity of rights more reasonable. Then, too, the ironic nature of "privilege" was much publicized by proponents of the Amendment.

Consequently, the argument for protection for women, both in labor and in their other social and biological roles, is really based on the belief that biological differences require differences in legal responsibilities and rights, an argument very much touted in the antifeminist sentiment of the 1940s. That women's legal nature is invariably connected to their biological nature was first stated authoritatively by Felix Frankfurter in 1923 while he was still at Harvard Law School. He insisted that women's position in the community was complicated because it involved so many relations—that is, individual, worker, wife, mother, citizen—and "the law must accommodate itself to the immutable differences of Nature."[10] For some purposes men and women could be seen as equal persons, having the same rights and responsibilities, but for other purposes, they must be subjected to different rules of legal conduct.

It is by now apparent that all the arguments which clustered around differences in the means to achieve equality were pretty much of a camouflage for a basic prejudice toward women and a belief in their inferiority as a class. Nevertheless, we must look at what was the declared motivation of these arguments. Opponents considered the ERA a hazardous method of obtaining equality because it would cancel women's protections and privileges, because its effects would be unpredictable, and because it would give the courts undefined powers for nullifying legislation. Moreover, opponents felt that the courts would be less likely to interpret equal rights for the benefit of women, since they were not controlled by women's votes, as were legislators. Those who accepted this argument offered alternatives in specific federal and state legislation and in alterations of the Amendment itself. The NWP argued that the reform of laws one by one on both federal and state levels had not only failed very often but was cumbersome, time consuming, expensive, and impermanent, since state laws could be and had been easily reversed. Of course, the irreversibility of a constitutional, amendment in contrast to the relative ease of repealing a state law, hardly appealed to ERA foes. In addition, the opponents' argument that the ERA would create legal chaos because of its conflict with state laws was easily countered, since state laws would ultimately be changed to conform to the ERA once it was passed. Opponents claimed that such conformance would involve endless litigation, hardly a point well taken in view of their state-by-state, statute-by-statute approach.

Because the moral argument for the ERA, based on the ideals of justice and democracy, was not in itself sufficient, the NWP was forced to resort to the insistence that the ERA was also expedient, that it would save campaign time, effort, and money by wiping out past and future discrimination with one fell swoop. It is an indication of the nature of the opposition that the NWP found itself in the position of having to temper justice and the moral imperative with expedience and the practical imperative. Principles per se were not at the heart of the opposing forces but rather the safest practical way of getting all they could without losing all they had. That is what the arguments over method really reveals.

Selfish motives also led to other inconsistent and specious arguments, such as that the ERA was unnecessary, since the real discrimination was in social custom, which the ERA would have no effect on. Consequently, the opponents' second alternative to constitutional amendment was general public reeducation. They might as well have argued against legal change altogether. Besides, no one argued against public reeducation; social and cultural attitudes are an issue apart, although proponents also argued that the ERA was needed precisely to improve women's self-image, to help them overcome their sense of inferiority, and that, in fact, its symbolic value would result in more equitable treatment by society. Enemies of the ERA insisted that this could be achieved in other ways.

The methods argument culminated in the constitutional law issue, which began to be connected to the ERA in the 1950s and became effective with the *Reed v. Reed* decision in 1971, in which the Supreme Court, for the first time, applied the Fourteenth Amendment to sex discrimination, although in the narrowest possible way. The use of constitutional law to support both sides increased after 1960 and especially after the President's Commission advocated the extension of judicial interpretation of the equal protection clause of the Fourteenth Amendment to women, arguing that it was preferable to change the interpretation of

constitutional law rather than the Constitution itself.[11] This method would have
been fine with proponents had it seemed likely that the Supreme Court would
actually give women the same status it accorded racial minorities, aliens, even
corporations. But such an approach was not forthcoming, so Amendment supporters saw the ERA as a means of modernizing constitutional law. Supporters
did not deny that the potential to protect women exists in the Fifth and Fourteenth Amendments, but saw that potential as dependent upon the subjective
nature of Court interpretation in each case it hears. ERA advocates considered
it faster and surer to use an Amendment to invalidate classifications based on sex.
Even in our time, however, constitutional lawyers against the ERA still insist
upon the distinction between being treated alike and being treated equally, although we have at least moved farther away from the social and cultural role
justification for this distinction toward areas that are clearly biological. The re-
finements of the argument have become increasingly sophisticated, and it is unnecessary to specify what they are here; but the argument still disguises a belief
in the relevance of one's biological nature to one's legal nature, of motherhood to
legal "rights."

The methods controversy also involves another issue which tends to duck the
principle of equal rights, that of state's rights. It has been argued that the ERA
would increase the power of the federal government and force every state to
have similar laws, especially in domains that belong rightfully to the states such
as domestic relations. On the other hand, the NWP had always argued that special legislation for women constituted an interference by the state. Furthermore,
ERA enemies have even advanced the argument that the entire matter of women's
rights is a "domestic" concern and the proper province of the states. The very
idea that because a legal question concerns women it is *ipso facto* "domestic" is
in itself the grossest kind of sexism and reveals the underlying hypocrisy of this
particular methods argument. But even further, it is logically inconsistent to also
argue that the Constitution already has the potential for equal rights and should
be so interpreted. Of course, if we simply deal with the facts rather than the arguments, it is clear that the ERA does not give Congress any powers that it does
not already have and could not have exercised without consulting the states at all.
The issue of state's rights has nothing to do with the principle of equal rights; it
was the entire methods argument, a camouflage for the prejudicial belief in equality without identity of rights.

The theory that equality is possible without identity of rights, based as it is on
a biological sanction for discrimination in the law and a belief in an absolute division of sex roles, does indeed conflict with the intent of the ERA as that intent
has been defined in the ERA's legislative history. An historical perspective on the
controversy does little to clarify the real and probable impact of the Amendment;
a brief, and therefore necessarily limited, statement about its meaning at the present time is, then, especially warranted as a conclusion to our discussion of its
history.

The ERA is a necessary clarification of the equal protection clause of the Four-

teenth Amendment. While the Fourteenth Amendment has been interpreted to define race as a "suspect" (that is, illegal) classification which cannot be used in making laws, the same has not been done for sex. Sex is, in fact, the only "class" not
covered explicitly by the Constitution as illegal; "equal protection of the laws"
has been explicitly extended to all other groups, to blacks, aliens, and corporations,
but sexual equality remains implicit and, therefore, debatable. A law or practice
involving race discrimination is "suspect" and must be subjected to a test known
as "strict scrutiny" by the Court before it can be upheld. Because this test is a
very stringent one and the burden is on the alleged discriminator to prove a serious
necessity for the classification, this standard of review has generally meant that
such laws are almost never upheld. On the other hand, when a classification like
sex is not "suspect," the standards of review under the Fourteenth Amendment
are far more lenient, and the showing that a "compelling state interest" is involved or that the classification bears merely a "rational relationship" to the purpose
of the law can easily uphold the classification. In this case, the burden is on the alleged victim of discrimination to prove the law or practice illegal. Because it is not
assumed to be illegal, as in the case of race, this standard of review has resulted in
a very uneven treatment by the Court.

The ERA, by defining sex as an equally "suspect" classification, will require at
least "strict scrutiny," thus making it far more difficult for the Court to use the
"compelling state interest" or "rational relationship" tests to uphold the law or
practice in question. If a law or practice is "neutral on its face" (that is, seemingly
not based on a sex classification) but it has a disproportionately discriminatory
impact upon one sex, that impact could be used to invalidate it under the ERA.
While hardly absolute in its practical, if not theoretical, meaning, the significance
of the ERA is that it provides a universal legal definition of female equality, outlawing distinctions between people on the basis of sex as a violation of constitutional rights, the most serious sanction in our legal system.

The more conservative method of specific legislation and specific challenge in
the lower courts or the Supreme Court under the Fifth and Fourteenth Amendments aims at retaining the right to redefine what actually constitutes discrimination in each specific case. A particular law or practice can then be determined as
"discriminatory" when it hurts women, "protective" when it benefits them, or a
"bona fide qualification" when it is seen as socially or biologically necessary. For
example, one Court decision under Title VII allowed motherhood as a bona fide
reason for an employer not to hire a woman.)

The application of "strict scrutiny" in sex discrimination cases is the very least
that the ERA will accomplish. Most recent legislative history and scholarship indi-
cate that the ERA will require the application of an even higher standard, one of
absolute prohibition of sex classifications in making laws. Not even a "compelling
state interest" could be used to justify sex classifications. While such justification
has been used only once in race discrimination, there is reason to believe that its
application in sex discrimination cases might be more lenient.[12] The absolute prohibition was therefore deemed necessary. The deeply entrenched nature of uncon-
scious sexist socialization, even in the Justices of the Supreme Court, is the target

of the ERA as the Amendment's meaning is being defined. Room for relativity is tantamount to room for discrimination, so the attempt has been made to narrow that space as far as possible.

But of necessity that space cannot be eliminated entirely. Two exceptions have been considered fair in defining the jurisdiction of the ERA. The first is the right of privacy, which would guarantee the individual's right to perform personal bodily functions without intrusion by the opposite sex. Thus, the whole rest room controversy is a red herring used by opponents to stir up emotional hostility and fear. As already mentioned, opponents care little about having their arguments based on facts and reason.

The Second is the exemption from the ERA of laws based on characteristics unique to one sex, and that exception is more complicated. Under the "unique physical characteristics" test, as it is called, physical (not social, cultural, psychological) traits found only in one sex may be used as a basis for legal classification. An example of such a law might be one that permits leaves of absence for women to bear, although not to rear, children. However, because in some areas, like that of pregnancy, the claim for exemption on this basis may be merely a cloak for discrimination, a guide for strictly scrutinizing such a law has already been developed to determine whether the law is fair or in fact discriminates against women or has a harmful impact on them. Thus, when discriminatory practices are challenged and one of those areas exempted from "absolute" prohibition is involved, the next level of Court analysis, "strict scrutiny," would be used and, hopefully, specifically defined and applied in a very narrow way.

In its jurisdiction, the ERA will apply only to the actions of government, federal and state, and those private institutions which are so involved with the government that they can be said to be acting for the state in some way. It will not apply to private individuals or groups. Sometimes there is a latitude of interpretation as to the degree of "state action" involved in certain enterprises, but it is generally agreed that the ERA will not reach private educational institutions, even if they receive federal or state money; religious institutions, even if they receive government tax exemptions, for jurisdiction over such institutions would conflict with the First Amendment right to establish religion; banks and savings and loan associations; insurance companies; private single-sex clubs; and most public accomodations, like bars, restaurants, nightclubs, hotels, and apartments.[13]

The ERA itself is not unlike the more conservative method of specific legislation and court challenge in that it involves exactly the same methods—minus the latitude of choice about which laws to change and challenge. It is not a law but will provide legal recourse in court and will require that all federal and state laws be changed to conform with the principle of equal rights. Such changes will involve more than making the laws sex neutral by altering pronouns; they will involve a deep analysis of the differential impact of facially neutral laws on the sexes in today's sociological reality. Court interpretation is neither guaranteed nor absolute, however, and it must be remembered that the meaning and scope of the ERA will only be defined in the litigation subsequent to its ratification.

The organization apparent in this introduction is indicative of the nature of
the material to be found in the bibliography. It is arranged by media, since the
overlapping of subjects made a topical arrangement haphazard at best, but the
media themselves tell a lot about the substance, as do the individual titles. The
researcher will find basically three types of material: reportage, which serves an
historical function; argumentation, which defines the controversy, especially regarding the ERA's assumed social impact; and analyses of the specifically legal effects of the Amendment.

Generally, the bulk of the material relating to this last area is to be found in
the legal periodical section, and it might be noted that the majority of the material
dates from 1971, when constitutional law and specifically legal analyses became
more important to the ERA controversy. The reportage function, that is, the
factual record of what happened with the ERA, when and who was involved, is
the overriding emphasis of both newspapers and newsletters, the latter proving
particularly useful for limited studies of the ERA's local fate. The comprehensive distribution of the major newspapers covered gives good insight into the nation's divergence: they cover the East Coast, West Coast, Midwest, and South effectively. They provide mini-histories of both fact and opinion regarding the ERA's
progress on the national and regional levels.

The organ of the National Woman's Party, *Equal Rights,* provides its own mini-
history. It has been set apart from the other periodicals because of its special nature as the closest source of information on the Amendment during the time of
its existence, 1923-1954. It combines the three types of material listed above,
but because it covers the ERA so intimately, it is the most detailed resource of
historical consequence. It is arranged chronologically, as are the newsletters and
newspapers, to give a sense of progress and history to the whole. When material
is reprinted from another source, it is given with the citation rather than with a
cross-reference number in order to keep the section more self-contained.

While no source limits itself to any one of the types of material mentioned,
both *Equal Rights* and the periodical section labeled academic journals, popular
magazines, and special interest newspapers emphasize the second type, that is,
argumentation defining the controversy. They combine this with a good deal of
historical reporting, but these are the sections of the bibliography one would
use the most in tracing the development of the arguments apart from the historical details, apart from facts.

The other sections of the bibliography are perhaps self-explanatory, but a word
should be said about each for comprehensiveness. The first covers the publications
of the House and Senate in their debates, their hearings, their reports resulting from
those hearings, and the materials read into the *Record* from other sources (listed
with the citation rather than cross-referenced, even if not precisely ERA-related).
The listing is complete, every mention of the ERA in Congress, except for very
minor procedural entries, being included. Since the listing is chronological within
each category, it is easy to locate the peak times of controversy. The most important coverage dates from 1970, when Congressional hearings finally led to ERA's

passage in March 1972. The debates, hearings, and reports during this period are crucial to any study of the ERA because they make up its legislative history and, consequently, its most probable meaning once ratified.

Other government publications, listed in Chapter 2, include studies by various federal agencies, most important of which are the Citizens' Advisory Council on the Status of Women and the Women's Bureau. These publications tend to be somewhere in between argumentation and legal analysis; that is, they are based on empirical facts and treated in a scholarly way but are not necessarily highly legal or technically sophisticated. State government publications are, for the most part, conformance studies, analyses of the ways in which state laws discriminate and would have to be changed upon ratification. These publications also study their own state ERAs. Only those code analyses explicitly related to the ERA are included here; many analyses have been done simply in terms of discrimination.

Chapter 3 covers books and dissertations, but only a very few of either are devoted entirely to the ERA; most citations are to essays or chapters within books and dissertations. The material is somewhat diverse and difficult to pinpoint, since the nature and thesis of the book determines the nature of its material on ERA. Most of the material probably belongs in the historical and argumentative categories, with very little on legal analyses, although there are notable exceptions. One excellent source for the latter is our own examination of the effects of the ERA prepared by Anne K. Bingaman (entry 400), it being the only one of its kind. Four important legal books deal significantly with the ERA: two by Leo Kanowitz (entries 464 and 465); one by Brown, Freedman, Norton, Holmes, and Ross (entry 441); and one by Davidson, Ginsburg, and Kay (entry 444). Catherine Stimpson (entry 485) has edited the Senate hearings, and that book is a good source of argumentation materials, as are all the books of Senate and House hearings since 1970. (These are listed in Chapter 1, Congressional publications.) The brief treatment generally accorded to the ERA in most of the books mentioned usually summarizes its historical progress over the years and the arguments for and against it. Loretta J. Blahna's dissertation (entry 437) summarizes well the history of the arguments themselves; that is, she treats the controversy itself from an historical perspective. The only book length study of the societal impact of the Amendment is the one done by our Project (entry 442).

The pamphlet and brochure section (Chapter 4) is mostly oriented toward the argumentative approach and is directed at the general public; it is generally lobbying material for one point of view or the other. Some of the brochures are merely status reports and, consequently, are of historical interest. More academic papers and reports are also included when they are not reproduced anywhere in periodical form.

This bibliography covers two microfilm collections of women's materials from the Women's Historical Research Center in Berkeley, California. These are *Herstory* and *Women and the Law* (of which only reel 1 is relevant to the ERA). At present these two collections are not topically indexed, nor are there complete and detailed reel guides available, so that we offer here the only entrance to the ERA material therein contained. In addition, the arrangement on these films is often haphazard and illogical, the filming itself often very poor. While a great deal of this material is somewhat trivial, we feel that the researcher must be given access to it in order to determine its particular usefulness to special areas of interest. Our own arrangement has been maintained and we have devised our own, hopefully more systematic or at least explainable, scheme of listing the material throughout the bibliography, which often differs from that of the collections; these are spelled out explicitly in the headnotes to each section. Our references are keyed to both series and reel number in order to avoid any possible confusion.

In addition, a system of cross-referencing of reprinted materials is provided. A separate entry has been included and cross-referenced when enough information about the primary source is given in the reprinted source; when the information is sufficient, it is simply given with the citation and no cross-reference appears. An attempt has been made to check the accuracy of the cross-references, but this effort was often impeded by either the unavailability of the materials or the inaccuracy of the data. In the latter case, the entries retain their independent listing, but a question mark signifies that they could not be located with the facts provided; perhaps the individual researcher should beware of citations to a primary source; they are inaccurate far more often than we would like to think. The *Congressional Record* (*CR*) and *Equal Rights* (*ER*) are self-contained: they include all the references to original sources in the citations; however, when complete information is given, those original sources are still listed elsewhere in the bibliography and cross-referenced to the *CR* or *ER* reprints. These sources, containing a great bulk of reprinted material in an easy-to-get-at, condensed form, are often to be recommended above the more obscure primary sources.

Also provided is a set of symbols which give details about the nature and source of the material. These are:

B	brochure, flyer, leaflet
Ed	editorial
H	*Herstory* (original set, followed by reel number, R)
H, Add	Addenda to the original set of *Herstory*
HU	*Herstory* Update (consists of two series, S1 and S2, followed by the reel number, R)
H2	*Herstory* 2 (consists of two series, S1 and S2, followed by the reel number, R)
H3	*Herstory* 3
LE	letter to the editor
N	newspaper or tabloid format
P	pamphlet, booklet
R	report, paper (unpublished as a pamphlet)
Rep.	reprinted
WL	*Women and the Law,* reel 1
*	See Addenda at end of chapter

We offer comprehensiveness in lieu of annotation and selection. We feel the great need is not so much for selected lists, abbreviated ones having been put together by various organizations and publications, but for a collection of all materials in one easily accessible reference work, since materials are so scattered at the present time. With such a controversial issue, a bibliographer could easily be accused of bias in selection, a result which comprehensiveness surely avoids. The time period covered is from 1914 (the year of the first citation) to the present time, generally January 1976 and in a few instances beyond that, when insertion has been possible. Both out-of-print and currently available material is included.

Our methodology has included coverage of all relevant indexes, firsthand coverage of the ninety-one microfilms, personal contact with women's organizations and publications, and our very own extensive network of contacts which automatically send in their publications. It should be noted that in each medium the bibliography covers not only whole pieces on the ERA but also items of which only a part concern the ERA specifically. This is why firsthand examination of the citations from indexes often became necessary. The determination of the "significance" of the ERA section of any one item is one area in which subjectivity inevitably crept in.

To increase the usefulness of the bibliography, we have prepared author and organization indices, including organization addresses for use in direct contact for available materials. Such a comprehensive list of groups which publish materials especially relevant to the ERA is also lacking in present resources. In addition, the indices complement the organization system within the bibliography proper and offer another way into the materials. Specifically, the author index is not only helpful in locating authors who straddle the various media; but for the newsletter, newspaper, and *Equal Rights* sections, in which the listing is chronological, and the pamphlet and government publications sections, in which the listing is primarily by organization name, it provides an entree to individual authors. Likewise, the organization index allows one not only to unite the contributions of an organization but also compensates for the fact that the very extensive newsletter section is arranged by publication title rather than by organization name, although these often coincide. For example, the index keys the NOW chapter names to the newsletter titles and thus offers another way of locating any particular NOW chapter's publication.

All alphabetizing is done by letter, as in a dictionary, rather than by word, as is often found in library card catalogs; the latter can be confusing and subjective.

It is our hope that whatever one's need for information or whatever one's approach to the ERA, this research tool will provide easy and complete access to the data available.

NOTES

1. Loretta J. Blahna, "The Rhetoric of the Equal Rights Amendment" (Ph.D. diss., University of Kansas, 1973), pp. 16-17.

2. James Stanley Lemons, "The New Woman in the New Era: The Woman Movement from the Great War to the Great Depression" (Ph.D. Diss., University of Missouri, 1967), p. 302.

3. Blahna, p. 23.

4. Ibid., p. 53.

5. Ibid. Quoted from hearings before Subcommittee No. 1 of the House Judiciary Committee, 1948, p. 89.

6. Ibid., p. 79.

7. Judith Hole and Ellen Levine, *Rebirth of Feminism* (New York: Quadrangle Books, 1971), p. 56. Quoted from hearings before the Senate Judiciary Committee, September 1970, p. 8.

8. Ibid., p. 57.

9. Blahna, p. 133.

10. Ibid., pp. 39-40. Quoted from "Senate Judiciary Committee Hears Arguments against the National Women's [*sic*] Party Amendment," March 1924, p. 3.

11. Ibid., p. 82.

12. For specific data proving this likely, see California Commission on the Status of Women, Equal Rights Amendment Project, *A Commentary on the Effect of the Equal Rights Amendment on State Laws and Institutions,* prepared by Anne K. Bingaman (Sacramento: California Commission on the Status of Women, Equal Rights Amendment Project, 1975), p. 20.

13. For an extensive discussion of the rationale behind the exemption of each and a general discussion of state action, see ibid., pp. 21-30.

THE EQUAL RIGHTS AMENDMENT

one

Congressional Publications

[The publications listed below include Senate and House debates, hearings, and reports. The coverage of the Congressional Record is complete, except for purely procedural matters which are not cited. When the debate is extensive, no attempt is made to annotate it to include the speakers or materials read into the Record during its course. However, when the citation is to an entry, the sole or main purpose of which is to read certain materials into the Record, then the primary source and author are included. The title of the original article is not repeated if it is the same as the Record subheading.]

The usual Chicago Manual of Style citation format has been amended slightly for the greater convenience of the reader. The citations are listed chronologically within each category of material and separately by Senate and House of Representatives.]

A. Senate

1. Debates and Materials Read into *The Congressional Record*

1. United States. Congress. Senate. "Equal Rights for Men and Women." CR, 68th Cong., 1st sess., 10 December 1923, 65, pt. 1: 150. Senator Curtis introduces the Equal Rights Amendment, S. J. Res. 21.

2. _____. "Equal Rights for Women." CR, 75th Cong., 3d sess., 13 January 1938, 83, pt. 9: 166 (Appendix). Contains: "Speech of Vera Brittain, British Author and Lecturer, Washington, D.C., December 14, 1937."

3. _____. "Proposed Equal-Rights Amendment to the Constitution." CR, 76th Cong., 3d sess., 18 March 1940, 86, pt. 3: 2967. Contains: "Resolution Unanimously Passed on February 15, 1940, at the Women's City Club, Detroit, Michigan."

4. _____. "Equal-Rights Amendment." CR, 76th Cong., 3d sess., 22 March 1940, 86, pt. 14: 1591 (Appendix). Contains: "Statement by Governor Moore of New Jersey."

5. _____. "Equal-Rights Amendment to the Constitution." CR, 76th Cong., 3d sess., 13 May 1940, 86, pt. 6: 5940. Contains a petition in Missouri.

6. _____. "The Equal Rights Amendment." CR, 77th Cong., 1st sess., 13 October 1941, 87, pt. 14: A4619. Contains: "Radio Discussion by Guy M. Gillette of Iowa and Mrs. Emma Guffey Miller, October 1, 1941."

7. _____. "Wyoming Territorial Laws and State Constitution--Precursors of the Equal Rights Amendment." CR, 77th Cong., 1st sess., 27 October 1941, 87, pt. 14: A4830-32. Contains an address by Senator Schwartz to National Woman's Party, 25 October 1941, "The Territorial Laws of 1869, and the Wyoming Constitution--Precursors of the Equal Rights Amendment."

8. _____. "Equal Rights for Men and Women--Constitutional Amendment." CR, 78th Cong., 1st sess., 21 January 1943, 89, pt. 1: 257, 271-73.

9. _____. "Equal Rights Amendment." CR, 78th Cong., 1st sess., 4 February 1943, 89, pt. 9: A440-41. Contains a letter from May G. Schaefer.

10. _____. "Equal Rights for Women on Senate Floor." CR, 78th Cong., 1st sess., 1 November 1943, 89, pt. 12: A4591-92. Contains: Hope Ridings Miller, "Wanted: Equal Rights on Senate Floor While Calendar Carries Equal Rights Amendment," Washington Post, 24 October 1943.

11. _____. "Emma Guffey Miller on Anniversary of the Birth of Elizabeth Cady Stanton." CR, 78th Cong., 1st sess., 16 November 1943, 89, pt. 12: A4893-94.

12. _____. "Equal Rights Amendment--Statement by National Consumers League." CR, 78th Cong., 2d sess., 2 February 1944, 90, pt. 1: 1038-39. Contains: "Definitely No!--Representative Professional and Working Women State Why They Are Opposed to the Proposed Equal Rights Amendment."

13. _____. "Proposed Equal Rights Amendment--Notice." CR, 78th Cong., 2d sess., 12 September 1944, 90, pt. 6: 7663-64.

14. _____. "Proposed Equal Rights Constitutional Amendment--Article from New York Herald Tribune." CR, 78th Cong., 2d sess., 19 September 1944, 90, pt. 6: 7903-907.

15. _____. "The Equal Rights Amendment." CR, 79th Cong., 1st sess., 1 March 1945, 91, pt. 10: A994-97. Contains an address by Emma Guffey Miller, 10 February 1945, to National Association of University Women.

16. _____. "Petitions and Memorials: A Resolution of the General Assembly of the State of New York." CR, 79th Cong., 1st sess., 30 April 1945, 91, pt. 3: 3940.

17. _____. "The Equal Rights Amendment." CR, 79th Cong., 1st sess., 18 June 1945, 91, pt. 12: A2902. Contains a letter from Mr. Guffey to Mrs. Thomas F. McAllister, Chairperson of National Committee to Defeat the Un-Equal Rights Amendment.

18. _____. "Equal Rights Amendment to the Federal Constitution." CR, 79th Cong., 2d sess., 7 May 1946, 92, pt. 11: A2492-93. Contains: Lena Madesin Phillips, Connecticut Bar Journal, January 1946.

19. _____. "The Equal Pay Bill and the Equal Rights Amendment." CR, 79th Cong., 2d sess., 14 May 1946, 92, pt. 11: A2662. Contains a letter from Mary Anderson to the Christian Science Monitor.

20. _____. "Proposed Equal-Rights Amendment to the Constitution." CR, 79th Cong., 2d sess., 1 July 1946, 92, pt. 6: 8018-19. Includes a statement by Paul Freund.

21. _____. "Equal Rights for Men and Women." CR, 79th Cong., 2d sess., 5 July 1946, 92, pt. 7: 8306. Contains a letter from William Green, President of American Federation of Labor, and a Resolution of 18th Biennial Convention of the International Glove Workers Union of America.

22. _____. "The Equal Rights Amendment." CR, 79th Cong., 2d sess., 5 July 1946, 92, pt. 12: A3934. Contains a letter from General Counsel of the Federal Security Agency.

23. _____. "Equal Rights for Men and Women." CR, 79th Cong., 2d sess., 17 July 1946, 92, pt. 7: 9219-20, 9223-29. See entry #2533.

24. _____. "Equal Rights for Men and Women." CR, 79th Cong., 2d sess., 18 July 1946, 92, pt. 7: 9293-97, 9302-35. See entry #2533.

25. _____. "Equal Rights for Men and Women." CR, 79th Cong., 2d sess., 19 July 1946, 92, pt. 8: 9397-405. See entry #2533.

26. _____. "Equal Rights." CR, 79th Cong., 2d sess., 26 July 1946, 92, pt. 12: A4451. Contains an editorial from the Washington Post, 21 July 1946.

27. _____. "Letter from Mrs. Emma Guffey Miller to Senator Barkley." CR, 79th Cong., 2d sess., 2 August 1946, 92, pt. 12: A4779.

28. _____. "Equal-Rights Amendment." CR, 79th Cong., 2d sess., 2 August 1946, 92, pt. 12: A4782. Contains a radio address by Florence L. C. Kitchelt, "Is the Equal-Rights Amendment Equitable to Women," 15 July 1946.

29. _____. "Equal Rights for Women." CR, 80th Cong., 2d sess., 19 June 1948, 94, pt. 7: 9044-45.

30. _____. "The Equal-Rights Amendment." CR, 81st Cong., 1st sess., 9 March 1949, 95, pt. 12: A1308.

31. _____. "Equal Rights for Men and Women--Proposed Amendment of Constitution." CR, 81st Cong., 1st sess., 11 April 1949, 95, pt. 4: 4246.

32. _____. "Equal Rights for Women--Concurrent Resolution of Minnesota Legislature." CR, 81st Cong., 1st sess., 29 April 1949, 95, pt. 4: 5289.

33. _____. "Procedure on Joint Resolutions Proposing Constitutional Amendments." CR, 81st Cong., 1st sess., 23 May 1949, 95, pt. 5: 6599.

34. _____. "Equal-Rights Amendment." CR, 81st Cong., 1st sess., 12 October 1949, 95, pt. 16: A6231-32. Contains: Helen Paul and Ernestine Hale Bellamy, "Equal-Rights Amendment Backers See Influential Groups Lending Support--Proponents Standing Behind Measure 26 Years Hold Equal-Status Bills to be Diametrically Opposed."

35. _____. "Eight Points on the Equal-Rights Amendment." CR, 81st Cong., 1st sess., 17 October 1949, 95, pt. 16: A6380-81. Contains: Florence A. Armstrong, Equal Rights, July/August 1949.

36. _____. "What Is the Constitution of the United States Worth to American Women?" CR, 81st Cong., 2d sess., 4 January 1950, 96, pt. 13: A34-36. Contains an address by Helen Elizabeth Brown to Lawyers' Civic Association of Maryland, 2 November 1949.

37. _____. "Equal Rights for Men and Women--Proposed Amendment to the Constitution--Amendments." CR, 81st Cong., 2d sess., 23 January 1950, 96, pt. 1: 724-25.

38. _____. "Equal Rights for Men and Women--Proposed Amendment to the Constitution." CR, 81st Cong., 2d sess., 23 January 1950, 96, pt. 1: 738-44, 758-62.

39. _____. "Equal Rights for Men and Women--Proposed Amendment to the Constitution." CR, 81st Cong., 2d sess., 24 January 1950, 96, pt. 1: 809-13, 826, 828-34, 861-73. Contains a review of state laws jeopardized by the Equal Rights Amendment.

40. _____. "Amendment of Constitution Affording Equal Rights for Women--Additional Cosponsors." CR, 82d Cong., 1st sess., 5 February 1951, 97, pt. 1: 911.

41. _____. "Printing of Manuscript Entitled 'Questions and Answers on Equal Rights Amendment' (S. Doc. No. 74)." CR, 82d Cong., 1st sess., 3 October 1951, 97, pt. 10: 12502.

42. _____. "Amendment of Constitution Relating to Equal Rights for Men and Women." CR, 83d Cong., 1st sess., 25 February 1953, 99, pt. 1: 1390-91.

43. _____. "Proposed Equal Rights Constitutional Amendment--Joint Resolution Passed Over." CR, 83d Cong., 1st sess., 8 June 1953, 99, pt. 5: 6173-75. Includes: Paul A. Freund, "Legal Implications of the Proposed Equal Rights Amendment."

44. _____. "Equal-Rights-for-Women Amendment." CR, 83d Cong., 1st sess., 1 July 1953, 99, pt. 6: 7763-64. Contains: "Relative to an Equal Rights Amendment Plank--Excerpts from a Brief Prepared by George Gordon Battle, Attorney at Law, New York City, on Behalf of the Equal Rights Amendment."

45. _____. "Equal Rights for Men and Women." CR, 83d Cong., 1st
    sess., 15 July 1953, 99, pt. 7: 8884-85.

46. _____. "Equal Rights for Men and Women." CR, 83d Cong., 1st
    sess., 16 July 1953, 99, pt. 7: 8954-74.

47. _____. "Petitions and Memorials: Joint Resolution 7 of
    Legislature of State of Colorado." CR, 85th Cong., 1st sess., 1 March
    1957, 103, pt. 3: 2850.

48. _____. "Proposed Amendment to Constitution, Relating to Equal
    Rights for Men and Women." CR, 85th Cong., 1st sess., 4 April 1957,
    103, pt. 4: 5093-95.

49. _____. "The Equal Rights Amendment, Senate Joint Resolution
    80." CR, 85th Cong., 1st sess., 10 April 1957, 103, pt. 4: 5441.
    Contains: "Equal Rights Amendment, Senate Joint Resolution 49,
    July 16, 1953."

50. _____. "The Case for the Equal Rights Amendment." CR, 85th
    Cong., 1st sess., 11 July 1957, 103, pt. 9: 11317-18. Contains:
    Senator John Marshall Butler, National Business Woman, July 1957.

51. _____. "Equal Rights--Resolution." CR, 85th Cong., 2d sess.,
    28 January 1958, 104, pt. 1: 1145. Contains a resolution of the
    Business and Professional Women's Club of New York State.

52. _____. "Equal Rights for Women." CR, 85th Cong., 2d sess.,
    26 February 1958, 104, pt. 3: 2855. Contains a letter from Mabel
    Purdy and Resolution of Business and Professional Women's Clubs of
    New York State.

53. _____. "AFL-CIO Opposition to Equal Rights." CR, 85th Cong.,
    2d sess., 16 August 1958, 104, Appendix: A7411-12. Contains a
    letter from Alma Lutz, "Hits AFL-CIO Opposition to Equal Rights,"
    Boston Sunday Herald, 13 July 1958.

54. _____. "The Supreme Court and Women." CR, 86th Cong., 1st
    sess., 10 April 1959, 105, Appendix: A2906. Contains: David Lawrence,
    "The Supreme Court and Women--Ruling for Segregation of Men or Women
    Is Compared to Integration Decision," Washington Evening Star, 8 April
    1959.

55. _____. "Printing as Separate Senate Documents Certain Informa-
    tion on Equal Rights Amendment and Federal Labor Laws." CR, 86th Cong.,
    1st sess., 14 September 1959, 105, pt. 15: 19629.

56. _____. "Equal Rights for Men and Women." CR, 86th Cong., 2d
    sess., 2 July 1960, 106, pt. 12: 15678-86.

57. _____. "Petitions and Memorials: House Joint Resolution of
    the State of New Hampshire." CR, 87th Cong., 2d sess., 11 January
    1962, 108, pt. 1: 82.

58. _____. "Concurrent Resolution of Louisiana Legislature." CR,
    87th Cong., 2d sess., 8 June 1962, 108, pt. 7: 9998.

59. _____. "Authorization for Printing as a Senate Document a
    Revised Edition of Senate Document No. 74, 82D Congress, Entitled
    'Equal Rights Amendment.'" CR, 87th Cong., 2d sess., 1 October 1962,
    108, pt. 16: 21162.

60. _____. "Equal Rights Amendment to the Constitution." CR,
    88th Cong., 1st sess., 18 February 1963, 109, pt. 2: 2405-406.
    Contains remarks of Senator Simpson and President Johnson.

61. _____. "Equal Rights for Women." CR, 88th Cong., 1st sess.,
    2 April 1963, 109, pt. 4: 5386-87. Contains: "Senator Keating Urges
    Progress in Ending Discrimination Against Women, March 31, 1963,
    address to B'nai B'rith in Washington."

62. _____. "Wisconsin Journal Praises Mrs. Peterson's Fight for
    Equal Rights for Women." CR, 88th Cong., 1st sess., 30 April 1963,
    109, Appendix: A2623. Contains: Harva Hachten, "Labor Department
    Aid Declares 'Myths' Plague United States Women--Conference Told
    They're Equal of Men as Labor," Wisconsin State Journal.

63. _____. "Petitions and Memorials: Assembly Joint Resolution 31
    of the State of Nebraska." CR, 88th Cong., 1st sess., 13 May 1963,
    109, pt. 6: 8263.

64. _____. "Equal Rights for Men and Women." CR, 88th Cong., 2d
    sess., 3 October 1964, 110, pt. 18: 24063-64. Contains excerpts from
    Senate Report No. 1558.

65. _____. "Proposed Amendment of Constitution Relating to Equal
    Rights for Women." CR, 89th Cong., 1st sess., 24 May 1965, 111, pt.
    8: 11350-51. Contains excerpts from Senate Report No. 1558 and
    Gould Lincoln, "Rights Laws by the Dozen, But--," Washington (D.C.)
    Star, 22 May 1965.   See entry #189.

66. _____. "Proposed Amendment to the Constitution Relating to
    Equal Rights for Men and Women." CR, 90th Cong., 1st sess., 13 March
    1967, 113, pt. 5: 6393-94.

67. _____. "Senate Joint Resolution 61--Introduction of a Joint
    Resolution to Propose a Constitutional Amendment Providing for Equal
    Rights for Men and Women." CR, 91st Cong., 1st sess., 28 February
    1969, 115, pt. 3: 4899-900.

68. _____. "The Equal Rights Amendment." CR, 91st Cong., 2d sess.,
    26 February 1970, 116, pt. 4: 4998-99. Contains: "Citizens' Advisory
    Council on the Status of Women Endorses Equal Rights Amendment,"
    13 February 1970. (WL)

69. _____. "Goodell Testimony on Constitutional Amendment on Equal
    Rights for Women." CR, 91st Cong., 2d sess., 5 May 1970, 116, pt. 11:
    14143-45. Contains: Charles E. Goodell, "Equal Rights for Women"
    (testimony before Judiciary Committee, 5 May 1970).

70. _____. "The Equal Rights Amendment." CR, 91st Cong., 2d sess.,
    12 May 1970, 116, pt. 11: 15065.

71. _____. "Equal Rights Amendment." CR, 91st Cong., 2d sess., 19 May 1970, 116, pt. 12: 16062.

72. _____. "Senator Murphy Joins Republican Woman in Urging the Enactment of Senate Joint Resolution 61." CR, 91st Cong., 2d sess., 22 June 1970, 116, pt. 15: 20727-28. Contains: Gladys O'Donnel, President of National Federation of Republican Women, testimony to Judiciary Committee, 7 May 1970.

73. _____. "Administration Stalls on Women's Rights." CR, 91st Cong., 2d sess., 27 July 1970, 116, pt. 19: 25913-22. (WL)

74. _____. "Equal Rights for Women--Address by Senator Tower." CR, 91st Cong., 2d sess., 10 August 1970, 116, pt. 21: 27911-13. Contains his speech before the American Bar Association in St. Louis.

75. _____. "Proposed Amendment to the Constitution Relative to Equal Rights for Men and Women." CR, 91st Cong., 2d sess., 12 August 1970, 116, pt. 21: 28375-76.

76. _____. "House Passage of Equal Rights for Women Amendment: First Step Toward Ratification of Political Rights of Women Treaty." CR, 91st Cong., 2d sess., 13 August 1970, 116, pt. 21: 28714.

77. _____. "Senate Should Act Quickly on Equal Rights for Women." CR, 91st Cong., 2d sess., 13 August 1970, 116, pt. 21: 28716.

78. _____. "Senate Joint Resolution 231--Introduction of a Joint Resolution Proposing an Amendment to the Constitution to Abolish Unfair Legal Discrimination Against Women." CR, 91st Cong., 2d sess., 19 August 1970, 116, pt. 22: 29444-45.

79. _____. "The House-Passed Equal Rights Amendment May End the Protection of Women." CR, 91st Cong., 2d sess., 20 August 1970, 116, pt. 22: 29566-67. Contains: Richard Wilson, "Women's Rights Amendment May End Protection," Washington Star, 14 August 1970.

80. _____. "The House-Passed Equal Rights Amendment: A Potentially Destructive and Self-Defeating Blunderbuss." CR, 91st Cong., 2d sess., 21 August 1970, 116, pt. 22: 29668-72.

81. _____. "Why the Majority and Minority Leaders of the Senate Ought to Comply with the Request of the Senate Judiciary Committee that the House-Passed Equal Rights Amendment Be Referred to the Senate Judiciary Committee for Study." CR, 91st Cong., 2d sess., 21 August 1970, 116, pt. 22: 29672-73.

82. _____. "The Equal Rights Amendment." CR, 91st Cong., 2d sess., 25 August 1970, 116, pt. 22: 29996-97.

83. _____. "The House-Passed Equal Rights Amendment: Whoso Diggeth a Pit Shall Fall Therein." CR, 91st Cong., 2d sess., 1 September 1970, 116, pt. 23: 30610-16.

84. _____. "Women Not Completely Sold on Equal Rights." CR, 91st
    Cong., 2d sess., 1 September 1970, 116, pt. 23: 30627-28. Contains:
    Lil Thompson, "Equal Rights? Women Not Completely Sold," Journal and
    Sentinel (North Carolina), 16 August 1970.

85. _____. "Statement of Professor Paul A. Freund of the Harvard
    Law School Before the Senate Judiciary Committee in Opposition to
    Senate Joint Resolution 61, the Equal Rights for Women Amendment."
    CR, 91st Cong., 2d sess., 10 September 1970, 116, pt. 23: 31131-33.

86. _____. "The Proposed Equal Rights Amendment." CR, 91st Cong.,
    2d sess., 10 September 1970, 116, pt. 23: 31137.

87. _____. "The Testimony of Professor Philip Kurland, of the
    University of Chicago Law School, in Opposition to Senate Joint
    Resolution 61, the Equal Rights for Women Amendment." CR, 91st Cong.,
    2d sess., 11 September 1970, 116, pt. 23: 31344-45.

88. _____. "Remarks by Professor Leo Kanowitz on the Equal Rights
    Amendment." CR, 91st Cong., 2d sess., 14 September 1970, 116, pt. 23:
    31533-37. Contains: Leo Kanowitz, "The Equal Rights Amendment and
    the Overtime Illusion." Rep. in entries #781, 3206

89. _____. "The Equal Rights Amendment." CR, 91st Cong., 2d sess.,
    16 September 1970, 116, pt. 24: 32028-32.

90. _____. "Women's Rights: A Matter of Simple Justice." CR,
    91st Cong., 2d sess., 17 September 1970, 116, pt. 24: 32396-97.

91. _____. "Statement by Hubert H. Humphrey on Equal Rights
    Amendment." CR, 91st Cong., 2d sess., 25 September 1970, 116, pt. 25:
    33832-33.

92. _____. "New York Times Magazine Article on the Equal Rights for
    Women Amendment." CR, 91st Cong., 2d sess., 1 October 1970, 116, pt.
    25: 34533-38. Contains: Robert Sherrill, "That Equal-Rights Amendment
    --What, Exactly Does It Mean?" New York Times Magazine, 20 September
    1970.

93. _____. "Equal Rights for Men and Women." CR, 91st Cong., 2d
    sess., 6 October 1970, 116, pt. 26: 35050.

94. _____. "Proposed Amendment to the Constitution Relative to
    Equal Rights for Men and Women--Amendment." CR, 91st Cong., 2d sess.,
    6 October 1970, 116, pt. 26: 35096.

95. _____. "Equal Rights for Men and Women." CR, 91st Cong., 2d
    sess., 7 October 1970, 116, pt. 26: 35448-75.

96. _____. "Consideration of House Joint Resolution 264 Tomorrow."
    CR, 91st Cong., 2d sess., 7 October 1970, 116, pt. 26: 35560. (WL)

97. _____. "Equal Rights for Men and Women." CR, 91st Cong., 2d
    sess., 8 October 1970, 116, pt. 26: 35621-28.

98. _____. "Equal Rights for Men and Women." CR, 91st Cong., 2d
    sess., 9 October 1970, 116, pt. 27: 35934-37, 35943-66.

99. _____. "Equal Rights for Men and Women." CR, 91st Cong., 2d
    sess., 12 October 1970, 116, pt. 27: 36265-78, 36299-313, 36315.

100. _____. "Status of Unfinished Business." CR, 91st Cong., 2d
     sess., 12 October 1970, 116, pt. 27: 36318.

101. _____. "Equal Rights for Men and Women." CR, 91st Cong., 2d
     sess., 13 October 1970, 116, pt. 27: 36372-73, 36448-51, 36478-81,
     36482-505.

102. _____. "Equal Rights for Men and Women." CR, 91st Cong., 2d
     sess., 14 October 1970, 116, pt. 27: 36862-66. (WL)

103. _____. "Equal Rights for Men and Women." CR, 91st Cong., 2d
     sess., 16 November 1970, 116, pt. 28: 37268-69.

104. _____. "Proposed Amendment of the Constitution Relative to
     Equal Rights for Men and Women--Amendments." CR, 91st Cong., 2d sess.,
     16 November 1970, 116, pt. 28: 37280.

105. _____. "Equal Rights Amendment." CR, 91st Cong., 2d sess.,
     16 November 1970, 116, pt. 28: 37462.

106. _____. "Senate Joint Resolution 9--Introduction of a Joint
     Resolution Relative to Equal Rights for Men and Women." CR, 92d
     Cong., 1st sess., 25 January 1971, 117, pt. 1: 364-66.

107. _____. "Senate Joint Resolution 8--A Constitutional Amendment
     to Guarantee Equal Rights for Men and Women." CR, 92d Cong., 1st
     sess., 28 January 1971, 117, pt. 1: 931-36.

108. _____. "Statements on Introduced Bills and Joint Resolutions:
     Mr. Hartke on S. J. Res. 79." CR, 92d Cong., 1st sess., 1 April
     1971, 117, pt. 7: 9183-84.

109. _____. "Equal Rights Amendment." CR, 92d Cong., 1st sess.,
     5 April 1971, 117, pt. 8: 9657.

110. _____. "The Equal Rights Amendment." CR, 92d Cong., 1st
     sess., 23 April 1971, 117, pt. 9: 11719-22.

111. _____. "Equal Rights for Women." CR, 92d Cong., 1st sess.,
     15 July 1971, 117, pt. 19: 25349-50.

112. _____. "Statements on Introduced Bills and Joint Resolutions:
     by Mr. Miller on S. J. Res. 138." CR, 92d Cong., 1st sess., 22 July
     1971, 117, pt. 20: 26713-14.

113. _____. "Equal Rights for Men and Women." CR, 92d Cong., 1st
     sess., 5 August 1971, 117, pt. 23: 30046-48.

114. _____. "Senate Joint Resolution 150--Introduction of a Joint
     Resolution Proposing an Equal Rights Amendment to the Constitution."
     CR, 92d Cong., 1st sess., 6 August 1971, 117, pt. 23: 30213-15.

115. _____. "Senate Joint Resolution 150--Proposing an Equal Rights Amendment to the Constitution." CR, 92d Cong., 1st sess., 8 September 1971, 117, pt. 23: 30889-90.

116. _____. "Statements on Introduced Bills and Joint Resolutions: by Mr. Javits on S. J. Res. 159." CR, 92d Cong., 1st sess., 23 September 1971, 117, pt. 25: 33027.

117. _____. "Equal Rights for Women." CR, 92d Cong., 1st sess., 29 September 1971, 117, pt. 26: 33943. Contains: Resolution of Governor's Commission on the Status of Women of Nebraska.

118. _____. "Controversy Over Equal Rights for Women." CR, 92d Cong., 1st sess., 1 October 1971, 117, pt. 26: 34453.

119. _____. "Legal Analysis of the Equal Rights Amendment." CR, 92d Cong., 1st sess., 5 October 1971, 117, pt. 27: 35012-41. Contains: Brown, Emerson, Falk, and Freedman, "The Equal Rights Amendment: A Constitutional Basis for Equal Rights for Women," Yale Law Journal 80 (1971): 871-985.

120. _____. "Program." CR, 92d Cong., 1st sess., 19 October 1971, 117, pt. 28: 36771.

121. _____. "Proposed Equal Rights Amendment." CR, 92d Cong., 1st sess., 20 October 1971, 117, pt. 28: 37013. Contains: Resolutions of Governor's Commission on Status of Women of Arkansas.

122. _____. "The Equal Rights Amendment." CR, 92d Cong., 1st sess., 26 October 1971, 117, pt. 29: 37495.

123. _____. "Equal Rights in the Senate." CR, 92d Cong., 1st sess., 27 October 1971, 117, pt. 29: 37719.

124. _____. "Equal Rights for Women." CR, 92d Cong., 1st sess., 15 December 1971, 117, pt. 36: 47083. Contains letters from Eugene Business and Professional Women's Club and Virginia Fuller.

125. _____. "New York City Bar Association Opposes Equal Rights for Women Amendment." CR, 92d Cong., 2d sess., 2 February 1972, 118, pt. 2: 2325-30. Contains: Association of the Bar of the City of New York, Committee on Federal Legislation, "Amending the Constitution to Prohibit State Discrimination Based on Sex."

126. _____. "Yale Medical Professor Equates Equal Rights Amendment to Tonkin Gulf Resolution." CR, 92d Cong., 2d sess., 3 February 1972, 118, pt. 3: 2472-73. Contains: Jonathan H. Pincus, "Rights Amendment: Is It Constructive?"

127. _____. "University of Chicago Law Professor Opposes Equal Rights for Women Amendment." CR, 92d Cong., 2d sess., 4 February 1972, 118, pt. 3: 2708-10. Includes a statement by Philip B. Kurland.

128. _____. "Elmo Roper Poll Shows Women Against Equal Rights Amendment." CR, 92d Cong., 2d sess., 8 February 1972, 118, pt. 3: 3072-73.

129. _____. "University of California Librarian Opposes Equal Rights Amendment." CR, 92d Cong., 2d sess., 8 February 1972, 118, pt. 3: 3075. Contains: Laurel Burley, "Protective Laws."

130. _____. "Equal Rights for Men and Women, 1972." CR, 92d Cong., 2d sess., 8 February 1972, 118, pt. 3: 3103-105. Includes letters from Thomas I. Emerson and Norman Dorsen.

131. _____. "Harvard Law Professor Opposes Equal Rights Amendment." CR, 92d Cong., 2d sess., 9 February 1972, 118, pt. 3: 3347-49. Contains: Paul A. Freund, "The Equal Rights Amendment Is Not the Way."

132. _____. "Ervin Statement on the Equal Rights Amendment." CR, 92d Cong., 2d sess., 15 February 1972, 118, pt. 4: 3863-66. Contains: Sam Ervin, "The Equal Rights Amendment: An Atomic Mousetrap."

133. _____. "AFL-CIO Opposes Equal Rights for Women Amendment." CR, 92d Cong., 2d sess., 16 February 1972, 118, pt. 4: 4033-34. Contains: "Report to 9th Convention and Resolution No. 122" of AFL-CIO Executive Council.

134. _____. "Professor Paul Freund Says Equal Rights Amendment Is Unnecessary." CR, 92d Cong., 2d sess., 18 February 1972, 118, pt. 4: 4599. Contains a letter from Paul Freund to Sam Ervin.

135. _____. "Equal Rights Amendment." CR, 92d Cong., 2d sess., 18 February 1972, 118, pt. 4: 4599-604. Contains: Report on the Equal Rights Amendment by the Association of the Bar of the City of New York by its Committee on Civil Rights and Special Committee on Sex and Law.

136. _____. "Equal Rights Amendment." CR, 92d Cong., 2d sess., 24 February 1972, 118, pt. 5: 5448.

137. _____. "American Bar Association Favors Constitutional Equality for Men and Women." CR, 92d Cong., 2d sess., 28 February 1972, 118, pt. 5: 5766. Contains: Report of the American Bar Association, Section on Individual Rights and Responsibilities.

138. _____. "Equal Rights Amendment." CR, 92d Cong., 2d sess., 29 February 1972, 118, pt. 5: 5940.

139. _____. "Equal Rights for Women." CR, 92d Cong., 2d sess., 1 March 1972, 118, pt. 5: 6167.

140. _____. "A Matter of Simple Justice." CR, 92d Cong., 2d sess., 1 March 1972, 118, pt. 5: 6206-207. Contains: Marion Bell Wilhelm, "Equal Rights Drive Stirs Anew."

141. _____. "The Equal Rights Amendment and the Draft." CR, 92d Cong., 2d sess., 2 March 1972, 118, pt. 6: 6765. Contains an address of George Washington University Women's Liberation, 13 November 1970.

142. _____. "Equal Rights for Women." CR, 92d Cong., 2d sess., 7 March 1972, 118, pt. 6: 7321-25. Contains studies by Labor Department, Equal Employment Opportunity Commission, and excerpts from a speech by Wilma Scott Heide.

143. _____. "The Effect of the Equal Rights Amendment on Laws Which
Apply to Only One Sex." CR, 92d Cong., 2d sess., 9 March 1972, 118,
pt. 6: 7786-89. Contains: Memorandum of Subcommittee on Constitutional
Amendments on question of nullification or extension of laws; excerpts
from report of Committee on Civil Rights and Special Committee on Sex
and Law of Association of Bar of City of New York; excerpts of
statement of Professor Norman Dorsen before Judiciary Committee.

144. _____. "United Church of Christ Supports Equal Rights
Amendment." CR, 92d Cong., 2d sess., 15 March 1972, 118, pt. 7:
8416-18. Contains: Tilford E. Dudley, Council for Christian Social
Action, United Church of Christ, "Equal Rights Amendment to the
Constitution."

145. _____. "Los Angeles Times Supports Equal Rights Amendment."
CR, 92d Cong., 2d sess., 15 March 1972, 118, pt. 7: 8420. Contains:
"Equal Rights for Women."

146. _____. "Equal Rights for Men and Women." CR, 92d Cong.,
2d sess., 15 March 1972, 118, pt. 7: 8451, 8452.

147. _____. "Memorandum of Citizens' Advisory Council on the
Status of Women." CR, 92d Cong., 2d sess., 17 March 1972, 118, pt. 7:
8876-79. Contains: The Equal Rights Amendment and Alimony and Child
Support Laws. (WL)

148. _____. "Equal Rights Amendment." CR, 92d Cong., 2d sess.,
17 March 1972, 118, pt. 7: 8893-94.

149. _____. "Equal Rights for Men and Women." CR, 92d Cong.,
2d sess., 17 March 1972, 118, pt. 7: 8899-911. Contains: Citizens'
Advisory Council on the Status of Women, The Equal Rights Amendment
and Alimony and Child Support Laws. (WL)

150. _____. "Equal Rights for Men and Women." CR, 92d Cong.,
2d sess., 20 March 1972, 118, pt. 7: 9080-106. Contains letters
from J. Fred Buzhardt, statement by Paul A. Freund, etc.

151. _____. "Equal Rights for Men and Women." CR, 92d Cong.,
2d sess., 21 March 1972, 118, pt. 7: 9314-73.

152. _____. "Equal Rights for Men and Women." CR, 92d Cong.,
2d sess., 22 March 1972, 118, pt. 8: 9517-40, 9544-99.
Rep. in entry #3191.

153. _____. "The Equal Rights Amendment: A Potentially
Destructive and Self-Defeating Blunderbuss." CR, 92d Cong., 2d sess.,
28 March 1972, 118, pt. 8: 10450-56.

154. _____. "Address Before Phi Theta Kappa, April 15, 1972." CR,
92d Cong., 2d sess., 20 April 1972, 118, pt. 11: 13781-82.

155. _____. "The Equal Rights Amendment." CR, 92d Cong., 2d sess.,
1 May 1972, 118, pt. 12: 15088-89. Contains a speech by Senator
Marlow Cook.

156. _____. "The Equal Rights Amendment." CR, 92d Cong., 2d sess., 1 June 1972, 118, pt. 15: 19433. Contains: Giddy Dyer, "For Women and Men: Commonsense and Equal Rights."

157. _____. "The Equal Rights Amendment." CR, 92d Cong., 2d sess., 19 June 1972, 118, pt. 17: 21336-37. "Equal Rights Arrives, Editorial in Journal of American Bar Association for June 1972."

158. _____. "The Equal Rights Amendment." CR, 92d Cong., 2d sess., 7 September 1972, 118, pt. 23: 29717-18. Contains: John V. Tunney, "Remarks to State of California Commission on the Status of Women."

159. _____. "Indianapolis Star Supports the Equal Rights Amendment." CR, 93d Cong., 1st sess., 29 January 1973, 119, pt. 2: 2456-57. Contains: "Equality for Women."

160. _____. "Nebraska and the ERA." CR, 93d Cong., 1st sess., 8 May 1973, 119, pt. 12: 14727. Contains: Frank Van Der Lenden, "Equal Rights Amendment," 30 March 1973.

161. _____. "The Equal Rights Amendment." CR, 93d Cong., 1st sess., 21 June 1973, 119, pt. 16: 20673-74. Contains: Ladies Auxiliary of Veterans of Foreign Wars position on ERA.

162. _____. "Petitions: House Joint Resolution No. 11." CR, 93d Cong., 2d sess., 28 February 1974, 120: S2405. Contains: Petition of the General Assembly of Ohio.

163. _____. "Ratification of the Equal Rights Amendment." CR, 93d Cong., 2d sess., 6 March 1974, 120: S2966-71. Contains: Lynn A. Fishel, "Reversals in the Federal Constitutional Amendment Process: Efficacy of State Ratifications of the Equal Rights Amendment," Indiana Law Journal.

164. _____. "Ratification of the Equal Rights Amendment." CR, 94th Cong., 1st sess., 28 January 1975, 121: S1083-85. Contains: Lucy Komisar, "10 Myths About the Equal Rights Amendment," Family Circle, May 1974.

165. _____. "Equal Rights Amendment." CR, 94th Cong., 1st sess., 10 March 1975, 121: S3507-509. Contains: "Women's Equality Fight," editorial in Des Moines Register, 6 March 1975, and "The Equal Rights Amendment: What It Will and Won't Do," published by Iowa Commission on the Status of Women.

166. _____. "Ratification of the Equal Rights Amendment." CR, 94th Cong., 1st sess., 23 April 1975, 121: S6576. Contains: Tom Wicker, "One More Spring," New York Times, 18 April 1975.

2.   Hearings

167. United States. Congress. Senate. Committee on the Judiciary.
Subcommittee on Constitutional Amendments. Equal Rights Amendment:
Hearing on S. J. Res. 64, Proposing an Amendment to the Constitution
of the United States Relative to Equal Rights for Men and Women.
70th Cong., 2d sess., 1 February 1929. Washington, D.C.: Government
Printing Office, 1929.

168. _____. Equal Rights Hearing on S. J. Res. 52, Proposing an
Amendment to the Constitution of the United States Relative to Equal
Rights for Men and Women. 71st Cong., 3d sess., 6 January 1931.
Washington, D.C.: Government Printing Office, 1931.

169. _____. Equal Rights for Men and Women: Hearing on S. J.
Res. 1, Proposing an Amendment to the Constitution of the United States
Relative to Equal Rights for Men and Women. 73d Cong., 1st sess., 27
May 1933. Washington, D.C.: Government Printing Office, 1933.

170. _____. Equal Rights for Men and Women: Hearings on S. J.
Res. 65, Proposing an Amendment to the Constitution of the United
States Relative to Equal Rights for Men and Women. 75th Cong., 3d
sess., 7-10 February 1938 and Supplemental Statements, 7 March 1938.
Washington, D.C.: Government Printing Office, 1938.

171. _____. Equal Rights Amendment Hearings on S. J. Res. 61,
Proposing an Amendment to the Constitution of the United States
Relative to Equal Rights for Men and Women. 79th Cong., 1st sess.,
28 September 1945. Washington, D.C.: Government Printing Office,
1945.

172. _____. Hearings on S. J. Res. 39, Proposing an Amendment
to the Constitution of the United States Relative to Equal Rights for
Men and Women. 84th Cong., 2d sess., 11, 13 April 1956. Washington,
D.C.: Government Printing Office, 1956.

173. _____. The "Equal Rights" Amendment Hearings on S. J. Res. 61
to Amend the Constitution so as to Provide Equal Rights for Men and
Women. 91st Cong., 2d sess., 5-7 May 1970. Excerpted in entries
#439, 452, 485.

174. _____. Committee on the Judiciary. Equal Rights
1970: Hearings on S. J. Res. 61 and S. J. Res. 231,
Proposing an Amendment to the United States Constitution Relative to
Equal Rights for Men and Women. 91st Cong., 2d sess., 9-11, 15
September 1970. Washington, D.C.: Government Printing Office, 1970.

3.   Reports

175. United States. Congress. Senate. Committee on the Judiciary.
Equal Rights Amendment: Report to Accompany S. J. Res. 65. S. Rept.
1641, 75th Cong., 3d sess., 20 April 1938. [Cited CR, 83, pt. 5:
5684; not printed.]

176. _____. Report to Accompany S. J. Res. 8, Proposing an
Amendment to the Constitution of the United States Granting Equal
Rights to Women. S. Rept. 1321, 77th Cong., 2d sess., 11 May 1942.
[Cited CR, 88, pt. 3: 4033; not printed.]

177. _____. Report to Accompany S. J. Res. 25, Proposing an
Amendment to the Constitution of the United States Granting Equal
Rights to Men and Women. S. Rept. 267, 78th Cong., 1st sess., 28 May
1943. [Cited CR, 89, pt. 4: 5017.]

178. _____. Equal Rights Amendment: Report (and individual views)
to Accompany S. J. Res. 61. S. Rept. 1013, 2 pts., 79th Cong., 2d
sess., 5 March 1946. [Part 1 cited CR, 92, pt. 2: 1900; part 2 cited
CR, 92, pt. 2: 2142.]

179. _____. Senate. Equal Rights Amendment: Questions and
Answers Prepared by the Research Department of the National Woman's
Party. By Helena Hill Weed. S. Doc. 209, 79th Cong., 2d sess., 1946.

180. _____. Committee on the Judiciary. Proposing an Amendment
to the Constitution of the United States Relative to Equal Rights for
Men and Women: Report to Accompany S. J. Res. 76. S. Rept. 1208,
80th Cong., 2d sess., 30 April 1948. [Cited CR, 94, pt. 4: 5090.]

181. _____. "Equal Rights": Report to Accompany S. J. Res. 25.
S. Rept. 137, 81st Cong., 1st sess., 22 March 1949. [Cited CR, 95,
pt. 3: 2887.]

182. _____. Equal Rights Amendment: Report to Accompany S. J.
Res. 3. S. Rept. 356, 82d Cong., 1st sess., 23 May 1951. [Cited
CR, 97, pt. 4: 5663.]

183. _____. Equal Rights for Men and Women: Report to Accompany
S. J. Res. 49. S. Rept. 221, 83d Cong., 1st sess., 4 May 1953.
[Cited CR, 99, pt. 4: 4313.]

184. _____. Equal Rights for Men and Women: Report to Accompany
S. J. Res. 39. S. Rept. 1991, 84th Cong., 2d sess., 14 May 1956.
[Cited CR, 102, pt. 6: 8018.]

185. _____. Equal Rights for Men and Women: Report to Accompany
S. J. Res. 80. S. Rept. 1150, 85th Cong., 1st sess., 27 August 1957.
[Cited CR, 103, pt. 12: 15999.]

186. _____. Equal Rights for Men and Women: Report to Accompany
S. J. Res. 69. S. Rept. 303, 86th Cong., 1st sess., 20 May 1959.
[Cited CR, 105, pt. 7: 8555.]

187. _____. Equal Rights for Men and Women: Report to Accompany
S. J. Res. 142. S. Rept. 2192, 87th Cong., 2d sess., 28 September
1962. [Cited CR, 108, pt. 16: 21161.]

188. _____. Committee on Rules and Administration. Equal Rights
Amendment: Questions and Answers: Report to Accompany S. Res. 410,
Authorizing the Printing of a Senate Document of a Revised Edition of
Senate Document No. 74, 82D Congress, Entitled "Equal Rights
Amendment." S. Rept. 2256, 87th Cong., 2d sess., 1 October 1962.
[Cited CR, 108, pt. 16: 21410.]

189. _____. Committee on the Judiciary. Equal Rights for Men and
Women: Report to Accompany S. J. Res. 45. S. Rept. 1558, 88th Cong.,
2d sess., 14 September 1964. [Cited CR, 110, pt. 17: 22025; excerpted
in CR, 89th Cong., 1st sess., 24 May 1965, pt. 8: 11350-51.]

190. _____. Report to Accompany S. J. Res. 8, S. J. Res. 9, H. J.
Res. 208, Joint Resolutions Proposing an Amendment to the Constitution
Relative to Equal Rights for Men and Women. S. Rept. 92-689, 92d
Cong., 2d sess., 14 March 1972. [Cited CR, 118, pt. 7: 8224.]

191. _____. Subcommittee on Constitutional Amendments. Annual
Report. No. 91-1367, 91st Cong., 2d sess., 23 November 1970. [Cited
CR, 116, pt. 28: 38445.]

B. House of Representatives

1. Debates and Materials Read into the *Congressional Record*

192. United States. Congress. House. "Public Bills, Resolutions, and
Memorials." CR, 68th Cong., 1st sess., 13 December 1923, 65, pt. 1:
285. Representative Anthony introduces the Equal Rights Amendment,
H. J. Res. 75.

193. _____. "Progress Registered in Campaign for Equal-Rights
Amendment." CR, 74th Cong., 2d sess., 8 June 1936, 80, pt. 9: 9287-89.

194. _____. "Mr. Bigelow's Statement on Equal Rights." CR, 75th
Cong., 1st sess., 15 April 1937, 81, pt. 9: 856-57 (Appendix).
Contains: "Statement of Hon. Herbert S. Bigelow, of Ohio."

195. _____. "Susan B. Anthony." CR, 77th Cong., 1st sess., 24
March 1941, 87, pt. 11: A1364-67. Contains: "Memorial Services to
Susan B. Anthony," Equal Rights, 15 February 1941; and Amelia Himes
Walker, "The Trial of Susan B. Anthony," Equal Rights, March 1941.

196. _____. "Katharine Hepburn on Equal Rights." CR, 77th Cong.,
2d sess., 27 March 1942, 88, pt. 8: A1241.

197. _____. "Equality for Women." CR, 77th Cong., 2d sess.,
25 May 1942, 88, pt. 9: A1897-98. Contains: "World Woman's Party
Demands of the United Nations Freedom and Equality for Women."

198. _____. "The Equal Rights Amendment." CR, 78th Cong., 1st
sess., 6 January 1943, 89, pt. 1: 13-14.

199. _____. "Equal Rights for Whom?" CR, 78th Cong., 1st sess., 22 March 1943, 89, pt. 9: A1326-27. Contains a letter from Mrs. James A. Starr; and a circular from the Michigan League of Women Voters, "Look Twice at the Equal-Rights Amendment."

200. _____. "Misleading Equal Rights Amendment." CR, 78th Cong., 1st sess., 12 April 1943, 89, pt. 10: A1771-72.

201. _____. "Equal Rights Amendment." CR, 78th Cong., 1st sess., 3 May 1943, 89, pt. 10: A2091-92. Contains: "Resolution of Executive Board of Wayne County CIO Council, Detroit, Michigan, April 13, 1943."

202. _____. "Equality Before the Law." CR, 78th Cong., 1st sess., 21 September 1943, 89, pt. 11: A3929. Contains an article from the New York Herald Tribune, 20 September 1943.

203. _____. "Equal Rights Amendment--Discharge Petition." CR, 78th Cong., 2d sess., 15 February 1944, 90, pt. 2: 1676-78.

204. _____. "Address by Judge Chamberlin on Equal Rights Amendment." CR, 78th Cong., 2d sess., 3 June 1944, 90, pt. 9: A2760-62. Contains: Harry O. Chamberlin, address to National Association of Women, 23 May 1944.

205. _____. "Equal-Rights Amendment." CR, 79th Cong., 1st sess., 29 January 1945, 91, pt. 1: 562-64.

206. _____. "Sponsors of the Equal Rights Amendment." CR, 79th Cong., 1st sess., 31 January 1945, 91, pt. 1: 669-70.

207. _____. "Child-Care Program--Equal-Rights Amendment." CR, 79th Cong., 1st sess., 19 February 1945, 91, pt. 10: A700. Contains a letter from R. J. Thomas, International President of UAW-CIO; and a resolution adopted at National UAW-CIO Conference, 8-9 December 1944.

208. _____. "New York Legislature Approves Equal Rights Amendment." CR, 79th Cong., 1st sess., 17 April 1945, 91, pt. 11: A1780-81. Includes: "New York for Equal Rights," New York Herald Tribune, 29 March 1945.

209. _____. "Equal Rights for Women." CR, 79th Cong., 1st sess., 3 May 1945, 91, pt. 11: A2038. Contains a resolution of the New York State Assembly.

210. _____. "Equal Rights Amendment." CR, 79th Cong., 1st sess., 9 May 1945, 91, pt. 4: 4340.

211. _____. "Equal Rights Amendment." CR, 79th Cong. 1st sess., 9 May 1945, 91, pt. 11: A2182-83. Contains: Grace B. Doering, "Saturday Town Meeting--Equal Rights for Women." Cleveland (Ohio) News; and Mrs. Charles Bang (National Women's Trade Union League of America), "Why Take Off Your Head to Cure a Headache."

212. _____. "The Equal Rights Amendment." CR, 79th Cong., 1st sess., 2 July 1945, 91, pt. 12: 3212-14. Contains a memorandum by Marvin Harrison.

213. _____. "Equal Rights Amendment." CR, 79th Cong., 1st sess.,
3 July 1945, 91, pt. 12: A3234-36. Contains: Marvin Harrison, "The
Equal-Rights Amendment Would Wipe Off the Statute Books All Laws Which
Now Give Needed and Special Protection to Women."

214. _____. "The Equal-Rights Amendment." CR, 79th Cong., 1st
sess., 9 July 1945, 91, pt. 12: A3343-44. Contains: Nora Stanton
Barney, "Why I Am for the Equal-Rights Amendment."

215. _____. "Equal Rights Amendment." CR, 79th Cong., 1st sess.,
20 July 1945, 91, pt. 12: A3565. Contains a statement by Worth M.
Tippy.

216. _____. "Illusory Women's Rights." CR, 79th Cong., 1st sess.,
21 July 1945, 91, pt. 12: A3599-3600. Contains an article from the
Washington Post, 19 July 1945.

217. _____. "Equal Rights Amendment." CR, 79th Cong., 1st sess.,
21 July 1945, 91, pt. 12: A3601-602. Contains minority views relating
to House Report No. 907.

218. _____. "Equal Rights Amendment." CR, 79th Cong., 1st sess.,
14 September 1945, 91, pt. 12: A3897-98. Contains: Chase Going
Woodhouse, Union Times (New Haven, Connecticut), 21 July 1945.

219. _____. "The Equal Rights Amendment--Article from the New York
Herald Tribune with Introductory Statement by Mrs. Florence L. C.
Kitchelt." CR, 79th Cong., 1st sess., 24 September 1945, 91, pt. 12:
A4020-21.

220. _____. "Women Go to Washington." CR, 79th Cong., 1st sess.,
10 October 1945, 91, pt. 12: A4247. Contains an editorial from
Waterloo Daily Courier (Iowa), 5 October 1945.

221. _____. "Address of Mrs. Harvey W. Wiley." CR, 79th Cong.,
2d sess., 3 April 1946, 92, pt. 10: A1894-96. Includes a foreword
by George Gordon Battle; address is to Berks County, Pennsylvania
Federation of Women's Clubs.

222. _____. "Misleading Amendment Dies." CR, 79th Cong., 2d sess.,
24 July 1946, 92, pt. 12: A4364. Contains an article from the
Cleveland Plain Dealer, 22 July 1946.

223. _____. "Unfinished Business." CR, 79th Cong., 2d sess., 30
July 1946, 92, pt. 12: A4615. Contains an editorial from the
New York Herald Tribune, 20 July 1946.

224. _____. "Equal Rights for Women." CR, 79th Cong., 2d sess.,
1 August 1946, 92, pt. 12: A4720-21. Contains: Mary Hornaday,
"Another Way to Women's Equal Rights," Christian Science Monitor.

225. _____. "Equal Rights Amendment." CR, 80th Cong., 2d sess.,
19 January 1948, 94, pt. 9: A267-68. Contains: Clifford Davis,
speech to Business and Professional Women's Clubs of Memphis.

226. _____. "Equal Rights Amendment." CR, 80th Cong., 2d sess.,
11 March 1948, 94, pt. 10: A1541.

227. _____. "Equal Rights for Men and Women." CR, 81st Cong.,
     1st sess., 8 February 1949, 95, pt. 1: 981.

228. _____. "Equal Rights." CR, 81st Cong., 1st sess., 12 April
     1949, 95, pt. 13: A2214-15. Contains an article from the Washington
     Post, 1 April 1949.

229. _____. "Equal Rights for Men and Women." CR, 81st Cong.,
     2d sess., 6 March 1950, 96, pt. 3: 2855.

230. _____. "Equal Rights Amendment." CR, 81st Cong., 2d sess.,
     6 March 1950, 96, pt. 14: A1686-87.

231. _____. "Equal Rights for Women." CR, 81st Cong., 2d sess.,
     7 March 1950, 96, pt. 3: 2953.

232. _____. "Equal Perils--Not Equal Rights." CR, 81st Cong.,
     2d sess., 7 March 1950, 96, pt. 14: A2053-54. Contains: Emanuel
     Celler, "Amendment Represents Neither Sound Law Nor Sound Behavior."
     Daily Compass, 17 March 1950.

233. _____. "Equal Rights for Women." CR, 81st Cong., 2d sess.,
     8 March 1950, 96, pt. 3: 3041.

234. _____. "Equal Rights Amendment." CR, 81st Cong., 2d sess.,
     22 March 1950, 96, pt. 14: A2156-57.

235. _____. "Equal Rights for Women." CR, 82d Cong., 1st sess.,
     2 February 1951, 97, pt. 1: 901-902.

236. _____. "Equal Rights." CR, 82d Cong., 1st sess., 12 March
     1951, 97, pt. 11: A1330-31. Contains: Florence A. Armstrong, "Equal
     Rights for Men and Women in the States," Shell Rock (Iowa) News.

237. _____. "Free the Women, by Dr. Florence A. Armstrong." CR,
     82d Cong., 1st sess., 25 July 1951, 97, pt. 14: A4670-71.

238. _____. "The Equal-Suffrage Amendment." CR, 83d Cong., 1st
     sess., 16 March 1953, 99, pt. 2: 1994-95.

239. _____. "Community Property Laws and the Equal Rights Amend-
     ment." CR, 83d Cong., 1st sess., 15 June 1953, 99, pt. 11: A3423-24.

240. _____. "The Equal Rights Amendment." CR, 83d Cong., 1st sess.,
     31 July 1953, 99, pt. 12: A4922-24. Contains a letter from Hazel
     Palmer.

241. _____. "Protecting Widow's Rights under the Equal Rights
     Amendment." CR, 83d Cong., 2d sess., 27 January 1954, 100, pt. 13:
     A627-28. Contains an essay by Marjorie Temple.

242. _____. "Equal Rights and the Hayden Rider." CR, 83d Cong.,
     2d sess., 14 April 1954, 100, Appendix: A2844-45. Contains: Alma
     Lutz, New York Herald Tribune, 1 August 1953.

243. _____. "The Equal Rights Amendment." CR, 84th Cong., 1st
     sess., 8 February 1955, 101, pt. 1: 1339-41.

244. _____. "Equal Rights for Women." CR, 84th Cong., 1st sess.,
20 July 1955, 101, pt. 9: 11088-89.

245. _____. "The Anniversary of the Birth of Susan B. Anthony."
CR, 84th Cong., 2d sess., 20 February 1956, 102, pt. 3: 2921-26.

246. _____. "Sponsors of the Equal Rights Amendment." CR, 84th
Cong., 2d sess., 19 July 1956, 102, pt. 10: 13554.

247. _____. "Equal Rights for Women." CR, 85th Cong., 1st sess.,
14 February 1957, 103, Appendix: A1094-95. Contains a statement by
Hazel Palmer.

248. _____. "A Brief Summary by the National Federation of
Business and Professional Women's Clubs, Inc., of the Reasons Why Its
Membership Urges Passage of the Equal Rights Amendment." CR, 85th
Cong., 1st sess., 20 February 1957, 103, Appendix: A1308-309.

249. _____. "Work for Equal Legal Rights." CR, 85th Cong., 1st
sess., 28 March 1957, 103, Appendix: A2522-23. Contains an essay by
Hazel Palmer.

250. _____. "Equal Rights for Men and Women." CR, 85th Cong.,
1st sess., 17 July 1957, 103, pt. 9: 12043.

251. _____. "Equal Rights Amendment." CR, 85th Cong., 1st sess.,
19 July 1957, 103, pt. 9: 12236-40.

252. _____. "Rights for Women." CR, 85th Cong., 1st sess.,
24 July 1957, 103, Appendix: A5994-95.

253. _____. "Equal Rights for Women." CR, 85th Cong., 1st sess.,
29 July 1957, 103, pt. 10: 12959.

254. _____. "Equal Rights for Women." CR, 85th Cong., 1st sess.,
1 August 1957, 103, pt. 10: 13414.

255. _____. "Equal Rights Amendment." CR, 85th Cong., 1st sess.,
19 August 1957, 103, Appendix: 6798. Contains a letter from R. N.
Longwell, California Chair of National Woman's Party.

256. _____. "Equal Rights Amendment." CR, 85th Cong., 1st sess.,
22 August 1957, 103, pt. 12: 15709-10.

257. _____. "Susan B. Anthony." CR, 86th Cong., 1st sess.,
16 February 1959, 105, pt. 2: 2414-20.

258. _____. "The Proposed Equal Rights Amendment to the U. S.
Constitution." CR, 86th Cong., 1st sess., 12 May 1959, 105, Appendix:
A3998. Contains an essay by Sarah Jane Cunningham.

259. _____. "The Equal Rights Movement." CR, 86th Cong., 1st
sess., 21 July 1959, 105, pt. 11: 13929. Contains: Katharine St.
George, "The Equal Rights Amendment," address at 111th birthday
celebration of Seneca Falls, in Washington, 19 July 1959.

260. _____. "Equal Economic and Political Rights." CR, 86th Cong., 2d sess., 11 January 1960, 106, Appendix: A154. Contains a resolution by the National Association of Women Lawyers, 23 August 1959.

261. _____. "Equal Rights." CR, 87th Cong., 1st sess., 20 July 1961, 107, pt. 10: 13122.

262. _____. "Equal Rights for Women." CR, 87th Cong., 1st sess., 25 July 1961, 107, pt. 10: 13444.

263. _____. "Connecticut Memorializes Congress for Equal Rights Amendment." CR, 87th Cong., 1st sess., 27 July 1961, 107, pt. 10: 13830-31.

264. _____. "Equal Rights for Women." CR, 87th Cong., 1st sess., 30 August 1961, 107, pt. 13: 17644.

265. _____. "Susan B. Anthony." CR, 87th Cong., 2d sess., 15 February 1962, 108, pt. 2: 2262. Contains a resolution of Susan B. Anthony Memorial, Inc.

266. _____. "Equal Rights for Men and Women." CR, 88th Cong., 1st sess., 21 February 1963, 109, pt. 2: 2712.

267. _____. "The Equal Rights for Women Amendment." CR, 88th Cong., 1st sess., 9 April 1963, 109, Appendix: A2157-58. Contains a resolution of the Fairfield County Republican Women's Association.

268. _____. "Horton Amendment for Women's Rights." CR, 89th Cong., 1st sess., 18 February 1965, 111, pt. 3: 2990.

269. _____. "Equal Rights for Men and Women." CR, 89th Cong., 1st sess., 30 March 1965, 111, pt. 5: 6357.

270. _____. "New York State Legislature Adopts Resolution Calling for Constitutional Amendment to Prohibit Discrimination on Account of Sex." CR, 89th Cong., 1st sess., 2 June 1965, 111, Appendix: 2837.

271. _____. "The Sex Amendment--Equality for Gals." CR, 89th Cong., 1st sess., 7 July 1965, 111, Appendix: 3588-89. Contains an article by Dorothy Daniel (Publisher's Auxiliary), 3 July 1965.

272. _____. "Equality under the Law." CR, 89th Cong., 2d sess., 10 February 1966, 112, pt. 3: 2827-28.

273. _____. "Introduction of Joint Resolution to Guarantee Equal Rights for Men and Women." CR, 89th Cong., 2d sess., 19 April 1966, 112, pt. 7: 8452.

274. _____. "Guaranteeing Equal Rights for Men and Women." CR, 90th Cong., 1st sess., 12 January 1967, 113, pt. 1: 406-409. Contains: Howard G. Earl, "Your Next Nurse May Be a Man," Today's Health, February 1966.

275. _____. "Equal Rights for Women." CR, 90th Cong., 1st sess., 17 January 1967, 113, pt. 1: 684.

276. _____. "Equal Rights for Women." CR, 90th Cong., 1st sess., 21 February 1967, 113, pt. 3: 4174.

277. _____. "Equal Rights for Women." CR, 90th Cong., 1st sess., 28 February 1967, 113, pt. 4: 4812-18.

278. _____. "Joint Resolution to Provide First-Class Citizenship for the Ladies." CR, 90th Cong., 1st sess., 2 March 1967, 113, pt. 4: 5107.

279. _____. "Congressman Claude Pepper Proposes Legislation to Guarantee Equal Rights for Men and Women--Regardless of Sex or Age." CR, 90th Cong., 1st sess., 26 April 1967, 113, pt. 8: 10882-83.

280. _____. "Equal Rights for Women." CR, 90th Cong., 1st sess., 16 October 1967, 113, pt. 21: 28948-49.

281. _____. "A Tribute to Maine's Women." CR, 91st Cong., 1st sess., 19 March 1969, 115, pt. 5: 6882.

282. _____. "Equal Rights for Women." CR, 91st Cong., 1st sess., 21 May 1969, 115, pt. 10: 13380-81.

283. _____. "Constitutional Amendment to Provide Equal Rights for the Nation's Women." CR, 91st Cong., 1st sess., 30 June 1969, 115, pt. 13: 17934.

284. _____. "Equal Rights Amendment." CR, 91st Cong., 1st sess., 26 November 1969, 115, pt. 27: 35964. Contains: Adele Weaver's memorandum (National Association of Women Lawyers and Florida Federation of Business and Professional Women's Clubs).

285. _____. "Equal Rights for Men and Women." CR, 91st Cong., 1st sess., 8 December 1969, 115, pt. 28: 37658.

286. _____. "Equal Rights for Men and Women." CR, 91st Cong., 2d sess., 16 March 1970, 116, pt. 6: 7559. Contains: "Citizens' Advisory Council on the Status of Women Endorses Equal Rights Amendment." (WL)

287. _____. "A Memorandum on the Proposed Equal Rights Amendment to the Constitution." CR, 91st Cong., 2d sess., 26 March 1970, 116, pt. 7: 9684-88. Contains: Citizens' Advisory Council on the Status of Women, "The Proposed Equal Rights Amendment to the United States Constitution--A Memorandum," March 1970. (WL)

288. _____. "Women's Rights Recommendations." CR, 91st Cong., 2d sess., 29 April 1970, 116, pt. 10: 13524-25. Contains: Elizabeth Shelton, Washington Post, 23 April 1970.

289. _____. "Legal Impact on Proposed Equal Rights Amendment by Adele T. Weaver." CR, 91st Cong., 2d sess., 20 May 1970, 116, pt. 12: 16300-302. Contains a statement made by Claude Pepper, 21 January 1943, 78th Cong., on S. J. Res. 25; and Adele Weaver's testimony before the Senate Judiciary Committee.

290. _____. "Marguerite Rawalt." CR, 91st Cong., 2d sess., 10 June 1970, 116, pt. 14: 19349-52. Contains her testimony before the Senate Judiciary Committee, "Support of the 'Equal Rights Amendment' to the Constitution." This has been reprinted by KNOW, Inc. (WL)

291. _____. "Providing for Consideration of H. R. 17970, Military Construction Appropriations, 1971." CR, 91st Cong., 2d sess, 11 June 1970, 116, pt. 14: 19356.

292. _____. "Women's Equality Act of 1970." CR, 91st Cong., 2d sess., 2 July 1970, 116, pt. 17: 22681-82.

293. _____. "Motion to Discharge Committee." CR, 91st Cong., 2d sess., 20 July 1970, 116, pt. 18: 24999-25000.

294. _____. "Tribute to the Honorable Martha W. Griffiths." CR, 91st Cong., 2d sess., 28 July 1970, 116, pt. 19: 25998-99.

295. _____. "Albert Supports Women's Rights Amendment." CR, 91st Cong., 2d sess., 28 July 1970, 116, pt. 19: 26252.

296. _____. "Equality of Opportunity for Women." CR, 91st Cong., 2d sess., 4 August 1970, 116, pt. 20: 27358-59.

297. _____. "The Equal Rights Amendment." CR, 91st Cong., 2d sess., 5 August 1970, 116, pt. 20: 27447.

298. _____. "Women's Rights Amendment." CR, 91st Cong., 2d sess., 5 August 1970, 116, pt. 20: 27512-13. Contains an essay by Dr. and Mrs. Robert Logan.

299. _____. "The Equal Rights Amendment." CR, 91st Cong., 2d sess., 6 August 1970, 116, pt. 20: 27769-71. Contains a letter from Virginia R. Allan (Chair of President's Task Force on Women's Rights and Responsibilities), 15 December 1969; and Congressperson Dwyer's testimony before Senate Judiciary Committee, May 1970.

300. _____. "Amendment to the Constitution of the United States Relative to Equal Rights for Men and Women." CR, 91st Cong., 2d sess., 10 August 1970, 116, pt. 21: 27999-28037.

301. _____. "By a Vote of 350 to 15, Congress Downgrades the American Woman." CR, 91st Cong., 2d sess., 11 August 1970, 116, pt. 21: 28199.

302. _____. "The Equal Rights Amendment." CR, 91st Cong., 2d sess., 11 August 1970, 116, pt. 21: 28335-36.

303. _____. "Amendment to the Constitution of the United States Relative to Equal Rights for Men and Women." CR, 91st Cong., 2d sess., 14 August 1970, 116, pt. 21: 29056-57.

304. _____. "Equal Rights." CR, 91st Cong., 2d sess., 25 August 1970, 116, pt. 22: 30033.

305. _____. "Women's Rights Amendment May End Protection." CR, 91st Cong., 2d sess., 14 September 1970, 116, pt. 23: 31656. Contains Richard Wilson, Evening Star (Washington, D.C.), 14 August 1970.

306. _____. "The Equal Rights Amendment--What It Will and Will Not Do." CR, 91st Cong., 2d sess., 18 September 1970, 116, pt. 24: 32669-70. Publication of the Citizens' Advisory Council on the Status of Women. (WL)

307. _____. "Equal Rights Amendment Hearings." CR, 91st Cong., 2d sess., 29 September 1970, 116, pt. 25: 34023-25. Contains a letter from the National Association of Women Lawyers, 14 September 1970, to the Senate Judiciary Committee; and "Equal Rights: Who Is Against It and Why," New York Times, 13 September 1970.

308. _____. "Horton Seeks Amendment for Women's Rights." CR, 92d Cong., 1st sess., 21 January 1971, 117, pt. 1: 43. Contains: Congressperson Horton, "Women Ask Freedom to Develop Their Own Potential: Horton Says Equal Rights Amendment Would Afford Women Full Equal Opportunity," July 1970.

309. _____. "Equal Rights for Women." CR, 92d Cong., 1st sess., 10 February 1971, 117, pt. 2: 2382-83.

310. _____. "Fascell Introduces Equal Rights Amendment." CR, 92d Cong., 1st sess., 1 March 1971, 117, pt. 4: 4215.

311. _____. "Equal Rights Amendment." CR, 92d Cong., 1st sess., 10 March 1971, 117, pt. 5: 5897.

312. _____. "Women's Equality Act of 1971." CR, 92d Cong., 1st sess., 25 March 1971, 117, pt. 5: 8137-38.

313. _____. "Equal Rights Amendment." CR, 92d Cong., 1st sess., 20 April 1971, 117, pt. 9: 11021-23. Contains: Adele T. Weaver, "Statement Favoring Proposed Equal Rights Amendment," testimony before Judiciary Committee, 31 March 1971.

314. _____. "Congressman Dingell Opposes the So-Called Equal Rights Amendment for Women." CR, 92d Cong., 1st sess., 23 April 1971, 117, pt. 10: 11766-70. Contains: Myra K. Wolfgang, "Testimony on Women's Equality Act and Equal Rights Amendment," before Judiciary Committee, 31 March 1971.

315. _____. "Equal Rights Amendment." CR, 92d Cong., 1st sess., 5 May 1971, 117, pt. 10: 13664-65. Contains: Marguerite Rawalt (National Association of Women Lawyers), "Equal Rights Amendment."

316. _____. "The Equal Rights Amendment." CR, 92d Cong., 1st sess., 10 June 1971, 117, pt. 15: 19402-403.

317. _____. "Congressman McClory Addresses Chicago Rotarians on
   Equal Rights for Women." CR, 92d Cong., 1st sess., 23 June 1971, 117,
   pt. 16: 21722-23. Contains: "The Equal Rights Amendment--Will It Make
   Women More Equal?"

318. _____. "Equal Rights for Women." CR, 92d Cong., 1st sess.,
   15 July 1971, 117, pt. 19: 25276.

319. _____. "Equal Rights Amendment." CR, 92d Cong., 1st sess.,
   15 July 1971, 117, pt. 19: 25490.

320. _____. "Women and Constitutional Rights." CR, 92d Cong.,
   1st sess., 20 July 1971, 117, pt. 20: 26319-20. Contains an essay by
   Eulah Laucks.

321. _____. "Equal Rights for Men and Women Supported." CR, 92d
   Cong., 1st sess., 22 July 1971, 117, pt. 20: 26836. Contains a
   resolution of the National Association of Women Lawyers.

322. _____. "Equal Rights for Men and Women Amendment." CR, 92d
   Cong., 1st sess., 27 July 1971, 117, pt. 21: 27399-400.

323. _____. "Equal Rights Amendment." CR, 92d Cong., 1st sess.,
   29 July 1971, 117, pt. 21: 28107.

324. _____. "Church and Society Task Force Reports on Equal Rights
   Amendment." CR, 92d Cong., 1st sess., 16 September 1971, 117, pt. 24:
   32280-81. Contains: Mrs. Virginia K. Mills, "Church and Society Task
   Force Report to Presbytery of Washington City."

325. _____. "Equal Rights for Women--Heard, But Not Seen." CR,
   92d Cong., 1st sess., 21 September 1971, 117, pt. 25: 32717.

326. _____. "Women United for the Equal Rights Amendment Without
   Wiggins' Amendment." CR, 92d Cong., 1st sess., 28 September 1971,
   117, pt. 26: 33744-45.

327. _____. "About 180,000 Working Women Support Equal Rights
   Amendment." CR, 92d Cong., 1st sess., 4 October 1971, 117, pt. 26:
   34851-52. Contains a letter from Osta Underwood (Business and
   Professional Women's Clubs).

328. _____. "Liz Carpenter Seeks Passage of Equal Rights
   Amendment without Wiggins Amendment." CR, 92d Cong., 1st sess.,
   4 October 1971, 117, pt. 26: 34852.

329. _____. "UAW Charges Wiggins Amendment Would Perpetuate
   Discrimination." CR, 92d Cong., 1st sess., 4 October 1971, 117, pt.
   26: 34852. Contains a letter from Olga M. Madar; and "What 'BFOQ'
   Means to You," McCalls, September 1971.

330. _____. "President Nixon Supports ERA." CR, 92d Cong., 1st
   sess., 5 October 1971, 117, pt. 27: 35078.

331. _____. "Providing for Consideration of House Joint Resolution 208, Equal Rights for Men and Women." CR, 92d Cong., 1st sess., 6 October 1971, 117, pt. 27: 35289-90.

332. _____. "Equal Rights for Men and Women." CR, 92 Cong., 1st sess., 6 October 1971, 117, pt. 27: 35295-326.

333. _____. "Equal Rights for Men and Women." CR, 92d Cong., 1st sess., 12 October 1971, 117, pt. 27: 35782-815.

334. _____. "Women's Equal Rights Amendment." CR, 92d Cong., 1st sess., 18 October 1971, 117, pt. 28: 36588-89.

335. _____. "Equality of Women." CR, 92d Cong., 1st sess., 2 November 1971, 117, pt. 30: 38940-42. Contains: Jane Fonda, "I Want to Work with Women," New York Times, 31 October 1971.

336. _____. "Palo Alto Times Supports Equal Rights Amendment." CR, 92d Cong., 1st sess., 9 November 1971, 117, pt. 31: 40253. Contains: "On With Women's Rights Amendment," Palo Alto Times, 15 October 1971.

337. _____. "Constitutional Rights of Women." CR, 92d Cong., 1st sess., 30 November 1971, 117, pt. 33: 43423.

338. _____. "The Equal Rights Amendment." CR, 92d Cong., 2d sess., 29 February 1972, 118, pt. 5: 6143.

339. _____. "The Equal Rights Amendment: A Beginning." CR, 92d Cong., 2d sess., 30 March 1972, 118, pt. 9: 11321. Contains: "A Matter of Simple Justice," Washington Post.

340. _____. "The Concept of Equal Rights." CR, 92d Cong., 2d sess., 1 May 1972, 118, pt. 12: 15022-24. Contains an article by NettaBell Girard Larson.

341. _____. "Poor Women and the Equal Rights Amendment." CR, 92d Cong., 2d sess., 7 June 1972, 118, pt. 16: 20135-36. Contains: Elizabeth Duncan Koontz, "ERA and Upward Mobility for Women."

342. _____. "Equal Rights Amendment." CR, 93d Cong., 1st sess., 1 February 1973, 119, pt. 3: 3112-13. Contains: Bob Yeargin, "Discrimination: Sexual As Well As Racial" and "ERA's Effect... Really a Nagging Question," Las Vegas Sun, December 1972.

343. _____. "Equal Rights Amendment." CR, 93d Cong., 1st sess., 5 February 1973, 119, pt. 3: 3381-82. Contains: Bob Yeargin, "ERA Has Been Around" and "Split Personality--Women in Gaming," Las Vegas Sun, December 1972.

344. _____. "Equal Rights Amendment." CR, 93d Cong., 1st sess., 6 February 1973, 119, pt. 3: 3639-41. Contains: Bob Yeargin, "Like Women--They Do Not Agree," Las Vegas Sun, 28 December 1972; and "Legislature's Reaction to ERA--Uncertain," Las Vegas Sun, 29 December 1972.

345. _____. "Equal Rights in Virginia?" CR, 93d Cong., 1st sess., 8 February 1973, 119, pt. 4: 4155-56. Contains: Helen Dewar, "Women's Rights Bid Dies in Virginia Assembly," and Joseph D. Whitaker, "A Teacher Beats the Law--Virginian's Lost Residence Status Restored." Washington Post, 7 February 1973.

346. _____. "Information on the State of the Union--Message from the President of the United States." (H. Doc. No. 93-52) CR, 1 March 1973, 119, pt. 5: 6017.

347. _____. "Women's Rights and Women's Lib." CR, 93d Cong., 1st sess., 30 April 1973, 119, pt. 11: 13677-78. Contains an article from the Christian Science Monitor, 16 April 1973.

348. _____. "Frontiero Against Richardson." CR, 93d Cong., 1st sess., 16 May 1973, 119, pt. 13: 15853.

349. _____. "Equal Rights Amendment." CR, 93d Cong., 1st sess., 16 May 1973, 119, pt. 13: 15861.

350. _____. "Does ERA Illustrate 'Representation Gap'?" CR, 93d Cong., 1st sess., 13 June 1973, 119, pt. 15: 19380-82.

351. _____. "Business and Professional Women's Clubs, Inc., of America, October 23, 1973." CR, 93d Cong., 1st sess., 23 October 1973, 119, pt. 27: 34880-81.

352. _____. "Endorsement of Equal Rights Amendment by AFL-CIO." CR, 93d Cong., 1st sess., 31 October 1973, 119, pt. 27: 35602. Contains: "Equal Rights Amendment," 22 October 1973.

353. _____. "Equal Rights Amendment." CR, 93d Cong., 2d sess., 31 July 1974, 120: E5158-60. Contains: Lisa Cronin Wohl, Ms., March 1974.

354. _____. "The Equal Rights Amendment." CR, 94th Cong., 1st sess., 10 April 1975, 121: E1694-95. Contains: Ruth Bader Ginsburg, "The Fear of the Equal Rights Amendment," Washington Post, 7 April 1975.

355. _____. "The Story of the Equal Rights Amendment in New York State." CR, 94th Cong., 1st sess., 24 April 1975, 121: E1985-86. Contains: League of Women Voters pamphlet, and "The Story of the Equal Rights Amendment in New York State."

356. _____. "Equal Rights Amendment." CR, 94th Cong., 1st sess., 9 October 1975, 121: E5365.

357. _____. "ERA Defeat May Be a Boon to Womanhood." CR, 94th Cong., 1st sess., 14 November 1975, 121: H11183.

358. _____. "The Women's Movement Is Still Moving." CR, 94th Cong., 2d sess., 28 January 1976, 122: E255-56. Contains: Bella Abzug, Village Voice, 22 December 1975.

2.   Hearings

359.   United States. Congress. House. Committee on the Judiciary.
Equal Rights Amendment to the Constitution: Hearing on H. J. Res. 75.
68th Cong., 2d sess., 4-5 February 1925.   Washington, D.C.:
Government Printing Office, 1925.

360.   _____. Equal Rights Amendment to the Constitution: Hearing
on H. J. Res. 197, Proposing an Amendment to the Constitution of the
United States Relative to Equal Rights for Men and Women.   72d Cong.,
1st sess., 16 March 1932. Washington, D.C.: Government Printing
Office, 1932.

361.   _____. Subcommittee No. 2. Amend the Constitution Relative
to Equal Rights for Men and Women: Statements Presented on H. J. Res.
1 (and Other Resolutions), Proposing an Amendment to the Constitution
of the United States Relative to Equal Rights for Men and Women.
79th Cong., 1st sess., 21 February - 31 March 1945. Washington, D.C.:
Government Printing Office, 1945.

362.   _____. Subcommittee No. 1. Equal Rights Amendment to the
Constitution and Commission on Legal Status of Women: Hearings on
H. J. Res. 49, 62, 85, 86, 89, 104, and 110, and H. R. 1972, 1996,
2003, 2007, 2035, 2323, and 3028.   80th Cong., 2d sess., 10 and 12
March 1948. Washington, D.C.: Government Printing Office, 1948.

363.   _____. Committee on Education and Labor. Special Subcommittee
on Education. Discrimination Against Women: Hearings on Section 805
of H. R. 16098, to Prohibit Discrimination Against Women in Federally
Assisted Programs and in Employment in Education; to Extend the Equal
Pay Act so as to Prohibit Discrimination in Administrative Professional
and Executive Employment; and to Extend the Jurisdiction of the
United States Commission on Civil Rights to Include Sex.   2 pts. 91st
Cong., 2d sess., 17, 19, 26, 29, 30 June 1970. Washington, D.C.:
Government Printing Office, 1970. Abridged in entry #484.

364.   _____. Committee on the Judiciary. Subcommittee No. 4.
Equal Rights for Men and Women 1971: Hearings on H. J. Res. 35, 208,
and Related Bills, Proposing an Amendment to the Constitution of the
United States Relative to Equal Rights for Men and Women.   92d Cong.,
1st sess., 24, 25, 31 March and 1, 2, 5 April 1971. Washington, D.C.:
Government Printing Office, 1971. Excerpts in WL and entry #449.

3.   Reports

365.   United States. Congress. House. Committee on the Judiciary.
Equal-Rights Amendment: Report to Accompany H. J. Res. 49, Proposing
Equal-Rights Amendment to the Constitution. H. Rept. 907, 79th Cong.,
1st sess., 12 July 1945. [Cited CR, 91, pt. 6: 7505.]

366. _____. Report to Accompany H. J. Res. 397, Proposing an Amendment to the Constitution of the United States Relative to Equal Rights for Men and Women. H. Rept. 2196, 80th Cong., 2d sess., 4 June 1948. [Cited CR, 94, pt. 6: 7218.]

367. _____. Report to Accompany H. J. Res. 208, Proposing an Amendment to the Constitution of the United States Relative to Equal Rights for Men and Women. H. Rept. 92-359, 92d Cong., 1st sess., 14 July 1971. [Cited CR, 117, pt. 19: 24935.]

368. _____. Committee on Rules. Report to Accompany H. R. 548, Providing for the Consideration of H. J. Res. 208. H. Rept. 92-365, 92d Cong., 1st sess., 19 July 1971. [Cited CR, 117, pt. 20: 25783.]

two

Other Government Publications

A. Federal Government

369. Citizens' Advisory Council on the Status of Women. "Endorses Equal Rights Amendment." Press Release, 13 February 1970. (WL) Rep. in entries #68, 286.

370. _____. The Equal Rights Amendment and Alimony and Child Support Laws. Washington, D.C.: Government Printing Office, January 1972. (WL) Rep. in entries #147, 149.

371. _____. The Equal Rights Amendment--Senator Ervin's Minority Report and the Yale Law Journal. Washington, D.C.: Government Printing Office, 1972.

372. _____. The Equal Rights Amendment--What It Will and Won't Do. Washington, D.C.: Government Printing Office, 1970. (WL) Rep. in entries #306, 2983, 4074.

373. _____. Interpretation of the Equal Rights Amendment in Accordance with Legislative History. Washington, D.C.: Government Printing Office, 1974. (WL)

374. _____. Only the Equal Rights Amendment Will Promptly End Prison Sentence Discrimination Because of Sex. Washington, D.C.: Government Printing Office, February 1972.

375. _____. The Proposed Equal Rights Amendment to the United States Constitution: A Memorandum. Washington, D.C.: Government Printing Office, March 1970. (WL) Rep. in entries #147, 287.

376. _____. Statement on Bayh Substitute and Ervin Amendment to the Equal Rights Amendment. Washington, D.C.: Government Printing Office, 29 October 1970.

377. _____. Women in 1970. Washington, D.C.: Government Printing Office, 1971.

378. _____. Women in 1971. Washington, D.C.: Government Printing Office, 1972.

379. _____. Women in 1972. Washington, D.C.: Government Printing Office, 1973.

380. _____. Women in 1973. Washington, D.C.: Government Printing Office, 1974.

381. _____. Women in 1974. Washington, D.C.: Government Printing
     Office, 1975.

382. Clark, Tom C. ["Equal Rights for Women in America."] Address to
     National Woman's Party, 2 April 1949. Mimeographed. Washington,
     D.C.: Department of Justice, 1949.

383. Commission on Civil Rights. The Equal Rights Amendment: What's In
     It for Black Women? By Frankie Muse Freeman. Washington, D.C.:
     Government Printing Office, 1973. (B) Rep. from entry #1153.

384. _____. Statement of U.S. Commission on Civil Rights on the
     Equal Rights Amendment: June 1973. Washington, D.C.: Government
     Printing Office, July 1973. (B)

385. Congress. Special Issues of Congressional Record on ERA: 23-25
     January 1950; 10 August 1970; 7-9, 12-14 October 1970; 6, 12 October
     1971; 17, 21-22 March 1972. Washington, D.C.: Government Printing
     Office.

386. Library of Congress. Congressional Research Service. Equal Rights
     Amendment Issue Brief. #74122. By Morrigene Holcomb. Washington,
     D.C.: Government Printing Office, 5 February 1976 (continually
     updated).

387. _____. The Equal Rights Amendment: Its Implications and
     Intent. By Barbara Dixon. Washington, D.C.: Government Printing
     Office, 1 February 1973. Replaced by Equal Rights Amendment:
     Selected Floor Debate and Votes. By Morrigene Holcomb. Washington,
     D.C.: Government Printing Office, 21 December 1974.

388. _____. The Proposed Equal Rights Amendment. By Morrigene
     Holcomb. Washington, D.C.: Government Printing Office, 15 January
     1971; rev. 24 March 1972. Rep. in entry #440.

389. President's Commission on the Status of Women. Report of the
     Committee on Civil and Political Rights. Washington, D.C.:
     Government Printing Office, October 1963. Rep. in entry #471.

390. President's Task Force on Women's Rights and Responsibilities. A
     Matter of Simple Justice. Washington, D.C.: Government Printing
     Office, April 1970.

391. Women's Bureau. Comments by Secretary of Labor, Frances Perkins,
     to Judiciary Committee of House of Representatives on Equal Rights
     Amendment, 1945. Washington, D.C.: Government Printing Office, 1949.

392. _____. Don't Buy a Gold Brick: Proposed Equal Rights Amend-
     ment to United States Constitution. Washington, D.C.: Government
     Printing Office, 1945.

393. _____. Do Women Really Want Equal Rights? By Joan and David
     Landman. Washington, D.C.: Government Printing Office, 1953.
     Rep. from entry #1245.

394. _____. Equal Rights Amendment. Washington, D.C.: Government
     Printing Office, May 1961.

395. _____. State Equal Rights Amendments. Washington, D.C.:
Government Printing Office, 1973. (B)

B. State Government

[Only those government analyses based specifically on ERA
conformance have been included; many more general reviews of
sex discriminatory laws have also been done. Both mimeographed and published material is included. (B) indicates
that the item is a brochure rather than a full report or
pamphlet.]

396. Arizona. Legislative Council. Arizona Laws Which May Discriminate
under ERA. Phoenix: ALC, n.d. Reprinted by League of Women Voters
of Arizona.

397. Arkansas. Legislative Council. "The Effects of the ERA on
Arkansas Law." Information Memo 199. Mimeographed. Little Rock:
ALC, 19 July 1974.

398. California. Assembly Judiciary Committee. Analysis of AJR17/
Karabian: Equal Rights for Men and Women. Sacramento: CAJC, 17 April
1972.

399. California Commission on the Status of Women. Successful Advocacy.
Sacramento: CCSW, 1975. (B)

400. _____. Equal Rights Amendment Project. A Commentary on the
Effect of the Equal Rights Amendment on State Laws and Institutions.
By Anne K. Bingaman. Sacramento: CCSWERAP, 1975.

401. _____. ERA Conformance: An Analysis of the California State
Codes. Sacramento: CCSWERAP, 1975.

402. _____. "Economic Impact of the Equal Rights Amendment."
Unpublished paper on file at Project Office. 1974.

403. _____. Spirit of '76: Equality. Sacramento: CCSWERAP,
1975. (B)

404. Colorado Commission on the Status of Women. The Colorado Equal
Rights Amendment. Denver: CCSW, n.d. (B)

405. _____. Five Year Report: 1967-72. Denver: CCSW, 1972.

406. Colorado. Legislative Council. "Survey of Colorado Revised
Statutes 1975--Categorization of Statutes by Sex-Neutrality or Sex-
Distinctions." Mimeographed. Denver: CLC, 3 October 1975.

407. Connecticut. Office of Legislative Research. The Potential Impact
of the Proposed Equal Rights Amendment on Connecticut Statutes.
Hartford: Connecticut General Assembly Monograph, 7 March 1973.

408. Florida. Office of Attorney General. "Position Paper of Attorney
General on Ratification of the Equal Rights Amendment." By Robert L.
Shevin. Mimeographed. Tallahassee: Department of Legal Affairs, n.d.

409. Georgia Commission on the Status of Women. "The Equal Rights
Amendment and Georgia Law." By Barbara S. Bent and Rose M. Higby.
Mimeographed. Atlanta: GCSW, 1972. (WL)

410. Illinois. Legislative Council. Methods of Implementing "Equal
Rights" Amendment, If Adopted. Springfield: ILC, December 1972.

411. Iowa Commission on the Status of Women. The Equal Rights
Amendment: What It Will and Won't Do. Des Moines: ICSW, 1975.
Rep. in entry #165.

412. Maryland Commission on the Status of Women. "List of Sections of
Maryland Annotated Code Which May Be Affected by the Adoption of the
Proposed Equal Rights Amendments to the United States and Maryland
Constitutions." Mimeographed. Baltimore: MCSW, n.d.

413. Michigan Women's Commission. The ERA Questions and Answers.
Lansing: MWC, 1973. (WL)

414. Missouri Commission on the Status of Women. ERA in Missouri: 9
Questions and Answers. Jefferson City: MCSW, n.d. (B)

415. _____. Impact of ERA on Missouri Statutes. By Providence
Fink. Jefferson City: MCSW, n.d.

416. New Jersey. Assembly Judiciary Committee. Public Hearing on
Assembly Concurrent Resolution No. 67, Proposing Constitutional
Amendment to Provide Equality of Rights of Women. Trenton: NJAC,
2 May 1974.

417. _____. Department of Community Affairs. Division on Women.
The Most Frequently Asked Questions about the New Jersey Equal Rights
Amendment. Trenton: NJDCADW, October 1975. (B)

418. New York. Women's Division. "ERA--Its Legal Effect." By Linda
Winikow and Karen Burstein. Colloquy between New York State Senators
during floor debate on ERA to State Constitution. Mimeographed.
New York City: NYWD, 21 May 1975.

419. Ohio Commission on the Status of Women. Equality of Rights . . .
Shall Not Be Denied or Abridged . . . On Account of Sex. Columbus:
OCSW, 1 September 1973. (B)

420. Ohio. Legislative Service Commission. "Memorandum on Equal Rights
Amendment and Ohio Law." Mimeographed. Columbus: OLSC, 10 April 1973.

421. South Carolina. Office of the Attorney General. "Effect of Equal
Rights Amendment on South Carolina Statutes." Mimeographed. Submitted
by S.C. Coalition for the ERA to Hearing on Proposed ERA, 25 February
1975. Columbia: SCOAG, March 1973.

422. Tennessee Commission on the Status of Women. "The Equal Rights Amendment and the Tennessee Code." Mimeographed. Nashville: TCSW, n.d.

423. Texas. Subcommittee on H.C.R. 57 of House Committee on Constitu-
     tional Revision. "Staff Report on Legal Issues Surrounding H.C.R. 57."
     Mimeographed. Austin: HCCR, 12 May 1975.

424. Utah. Governor's Committee on the Status of Women. Utah and the
     Equal Rights Amendment. Salt Lake City: GCSW, n.d. (B)

425. _____. Office of Legislative Research. "Statutory Sex
     Discrimination in Utah." Mimeographed. Salt Lake City: UOLR, August
     1975.

426. Vermont. Legislative Council. "Report of Joint Committee to Study
     Equal Rights of Women." Mimeographed. Montpelier: VLC, October 1972.

427. Washington. Legislative Council. Judiciary Committee. The
     Potential Impact of House Joint Resolution No. 61--The Equal Rights
     Amendment--On Laws of the State of Washington. Seattle: WLC, 16
     October 1972.

428. Wisconsin. Governor's Commission on the Status of Women. Wisconsin
     Women and the Law. Madison: University of Wisconsin Extension, 1975.

429. _____. Legislative Council. "Background and Highlights of
     1975 Assembly Bill 431, as Amended and Passed by the Assembly, Relating
     to Equal Rights for Men and Women." Mimeographed. Madison: WLC,
     3 March 1975; rev. 11 September 1975. Replaced by "Summary and Analysis
     of Chapter 94: Laws of 1975 Relating to Equal Rights for Men and
     Women," 31 October 1975.

430. _____. Report to the 1973 Legislature on Equal Rights.
     By Special Committee on Equal Rights. Madison: WLC, February 1973.

431. _____. A Summary of Wisconsin Laws Which Treat Men and Women
     Differently; Background Information for the Special Committee on Equal
     Rights. Staff Brief 72-10. Madison: WLC, 22 June 1972.

432. _____. Legislative Reference Bureau. The Equal Rights
     Amendment: How Would It Affect Wisconsin Statutes? Research Bulletin
     70-3. Madison: WLRB, December 1970.

433. _____. "Women's Equal Rights Amendment and the Wisconsin
     Equal Rights Law: List of Material in the Wisconsin Legislative
     Reference Library." Mimeographed. Madison: WLRB, 1926.

three

Books, Articles, and Discussions in
Books, and Dissertations

[This section includes entire books and dissertations on the
ERA, articles in books and dissertations on the ERA, and
whole chapters on or extended discussions of the ERA in books
and dissertations. Pagination is only indicated in the case
of separate articles.]

434. Antieau, Chester James. "The ERA." In Modern Constitutional Law,
vol. 2, pp. 711-15. Rochester, New York: Lawyers Co-operative
Publishing Co., 1969.

435. Beard, Charles A., and Beard, Mary R. "Equal Rights Amendment in
American History." In History of the United States, pp. 554-68. N.Y.:
Macmillan, 1925.

436. Bird, Caroline. Born Female. New and rev. ed. New York: Pocket
Books, 1971. (Orig. David McKay, 1968)

437. Blahna, Loretta J. "The Rhetoric of the Equal Rights Amendment."
Ph.D. dissertation, University of Kansas, 1973.

438. Boles, Janet. "The Coalescence of Controversy: Conditions
Surrounding the Proposed Equal Rights Amendment." Dissertation
project in progress. (2812 Rio Grande, #205, Austin, Texas)

439. Bosmajian, Hamida, and Bosmajian, Haig, eds. This Great Argument:
The Rights of Women. Menlo Park, California: Addison-Wesley
Publishing Co., 1972. Excerpts from entry #173.

440. Boylan, Brian Richard. The Legal Rights of Women. New York:
Award Books, 1971. Appendices B and C rep. entry #388 and Martha
Griffiths' testimony to the Senate Judiciary Committee, Subcommittee
on Constitutional Amendments, 5 May 1970, and to the House Judiciary
Committee, Subcommittee No. 4, 24 March 1971. See entries #173, 364.

441. Brown, Barbara Allen; Freedman, Ann E.; Norton, Eleanor Holmes;
and Ross, Susan D. Sex Discrimination and the Law: Causes and
Remedies. Boston: Little, Brown and Company, 1975.

442. California Commission on the Status of Women, Equal Rights
Amendment Project, ed. Impact ERA: Limitations and Possibilities.
Millbrae, California: Les Femmes Publishing, 1976.

443. Chafe, William H. The American Woman: Her Changing Social,
Economic, and Political Role, 1920-1970. New York: Oxford
University Press, 1972.

444. Davidson, Kenneth M.; Ginsburg, Ruth Bader; and Kay, Herma Hill.
Sex-Based Discrimination: Text, Cases and Materials. St. Paul,
Minnesota: West Publishing Co., 1974.

445. Deckard, Barbara. The Women's Movement: Political, Socioeconomic,
and Psychological Issues. New York: Harper and Row, 1975.

446. DeCrow, Karen. Sexist Justice: How Legal Sexism Affects You.
New York: Random House, 1974.

447. Delsman, Mary Ann. Everything You Need to Know about ERA.
Riverside, California: Meranza Press, 1975.

448. "Equal Rights Amendment." In University Debaters' Annual 1926-1927,
edited by Edith M. Phelps. New York: H. W. Wilson, 1927.

449. "Equal Rights and Women." In Issues 71-72: Documents in Current
American Government and Politics, edited by Sidney Wise, pp. 1-14.
New York: Thomas Crowell, 1971. (WL) Contains: Sam Ervin, Jr.,
"The Equal Rights Amendment: An Atomic Mousetrap"; and Norman Dorsen,
"The Equal Rights Amendment: The Case For"--testimony before House
Judiciary Committee, Subcommittee No. 4, 23 and 25 March 1971. See
entry #364 for complete hearings; also entries #132, 143.

450. "Equal Rights for Women." In Congressional Quarterly's Guide to
the Congress of the United States, p. 294. Washington, D.C.:
Congressional Quarterly Service, 1971.

451. Farnham, Marynia F., and Lundberg, Ferdinand. Modern Woman: The
Lost Sex. New York: Harper, 1947.

452. Ford, Lee Ellen, ed. Equal Rights Amendment. Women's Legal
Handbook Series on Job and Sex Discrimination, vol. 5. Butler,
Indiana: Ford Associates, 1974.

453. Freeman, Jo. The Politics of Women's Liberation: A Case Study
of an Emerging Social Movement and Its Relation to the Policy Process.
New York: David McKay, 1975.

454. _____, ed. Women: A Feminist Perspective. Palo Alto,
California: Mayfield Publishing, 1975.

455. Gager, Nancy, ed. Women's Rights Almanac: 1974. Bethesda,
Maryland: Elizabeth Cady Stanton Publishing Co., 1974; Harper
Colophon Book, 1975.

456. Gardner, Jo-Ann Evans, comp. The Equal Rights Amendment: A
National Issue Around Which Women Can Unite! Pittsburgh, Pennsylvania:
KNOW, Inc., n.d. Contains a collection of position papers and
editorials.

457. Getman, Julius G. "The Emerging Constitutional Principle of Sexual
Equality." In The Supreme Court Review, 1972, edited by Philip B.
Kurland, pp. 157-80. Chicago, Illinois: University of Chicago Press,
1973.

458. Grossman, Joel B., and Wells, Richard S., eds. Constitutional Law and Judicial Policy-Making. New York: John Wiley, 1972.

459. Heide, Wilma Scott. "Equal Rights Amendment." In Women's Role in Contemporary Society: The Report of the New York City Commission on Human Rights, September 21-25, 1970, pp. 618-23. New York: Avon, 1972.

460. Hole, Judith, and Levine, Ellen. Rebirth of Feminism. New York: Quadrangle, 1971.

461. Irwin, Inez Haynes. Angels and Amazons: A Hundred Years of American Women. New York: Arno Press, 1974.

462. _____. Up Hill with Banners Flying: The Story of the Woman's Party. Penobscot, Maine: Traversity Press, 1964.

463. Johnsen, Julia E., comp. Special Legislation for Women. The Reference Shelf, vol. 4, no. 7. New York: H.W. Wilson, 1926.

464. Kanowitz, Leo. Sex Roles in Law and Society: Cases and Materials. Albuquerque: University of New Mexico Press, 1973; Supplement, 1974.

465. _____. Women and the Law: An Unfinished Revolution. Albuquerque: University of New Mexico Press, 1969.

466. Kraditor, Aileen S. Up from the Pedestal: Selected Writings in the History of American Feminism. Chicago, Illinois: Quadrangle, 1970.

467. Lemons, James Stanley. "The New Woman in the New Era: The Woman Movement from the Great War to the Great Depression." Ph.D. dissertation, University of Missouri, 1967.

468. _____. The Woman Citizen: Social Feminism in the 1920s. Urbana: University of Illinois Press, 1973.

469. "The Lucretia Mott Amendment." In Women of 1924 International, edited by Ida Clyde Clark and Lillian Ballance Sheridan, pp. 200-203. New York: Women's News Service, 1924.

470. Lund, Caroline, and Stone, Betsey. Women and the Equal Rights Amendment. New York: Pathfinder Press, 1970.

471. Mead, Margaret, and Kaplan, Frances Balgley, eds. American Women: The Report of the President's Commission on the Status of Women and Other Publications of the Commission. New York: Scribners' Sons, 1965. Rep. from entry #389.

472. Murphy, Irene. Public Policy on the Status of Women: Agenda and Strategy for the Seventies. Lexington, Massachusetts: D. C. Heath, Lexington Books, 1973.

473. Murray, Pauli. "Equal Rights Amendment." In Women's Role in Contemporary Society: The Report of the New York City Commission on Human Rights, September 21-25, 1970, pp. 612-18. New York: Avon, 1972.

474. _____. "The Rights of Women." In The Rights of Americans: What They Are and What They Should Be, edited by Norman Dorsen, pp. 521-45. New York: Pantheon, 1971.

475. Ondercin, David G. "The Compleat Woman: The Equal Rights Amendment and Perceptions of Womanhood, 1920-1972." Ph.D. dissertation, University of Minnesota, 1973.

476. O'Neill, William. Everyone Was Brave: A History of Feminism in America. Chicago: Quadrangle, 1971. (orig. The Woman Movement: Feminism in the United States and England. New York: Franklin Watts, 1969.)

476a. Pogrebin, Letty Cottin. Getting Yours: How to Make the System Work for the Working Woman. New York: Avon, 1975.

477. Ross, Susan D. The Rights of Women: A Basic ACLU Guide to a Woman's Rights. New York: Avon, 1973.

478. Ryan, John Augustine. "Equal Rights for Women." In Declining Liberty and Other Papers, pp. 101-14. New York: Macmillan, 1927.

479. Scheinfeld, Amram. "Equality for Women." In Women and Men, pp. 347-57. New York: Harcourt, Brace and Co., 1943.

480. Shaffer, Helen. "Status of Women." In Editorial Research Reports on the Women's Movement, pp. 41-63. Washington, D.C.: Congressional Quarterly, 1973. Rep. from entry #1425.

481. Smith, Cyril J. Tradition of Eve. San Antonio, Texas: The Naylor Co., 1961.

482. Smith, Ethel M. Toward Equal Rights for Men and Women. Washington, D.C.: National League of Women Voters, 1929.

483. Sochen, June. Movers and Shakers: American Women Thinkers and Activists, 1900-1970. New York: Quadrangle/New York Times Book Co., 1973.

484. Stimpson, Catharine R., and Congressional Information Service, eds. Discrimination against Women: Congressional Hearings on Equal Rights in Education and Employment. New York: Bowker, 1973. Excerpts from entry #363.

485. _____. Women and the "Equal Rights" Amendment: Senate Sub-committee Hearings on the Constitutional Amendment, 91st Congress. New York: Bowker, 1972. Excerpts from entry #173.

486. Suelzle, Marijean. "The Politics of the Equal Rights Amendment." In Women on the Move: A Feminist Perspective, edited by Jean Ramage Leppalvoto, Joan Acker, Claudeen Naffziger, Karla J. H. Brown, Catherine M. Porter, Barbara A. Mitchell, and Roberta Hanna. A report on the sixth annual conference of the Lila Acheson Wallace School of Community Service and Public Affairs, University of Oregon, Eugene. Pittsburgh, Pennsylvania: KNOW, Inc., 1973.

487. _____. What Every Woman Should Know about the Women's Liberation Movement. Privately published, 1971. Rep. from entry #5745.

488. Taylor, Charlene M., and Herzog, Stuart. <u>Impact Study of the Equal Rights Amendment--Subject: The Arizona Constitution and Statutes</u>. Tucson: Privately published, January 1973.

489. Tolchin, Susan, and Tolchin, Martin. <u>Clout: Womanpower and Politics</u>. New York: Coward, McCann and Geoghegan, 1973.

490. Turner, Jennie McMullin. "Paper Equality." In <u>Special Legislation for Women</u>, compiled by Julia E. Johnsen, pp. 69-86. New York: H. W. Wilson, 1926.

491. <u>Women: Their Changing Roles</u>. New York: Arno Press, 1973.

492. Young, Louisa M., ed. <u>Women's Opportunities and Responsibilities</u>, vol. 251. Philadelphia, Pennsylvania: American Academy of Political and Social Sciences, 1947. See entries #930, 1281.

four

Pamphlets, Brochures, Reports, Papers, and Other Documents

[These are the most difficult types of material to select and
classify because their status as "publications" is often
dubious and always arguable. Therefore, arbitrary lines had
to be drawn in order to define "publication" for the purposes
of this bibliography. In general, this section includes
independent pamphlets (P), self-contained brochures, flyers,
and leaflets (B), and published and mimeographed reports or
papers of some length (R). It excludes mimeographed or type-
written "handouts" resembling organization memoranda more than
brochures; such handouts are not considered independent publications and are only included if they appear on microfilm in the
Herstory (H) or Women and the Law (WL) collections. The line
between a brochure and a handout is not easy to draw, so we
have tried to err on the side of inclusion. The point of
division is to separate the relatively short-lived and narrowly
circulated in-group publications from the more permanent,
widely circulated ones. Also excluded are materials individually
authored and merely reprinted by the organization rather than
prepared for or at the request of the organization. The former
usually appear elsewhere in the bibliography.

The arrangement, due to the nature of the bulk of the material,
is alphabetically by organization (as author) or, when there is
no organization involved, by individual author. Where both
appear, it is assumed that, as already stated, the author has
prepared it for or at the request of the organization.

Within each organization, the arrangement is alphabetical by
title, except that the national chapter is grouped first,
followed by state chapters in alphabetical order.

In most cases the organization-author and publisher are the
same; therefore, the publisher's name in the citation is
merely abbreviated by the initials of the organization.]

493. American Association of University Women. Against an Unqualified
ERA. Washington, D.C.: AAUW, March 1950. (P)

494. _____ . ERA: A Bread and Butter Issue. Washington, D.C.:
AAUW, n.d. (B)

495. _____ . The ERA--A Pro-Con Study. Prepared by Rosamonde
Ramsay Boyd and Dorothy McCullough Lee. Washington, D.C.: AAUW,
c.1953. (P)

496. _____. California Division. <u>What Shall the AAUW Convention</u>
<u>Write to Susan</u>? California: AAUW, June 1971. (P)

497. _____. Illinois Division. Equal Rights Amendment: <u>What It</u>
<u>Is . . . What It Will Do . . . What It Won't Do . . . Right Here in</u>
<u>Illinois</u>! Macomb: AAUW, n.d. (B)

498. _____. North Carolina Division. <u>Revised Manual of Selected</u>
<u>Questions and Answers on the ERA</u>. Compiled by Elizabeth Welch and
Mrs. B. Edward Ritter. Winston-Salem: AAUW, n.d. (P)

499. _____. North Dakota Division and Coordinating Council for
the ERA. <u>Discussion Packet on the Equal Rights Amendment and the</u>
<u>Laws Affecting Men and Women</u>. Largo: CCERA, 1974. (P)

500. _____. Texas Division. <u>Legal Rights of Texas Women</u>. 2d ed.
Houston: AAUW, 1974. (P)

501. _____. Utah Division. <u>Utah Women and the Law: An Analysis</u>
<u>of the Utah Code Annotated</u> (1953). Salt Lake City: AAUW, November
1974. (P)

502. American Civil Liberties Union. Women's Rights Project. "Equal
Rights Amendment." Mimeographed. New York: ACLU, June 1973. (WL)

503. _____. "Equal Rights Amendment." By Brenda Feigen Fasteau
and Ruth Bader Ginsburg. Mimeographed. New York: ACLU, 17 April
1972. (WL)

504. _____. "Equal Rights Amendment Report." Mimeographed.
New York: ACLU, 29 September 1972. (WL)

505. _____. "Memorandum on Efficacy of a State's Attempt to
Withdraw Ratification of ERA." Prepared by Jane Booth. Mimeographed.
New York: ACLU, 1 December 1975. (R)

506. _____. Press Release. Mimeographed. New York: ACLU,
2 October 1970. (WL)

507. _____. Two letters by Ruth Bader Ginsburg. Mimeographed.
New York: ACLU, 3 July 1973. (WL)

508. _____. "Women's Rights Project Director Challenges Phyllis
Schlafly to Debate the Equal Rights Amendment." Press Release.
Mimeographed. New York: ACLU, 18 March 1974. (WL)

509. American Federation of State, County and Municipal Employees.
<u>Sex: It's No Reason to Discriminate against More Than Half of All</u>
<u>Americans</u>. Washington, D.C.: AFSCME, c.1975. (B)

510. Board of Church and Society. <u>Resolution on Equal Rights of Women</u>.
Washington, D.C.: BCS, 1972. (B)

511. Coalition for the Passage of the Equal Rights Amendment in Arkansas.
<u>The ERA: What It Means to Men and Women in Arkansas</u>. Little Rock:
CPERAA, n.d. (B)

512. _____. Who Needs the Equal Rights Amendment? Little Rock:
     CPERAA, n.d. (B)

513. Committee for the Protection of Women and Children. E.R.A.: The
     Facts. Jefferson City, Missouri: CPWC, n.d. (B)

514. Committee to Ratify the Massachusetts State Equal Rights Amendment.
     A Report on the History and Impact of the Massachusetts State Equal
     Rights Amendment. Cambridge: CRMSERA, 1975. (R)

515. Committee to Restore Women's Rights. "Letter-Writing." Mimeo-
     graphed. San Antonio, Texas: CRWR, n.d. (B)

516. Common Cause. Action Program for Ratification of the Equal Rights
     Amendment. Washington, D.C.: CC, 1973. (P)

517. _____. Equality of Rights . . . Shall Not Be Abridged . . .
     on Account of Sex. Washington, D.C.: CC, n.d. (B) (WL)

518. _____. The Equal Rights Amendment: A Report on the
     Proposed 27th Amendment to the Constitution. Washington, D.C.: CC,
     [1975]. (B)

519. _____. Questions and Answers on the Proposed 27th Amendment
     to the Constitution, Now before the States for Ratification.
     Washington, D.C.: CC, n.d. (B)

520. _____. Status Report on ERA. Washington, D.C.: CC, 1973. (B)

521. _____. Status Report on the Ratification of the Equal Rights
     Amendment. Washington, D.C.: CC, April 1972; 15 February 1973; 12
     March 1974; 22 April 1974; 13 May 1974; 28 July 1974; 2 October 1974;
     9 December 1974; 6 February 1975; 20 February 1975; 7 March 1975;
     16 April 1975; 2 July 1975. (B) (WL)

522. Communication Workers of America. Brochure on the ERA. Washington,
     D.C.: CWA, n.d.

523. Council of State Governments. All Are Created Equal: The States
     and the Equal Rights Amendment. Iron Work Pike, Lexington, Kentucky:
     CSG, December 1973. (P)

524. Democratic National Committee. Work for the Equal Rights
     Amendment. Washington, D.C.: DNC, n.d. (Postcard)

525. The Equal Rights Amendment. Transcript of the debate between
     Ann Scott and Phyllis Schlafly on Firing Line. Moderated by William
     F. Buckley. Southern Educational Communications Association, 1973.

526. "Equal Rights Amendment for Women." Mimeographed. 1970. (WL)

527. Equal Rights Amendment Project. Equal Rights Amendment: Questions
     and Answers. Sacramento, California: ERAP, [1976]. (B)

528. Equal Rights Coalition of Utah. Utah and Equal Rights. Salt Lake
     City: ERCU, n.d. (B)

529. E.R.A. Central. <u>Facts and Myths about the Equal Rights Amendment</u>.
     Prepared by Giddy Dyer. Chicago, Illinois: ERAC, [1973]. (B)

530. _____. <u>Test Your Activity Quotient</u>. Chicago, Illinois: ERAC,
     n.d. (B)

531. _____. <u>What Is the STOP ERA Movement and Why Is It Saying All
     Those Terrible Things about Us?</u> Prepared by Linda Hirshman and Judy
     Lonnquist. Chicago, Illinois: ERAC, n.d. (B)

532. ERA United. <u>Before and After the Equal Rights Amendment: The
     Current Status of Women and the Expected Effects of ERA Ratification
     in North Carolina</u>. By Cher Brooks, et al. Edited by Howard F. Twiggs.
     Rev. ed. Raleigh, North Carolina: ERAU, January 1975. (P)

533. _____. <u>The Potential Impact of the Equal Rights Amendment on
     the Laws of the State of North Carolina</u>. By Cher Brooks, et al.
     Raleigh, North Carolina: ERAU, 1975. (P)

534. _____. <u>Who Supports ERA</u>? Raleigh, North Carolina: ERAU,
     n.d. (B)

535. ERA United of Louisiana. <u>Men and ERA</u>. Prepared by Common Cause.
     Baton Rouge: ERAUL, January 1975. (B)

536. Feeley, Dianne. <u>Why Women Need the Equal Rights Amendment</u>. New
     York: Pathfinder, 1973. Abridged from entry #1135.

537. "A Few Questions and Answers about the Proposed California Equal
     Rights Amendment." Mimeographed. (WL)

538. Flexner, Eleanor. <u>Women's Rights--Unfinished Business</u>. New York:
     Public Affairs Committee, Pamphlet No. 469, October 1971. (P)

539. Hoosiers for ERA. <u>ERA the Hoosier Way: Ten Reasons Why Indiana
     Should Ratify the Equal Rights Amendment</u>. Indianapolis, Indiana:
     HERA, n.d. (B)

540. Housewives for ERA. <u>Homemakers Need the Equal Rights Amendment</u>.
     Evanston, Illinois: E.R.A. Central, n.d. (B)

541. _____. <u>Housewives for E.R.A.</u> Evanston, Illinois: E.R.A.
     Central, n.d. (B)

542. Jordan, Joan. <u>Amend the Equal Rights Amendment to Extend the State
     Protective Laws to Men</u>. San Francisco, California: Women, Inc., and
     San Francisco Women's Liberation Intergroup Council, 1970. (WL)

543. Krauskopf, Joan M. "A Woman's Right to Support: Homemakers Need
     the ERA." Mimeographed. Columbia: University of Missouri, n.d.

544. League of Women Voters of the United States. <u>Against Equal Rights
     by Constitutional Amendment</u>. By Gladys Amelia Harrison. Washington,
     D.C.: LWVUS, 1928. (P)

545. _____. <u>Equal Rights, How Not to Get Them</u>. Washington, D.C.:
     LWVUS, n.d. (P)

546. _____ . *ERA Campaign Countdown Kit.* Washington, D.C.: LWVUS, n.d.

547. _____ . *The ERA: What It Means to Men and Women.* Pub. No. 272. Washington, D.C.: LWVUS, 1975. (B) (WL)

548. _____ . *The Proposed Equal Rights Amendment: A Brief in Support of Its Ratification.* Prepared by Bellamy, Blank, Goodman, Kelly, Ross, and Stanley. Washington, D.C.: LWVUS, 22 March 1974. (P)

549. _____ . *Some Questions and Answers about the Equal Rights Amendment.* Washington, D.C.: LWVUS, n.d. (B)

550. _____ . *Women in the '70s: Black Women and the Equal Rights Amendment.* Excerpts from a speech by Frankie M. Freeman. Pub. No. 527. Washington, D.C.: LWVUS, August 1975. (B)

551. _____ . California League. *The Equal Rights Action Kit.* San Francisco: LWVC, February 1974. (P)

552. _____ . Indiana League. *Discover ERA: A Place to Grow.* Indianapolis: LWVI, 1973; rev. ed. 1975. (P)

552a. _____ . Jefferson Parish. *Equal Rights Amendment Information.* Metairie, Louisiana: LWVJP, 1976. (B)

553. _____ . Louisiana League. *The ERA: What It Means to Louisiana Men and Women.* Baton Rouge: LWVL, May 1973; rev. September 1974. (B)

554. _____ . Massachusetts League. *Background Paper on the Equal Rights Amendment.* Boston: LWVM, 22 May 1972. (B)

555. _____ . New Mexico League. *The ERA: What It Will and Will Not Do.* Santa Fe: LWVNM, January 1975. (B)

556. _____ . *New Mexico Statute Revisions under ERA 1973-75 Summarized.* Santa Fe: LWVNM, 1975. (B)

557. _____ . *With Rights Come Responsibilities.* Santa Fe: LWVNM, July 1973. (B)

558. _____ . New York League. *ERA Campaign Kit.* New York City: New York Coalition for Equal Rights, 1975. (P)

559. _____ . *Fables and Facts: The Story of the Equal Rights Amendment in New York State.* New York City: LWVNY, n.d. (B) Rep. in entry #355.

560. _____ . North Carolina League. *Woman's Suffrage, the Equal Rights Amendment, Equal Pay for Equal Work, and Other Such Revolutionary Ideas: A Survey of the Status of Women in North Carolina.* By Margaret A. Blanchard. Greenville: LWVNC, 1974. (P)

561. _____ . Ohio League. *What You Can Do about Equal Rights.* Columbus: LWVO, April 1975. (B)

562. _____ . San Diego League. *200 Years and Holding: A Look at the Legal Rights of American Women.* San Diego, California: LWVSD, 1973. (P)

563. _____. Washington League. Status of Women in Washington State. Seattle: LWVW, 1972. (P)

564. Lillie, Alice. ERA! The Individualist Case. Columbus, Ohio: Feminists for Life, 1974. (P) (H2,S2,R10) Rep. from entry #1256.

565. Livesey, Sharon. Survey of the Legal Literature on Women Offenders. Pittsburgh, Pennsylvania: Entropy Limited, June 1975. (P)

566. "Lobbying Drive Sought on Women's Rights Bill." Mimeographed. 1971. (WL)

567. Longwell, Marjorie R. "Statement of the Equal Rights Amendment to the Constitution." Mimeographed. 1970. (WL)

568. Massachusetts Committee for the Equal Rights Amendment. Why the Equal Rights Amendment? Boston: MCERA, n.d. (B)

569. Minnesota Coalition to Support the ERA. Equal Rights Amendment. St. Paul: MCSERA, n.d. (B)

570. Montana ERA Ratification Council. The ERA Way (ERA Action Handbook). Helena: MERARC, October 1973. (P)

571. _____. "Equality of Rights under the Law Shall Not Be Denied or Abridged by the United States or by Any State on Account of Sex." Helena: MERARC, 1974. (P)

572. _____. Facts and History of ERA. Helena: MERARC, Fall 1973. (P)

573. _____. Legislative Strategy, Public Education, Fund Raising. Helena: MERARC, Fall 1973. (P)

574. _____. Montana and the Equal Rights Amendment. Helena: MERARC, October 1973; rev. 1974. (B)

575. "Mrs. Nixon Speaks, a Little, on Women." Mimeographed. Liberation News Service, 29 April 1970. (WL)

576. Murphy, Irene L. "Strategy for Ratification of the Equal Rights Amendment." Paper read at the Annual Conference of National Capitol Area Political Science Association, 27 April 1974. Mimeographed. Washington, D.C.: American University, 1974.

577. Murray, Pauli. ERA Testimony. Special Subcommittee on Education, 91st Congress, June 1970. Pittsburgh, Pennsylvania: KNOW, Inc., n.d. (WL)

578. _____. "Statement on the Equal Rights Amendment (S. J. Res. 61) Submitted to the Senate Judiciary Committee, September 16, 1970." Mimeographed. (WL)

579. National Association of Women Lawyers. What the Equal Rights Amendment Means. Chicago, Illinois: NAWL, n.d. (B)

580. National Ad Hoc Committee for the Equal Rights Amendment. Is the
Equal Rights Amendment Dead for This 91st Session of the Senate?
Mimeographed. Falls Church, Virginia: NAHCERA, 30 November 1970.
(B) (H,R16) Contains: Flora Crater's "Statement Re: The Equal Rights
Amendment and the Senate of the 91st Session of Congress"; Joan
Higbee's "Press Conference Statement"; George Washington University
Women's Liberation's "The Equal Rights Amendment and the Draft" (WL);
Vicki Lathom's "Statement of National Organization for Women; and
Carthuers Gholson Berger's "The Equal Rights Amendment." Press Confer-
ence material, 13 November 1970. See entries #141, 1161, 3208-10.

581. National Consumer's League. Blanket Equality Bill: Why It Should
Not Pass. New York: NCL, April 1922. (P)

582. _____. Twenty Questions about the Proposed Equal Rights
Amendment of the Woman's Party, 1923-1924. Compiled by Florence Kelley.
New York: NCL, 1924. (P)

583. National Federation of Business and Professional Women's Clubs.
"A Brief in Favor of the Equal Rights Amendment to the United States
Constitution and Its Effect on Alimony, Custody of Children,
Differential Age of Marriage and Protective Labor Legislation for
Women." Prepared by Libby E. Sachar and Joyce Capps for the Civil and
Political Rights Committee of the President's Commission on the Status
of Women. Mimeographed. Washington, D.C.: Women's Bureau, April 1963.

584. _____. Bringing Home Equality. Washington, D.C.: NFBPW, n.d.
(B)

585. _____. Equality. Washington, D.C.: NFBPW, n.d. (B)

586. _____. "Equal Rights Amendment." In Spanning Half a Century
of Legislation, pp. 12-15. Washington, D.C.: NFBPW, 1970. (P)

587. _____. "Equal Rights Amendment Background Material."
Mimeographed. Washington, D.C.: NFBPW, n.d. (P)

588. _____. How and Why to Ratify the ERA. Washington, D.C.:
NFBPW, 1973. (B)

589. _____. Osta Underwood's Reply to STOP ERA. Washington, D.C.:
NFBPW, n.d. (P)

590. _____. What's in It for Men? Washington, D.C.: NFBPW, n.d.
(B)

591. _____. Who Will Defend America? Washington, D.C.: NFBPW,
n.d. (B)

592. _____. California Federation. "The Equal Rights Amendment."
By Ruth Church Gupta. Mimeographed. San Francisco: CFBPW, March
1971. (P)

593. National Organization for Women. The American Way: Ratify the ERA.
Washington, D.C.: NOW, n.d. (B)

594. _____. August 1974 ERA Status for Unratified States.
Washington, D.C.: NOW, 1974. (B)

595. _____. The Equal Rights Amendment: Features from the N.O.W.
News Service. Edited by Dian Terry. New York: NOW National Public
Information Office, c.1974. (P)

596. _____. The Equal Rights Amendment: What Does It Mean to You?
New York: NOW Public Information Office, n.d. (B)

597. _____. Letter by Wilma Scott Heide. Mimeographed. Chicago,
Illinois: NOW, 1972. (WL)

598. _____. NOW ERA Information Kit. Washington, D.C.: NOW, n.d.

599. _____. NOW ERA Status Report. Washington, D.C.: NOW,
regularly updated.

600. _____. NOW ERA Two Year Strategy. Washington, D.C.: NOW,
May 1973. (B)

601. _____. Illinois ERA/NOW. ERA Kit. Chicago: NOW, n.d.

602. _____. Lincoln Chapter and National Legislative Office. The
Insurance Connection with STOP ERA Forces. Edited by Ann K. Justice.
Lincoln, Nebraska: NOW, n.d. (R)

603. _____. Virginia Chapter. The Equal Rights Amendment
Supporter's Handbook. Richmond: NOW, September 1974. (P)

604. _____. Rebirth and Growth through Equality: Equal Rights
Amendment. Richmond: NOW, n.d. (P)

605. National Woman's Party, Answers to Questions on the Equal Rights
Amendment. Washington, D.C.: NWP, 1938. (B)

606. _____. Answers to Questions about the Equal Rights Amendment.
Washington, D.C.: NWP, 1974. (B) (WL)

607. _____. Endorsement of the Equal Rights Amendment by
Prominent People--Leaflets. Washington, D.C.: NWP, c.1950. Contains
endorsements by Dennis, Cardinal Dougherty, Dr. Worth M. Tippy,
Rabbi Emeritus Jacob S. Raisin, Margaret Culkin Banning, Pearl Buck,
James Truslow Adams, Irving Fisher, Raymond Gram Swing, Samuel Gompers,
Governors, and Religious Leaders.

608. _____. Equal Rights Amendment: Questions and Answers.
Prepared by Helena Hill Weed. Washington, D.C.: Government Printing
Office, 1943. (U.S., 78th Cong., 1st sess., S. doc. no. 97) Rev.
1946 (U.S., 79th Cong., 2d sess., S. doc. no. 209) (P)

609. _____. Equal Rights Amendment: Questions and Answers.
Edited by Ethel Ernest Murrell. Washington, D.C.: Government
Printing Office, 1951. (U.S., 82d Cong., 1st sess., S. doc. no. 74)
(P)

610. _____ . Equal Rights Amendment: Questions and Answers.
Edited by Margery C. Leonard. Washington, D.C.: Government Printing
Office, 1963. (U.S., 87th Cong., 2d sess., S. doc. no. 164) (P)

611. _____ . Equal Rights by National Amendment. Washington, D.C.:
NWP, 1927. (P) Rep. from entry #1815.

612. _____ . How the Woman's Rights Bill Works in Wisconsin.
Washington, D.C.: NWP, c.1922. (P)

613. _____ . Men Speak for the Equal Rights Amendment. Statements
by prominent men. Washington, D.C.: NWP, c.1944. (B)

614. _____ . The Present Campaign for Equality of Rights for Women.
Washington, D.C.: NWP, 1945. (P)

615. _____ . Some Recent Editorials and Press Comments on the
Equal Rights Amendment, September 1943–January 1944. Washington, D.C.:
NWP, 1944. (P)

616. _____ . Statements on the Equal Rights Amendment. By Irving
Fisher, Helen Hayes, Mary E. Wooley, Gladys Swarthout, Katharine
Hepburn, Pearl Buck, Jeannette Marks, James Truslow Adams, Raymond
Gram Swing, Arthur M. Schlesinger. Washington, D.C.: NWP, c.1944. (B)

617. _____ . Text of Equal Rights Amendment with Platform Pledges
by Republican and Democratic Parties. Washington, D.C.: NWP, c.1950.
(B)

618. _____ . Women Are Not Persons--A Short Version of Questions
and Answers. Washington, D.C.: NWP, c.1944. (B)

619. National Trade Union League of America. Protective Legislation in
Danger. Chicago, Illinois: NTULA, 1922. (P)

620. National Women's Trade Union League of America. Opposing the So-
Called Equal Rights Amendment. By Blanch Freedman. Washington, D.C.:
NWTULA, 193-(?). (P)

621. Network. Catholics and the Equal Rights Amendment. Washington,
D.C.: Network, n.d. (B)

622. Nevadans for E.R.A. Nevada ERA. Carson City: NERA, 1974. (B)

623. New Mexico Equal Rights Legislation Committee. General Information--
New Mexico Equal Rights Amendment. Albuquerque: NMERLC, 1972. (B)

624. _____ . "A Report on the Possible Effects of the Equal Rights
Amendment." Researched and compiled by University of New Mexico Law
Students. Mimeographed. Albuquerque: NMERLC, 5 April 1972. (R)

625. _____ . Vote for the Proposed Equal Rights Amendment to the
New Mexico Constitution. Albuquerque: NMERLC, 1972. (B)

626. New York Coalition for Equal Rights. Equal Rights Amendment. New
York City: NYCER, 1975. (B)

627. "1970's Most Significant Accomplishment: The Equal Rights
    Amendment." Mimeographed. Prepared for Congress to Unite Women,
    November 1969. (WL)

628. Novick, Lee. "The Political History of the Equal Rights Amendment,
    1923-1972." Mimeographed. New Haven: Yale University, 1972.

629. Ohio Coalition for Equal Rights Amendment. Action Manual.
    Columbus: OCERA, 1974. (P)

630. Ohio Task Force for the Implementation of the Equal Rights
    Amendment. A Report. Columbus: OTFIERA, July 1975. (P)

631. Pro ERA Alliance. Questions and Answers for Kentuckians about the
    Equal Rights Amendment. Louisville: PERAA, n.d. (B)

632. Provinzano, Madeleine. "Equality for What?" Mimeographed. (WL)

633. Rabin, Jack, and Dodd, Donald B. "The 'ERA' Comes to New Columbia."
    Washington, D.C.: ERIC, 1973. (P)

634. Rawalt, Marguerite. Testimony on the Equal Rights Amendment.
    (91st Cong., 2d sess., 1970) Pittsburgh, Pennsylvania: KNOW, Inc.,
    n.d. (P) (WL) Rep. in entry #290.

635. Republican National Committee. Ten Reasons Why the Equal Rights
    Amendment Should Be Ratified. Washington, D.C.: RNC, [1973].
    (Pocket Card)

636. Rogers, J. Earl, Jr. "Equal Rights Amendment and Labor."
    Mimeographed. San Diego, California: Cal-Western School of Law,
    1974. (R)

637. Rosenwasser, Marie E. J. "Growing Up from Another Perspective:
    The Countermovement." Paper read at the Annual Meeting of the Speech
    Communications Association, December 1972, in Chicago. Washington,
    D.C.: ERIC, December 1972.

638. Ross, Susan Deller. "Sex Discrimination and 'Protective' Labor
    Legislation." Mimeographed. New York: New York University Law
    School, 1970. (R) (WL)

639. Ryan, John Augustine. Equal Rights Amendment in Relation to
    Protective Legislation for Women. Washington, D.C.: Catholic
    Welfare Conference, 1930. (P)

640. Sandler, Bernice. The Equal Rights for Women Amendment: Statement
    before Senate Judiciary Committee, Subcommittee on Constitutional
    Amendments, 6 May 1970. Pittsburgh, Pennsylvania: KNOW, Inc., n.d.
    (P) (WL)

641. Schurr, Cathleen. "Testimony before the Pennsylvania Senate
    Committee on Constitutional Changes and Federal Relations," 1 June
    1972. Mimeographed. (WL)

642. South Carolina Coalition for the ERA. Coalition Countdown.
    Columbia: SCCERA, 31 March 1975. (B)

643. _____. The Equal Rights Amendment and South Carolina Laws.
     Edited by Mary Lowndes Bryan. Columbia: SCCERA, January 1975. (P)

644. _____. The ERA and the People of South Carolina. Columbia:
     SCCERA, n.d. (B)

645. _____. ERA Victory Book. Columbia: SCCERA, May 1974. (P)

646. _____. "Sermon on Equal Rights." Mimeographed. Columbia:
     SCCERA, October 1974. (B)

647. _____. South Carolina Christians Support the ERA. Columbia:
     SCCERA, January 1975. (B)

648. "Statement of the National Women's Commission of the C.P.U.S.A. on
     the Equal Rights Amendment." Mimeographed. (WL)

649. STOP ERA. Various untitled brochures.

650. _____. Illinois Division. What the Equal Rights Amendment
     Means. Alton: STOP ERA, n.d. (B)

651. _____. Texas Division. The Equal Rights Amendment Can Be
     Rescinded. Austin: STOP ERA, n.d. (B)

652. "Testimony to House Judiciary Committee," 2 April 1971. (WL)

653. Texans for Equal Rights Amendment. Equal Rights Amendment. By
     Hermine D. Tobolowsky. Austin: TERA, n.d. (B)

654. Thomas, Alice. "Sex Based Discrimination under American Law and the
     Equal Rights Amendment." Mimeographed. California: Valparaiso
     University, 1971. (R) (WL)

655. United Methodist ERA Support Project. The Church, Religion, and
     the Equal Rights Amendment. Washington, D.C.: UMERASP, August 1975.
     (B)

656. _____. Equality of Women and Men: God's Plan at Creation.
     By Katherine A. Shindel. Washington, D.C.: UMERASP, n.d. (B)

657. Wisconsin Equal Rights Coalition. Comprehensive Equal Rights
     Legislation. Madison: WERC, August 1975. (B)

658. _____. The Wisconsin Equal Rights Amendment. Madison: WERC,
     n.d. (B)

659. _____. The Equal Rights Implementation Package. Madison:
     WERC, January 1973. (B)

660. "Women at Dodge Main Speak Out: An Interview." Liberation News
     Service, 1 October 1970, pp. 13-15. (WL)

661. Women's Bar Association of the District of Columbia. Statement
     in Support of the ERA. Arlington, Virginia: WBADC, August 1974. (R)
*

662. Women's Political Caucus. New Mexico Chapter. The Equal Rights
Amendment. Albuquerque: NMWPC, n.d. (B)

663. _____. Oregon Chapter. Quick Look: A Summary of Women's
Issues in the 1973 Oregon Legislature. Corvallis: OWPC, October 1973.
(P)

664. _____. Wisconsin Chapter. The Wisconsin Equal Rights
Amendment. Madison: WWPC, n.d. (B) (WL)

665. Women United. "Ervin Tramples on Women's Rights . . ." Release
No. 17. Washington, D.C.: WU, 14 December 1971. (B)

666. _____. Is a Woman a Person? Prepared by Washington Forum.
Washington, D.C.: WU, 1971. (B)

667. _____. This Is It! Washington, D.C.: WU, n.d. (B)

668. _____. Virginia Chapter. Women and the Draft: What Does
"Equal Rights" Mean? Arlington: WU, 1972. (B)

669. Women Who Want to Be Women. Churches. Ft. Worth, Texas: WWWW,
n.d. (B)

670. _____. Equality without ERA. Ft. Worth, Texas: WWWW, n.d. (B)

671. _____. Equal Rights in Action--The Effect on Men. Ft. Worth,
Texas: WWWW, n.d. (B)

672. _____. ERA--Myth or Fact. Ft. Worth, Texas: WWWW, n.d. (B)

673. _____. "ERA Speech." Mimeographed. Ft. Worth, Texas: WWWW,
n.d.

674. _____. Harmful Effects of ERA. Ft. Worth, Texas: WWWW,
n.d. (B)

675. _____. How About That??? Ft. Worth, Texas: WWWW, n.d. (B)

676. _____. Ladies! Have You Heard? Ft. Worth, Texas: WWWW,
n.d. (B)

677. _____. Legalize Homosexuality? Ft. Worth, Texas: WWWW,
n.d. (B)

678. _____. Marriage and the Family. Ft. Worth, Texas: WWWW,
n.d. (B)

679. _____. May a State Rescind Its Ratification of ERA? Ft. Worth,
Texas, n.d. (B)

680. _____. The Right to Privacy. Ft. Worth, Texas: WWWW, n.d. (B)

681. _____. Status of ERA. Ft. Worth, Texas: WWWW, 1 March 1975.
(B)

682. _____. "Things to Do Immediately." Mimeographed. Ft. Worth,
     Texas: WWWW, n.d.

683. _____. Warning! ERA Is Dangerous to Women!!! Ft. Worth,
     Texas: WWWW, n.d. (B)

684. _____. Who Are the Proponents of ERA, the "Women Libbers,"
     and Do They Speak for You? Ft. Worth, Texas: WWWW, n.d. (B)

                          *Addendum

661a. Women's Equity Action League. ERA Kit. Washington, D.C.: WEAL,
     n.d.

five

Periodical Material

[While there are no selection problems in this group, as there
was with pamphlets, the classification difficulties are as
great. Again, the lines between the various media--scholarly
journals, popular magazines, special interest magazines and
newspapers, and even newsletters--are often arbitrarily drawn.
Sourcebooks differ in their classifications of many of these;
then, too, many of them evolve from newsletters to journals
or papers, for example, so that the media change. We see no
value, therefore, in making arbitrary distinctions in most
cases: scholarly journals, popular magazines, and special
interest (especially feminist) magazines and newspapers are
grouped together and arranged alphabetically by author and/or
title. A periodical with a newspaper format is so indicated
(N). In general, the style of citation separates journals
from magazines.

Newsletters, narrowly dependent on organizations and of limited
circulation, are separated from more widely distributed periodicals. They are listed alphabetically by title with the organization indicated in parenthesis and the entries arranged
chronologically.

Legal periodicals are grouped separately and arranged like the
periodicals, alphabetically by author and title. This is very
specialized material, so some advantage is gained by grouping
them separately.

Newspapers often provide mini-histories of the ERA, especially
the New York Times which is indexed back to the ERA's introduction. Other major newspapers are indexed only since 1972,
the year of ERA's passage, but a crucial period in its
history nevertheless. These major newspapers are grouped
together and arranged chronologically to provide that historical
perspective. Geographically they represent the full sweep of
the country and differ quite a bit in the quality and quantity
of their coverage. Newspapers which are not currently indexed
are grouped at the end and arranged alphabetically by title
and author.

Equal Rights, the magazine of the National Woman's Party which
introduced the ERA, provides the most excellent resource on the
ERA, both in terms of analysis, argumentation, and reportage
during its life from 1923 to 1954. For this reason, it is
separated from the other periodicals and arranged chronologically.]

A. Legal Periodicals

[Comments and Notes are listed alphabetically by title;
authors are not indicated, nor are the words "comment" or
"note."]

685. "ABA and Sex Discrimination." Women Law Reporter, 15 October 1974,
p. 1.49.

686. Alvarez, Edna R. S. "Discrimination on the Basis of Sex and Marital
Status in Tax and Related Laws." Connecticut Bar Journal 46 (1972):
496-505.

687. Anderson, Lee Berger. "NAWL Driving for Ratification of Equal
Rights Amendment." Women Lawyers Journal 59 (1973): 3.

688. Anthony, S. B., II. "The 'Equal Rights' Amendment: An Attack on
Labor." Lawyers Guild Review 3 (January 1943): 12-17.

689. Association of the Bar of the City of New York. Committee on Civil
Rights and Special Committee on Sex and Law. "The Equal Rights
Amendment." Record of the Association of the Bar of the City of New
York 27 (1972): 172-87; Bulletin 2 (September 1972): 22-37. Also
published separately. Rep. in entries #135, 143.

690. _____. Committee on Federal Legislation. "Amending the
Constitution to Prohibit State Discrimination Based on Sex." Record
of the Association of the Bar of the City of New York 26 (1971): 77-89.
Rep. in entry #125.

691. _____. "The Equal Rights Amendment--As of 1972." Bulletin 2
(September 1972): 38-44.

692. Barham, Mack E. "Introduction: Equal Rights for Women Versus the
Civil Code." Tulane Law Review 48 (1974): 560-66.

693. Bayh, Birch. "Equal Rights Amendment." Indiana Law Review 6
(1972): 1-18.

694. _____. "The Need for the Equal Rights Amendment." Notre
Dame Lawyer 48 (1972): 80-91.

695. Behles, Jennie D., and Behles, Daniel J. "Equal Rights in Divorce
and Separation." New Mexico Law Review 3 (1973): 118-35. See
entry #810.

696. Bilbe, George L. "Constitutionality of Sex-Based Differentiations
in the Louisiana Community Property Regime." Loyola Law Review 19
(1972/73): 373-99.

697. Bingaman, Anne K. "The Effects of an Equal Rights Amendment on the
New Mexico System of Community Property: Problems of Characterization,
Management, and Control." New Mexico Law Review 3 (1973): 11-56.
See entry #810.

697a. _____. "Impact of the Equal Rights Amendment on Married
Women's Individual Rights." Pepperdine Law Review 3 (1975): 26-41.
A slightly amended version appears in entry #442.

698. Blank, Diane Serafin, and Rone, Jemera. "Enforcement of Inter-
Spousal Support Obligations: A Proposal." Women's Rights Law Reporter
2 (June 1975): 13-25.

699. Bonnano, Jack F. "The Constitution and 'Liberated' Community
Property in California--Some Constitutional Issues and Problems under
the Newly Enacted Dymally Bill." Hastings Constitutional Law Quarterly
1 (1974): 97-131.

700. Brophy, Mary L. "An Equal Rights Amendment: Would It Benefit
Women." American Bar Association Journal 38 (1952): 393-95.

701. Brown, Barbara A.; Emerson, Thomas I; Falk, Gail; and Freedman,
Ann E. "The Equal Rights Amendment: A Constitutional Basis for
Equal Rights for Women." Yale Law Review 80 (1971): 871-985. Rep.
in entry #119.

702. Brown, Barbara A., and Freedman, Ann E. "Equal Rights Amendment:
Growing Impact on the States." Women Law Reporter, 15 November 1974,
pp. 1.63-65.

703. _____. "Sex Averaging and the Equal Rights Amendment."
Women's Rights Law Reporter 2 (June 1975): 35-49. A slightly amended
version also appears in entry #442.

704. Brown, David Ira. "The Discredited American Woman: Sex Discrimination in Consumer Credit." University of California Davis Law Review
6 (1973): 61-82.

705. Brown, Helen Elizabeth. "Woman Lawyer Defends Proposed 'Equal
Rights' Amendment." American Bar Association Journal 26 (1940):
356-58.

706. Bysiewicz, Shirley Raissi, and MacDonnell, Gloria Jeanne Stillson.
"Married Women's Surnames." Connecticut Law Review 5 (1973): 598-621.

706a. California Commission on the Status of Women, Equal Rights
Amendment Project. "General and Code-Indexed Equal Rights Amendment
Bibliography Prepared by the Commission on the Status of Women, Equal
Rights Amendment Project." Pepperdine Law Review 3 (1975): 69-81.

707. Chittick, Elizabeth L. "Questions and Answers Most Frequently
Asked about the Equal Rights Amendment." Women Lawyers Journal 59
(1973): 11-14.

708. Clark, Marylou; Semmelhack, Tricia; and Steinbock, Sara. "The
Equal Rights Amendment: Constraint on Discretion in Family Law."
Buffalo Law Review 22 (1973): 917-46.

709. "Congress: Women and the Military." Women Law Reporter, 15
October 1974, pp. 1.45-1.46.

710. Conlin, R. B. "Equal Protection Versus Equal Rights Amendment--
Where Are We Now?" Drake Law Review 24 (1975): 259-35.

711. Connelly, Mary M. "Equal Rights Amendment." Women Lawyers Journal
41 (Fall 1955): 18-19.

712. "Constitutional Law--Divorce--Pendente lite Awards--Counsel Fees--
Costs--Alimony--Effect of Equal Rights Amendment." Akron Law Review
8 (1974): 171-79.

713. "Constitutional Law: The Equal Protection Clause and Women's
Rights." Loyola Law Review 19 (1973): 542-51.

714. "Contact Persons Carrying on ERA Ratification Efforts, ERA
Ratification Council, Washington, D.C., as of September 1, 1975."
Women Lawyers Journal 62 (Winter 1976): 62.

715. Copelon, Rhonda; Schneider, Elizabeth M.; and Stearns, Nancy.
"Constitutional Perspectives on Sex Discrimination in Jury Selection."
Women's Rights Law Reporter 2 (June 1975): 3-12.

716. Coyne, Mary Jeanne. "The Equal Rights Amendment--Is It Needed?"
Women Lawyers Journal 58 (1972): 4-6.

717. Crable, Elizabeth C. "Pros and Cons of the Equal Rights Amendment."
Women Lawyers Journal 35 (Summer 1949): 7-9. Rep. as a separate by
the National Woman's Party.

718. Cross, Harry M. "Equality for Spouses in Washington Community
Property Law--1972 Statutory Changes." Washington Law Review 48 (1973):
527-53.

719. Crump, S. "Overview of Equal-Rights Amendment in Texas." Houston
Law Review 11 (1973): 136.

720. "Custody Rights of Unwed Fathers." Pacific Law Journal 4 (1973):
922-42.

721. Daniels, Charles. "The Impact of the Equal Rights Amendment on the
New Mexico Criminal Code." New Mexico Law Review 3 (1973): 106-17.
See entry #810.

722. Davis, Samuel M., and Chaires, Susan C. "Equal Protection for
Juveniles: The Present Status of Sex-Based Discrimination in Juvenile
Court Laws." Georgia Law Review 7 (1973): 494-532.

723. "Domestic Relations: Pennsylvania Declares the Wife's Rights to
Divorce from Bed and Board and Alimony Pendente Lite Unconstitutional
in Light of the Equal Rights Amendment." Dickinson Law Review 78
(1973): 402-14.

724. Dorsen, Norman, and Ross, Susan. "The Necessity of a Constitutional
Amendment." Harvard Civil Rights/Civil Liberties Review 6 (1971):
216-24. See entry #750.

724a. Dunlap, Mary. "The Equal Rights Amendment and the Courts."
Pepperdine Law Review 3 (1975): 42-68. Also appears in entry #442.

725. Dybwad, Linda H. "Implementing Washington's ERA: Problems with
     Wholesale Legislative Revision." Washington Law Review 49 (1974):
     571-602.

726. Eastwood, Mary. "The Double Standard of Justice: Women's Rights
     under the Constitution." Valparaiso University Law Review 5 (1971):
     281-317.

727. "The Effect of Title VII and the Proposed Equal Rights Amendment
     on Mandatory Maternity Leaves for Teachers." Journal of Family Law
     12 (1972/73): 447-58.

728. "The Effect of the Equal Rights Amendment on Kentucky's Domestic
     Relations Law." Journal of Family Law 12 (1972/73): 151-59.

729. "The Effect of the Equal Rights Amendment on Minnesota Law."
     Minnesota Law Review 57 (1973): 771-806.

730. "The Elimination of Sex Discrimination in Employment: Alternatives
     to a Constitutional Amendment." Boston College Industrial and
     Commercial Law Review 12 (1971): 723-36.

731. Ellis, Willis H. "Equal Rights and the Debt Provisions of New
     Mexico Community Property Law." New Mexico Law Review 3 (1973):
     57-68. See entry #810.

732. Emerson, Thomas I. "The Equal Rights Amendment: The Legal Basis."
     Women Lawyers Journal 57 (1971): 12-16.

733. _____. "In Support of the Equal Rights Amendment." Harvard
     Civil Rights/Civil Liberties Review 6 (1971): 225-33. Rep. in
     entry #1010. See entry #750.

734. "Employment Practices and Sex Discrimination: Judicial Extension
     of Beneficial Female Protective Labor Laws." Cornell Law Review 59
     (1973): 133-57.

735. "Equal Justice for Women--Update the Constitution." New York Law
     Forum 17 (1971): 528-42.

735a. "The Equal Rights Amendment." American Bar Association Journal
     38 (1952): 45-46. (Ed) Rep. in entry #2653.

736. "Equal Rights Amendment." Human Rights 1 (1971): 54-85.
     Symposium of Rita E. Hauser, Mort Furay, Adele T. Weaver; Selected
     bibliography.

737. "The Equal Rights Amendment and Inequality between Spouses under
     the California Community Property System." Loyola of Los Angeles Law
     Review 6 (1973): 66-96.

738. "Equal Rights Amendment: A New Reasonableness Test for Viewing
     Sex-Based Classifications." Loyola University of Chicago Law Journal
     4 (1973): 69-108.

739. "The Equal Rights Amendment and the Military." Yale Law Journal 82
     (1973): 1533-57.

740. "Equal Rights Amendment and the Right of Privacy." Emory Law Journal 23 (1974): 197-209.

740a. "Equal Rights Amendment Arrives." American Bar Association Journal 58 (1972): 604-605. (Ed) Rep. in entry #157.

741. "Equal Rights Amendment: Constraint on Discretion in Family Law." Buffalo Law Review 22 (1973): 917-46.

742. "Equal Rights Amendment: Its Meaning and Its Impact on Missouri Law." Missouri Law Review 39 (1974): 553-72.

743. "The 'Equal Rights' Amendment--Positive Panacea or Negative Nostrum?" Kentucky Law Journal 59 (1971): 953-89.

744. "'Equal Rights' Amendment--Pro and Con: A Panel." Kappa Beta Pi Quarterly 42 (1958): 25ff. Symposium by Avery, O'Neil, Hurney, Earley, and Steinbinder.

745. "The Equal Rights Amendment Tally Sheet." Women's Rights Law Reporter 1 (Spring 1973): 104.

746. "Equal Rights Amendment: The Need for a National Policy." Indiana Law Journal 46 (1971): 373-91.

747. "The Equal Rights Amendment: Women Lawyers Examine Its Implications." Student Lawyer 1 (1973): 6-9, 52-54. (WL) Excerpted from ABA Section of Individual Rights and Responsibilities panel on the Impact of the Equal Rights Amendment held at the 1972 Annual Meeting. See entry #137.

748. "Equal Rights and Equal Protection: Who Has Management and Control?" Southern California Law Review 46 (1973): 892-921.

749. "Equal Rights for Women." University of Florida Law Review 15 (1962): 134-42.

750. Equal Rights for Women: A Symposium on the Proposed Constitutional Amendment. Harvard Civil Rights/Civil Liberties Law Review 6 (1971): 215-87. See entries #724, 733, 760, 806.

751. "Equal Rights for Women: The Need for a National Policy." Indiana Law Journal 46 (1971): 373-91.

752. "ERA and Child Support." Women Law Reporter, 15 November 1974, p. 1.65.

753. "ERA Tally Sheet." Women's Rights Law Reporter 2 (April 1974): 40-41.

754. "ERA Tally Sheet: Ratification by Four States Needed." Women's Rights Law Reporter 2 (March 1975): 46.

755. Ferrell, Ruth M. "Equal Rights Amendment to the United States Constitution--Areas of Controversy." Urban Lawyer 6 (1974): 853-91.

756. _____. "Sex Discrimination in Employment by the State and
    Local Governments: Procedures and Remedies." Urban Lawyer 5 (1973):
    307-26.

757. Fishel, Lynn A. "Reversals in the Federal Constitutional Amendment
    Process: Efficacy of State Ratification of the Equal Rights Amendment."
    Indiana Law Journal 49 (1973): 147-66. Rep. in entry #163.

758. Forrester, William Ray. "The Feminists--Why Have They Not Yet
    Succeeded?" American Bar Association Journal 61 (1975): 333-37.

759. Freund, Ernst. "Proposed Women's Rights Amendment--Legislation
    through the Constitution." American Bar Association Journal 7 (1921):
    658.

760. Freund, Paul A. "The Equal Rights Amendment Is Not the Way."
    Harvard Civil Rights/Civil Liberties Law Review 6 (1971): 234-42.
    Rep. in entries #131, 1154. See entry #750.

761. Gabler, Ronald G. "The Impact of the ERA: Specific Focus on
    California." Family Law Quarterly 8 (1974): 51-90.

762. Gale, Zona. "Status of Wisconsin Women under the Equal Rights Law."
    State Bar Association of Wisconsin Proceedings 14 (1922): 168-85.

763. Gallagher, Monica. "Desegregation: The Effect of the Proposed
    Equal Rights Amendment on Single-Sex Colleges." St. Louis University
    Law Journal 18 (1973): 41-74.

764. Ginsburg, Ruth Bader. "Comment: Frontiero v. Richardson."
    Women's Rights Law Reporter 1 (Summer 1973): 2-4.

765. _____. "Gender and the Constitution." University of
    Cincinnati Law Review 44 (1975): 1-42.

766. _____. "The Need for the Equal Rights Amendment." American
    Bar Association Journal 59 (1973): 1013-19; Women Lawyers Journal 60
    (1974): 4-15. (WL)

767. Goldberg, Joseph, and Hale, Mariclaire. "The Equal Rights Amendment
    and the Administration of Income Assistance Programs in New Mexico."
    New Mexico Law Review 3 (1973): 84-105. See entry #810.

768. Griffiths, Martha W. "International Women's Year Is Just the
    Beginning." American Bar Association Journal 60 (1974): 1237-39.

769. _____. "The Law Must Reflect the New Image of Women."
    Hastings Law Journal 23 (1971): 1-14.

770. Grinnell, F. W. "Constitutional Thinking Needed from Women
    Lawyers." Massachusetts Law Quarterly 7 (1922): 164-66.

771. Gunther, Gerald. "Foreword: In Search of Evolving Doctrine on a
    Changing Court: A Model for a Newer Equal Protection." Harvard Law
    Review 86 (1972): 1-48.

772. Hale, Mariclaire, and Kanowitz, Leo. "Women and the Draft: A
Response to Critics of the Equal Rights Amendment." Hastings Law
Journal 23 (1971): 199-220.

773. Harte, Grace H. "Political and Civil Equality Versus Equal Rights."
Women Lawyers Journal 27 (1941): 19, 25.

774. Heckman, J. William, Jr. "Ratification of a Constitutional Amendment: Can a State Change Its Mind?" Connecticut Law Review 6 (1973):
28-35.

775. Heft, Carroll R. "Women's Equality Legislation in Wisconsin."
Wisconsin Law Review 2 (1924): 350-62.

776. Hillman, Jordan Jay. "Sex and Employment under the Equal Rights
Amendment." Northwestern University Law Review 67 (1973): 789-841.

777. "Impact of the Equal Rights Amendment." Human Rights 3 (1973):
125-54. Symposium of Eleanor Holmes Norton, Barbara Allen Babcock,
Catherine East, Marguerite Rawalt; Selected bibliography.

778. "In Brief: Equal Rights Amendment." Women Law Reporter, 15
February 1975, p. 1.150.

779. "Is the Texas Equal Rights Amendment the Answer?" South Texas Law
Journal 15 (1974): 111-28.

780. Kanowitz, Leo. "Constitutional Aspects of Sex-Based Discrimination
in American Law." Nebraska Law Review 48 (1968): 131-82.

781. _____. "The Equal Rights Amendment and the Overtime Illusion."
New Mexico Law Review 1 (1971): 461-78. (WL) Rep. from entries
#88, 144.

782. _____. "The New Mexico Equal Rights Amendment: Introduction
and Overview." New Mexico Law Review 3 (1973): 1-10. See entry #810.

783. Karabian, Walter. "Equal Rights Amendment: The Contribution of
Our Generation of Americans." Pepperdine Law Review 1 (1974): 327-54.

784. Kendig, Dennis. "Discrimination against Women in Home Mortgage
Financing." Yale Review of Law and Social Action 3 (1973): 166-80.

785. Krauskopf, Joan M. "The Equal Rights Amendment." Missouri Bar
Journal 29 (1973): 85-93.

786. _____. "Equal Rights Amendment: Its Political and Practical
Contexts." California State Bar Journal 50 (1975): 78-84, 136-41.

787. _____. "Sex Discrimination--Another Shibboleth Legally
Shattered." Missouri Law Review 37 (1972): 377-408.

788. _____, and Thomas, Rhonda C. "Partnership Marriage:
The Solution to an Ineffective and Inequitable Law of Support." Ohio
State Law Journal 35 (1974): 558-600.

789. Kurland, Philip B. "The Equal Rights Amendment: Some Problems of Construction." Harvard Civil Rights/Civil Liberties Law Review 6 (1971): 243-52. See entry #750.

790. Larson, NettaBell Girard. "Concept of Equal Rights." Women Lawyers Journal 58 (1972): 95-103.

791. "The Legality of Homosexual Marriage." Yale Law Journal 82 (1973): 583-89.

792. Levitt, Albert. "Privileges--Or Rights and Duties?" American Bar Association Journal 11 (1925): 783-85. Rep. in entry #1781.

793. Lexcen, Esther Helms. "The Equal Rights Amendment." Federal Bar Journal 31 (1972): 247-57.

794. Luff, Ellen. "Maryland ERA Applied in Court." Women Law Reporter, 15 November 1974, pp. 1.67-68.

795. _____. "Rape Developments: Maryland Court Rules Crime of Common Law Rape Not Violative of State Equal Rights Amendment." Women Law Reporter, 15 March 1975, p. 1.172.

796. Lukens, Edward Clark. "Shall Women Throw Away Their Privileges?" American Bar Association Journal 11 (1925): 645-46. Rep. in entry #463.

797. Martin, Philip L. "The Equal Rights Amendment: An Overview." St. Louis University Law Journal 17 (1972): 1-16.

798. _____. "Equal Rights Amendment: Legislative Background." Journal of Family Law 11 (1971): 363-74.

799. Matheson, Alexander E. "Status of Women under the Equal Rights Law: Discussion of Chapter 529 of the Wisconsin Laws of 1921." State Bar Association of Wisconsin Proceedings 14 (1922): 186-97.

800. Matthews, Burnita Shelton. "Women Should Have Equal Rights with Men: A Reply." American Bar Association Journal 12 (1926): 117-20. Rep. in entries #463, 1797.

801. McDougal, Myres S., et al. "Human Rights for Women and World Public Order: The Outlawing of Sex-Based Discrimination." American Journal of International Law 69 (1975): 497-533.

802. "Men, Women, and the Constitution: The Equal Rights Amendment." Columbia Journal of Law and Social Problems 10 (1973): 77-112.

803. Mink, Patsy T. "Federal Legislation to End Discrimination against Women." Valparaiso Law Review 5 (1971): 397-414.

804. Murphy, R. H. "Impact of Equal-Rights Amendment on New-York-State Alimony Statute." Buffalo Law Review 24 (1975): 395-418.

805. Murphy, Thomas E. "Sex Discrimination in Employment: Can We Legislate a Solution." New York Law Forum 17 (1971): 437-79.

806. Murray, Pauli. "The Negro Woman's Stake in the Equal Rights Amendment." Harvard Civil Rights/Civil Liberties Law Review 6 (1971): 253-59. See entry #750.

807. Murrell, Ethel Ernest. "Equality--The Leading Question." Women Lawyers Journal 31 (Winter 1945): 9.

808. _____. "Full Citizenship for Women: An Equal Rights Amendment." American Bar Association Journal 38 (1952): 47-49. Rep. in entry #2652.

809. "Name Change: Hawaii Name Change Laws Voided under State ERA." Women Law Reporter, 1 March 1975, p. 1.162.

810. The New Mexico Equal Rights Amendment--Assessing Its Impact. New Mexico Law Review 3 (1973). See entries #695, 697, 721, 731, 767, 782, 829.

811. Oakley, Mary Ann B. "The Equal Rights Amendment and the Right to Privacy." Emory Law Journal 23 (1974): 196-209.

812. "On the ERA Front." Women Lawyers Journal 62 (Winter 1976): 41-42.

813. "Overview of the Equal Rights Amendment in Texas." Houston Law Review 11 (1973): 136-67.

814. Peratis, Kathleen, and Rindskopf, Elisabeth. "Pregnancy Discrimination as a Sex Discrimination Issue." Women's Rights Law Reporter 2 (June 1975): 26-34.

815. Phillips, Lena Madesin, and Tilson, C. J. "Equal Rights Amendment to the Federal Constitution." Connecticut Bar Journal 20 (1946): 62-74. Phillips piece in favor rep. in entry #18.

816. Planell, Raymond M. "The Equal Rights Amendment: Will States Be Allowed to Change Their Minds?" Notre Dame Lawyer 49 (1974): 657-70.

817. "Pregnancy and the Constitution: The Uniqueness Trap." California Law Review 62 (1974): 1532-66.

818. "Protection, Poverty and the Woman Worker." Suffolk University Law Review 5 (1970): 139-60.

819. Rawalt, Marguerite. "Equal Justice for Women--Update the Constitution." New York Law Forum 17 (1971): 528-42.

820. _____. "The Equal Rights Amendment: Legislative History." Women Lawyers Journal 57 (1971): 19-20.

821. _____. "The Equal Rights Amendment: The 'Why.'" Women Lawyers Journal 57 (1971): 7-11.

822. _____. "The Equal Rights for Men and Women Amendment Is Needed." Women Lawyers Journal 59 (1973): 4-10.

823. _____. "Litigating Sex Discrimination Cases." Family Law Quarterly 4 (1970): 44-52.

824. "Recent Developments in the Area of Sex-Based Discrimination--The Courts, the Congress, and the Constitution." New York Law Forum 20 (1974): 359-80.

825. Rheinstein, M. "The Transformation of Marriage and the Law." Chicago: Northwestern University Law Review 68 (1973): 463-79.

826. Rynan, Arthur E., Jr. "A Comment on Family Property Rights and the Proposed 27th Amendment." Drake Law Review 22 (1973): 505-37.

827. Sampson, John J. "Texas Equal Rights Amendment and the Family: Litigation Ahead." Texas Tech Law Review 5 (1974): 631-43.

828. Schlafly, Phyllis, and Cook, Marlow W. "ERA: Loss of Protection or Promise of Equality." Trial 9 (1973): 18-22.

829. Schlenker, K. O. "Tax Implications of the Equal Rights Amendment." New Mexico Law Review 3 (1973): 69-83. See entry #810.

830. Search, Mabel. "Women's Rights in Wisconsin." Marquette Law Review 6 (1922): 164-69.

831. Sedler, Robert Allen. "Legal Dimensions of Womens Liberation: An Overview." Indiana Law Journal 47 (1971): 419-56.

832. "Sex Classifications in the Social Security Benefit Structure." Indiana Law Journal 49 (1973): 181-200.

833. "Sex Discrimination and Equal Protection: An Analysis of Constitutional Approaches to Achieve Equal Rights for Women." Albany Law Review 38 (1973): 66-83.

834. "Sex Discrimination and Equal Protection: Do We Need a Constitutional Amendment?" Harvard Law Review 84 (1971): 1499-1524.

835. "Sex, Discrimination, and the Constitution." Stanford Law Review 2 (1950): 691-730.

836. "Sex Discrimination in Interscholastic High School Athletics." Syracuse Law Review 25 (1974): 535-74.

837. "Sex Discrimination in the Criminal Law: The Effect of the Equal Rights Amendment." American Criminal Law Review 11 (1973): 469-510.

838. "Sexual Mythology and Employment Discrimination." Seton Hall Law Review 3 (1971): 108-29.

839. "The Sexual Segregation of American Prisons." Yale Law Journal 82 (1973): 1229-73.

840. "Source References on the Equal Rights Amendment." Women Lawyers Journal 59 (1973): 15-16.

841. "State ERA Cases." Women Law Reporter, 15 November 1974, pp. 1.69-1.75.

842. "State ERA Provisions." Women Law Reporter, 15 November 1974, p. 1.66.

843. Sullivan, Leo. "Same Sex Marriage and the Constitution." University of California Davis Law Review 6 (1973): 275-93.

844. "The Support Law and the Equal Rights Amendment in Pennsylvania." Dickinson Law Review 77 (1973): 254-76.

845. Temin, Carolyn E. "Discriminatory Sentencing of Women Offenders: The Argument for ERA in a Nutshell." American Criminal Law Review 2 (1973): 355-72.

846. "Tennessee Law and the Equal Rights Amendment, Domestic Relations, Property Law, Employment Relations and Juries." Memphis State University Law Review 3 (1973): 309-43.

847. "Trade Union Leader Speaks: An Interview with Doris Turner." Women's Rights Law Reporter 1 (Fall 1972/73): 73-76.

848. Trumbull, Terry A. "The Equal Rights Amendment and the Military." Women Lawyers Journal 57 (1971): 92-95.

849. Turner, Jennie McMullin. "Women's Rights by Blanket Legislation." Wisconsin Law Review 2 (1923): 103-9.

850. Uda, Joan. "Equality for Men and Women: Three Approaches: Frontiero, the Equal Rights Amendment, and the Montana Equal Dignities Provision." Montana Law Review 35 (1974): 325-39.

851. "United States: Equal Rights and Responsibilities for Women." International Labour Review 103 (1971): 195-96.

852. Weaver, Adele T. "The Equal Rights Amendment: The Practical Effects." Women Lawyers Journal 57 (1971): 17-18.

853. _____. "The Equal Rights Amendment: Update 1970." Women Lawyers Journal 57 (1971): 21-23.

854. Weitzman, Lenore J. "Legal Regulation of Marriage: Tradition and Change." California Law Review 62 (1974): 1169-1288.

855. Wells, Gladys. "A Critique of Methods for Alteration of Women's Legal Status." Michigan Law Review 21 (1923): 721-42.

856. Wheeler, Louise A. "Women under the Law: The Pedestal or the Cage?" Journal of the Kansas Bar Association 43 (1974): 25-29, 52-59.

857. Wohl, Lisa Cronin. "White Gloves and Combat Boots: The Fight for ERA." Civil Liberties Review 1 (Fall 1974): 77-86.

B. Academic Journals, Popular Magazines, and Special Interest Newspapers

858. AAUW Committee on the Economic and Legal Status of Women. "Next
Step in the Emancipation of Women--An Equal Rights Amendment?" AAUW
Journal, April 1938, pp. 160-64.

859. "AAUW Continues Campaign for ERA Passage." AAUW Journal Newspaper,
October 1975, pp. 1, 2.

860. Abbott, Elizabeth. "Big Campaign for Equal Rights." Jus Suffragii
(International Woman Suffrage News), February 1922, pp. 75-78.

861. Abzug, Bella. "The Women's Movement Is Still Moving." Village
Voice, 22 December 1975, pp. 33-34, 37. (N) Rep. in entry #358.

862. _____, and Edgar, Cynthia. "Women and Politics: The Struggle
for Representation." Massachusetts Review 13 (1972): 17-24.

863. Ackroyd, Margaret F., and Brown, Mary-Agnes. "The Equal Rights
Amendment: Is It the Next Step to Women's Freedom? Convention
Speakers Say Yes and No." AAUW Journal, October 1953, pp. 20-27.

864. AFL-CIO. "Equal Rights Amendment." Proceedings of the AFL-CIO 2
(1957): II, 269-70.

865. _____. "Equal Rights Amendment." Proceedings of the AFL-CIO
3 (1959): II, 236.

866. _____. "Women Workers." Proceedings of the AFL-CIO 1 (1955):
75-76.

867. "AFL for E.R.A." Majority Report, November 1973, p. 1. (N)
(HU, S2, R2)

868. "Again It Is the Time to Move Mountains." National Business Woman
(National Federation of Business and Professional Women's Clubs),
October 1970, pp. 4-5. Formerly Independent Woman.

869. "AHEA Supports Equal Rights Amendment on Capitol Hill." Journal of
Home Economics 63 (1971): 642.

870. "Air Vibes." Gold Flower (Minnesota Women's Political Caucus),
January 1973, p. 2. (N) (H2, S1, R5)

871. Albert, Marilyn. "E.R.A." Off Our Backs, 30 September 1970, p. 14.
(LE) (N) (H, R3)

872. _____. "No E.R.A. without Protection." Off Our Backs, 30
September 1970, p. 6. (N) (H, R3)

873. "All We Want for Christmas Is the Ratification of the 27th
Amendment." Liberator, December 1972, p. 3. (WL)

874. "Almost Home." National Business Woman (National Federation of
Business and Professional Women's Clubs), April 1972, p. 8.9. Formerly
Independent Woman.

875. American Federation of Labor. "Amendment for 'Equal Rights.'"
Report of the Proceedings of the American Federation of Labor 70 (1951):
141, 508.

876. _____. "Blanket Amendment." Report of the Proceedings of the
American Federation of Labor 44 (1924): 73, 186-87.

877. _____. "Equal Rights." Report of the Proceedings of the
American Federation of Labor 49 (1929): 86-87, 244.

878. _____. "Equal Rights." Report of the Proceedings of the
American Federation of Labor 50 (1930): 106-107, 234.

879. _____. "Equal Rights Amendment." Report of the Proceedings
of the American Federation of Labor 58 (1938): 166, 549.

880. _____. "Equal Rights Amendment." Report of the Proceedings
of the American Federation of Labor 64 (1944): 449, 559-60.

881. _____. "Equal Rights Amendment." Report of the Proceedings
of the American Federation of Labor 65 (1945): 227, 321, 470, 553.

882. _____. "Equal Rights Amendment." Report of the Proceedings
of the American Federation of Labor 72 (1953): 153-54, 499.

883. _____. "Equal Rights Amendment." Report of the Proceedings
of the American Federation of Labor 74 (1955): 150.

884. _____. "Fair Employment Practices Legislation" and "Equal
Rights Amendment." Report of the Proceedings of the American
Federation of Labor 73 (1954): 125, 552.

885. _____. "Protest against 'Blanket' Legislation." Report of the
Proceedings of the American Federation of Labor 43 (1923): 363.

886. _____. "Resolution No. 109--By Delegate Julia O'Connor of
Brotherhood of Electrical Workers" and "Women in Industry Endangered."
Report of the Proceedings of the American Federation of Labor 1922:
224, 476, 456-57.

887. _____. "Women's Blanket Amendment." Report of the
Proceedings of the American Federation of Labor 45 (1925): 55, 172.

887a. "Ancient Fake of the 'Equal Rights' Amendment." Labor (Washington,
D.C.), 19 October 1929. Rep. in entry #1918.

888. Anderson, Mary. "Which Road, Women Workers?" Christian Science
Monitor Magazine, 13 April 1946, p. 14 (LE) (N)

889. "Another E.R.A." Off Our Backs, 24 June 1971, p. 15. Contains a
letter from Seattle Radical Women, 5 March 1971, most of an article
by Joan Jordan in Up From Under, and a commentary of OOB. (N)
(H, R3)

890. "Answering Opponents of Equal Rights." Independent Woman (National
Federation of Business and Professional Women's Clubs), October 1947,
p. 302. Becomes National Business Woman.

891. Anthony, Susan B. II. "We Women Throw Our Votes Away."
     Saturday Evening Post, 17 July 1948, pp. 23, 119-20.

892. "Anti E.R.A. Tactics." Everywoman, 11 September 1970, p. 10. (N)
     (H, R1)

893. "Appeal at the Capitol for Women's Equal Rights" and "Legislative
     News: Some Questions and Answers on an Equal Rights Amendment."
     National Business Woman (National Federation of Business and Profession-
     al Women's Clubs), February 1969, pp. 8.3-8.5. Formerly Independent
     Woman.

894. Arbogast, Kate A. "Women in the Armed Forces: A Rediscovered
     Resource." Military Review 53 (1973): 9-19.

895. "As We See It: Support Women's Equal Rights." The Chieftain
     (Black Hawk College), 15 November 1972, p. 2. (N) Rep. in entry #3638.

896. Avery, Edwina Austin. "Let's Open the Mail." Think Tank
     (Atlanta, Georgia), 23 September 1943, p. 2. (LE) Rep. in entry
     #2392.

897. Avery, Patricia, and Oster, Patrick. "Equal Rights for Women--
     Doomed?" U.S. News and World Report, 28 April 1975, p. 45.

898. Baker, Elizabeth F. "About the Women's Charter." Independent
     Woman (National Federation of Business and Professional Women's Clubs),
     March 1937, pp. 72-74, 95. Becomes National Business Woman.

899. Baldwin, J. W. "Louisiana Defeats ERA." Progressive, September
     1974, p. 37.

900. Barclay, Robert W. "Equal Rights." Journal of Home Economics 62
     (1970): 572.

901. _____. "Equal Rights." Journal of Home Economics 64 (1972): 4.

902. _____. "Equal Rights for Women." Journal of Home Economics
     62 (1970): 152.

903. _____. "Equal Rights for Women." Journal of Home Economics
     62 (1970): 376.

904. _____. "ERA." Journal of Home Economics 65 (1973): 6.

905. Bayh, Birch; Griffiths, Martha; Chisholm, Shirley; Leonard, Margery
     C.; and Witter, Jean. "Should Congress Approve the 'Equal Rights
     Amendment?': Pro." Congressional Digest, January 1971, pp. 10-30
     (even numbered pages only). See entry #962.

906. "A Beginning and an End of an ERA." Big Mama Rag 1, no. 4 (1973):
     14.

907. Bellete, Ellen; Reverby, Susan; and Jordon, Joan. "The Equal Rights
     Controversy: Past and Present." Up from Under, August/September 1970,
     pp. 61-64. (H, R11) Rep. in Rat, 11-25 September [1970], pp. 18-19.
     (N)

908. Benson, Lucy Wilson. "ERA: State by State." The National Voter
     (League of Women Voters of the United States), April/May 1973, pp. 5-9.

909. Bent, Silas. "The Women's War." New York Times Magazine, 14
     January 1923, pp. 4, 15. (N)

910. Berman, Susan K. "Maureen Reagan: Why I Support the ERA." Ms.,
     November 1975, pp. 78-79.

911. Beyer, Clara Mortenson. "What Is Equality?" Nation, 31 January
     1923, p. 116.

912. "Bishop's Unit Raps Amendment on Women." National Catholic
     Reporter, 6 October 1972, p. 3. (N)

913. Biernacki, Carol. "ERA Opponents Denounced." Speakout, May/June
     1972, pp. 5, 6. (H2, S1, R15)

914. Bills, Nancy. "Women and Legislature." Big Mama Rag, April 1974,
     p. 3. (N)

915. Blanton, Angele. "Pushing ERA in Louisiana: An 11th Wheel's
     Weekend." Off Our Backs, May 1973, p. 25. (N) (HU, S1, R13)

916. Blatch, Harriet Stanton. "Can Sex Equality Be Legislated?" The
     Independent, 22 December 1923, p. 301.

917. "Board Establishes ERA Fund." AAUW Journal Newspaper, January 1974,
     p. 1.

918. Boeckel, Richard. "Sex Equality and Protective Laws." Editorial
     Research Reports, 13 July 1926, pp. 524-64, esp. 525-28.

919. Bohen, K. L. "Equal Rights Amendment: Questions and Answers."
     Seventeen, August 1974, p. 62.

920. Bonham, Kathy. "Woman's Rights by Law--The 19th Step Forward?"
     Big Mama Rag 1, no. 3 (1973): 8. (N)

921. Borman, Nancy. "Equal Rights--The Long Road to Ratification."
     Majority Report, 22 March 1975, p. 7. (N)

922. _____. "Gunning: 'I Didn't Leave the Party--They Left Me.'"
     Majority Report, 18 October-1 November 1975, pp. 3, 8. (N)

923. _____. "If You Don't Vote, You're Gambling Your Rights."
     Majority Report, 4-18 October 1975, p. 1. (N)

924. _____. "In New York, Equality Is Just Around the Corner."
     Majority Report, 26 July 1975, p. 6. (N)

925. Boyer, Gene. "There Ought to Be a Law! (Like the Equal Rights
     Amendment)." Forum (Wisconsin Psychiatric Institute), no. 2 (1971).
     (WL)
*
926. Brewer, F.M. "Equal Rights Amendment." Editorial Research Reports,
     4 April 1946, pp. 217-36.

927. Brownell, Susan. "Senate Relents, Ratifies ERA." Pandora, 3 April
     1973, pp. 3, 7. (N) (HU, S1, R13)

928. _____. "State House Passes E.R.A." Pandora, 20 February
     1973, p. 3. (N) (HU, S1, R13)

929. _____. "Why the ERA Failed." Pandora, 14 November 1972, p. 3.
     (N) (HU, S1, R13)

930. Bruton, Margaret Perry. "Present-Day Thinking on the Woman
     Question." Annals of the American Academy of Political and Social
     Science 251 (1947): 10-16. See entry #492.

931. Buckley, James. "The Equal Rights Amendment: The Legislative
     Aspect." Vital Speeches of the Day 38 (1 June 1972): 493-96.

932. Burke, Mary. "The Church and the Equal Rights Amendment."
     America, 17 May 1975, pp. 374-78.

933. Butler, John Marshall. "The Case for Equal Legal Rights." National
     Business Woman (National Federation of Business and Professional
     Women's Clubs), July 1957, pp. 6-7, 16. Formerly Independent Woman.
     Rep. in entry #50.

934. Byrns, Elinor, and Regan, Agnes G. "Should Women Have Identical
     Rights with Men?: Pro and Con." Congressional Digest, March 1924,
     p. 204. See entry #1022.

935. "California Ratifies ERA." National Business Woman (National
     Federation of Business and Professional Women's Clubs), January 1973,
     p. 8.3. Formerly Independent Woman.

936. "Campaign Headquarters Opened: To Work for the Equal Rights
     Amendment." Independent Woman (National Federation of Business and
     Professional Women's Clubs), April 1947, p. 112. Becomes National
     Business Woman.

937. Campos, Jeannie. "ERA Campaign Now Underway." Pandora, 13 June
     1972, pp. 3, 6. (N) (WL; HU, S1, R13)

938. Carruthers, Sue. "1972--The ERA for Personhood." Progressive
     Woman, December 1971, p. 5. (Ed) (HU, S1, R14)

939. Casey, Rick. "States Vote, Catholics Split on Women's Rights
     Measure." National Catholic Reporter, 16 February 1973, p. 1. (N)

940. Cassell, Kay Ann. "The Legal Status of Women." Library Journal,
     1 September 1971, pp. 2600-603.

941. "Catholic Spokesman Wary of Equal Rights for Women Effort."
     Catholic Herald-Citizen, 1 August 1970, p. 7. (N)

942. Catt, Carrie Chapman. "Too Many Rights: Women Leaders Who Would
     Go beyond All Decent Limits." Ladies Home Journal, November 1922,
     pp. 31, 68.

943. _____; Wells, Marguerite M.; Anderson, Mary; Frankfurter, Felix; Green, William; Ryan, John A.; National Council of Catholic Women; Stone, Mrs. J. Austin; American Association of University Women; Women's Trade Union League; Lane, Gertrude; National League of Women Voters; Congress of Women's Auxiliaries, C.I.O.; Washington Committee, Women's Trade Union League; Bassette, Linna E.; Straus, Dorothy; Pound, Roscoe; Rieve, Emil; and Laderman, Isador. "Should Congress Approve the Proposed Equal Rights Amendment to the Constitution?: Con." Congressional Digest, April 1943, pp. 118-28. See entry #1371.

944. "Challenge for Committment: Legislative Challenges." National Business Woman (National Federation of Business and Professional Women's Clubs), March 1973, pp. 14-15. Formerly Independent Woman.

945. Chew, Barbara. "Stopping ERA." Newsweek, 15 December 1975, p. 11. (LE)

945a. Chodorov, Frank. "Equal Rights for Women." Analysis 1 (January 1945): 4. Rep. in entry #2465.

946. Christy, Teresa. "Equal Rights for Women: Voices from the Past." American Journal of Nursing 71 (1971): 288-93.

947. "Church Support Sought for ERA." Pandora, 6 February 1973, p. 3. (N) (HU, S1, R13)

948. "Citizens for the ERA." Feminists for Life 1, no. 2 [1972], p. [9]. Becomes Sisterlife (Columbus, Ohio). (H2, S1, R5)

949. "Closer: Equality for Women." U.S. News and World Report, 3 April 1972, p. 58.

950. Cochrane, Elizabeth. "The Year Ahead for E.R.A." Majority Report, January 1974, pp. 5, 11. (N) (HU, S2, R2) Rep. in Changing Woman, 21 February 1974, p. 3. (N)

951. Cohn, Ellen. "Gazette." Ms., September 1974, p. 19.

952. Colorado Coalition for Equal Rights. "ERA Opponents' Figures Faulty." Big Mama Rag, January 1976, p. 12. (N)

953. Commons, Telah. "ERA." California Woman (California Federation of Business and Professional Women's Clubs), September/October 1974, pp. 4-5.

954. "Congress Approves 44 Percent of Nixon's 1972 Requests: Civil Rights." Congressional Quarterly Weekly Report, 16 December 1972, pp. 3138, 3142.

955. "Congress Passes ERA after Long Struggle." Pandora, 4 April 1972, p. 1. (N) (HU, S1, R13)

956. "Congress: Rights for Women." Newsweek, 29 July 1946, p. 17.

957. "Congress to Get Bills on Equal Treatment for Women." Congressional Quarterly Weekly Report, 28 December 1962, pp. 2298-300.

958. Connors, Joy. "The E.R.A.: Do We Need It?" Everywoman, 1 October 1971, pp. [24-25]. (N) (HU, S1, R3)

959. Conroy, Sarah Booth. "Set Stage for Equal Rights." McCalls, May 1971, p. 37.

960. "Constitutional Amendment." Congressional Quarterly Weekly Report, 14 August 1970, pp. 2041-42.

961. "Controversial Equal Rights Amendment before Senate." Congressional Quarterly Guide to Current American Government, Spring 1972, p. 65.

962. Controversy over the "Equal Rights for Women" Amendment. Congressional Digest, January 1971, pp. 1-32 (entire issue). (WL) See entries #905, 1132.

963. Cook, Marlow W., and Abernethy, Thomas G. "Do Women Need an Equal Rights Amendment? Yes and No." American Legion Magazine, December 1970, pp. 30-31.

964. "Cooperate to Legislate." National Business Woman (National Federation of Business and Professional Women's Clubs), July/August 1974, p. 6. Formerly Independent Woman.

965. Cooper, Carolyn L. "Equal Protection." New York Times Magazine, 15 July 1973, p. 21. (LE) (N)

966. Cooper, John M. "Newest Platform of the National Woman's Party." Catholic Charities Review, December 1922, pp. 359-61.

967. Copeland, Royal S., and Pepper, George Wharton. "Members of Congress Express Views on Equal Rights Amendment: Con." Congressional Digest, March 1924, p. 197. See entry #1022.

968. Corson, Rosalie. "ERA--How Effective Can It Be?" Progressive Woman, April (2) 1972, p. 4. (Ed) (HU, S1, R14)

969. "Courtship, Marriage, Divorce, and the ERA." Women in Business (American Business Women's Association), March/April 1973, pp. 10-11.

970. Cramer, Jane Smith, and Parkhurst, Genevieve. "Should Women Support the Equal Rights Amendment?" Independent Woman (National Federation of Business and Professional Women's Clubs), May 1935, pp. 148-49, 171-74. Becomes National Business Woman.

971. Crater, Flora. "The U.S. Senate and the Subjugation of Women." Second Wave, December 1971, pp. 11-12, 17. (HU, S1, R14).

972. Cravens, Fadjo; Pollitzer, Anita; Dickinson, Mrs. LaFell; Phillips, Lena M.; Butler, Sally; Sherwin, Ella M.; Avery, Nina Horton; Wiley, Anne Kelton; Smith, Jane Norman; Taylor, A. Elizabeth; and Lutz, Alma. "Should the U.S. Constitution Guarantee Equal Rights for Women under the Law?: Pro." Congressional Digest, December 1946, pp. 302-18 (even numbered pages only). See entry #996.

973. Cross, Robert. "Dialog: Esther Saperstein." Chicago Tribune
     Magazine, 7 September 1975, p. 56. (N)
*
974. Cukor, Janet. "ERA: Dispelling Crippling Myths." AAUW Journal
     Newspaper, May 1974, pp. 1, 4.

975. Cunningham, Sarah Jane. "To Break the Bars to Women's Equal Rights."
     National Business Woman (National Federation of Business and Profes-
     sional Women's Clubs), November 1969, pp. 5, 13-14. Formerly
     Independent Woman.

976. Curley, Suzanne. "Equal Rights Amendment for Women--When?"
     Washington Post Parade Magazine, 17 September 1972, p. 23. (N) (WL)

977. Curtis, Charles, and Anthony, Daniel R., Jr. "Members of Congress
     Express Views on Equal Rights Amendment: Pro." Congressional Digest,
     March 1924, p. 197. See entry #1022.

978. Danton, Marilyn. "Protective Legislation and the ERA." Workers'
     Power, no. 23 (9-22 October 1970), pp. 3-4. (N)

979. Davis, Eleanor R. "OCWE." Changing Woman, 31 March 1972, p. 2.
     (N) (H2, S1, R2)

980. "Dawn of a New ERA." The Lesbian Tide, April 1972, p. 18.
     (HU, S1, R6)

981. Dawson, John B. "Program of the National Woman's Party from the
     Point of View of Connecticut Social Workers." Family 3 (1923): 225-28.

982. "D-Day: Day of Decision." National Business Woman (National
     Federation of Business and Professional Women's Clubs), September 1975,
     p. 9. Formerly Independent Woman.

983. "Deep Concern for ERA Spurs Board Action on Funds, Site." AAUW
     Journal Newspaper, January 1976, p. 1.

984. Dekkers, Onka. "Death of an E.R.A." Off Our Backs, 8 November
     1970, p. 3. (N) (H, R3)

985. DeNoux, Bonnie. "ERA Central Up and at It." Distaff, November/
     December 1973, p. 14. (N) (H2, S2, R2)

986. De Santis, Marie. "Equal Rights No Rights?" Broadside, 16 February
     1973, p. 2. (N) (H2, S1, R2)

987. Deutch, Virginia L. "Equal Rights." Saturday Review of Literature,
     7 August 1948, p. 23. (LE)

988. "Discussion." Atlantic Monthly, July 1964, p. 24.

989. Dock, Lavinia L. "Lucretia Mott Amendment." Public Health
     Nursing 16 (1924): 135-36.

990. "Doctrinaire Equality." New Republic, 24 July 1929, p. 249.

991. "Double Talk or . . . The Equal Rights Amendment." Through the Looking Glass, February 1971, p. 6. (N) (H, R4)

992. "Do Women Have Equal Rights?" Good Housekeeping, December 1948, pp. 38-39, 264-68.

993. Draper, Anne. "Equal Rights for All." Union W.A.G.E., December 1971, pp. [3-4]. (N) (HU, S1, R16)

994. _____. Letter to Dianne Feinstein. Union W.A.G.E., July 1971, p. [7]. (N) (H, R22)

995. _____, and Hanberry, Luella. "ERA Delayed: Fight Goes on for Protective Legislation." Union W.A.G.E., May/June 1972, pp. 1, 4. (N) (HU, S1, R16)

996. The Drive to Secure for Women Equal Rights with Men under the Law. Congressional Digest, December 1946, pp. 289-320 (entire issue). See entries #972, 1175, 1196.

997. Dubrow, Evelyn. "'Equal Rights Amendment' Endangers U.S. Women's Gains." AFL-CIO Free Trade Union News, September 1970, p. 3.

998. Dunkle, Margaret C. "The Law Is on Your Side." Womensports, September 1974, pp. 44-53.

999. Dunlap, Mary C. "Political Bread-and-Butter and the Slow Starvation of the Equal Rights Amendment." Conspiracy (Bay Area National Lawyers Guild), August 1973, pp. 6, 15. (N) (WL)

1000. Durbin, Karen. "Why the ERA Frightens Women." Mademoiselle, February 1976, pp. 18, 70 (pt. 1); March 1976, pp. 54, 57 (pt. 2).

1001. Eagon, Betty J. "United Effort Needed for ERA." California Woman (California Federation of Business and Professional Women's Clubs), September/October 1975, pp. 4-5.

1001a. "Early Predictions and Unfinished Business." National Business Woman (National Federation of Business and Professional Women's Clubs), February 1975, p. 4. Formerly Independent Woman.

1002. East, Catherine. "Equal Protection." New York Times Magazine, 15 July 1973, p. 21. (LE) (N)

1003. East, Marjorie. "Statement in Support of ERA." Journal of Home Economics 65 (1973): 73.

1003a. Eastman, Crystal. "Equality or Protection." Time and Tide, 18 January 1924. Rep. in entry #1637.

1003b. _____. "Equal Rights Amendment." New Republic, 19 November 1924, p. 299. (LE) Rep. in entry #1713.

1004. "Education and the ERA: Reading, Writing, and Rights." Women in Business (American Business Women's Association), May 1973, pp. 8-9.

1005. Eisler, Riane. "To Kill or Not to Kill the ERA." Born a Woman, [Fall/Winter 1971], pp. 14-16. (H2, S1, R2)

1006. "Election Day for ERA." Pandora, 31 October 1972, p. 3. (N) (HU, S1, R13)

1006a. Elizabeth,Ann. "Equality under the Law More of the Same: Commentary on the Equal Rights Amendment." Ain't I a Woman?, 25 September 1970, p. 9. (N) (H, R1)

1007. _____. "The Equal Rights Amendment: Pro and Con." Everywoman, 2 October 1970, p. 8. (N) (H, R1) Rep. from entry #3083.

1008. Elliott, Linda. "Politics of the Equal Rights Amendment." Women's Press, August 1972, pp. 10, 14. (N) (HU, S1, R19)

1009. "Emergency for the ERA." NOW York Woman (Supplement to Manhattan Tribune), 1 May 1971, p. 8. (N) (H, R2)

1010. Emerson, Thomas I. "Supporting an Equal Rights Amendment." Current, no. 134 (1971): 25-32. Rep. from entry #733.

1011. "End of an ERA?" Time, 17 November 1975, p. 65.

1012. "Equality of Women." America, 26 October 1963, p. 473.

1013. "Equality Rip-off Amendment: Giant Step Backwards for Workers." Change, December 1972, p. 1. (N) (HU, S1, R1)

1014. "Equal Rights." Congressional Quarterly Almanac 9 (1953): 333, 386.

1015. "Equal Rights." Congressional Quarterly Weekly Report, 18 September 1970, pp. 2256-57.

1016. "Equal Rights." Congressional Quarterly Weekly Report, 2 April 1971, p. 744-45.

1017. "Equal Rights." Congressional Quarterly Weekly Report, 16 April 1971, p. 850.

1018. "Equal Rights." Congressional Quarterly Weekly Report, 23 July 1971, pp. 1562-63.

1019. "Equal Rights." Journal of Home Economics 64 (1972): 78.

1020. "Equal Rights." Woman's Home Companion, April 1939, p. 2.

1021. "The Equal Rights Alliance." Changing Woman, 28 February 1973, pp. 1-2. (N) (H2, S1, R3)

1022. "The Equal Rights Amendment." Congressional Digest, March 1924, pp. 192-207 (special feature of the issue). See entries #934, 967, 977, 1159, 1247, 1289, 1352, 1520, 1529, 1556.

1023. "Equal Rights Amendment." Congressional Quarterly Almanac 2 (1946): 540-41, 568, 759.

1024. "Equal Rights Amendment." _Congressional Quarterly Almanac_ 6 (1950): 419-22, 539.

1025. "Equal Rights Amendment." _Congressional Quarterly Weekly Report_, 9 June 1950, pp. 647-50.

1026. "Equal Rights Amendment." _Congressional Quarterly Weekly Report_, 15 January 1954, p. 51.

1027. "Equal Rights Amendment." _Congressional Quarterly Weekly Report_, 16 October 1970, p. 2550.

1028. "Equal Rights Amendment." _Congressional Quarterly Weekly Report_, 25 September 1971, p. 1982.

1029. "Equal Rights Amendment." _Congressional Quarterly Weekly Report_, 9 October 1971, p. 2107.

1030. "Equal Rights Amendment." _Congressional Quarterly Weekly Report_, 24 June 1972, p. 1529.

1031. "Equal Rights Amendment." _Congressional Quarterly Weekly Report_, 13 January 1973, p. 43.

1032. "Equal Rights Amendment." _Congressional Quarterly Weekly Report_, 10 February 1973, p. 305.

1033. "Equal Rights Amendment." _Congressional Quarterly Weekly Report_, 10 March 1973, p. 500.

1034. "Equal Rights Amendment." _Congressional Quarterly Weekly Report_, 14 April 1973, p. 820.

1035. "Equal Rights Amendment." _Congressional Quarterly Weekly Report_, 26 January 1974, p. 175.

1036. "Equal Rights Amendment." _Everywoman_, 23 October 1970.   (N)   (WL)

1037. "Equal Rights Amendment." _Focus: A Journal for Gay Women_, March 1974, p. 12.   (HU, S2, R1)

1038. "The Equal Rights Amendment." _Majority Report_, November 1972, p. 12.   (N)   (HU, S1, R6)

1039. "Equal Rights Amendment." _National Education Association Journal_, October 1944, p. 168.

1039a. "Equal Rights Amendment." _New Carolina Woman_, November 1970, p. 7.   (N)   (H, R2)

1040. _Equal Rights Amendment_. _Pennsylvania NOW_, January 1976, pp. 1-12 (entire issue).

1041. "Equal Rights Amendment a Dead Issue?" _Human Events_, 28 April 1973, p. 4.   (N)

1042. "Equal Rights Amendment Again before the Senate." Scholastic
Teacher, 26 February 1938, p. 16S. Becomes Senior Scholastic.

1043. "Equal Rights Amendment Alive and Support Growing." Bridge
(Unitarian Universalist Women's Federation), February 1971, p. 10.
Also in Program Builder, March 1971, p. 3. (H, R5)

1044. "The Equal Rights Amendment--All Men and Women Are Created Equal."
Women in Business (American Business Women's Association), January
1973, pp. 6-7.

1045. "Equal Rights Amendment: A Step Backwards for Working Women."
Change, May 1972, pp. 6-7. (N) (WL; HU, S1, R1)

1046. "The Equal Rights Amendment Congressional Jubilee and Ratification
Assembly." National Business Woman (National Federation of Business
and Professional Women's Clubs), June 1972, p. 12. Formerly Independent
Woman.

1047. "Equal Rights Amendment Fails in Two More States." Human Events,
10 March 1973, p. 4. (N)

1048. "Equal Rights Amendment: Opposition by Labor and Women's Groups."
Social Service Review 19 (1945): 111-13.

1049. "Equal Rights: Amendment Passed over Ervin Opposition."
Congressional Quarterly Almanac 28 (1972): 199-204, 17-18-S.

1050. "Equal Rights: Amendment Passed over Ervin Opposition."
Congressional Quarterly Weekly Report, 25 March 1972, pp. 692-95.

1051. "Equal Rights Amendment Ratification Rally Announced." St. Louis
Organization for Women's Rights, [September 1972], p. [6]. (N) (H2,
S1, R14)

1052. "The Equal Rights Amendment Revised: Have Recent Developments
Removed the Grounds for Opposition?" AAUW Journal, October 1943, pp.
10-14.

1053. "Equal Rights Amendment--Why It Is Needed." Bridge (Unitarian
Universalist Women's Federation), October 1970, pp. 8-9. (H, R5)

1054. "Equal Rights and Democracy: Proposed Equal Rights Amendment."
Independent Woman (National Federation of Business and Professional
Women's Clubs), December 1944, pp. 374-87. Becomes National Business
Woman.

1055. "The Equal Rights Controversy." Rat, 11-25 September [1970],
pp. 18-19. (N) (H, R3) Rep. from Up From Under, August/September
1970, pp. 61-64.

1056. "Equal Rights English." National Business Woman (National
Federation of Business and Professional Women's Clubs), January 1972,
p. 14. Formerly Independent Woman.

1057. "Equal Rights for Women?" America, 1 August 1953, p. 434.

1058. "Equal Rights for Women." Congressional Quarterly Weekly Report,
27 January 1950, pp. 96, 104.

1059. "Equal Rights for Women." Congressional Quarterly Weekly Report,
18 September 1964, p. 2184.

1060. "Equal Rights for Women." Congressional Quarterly Weekly Report,
15 May 1970, pp. 1292-93.

1061. "Equal Rights for Women." National Review, 14 April 1972, p. 383.

1062. "Equal Rights for Women?" New Republic, 16 February 1938, p. 34.

1063. "Equal Rights for Women." Scholastic Teacher, 15 February 1950,
pp. 10-11. Becomes Senior Scholastic.

1064. "Equal Rights for Women: ABC's of the Big Fight." U.S. News and
World Report, 26 March 1973, pp. 34-36. (WL)

1065. "The Equal Rights for Women Amendment." Bridge (Unitarian
Universalist Women's Federation), March 1970, p. 9. (H, R5)

1066. "Equal Rights for Women Amendment Dropped in Senate." Congressional
Quarterly Almanac 26 (1970): 706-709, 54-H, 60-S.

1067. "Equal Rights for Women--Is '75 the Year?" U.S. News and World
Report, 17 February 1975, pp. 49-50.

1068. "Equal Rights for Women? Pro and Con Discussion." Scholastic
Teacher, 6 May 1953, pp. 7-8. Becomes Senior Scholastic.

1069. "Equal Rights for Women? Things May Never Be the Same." U.S. News
and World Report, 24 August 1970, pp. 29-30.

1070. "Equal Rights Law Amended." Pandora, 27 July 1971, p. 4. (N)
(H, R20)

1071. "Equal Rights NOW." Newsweek, 2 March 1970, p. 75.

1072. "Equal Rights Soon." Lesbian Tide, September 1972, p. 11
(HU, S1, R6)

1073. "E.R.A." Everywoman, 21 August 1970, p. 3. (N) (H, R1) Rep.
from entry #4515.

1074. "ERA." Gold Flower (Minnesota Women's Political Caucus), July/
August 1972, p. 8. (N) (WL; H2, R5)

1075. "ERA." National Voter (League of Women Voters of the United
States), Spring 1975, p. 30.

1076. "ERA." Off Our Backs, December 1972, p. 18. (N) (HU, S1, R13)

1077. "ERA." Speakout, March 1973, p. 14. (H2, S1, R15)

1078. "E.R.A." What She Wants, February 1974, p. 4. (N) (H2, S2, R12)

1079. "E.R.A." Women's Press, April 1972, p. 5. (N) (HU, S1, R19)

1080. "E.R.A. and Abortion: Top Priority." Women's News Exchange,
17 March 1972, p. 1. (N) (H2, S1, R19)

1081. "The E.R.A. and Its Enemies." Majority Report, 25 January 1975,
pp. 1-10 (special issue). (N)

1082. "ERA and the Lesbian Ghetto." Lavender Woman, November 1973, p. 6.
(N) (H2, S2, R4)

1083. "E.R.A. and the State Senate." Goodbye to All That, 3-24 May 1972,
p. 3. (N) (HU, S1, R5)

1084. "ERA Benefit Party Planned." Pandora, 8 August 1972, p. 2.
(N) (HU, S1, R13)

1085. "ERA Beset by Anti-Equality Money." Majority Report, February
1973, p. 18. (N) (WL; HU, S1, R6)

1086. "ERA Breakthrough in California." Changing Woman, 1 November
1972, p. 2. (N) (H2, S1, R3) Rep. from entry # 3842.

1087. "ERA Congressional Jubilee." Journal of Home Economics 64 (1972):
31.

1088. "The ERA Defeat." Majority Report, 15-29 November 1975, p. 2. (Ed)
(N)

1089. "E.R.A. Defeat: Where Do We Go from Here?" Majority Report,
15-29 November 1975, p. 4. (N)

1090. "E.R.A., E.L.R.A.; Both Needed to Insure Fem Rights." Liberator,
August 1972, p. 2. (H2, S1, R7)

1091. "ERA Faces Long Uphill Battle in Five Still Unratified States."
AAUW Journal Newspaper, October 1974, p. 10.

1092. "ERA Fails Second Test in Virginia." Human Events, 9 March 1974,
p. 5. (N)

1093. "ERA: Failure Calls for Strategy." AAUW Journal Newspaper,
August 1975, p. 7.

1094. "ERA for Women." Economist, 15 March 1975, p. 70.

1095. "ERA Hearings." National Business Woman (National Federation of
Business and Professional Women's Clubs), June/July 1970, pp. 8.2-8.5.
Formerly Independent Woman.

1096. "ERA Implementation Bill Passed." Pandora, 17 April 1973, p. 2.
(N) (HU, S1, R13)

1097. "The ERA in 1974." Pandora, 22 January 1974, p. 2. (N) (HU, S2,
R6)

1098. "ERA Is Good Politics." National Business Woman (National Federation of Business and Professional Women's Clubs), May 1974, p. 8.2. Formerly Independent Woman.

1099. "E.R.A.: It Was Women or Willie's Woodpile." Majority Report, March 1974, p. 5. (N) (HU, S2, R2)

1100. "ERA Marches On." Ms., January 1974, p. 22. (HU, S2, R5)

1101. "An ERA Media Blitz." Newsweek, 26 January 1976, p. 15.

1102. "ERA Meeting Set." Pandora, 13 June 1972, p. 7. (N) (WL; HU, S1, R13)

1103. "ERA: More Freedom or a Fraud?" Senior Scholastic, 21 October 1975, pp. 12, 32. Formerly Scholastic Teacher.

1104. "ERA News." 51%, 1 December 1972, p. [5]. (N) (H2, S1, R5)

1105. "ERA: Not Dead in Missouri Despite Senate Setback." St. Louis Organization for Women's Rights, February 1973, p. [2]. (N) (H2, S1, R14)

1106. "ERA Not Insured." Big Mama Rag, February 1976, p. 14. (N)

1107. "E.R.A.--Only Five States to Go." 51%, March 1974, p. [2]. (N) (H2, S2, R3) Rep. from entry #2891.

1108. "ERA Opponents Deserve the Ax." FOCUS/Midwest 10 (1974): 5.

1109. "ERA or Error? Progress of the Equal Rights Amendment." Broadside, October [1970], p. 7. (N) (H, R1)

1110. "ERA Passes Senate." Progressive Woman, April (2) 1972, p. 3. (HU, S1, R14)

1111. "ERA Portends 'Dramatic Developments.'" Gold Flower (Minnesota Women's Political Caucus), September 1972, p. 5. (N) (H2, S1, R5)

1112. "ERA: Pro and Con." National Business Woman (National Federation of Business and Professional Women's Clubs), June 1971, pp. 6-7, 11. Formerly Independent Woman.

1113. "ERA Progress Report." National Business Woman (National Federation of Business and Professional Women's Clubs), April 1974, p. 5. Formerly Independent Woman.

1114. "ERA Rally in Miami." AAUW Journal Newspaper, May 1974, p. 3.

1115. "ERA Ratification Fight Continues." AAUW Journal Newspaper, March 1974, p. 1.

1116. "ERA Report." AAUW Journal Newspaper, January 1974, p. 2.

1117. "ERA Report." Big Mama Rag, March 1975, p. 13. (N) Rep. from Sister (Los Angeles).

1118. "ERA Roundup." National Business Woman (National Federation of Business and Professional Women's Clubs), December 1970, pp. 8.8-8.10. Formerly Independent Woman.

1119. "ERA Seminar." Pandora, 3 October 1972, p. 3. (N) (HU, S1, R13)

1120. "ERA '76: You Can Bank on It." Ms., September 1975, p. 21.

1121. "ERA: State by State." National Voter (League of Women Voters of the United States), April/May 1973, pp. 5-6.

1122. "ERA State Ratification Scorecard." National Business Woman (National Federation of Business and Professional Women's Clubs), June 1972, p. 8.2; July/August 1972, p. 8.2. Formerly Independent Woman.

1123. "ERA Still Alive?" Pandora, 20 March 1973, p. 6. (N) (HU, S1, R13)

1124. "ERA Struggling." Big Mama Rag 1, no. 3 (1973): 4. (N)

1125. "ERA Stuck in Senate." Pandora, 6 March 1973, p. 7. (N) (HU, S1, R13)

1126. "ERA Tally Rally." National Business Woman (National Federation of Business and Professional Women's Clubs), February 1974, p. 4. Formerly Independent Woman.

1127. "ERA: The Ratification of Change." County Manpower Report (National Association of Counties Research Foundation) 2 (August 1973): 15-17.

1128. "ERA Votes See-Saw" and "California Ratifies ERA." Pandora, 28 November 1972, p. 7. (N) (HU, S1, R13)

1129. "E.R.A.: What's in It for You?" National Voter (League of Women Voters of the United States), September 1972, pp. 24-25.

1130. "ERA: What We Have in Common." National Voter (League of Women Voters of the United States), Fall 1975, pp. 6-8.

1131. "ERA: Where Are You?" Pandora, 16 May 1972, p. 2. (N) (HU, S1, R13)

1132. Ervin, Sam J., Jr.; Biemiller, Andrew J.; Wolfgang, Myra K.; Freund, Paul A.; and Keyserling, Mary Dublin. "Should Congress Approve the 'Equal Rights Amendment'?: Con." Congressional Digest, January 1971, pp. 11-31 (odd numbered pages only). See entry #962.

1133. "Eve Battling On for Equal Rights." Literary Digest, 28 June 1924, pp. 11-12.

1134. "Facing Equality for Women: Proposed Constitutional Amendment." Time, 4 October 1971, pp. 58-59. (WL)
*
1135. Feeley, Dianne. "The Case for the Equal Rights Amendment." International Socialist Review 34 (1973): 6-9. Abridged as entry #536.

1136. _____. Letter to the Editor. Everywoman, 13 November 1970, p. 3. (N) (H, R1)

1137. "Feminism in the Federal Constitution." World's Work, November 1922, pp. 20-21.

1138. Field, Shirley A. "Facing Equality." Changing Woman, 31 March 1972, pp. 1-2. (N) (H2, S1, R2)

1139. "Fight Continues for 'Equal Rights' for Women." Congressional Quarterly Weekly Report, 9 May 1958, p. 575.

1140. "Fighting First Lady: B. Ford's Support of the Equal Rights Amendment." Time, 3 March 1975, p. 20.

1141. "Fighting for ERA." Editorial Research Reports Reminder Service, 17 August 1973.

1142. "Fight the ERA: The Ladies Mobilize." Texas Observer, 15 November 1974, pp. 1, 3-5. (N)

1143. Fisher, M. J. "Equal Rights by Constitutional Amendment." Social Science 26 (1951): 166-72.

1144. Fitzgerald, Laurine E. "Women's Changing Expectations: New Insights, New Demands." Counseling Psychologist 4 (1973): 90-95.

1145. "5 in '75: ERA Campaign Countdown." National Voter (League of Women Voters of the United States), Fall 1974, p. 17.

1146. "5 in '75: ERA Campaign Countdown." National Voter (League of Women Voters of the United States), Winter 1975, p. 3.

1147. "Five More in '74." National Business Woman (National Federation of Business and Professional Women's Clubs), April 1974, p. 4. Formerly Independent Woman.

1148. "Flash, AFL-CIO Support." National Business Woman (National Federation of Business and Professional Women's Clubs), November 1973, p. 5. Formerly Independent Woman.

1149. Ford, Gerald R. "Equal Rights for Women." Weekly Compilation of Presidential Documents, 21 July 1975, p. 739.

1150. _____. "The White House--Women's Equality Day, 1974--A Proclamation." National Business Woman (National Federation of Business and Professional Women's Clubs), October 1974, p. 4. Formerly Independent Woman.

1151. Fox, Nellie. "Union Women." Changing Woman, 31 March 1972, p. 1. (N) (H2, S1, R2)

1152. Fraser, Arvonne S. "Women: The New Image." Vital Speeches of the Day 37 (15 July 1971): 599-605.

1153. Freeman, Frankie Muse. "Equal Rights Amendment: What's in It for Black Women?" FOCUS/Midwest 9 (1973): 22-28. Rep. as entry #383.

1154. Freund, Paul A. "Achieving Equal Rights Other Ways." Current, no. 134 (November 1971): 32-39. Rep. from entry #760.

1155. Gabringer, Vicki. "ERA: Year of the Rabble." Quest 1 (Fall 1974): 62-73.

1156. Gage-Colby, Ruth. "Where Is the Equal Rights Amendment?" Broadside, December 1970, p. 13. (N) (H, R1)

1157. "Gains for Women Still Snowballing." U.S. News and World Report, 11 March 1974, p. 44.

1158. Gale, Zona. "What Women Won in Wisconsin." Nation, 23 August 1922, pp. 184-85. Rep. in entry #463 and as a separate by the National Woman's Party.

1159. _____; Turner, Jennie McMullin; and Hochstein, Irma. "Is Wisconsin Equal Rights Law Proving Beneficial to Women?: Pro and Con." Congressional Digest, March 1924, p. 205. See entry #1022.

1159a. Garvin, Florence. "Plea to Support Amendment." Birth Control Review, April 1924. Rep. in entry #1662.

1160. Gelder, Lindsy Van. "The 400,000 Vote Misunderstanding." Ms., March 1976, pp. 67-68.

1161. George Washington University Women's Liberation. "The Equal Rights Amendment and the Draft." Second Wave, Summer 1971, pp. 4-5. (H, R11) Rep. in entries #141, 580, 3209, 3939.

1162. Gillooly, Thomas J. "Equal Rights and Insurance." Journal of the American Society of Chartered Life Underwriters, 29 (January 1975): 37-41.

1163. Ginsburg, Ruth Bader. "ERA: Fiction and Fact." Ms., May 1973, pp. 119-21. (H2, S1, R9)

1164. Goldberger, Rita A. "E.R.A.: Coalition Active in Missouri." Lesbian Tide, February 1973, p. 13. (HU, S1, R6)

1165. Golick, Toby. "The Amendment: Do Women Need It?" American Journal of Nursing 71 (1971): 284-87.

1166. Goltz, Pat. "Equal Rights." Sisterlife, July 1973, pp. [1-2]. Formerly Feminists for Life (Columbus, Ohio). (H2, S2, R10)

1167. Goodman, L.V. "Women's New-Found Muscle: ERA." American Education 8 (December 1972): inside cover.

1168. Gordon, Elaine, and Camping, Trudy. "Equal Rights Amendment: Pro and Con." State Government 48 (1975): 104-108.

1169. Greathouse, Rebekah S. "The Effect of Constitutional Equality on
   Working Women." American Economic Review 34, pt. 2 (Papers and
   Proceedings of the 56th Annual Meeting of the American Economic
   Association) (March 1944): 227-36. Rep. in entry #2434.

1170. Grumbach, Doris. "Listening to Women." New Republic, 9 June
   1973, pp. 24-27.

1171. Gupta, Ruth Church. "The Saga of the Ratification of ERA--
   California Style." California Woman (California Federation of Business
   and Professional Women's Clubs), January/February 1973, p. 6.

1172. _____. "Testimony Regarding a Review of the Property Laws."
   California Woman (California Federation of Business and Professional
   Women's Clubs), January/February 1973, p. 13.

1173. Halberstam, Sandra. "Yes, Sisters, We Can Outnumber Them!"
   Majority Report, 26 July 1975, p. 7. (N)

1174. Hamilton, Alice. "The 'Blanket' Amendment--A Debate: Protection
   for Women Workers." Forum 72 (1924): 152-60. See entry #1455 for
   companion article.

1175. _____. "Why I Am against the Equal Rights Amendment."
   Ladies Home Journal, July 1945, pp. 23, 123. Abridged in entry #996.

1176. "Happy New Era." Progressive Woman, December 1972, p. 8.
   (HU, S1, R14)

1177. Hardesty, Doris Gibson. "The Continuing Fight for Women's Rights."
   American Federationist (American Federation of Labor and Congress of
   Industrial Organizations), January 1971, pp. 12-20.

1178. Hartz, Mrs. A. Paul. "Is a Woman a Person?" Clubwoman (General
   Federation of Women's Clubs), November 1971, pp. 20-21.

1179. Hastings, Dorian. "E.R.A. Workshop Plans Strategy." Distaff,
   April 1974, p. 8. (N) (H2, S2, R2)

1180. Hastings, Mary. "ERA Passes House, Faces Senate--Will Bill's Fate
   Affect Future Women's Lobbying." Gold Flower (Minnesota Women's
   Political Caucus), January 1973, p. [4]. (N) (H2, S1, R5)

1181. "Has Your State Ratified the Equal Rights Amendment?" National
   Business Woman (National Federation of Business and Professional
   Women's Clubs), November 1972, p. 15. Formerly Independent Woman.

1182. Hathaway, Carson C. "Woman's Demand for Man's Full Civil Rights."
   Current History Magazine 17 (1923): 642-45.

1183. "Hearing on the Equal Rights Amendment." Independent Woman
   (National Federation of Business and Professional Women's Clubs),
   March 1938, pp. 88-89. Becomes National Business Woman.

1184. Heide, Wilma Scott. "Feminism: The Sine Qua Non for a Just
   Society." Vital Speeches of the Day 38 (15 April 1972): 403-408.

1185. Helmes, Winifred G. "Equal Rights, Where Do We Stand?" AAUW
Journal, March 1953, p. 165.

1186. "Helwig Speech on the ERA." Distaff, November/December 1973,
pp. 12-13. (N) (H2, S2, R2)

1187. Hentoff, Nat. "The Law Is an Ass [Male]." Evergreen, November
1970, pp. 49-51, 74. (WL)

1188. Herrick, Elinore M.; Banning, Margaret Culkin; Lutz, Alma; Miller,
Frieda; and Randall, Ollie A. "How Can We Raise Women's Status?"
Independent Woman (National Federation of Business and Professional
Women's Clubs), September 1938, pp. 280-81, 301-302. Becomes National
Business Woman.

1189. Herzfeld, Norma Krause. "The Status of Women." Commonweal,
5 February 1960, pp. 515-18.

1190. Hesburgh, Theodore. "Guess Who's for the ERA?" Ms., January
1976, p. 60.

1191. Heyer, Shirley. "'Let the Women Wait...'" Gold Flower (Minnesota
Women's Political Caucus), July/August 1972, pp. 5, 15. (N) (WL)

1192. Hille, Carol. "IWY Co-opted Again." Big Mama Rag, September
1975, p. 1. (N)

1193. _____. "Logic Proves Wrong Tactic in ERA Fight." Big
Mama Rag, February 1976, p. 1. (N)

1194. Hill, Elsie, and Kelley, Florence. "Shall Women Be Equal before
the Law." Nation, 12 April 1922, pp. 419-21.

1195. Hirshman, Linda R. "The Constitution and Women's Liberation."
Social Education 37 (1973): 381-86.

1196. Hobbs, Sam; Strauss, Anna Lord; Miller, Frieda; Morrissey,
Elizabeth; Hamilton, Alice; Stone, Margaret F.; Kenyon, Dorothy;
Fowler, Eleanor; Freund, Paul; Tate, Jack B.; and Welt, Mrs. Joseph M.
"Should the U.S. Constitution Guarantee Equal Rights for Women under
the Law?: Con." Congressional Digest, December 1946, pp. 303-20 (odd
numbered pages only). See entry #996.

1197. Hornaday, Mary. "Showdown on Equal Rights: Amending the
Constitution." Christian Science Monitor Magazine, 9 October 1943,
p. 5. (N)

1198. Horowitz, Peggy. "Reagan to Speak on ERA Here." California Aggie
(University of California, Davis), 19 February 1976, p. 1. (N)

1199. "House Approves Equal Rights for Women." Pandora, 19 October 1971,
p. 1. (N) (HU, S1, R13)

1200. "House Passes Equal Rights Constitutional Amendment."
Congressional Quarterly Almanac 27 (1971): 656-58, 68-H.

1201. "House Passes Equal Rights Constitutional Amendment." Congressional Quarterly Weekly Report, 16 October 1971, p. 2145.

1202. Hymer, Esther W. "Equal Rights--A World Issue." Independent Woman (National Federation of Business and Professional Women's Clubs), January 1954, pp. 20-22, 38. Becomes National Business Woman.

1203. "'I Didn't Raise My Girl to Be a Soldier'! Sense and Nonsense about the ERA." Christian Century, 25 October 1972, pp. 1056-58.

1204. "If He Were We." Women's Free Express, April 1974, pp. 4-5. (H3, R5)

1205. Irwin, Inez Haynes. "The Equal Rights Amendment: Why the Woman's Party Is for It." Good Housekeeping, March 1924, pp. 18, 158-61. See entry #1223 for companion article.

1206. "Is this Amendment Necessary." Editorial Research Reports Daily Service, 19 November 1974.

1207. It's Touch and Go with E.R.A." Liberator, February 1973, p. 2. (H2, S1, R7)

1208. "It's Up to You." Majority Report, 26 July 1975, p. 2. (Ed) (N)

1209. Jacobson, Carolyn J. "ERA: Ratifying Equality." American Federationist (American Federation of Labor and Congress of Industrial Organizations), January 1975, pp. 9-13.

1210. "January 20 Is the Day." National Business Woman (National Federation of Business and Professional Women's Clubs), January 1972, pp. 4-5. Formerly Independent Woman.

1211. Javits, Jacob K. "Women's Lib in Congress." Esquire, October 1971, pp. 76-84.

1212. "J. B. Stoner Exposes ERA." The Thunderbolt, April 1973, p. 9. (N)

1213. Jerard, Elise. "That Equal-Rights Amendment." New York Times Magazine, 25 October 1970, p. 89. (LE) (N)

1214. Jirak, Yvonne. "ERA Holds Ground in Minnesota Despite Opposition Efforts." Gold Flower (Minnesota Women's Political Caucus), March 1974, p. 11. (N) (H2, S2, R3)

1215. Joan J. "Protection?: It Ain't Me Babe, 21 August-3 September 1970, pp. 4, 18. (N) (H, R2) Rep. in entry #1219.

1216. Johnson, Ethel M. "Why 'Protection.'" Woman Citizen, 9 August 1924, pp. 16-17.

1217. Johnson, Susan Mallula. "E.R.A. Is Not 'Earned Run Average!'" Cleveland Feminist, August 1973, pp. 10-11. (H3, R1)

1218. Jordan, Joan. "Comment: Working Women and the Equal Rights Amendment." Trans-Action 8 (November/December 1970): 16-22.

1219. _____. "New Era for Whom, Now?" Great Speckled Bird,
14 September 1970, p. 9. (N) (WL) Rep. from entry #1215.

1220. Kafoury, Gretchen. "ERA." Changing Woman, 15 April 1972, p. 2.
(N) (H2, S1, R2)

1221. Kanowitz, Leo. "End to Discrimination? Proposed Equal Rights
Amendment." McCalls, August 1972, pp. 36-37, 38.

1222. Kelley, Florence. "Equal Rights Amendment: Reply to L. L. Dock."
Public Health Nursing 16 (1924): 191-92.

1223. _____. "The Equal Rights Amendment: Why Other Women Groups
Oppose It." Good Housekeeping, March 1924, pp. 19, 162-65. See entry
#1205 for companion article.

1224. _____. "The Right to Differ." Survey, 15 December 1922,
pp. 375-76.

1225. _____. "Should Women Be Treated Identically with Men by the
Law?" American Review 1 (1923): 276-84. Rep. in entry #463.

1226. _____, and Catt, Carrie Chapman. "Blanket Equality Bill: A
Frank Discussion of the Legislation Now Being Urged by the National
Woman's Party." Woman's Home Companion, August 1922, pp. 4, 89.

1227. Kenton, Edna. "Four Years of Equal Suffrage." Forum 72 (1924):
37-44.

1228. _____. "Ladies Next Step: Case for the Equal Rights
Amendment." Harper's Monthly Magazine, February 1926, pp. 366-74.

1229. Kenyon, Dorothy. "To End Discrimination against Women: Specific
Bills." Independent Woman (National Federation of Business and
Professional Women's Clubs), May 1937, pp. 132, 151, 159. Becomes
National Business Woman.

1230. Kerr, Virginia, and Sudow, Ellen. "A Legislative Agenda for the
93rd Congress: Beyond Constitutional Amendments." Ms., January 1973,
pp. 81, 84, 127-29. (H2, S1, R9)

1231. Keyes, Francis Parkinson. "Equal Rights Bill." Good Housekeeping,
February 1923, pp. 28-29, 180, 182-85.

1232. "Key Votes 1972: 3. Equal Rights." Congressional Quarterly
Weekly Report, 28 October 1972, pp. 2802, 2807.

1233. Kilpatrick, James J. "The Case against ERA." Nation's Business,
January 1975, pp. 9-10.

1234. Kinsella, Margie. "Why the ERA Controversy?" The Feminist Voice
1, no. 10 (1972), pp. 3-4, 10. (N) (HU, S1, R4)

1235. Kitchelt, Florence L. C. "Equal Rights Amendment." Independent
Woman (National Federation of Business and Professional Women's Clubs),
April 1946, p. 122. Becomes National Business Woman.

1236. _____. "Equal-Rights Amendment: With Reply." New
   Republic, 17 December 1945, pp. 840-41.

1237. _____. "Letters: Which Road, Women Workers?" Christian
   Science Monitor Magazine, 11 May 1946, p. 21. (LE) (N)

1238. "Know Your Enemies." Progressive Woman, May (2) 1972, p. 3.
   (HU, S1, R14)
*
1239. Komisar, Lucy. "Ten Myths about the Equal Rights Amendment."
   Family Circle, May 1974, pp. 46, 160. Rep. in entry #164.

1240. Koontz, Elizabeth Duncan. "The Women's Bureau Looks to the Future."
   Monthly Labor Review 93, pt. 1 (June 1970): 3-9.

1241. Krauskopf, Joan. "Distortion a La [Phyllis] Schlafly." FOCUS/
   Midwest 9 (1973): 23.

1242. Kuhne, Catherine. "Equal Rights Amendment before New Congress."
   Independent Woman (National Federation of Business and Professional
   Women's Clubs), March 1955, pp. 91, 118. Becomes National Business
   Woman.

1243. "Labor Legislation and the Rights of Women." Journal of Home
   Economics 21 (1929): 664-66.

1244. "Ladies Day: House Approves Constitutional Amendment." Newsweek,
   24 August 1970, pp. 15-16. (WL)

1245. Landman, Joan, and Landman, David. "Do Women Really Want Equal
   Rights?" Today's Woman, February 1953. Rep. as entry #393.
*
1246. Latimer, Clay. "ERA in 1974." Distaff, February 1974, pp. 2, 11.
   (N) (H2, S2, R2)

1247. Laughlin, Gail; Graves, Rowena Dashwood; and Anderson, Mary. "Do
   Special Labor Laws for Women Curtail Their Opportunities?: Pro and
   Con." Congressional Digest, March 1924, pp. 201, 207. See entry #1022.

1248. League of Women Voters of Arizona. "Rights and Responsibilities."
   Arizona Voter, November/December 1972.

1249. Lease, Carol. "The ERA: What It Will and Won't Do." Big Mama
   Rag, April 1975, p. 5. (N)

1250. _____. "Self-Destructive Women's Group Spreads Anti-Woman's
   Line." Big Mama Rag, April 1975, p. 5. (N)

1251. "Legislative Process." National Business Woman (National
   Federation of Business and Professional Women's Clubs), May 1970, p.
   8.2. Formerly Independent Woman.

1252. "Legislative Recap." National Business Woman (National Federation
   of Business and Professional Women's Clubs), November 1970, pp. 8.6-
   8.7. Formerly Independent Woman.

1253. "The Legislature Adrift." Texas Observer, 9 May 1975, pp. 5-6. (N)

1254. Leon, Barbara. "The Equal Rights Amendment." Woman's World,
   July/September 1972, pp. 1, 18-19. (N) (HU, S1, R17)
*
1255. Lewis, Alice Shannon. "B and PW Sponsor Picnic-Rally to Promote
   E.L.R.A." Liberator, August/September 1972, p. 7. (H2, S1, R7)

1256. Lillie, Alice. "ERA! The Individualist Case." New Guard (Young
   Americans for Freedom), March 1974, pp. 19ff. Rep. as entry #564.

1257. Lulkin, Sheli A. "Fight for ERA Reaches Crucial Stage." American
   Teacher, March 1973, p. 4. (N) Rep. as a separate by the Women's
   Rights Committee, American Federation of Teachers.

1258. Lund, Caroline. "Women: The Insurgent Majority." Militant,
   22 October 1971, p. 17. (N) (WL)

1259. Lutz, Alma. "Equal Rights, A Protest." AAUW Journal, January
   1954, pp. 131-32. (LE)

1260. _____. "Only One Choice: Taft-Wadsworth Legal Status Bill
   vs. Equal Rights Amendment." Independent Woman (National Federation
   of Business and Professional Women's Clubs), July 1947, pp. 199, 205.
   Becomes National Business Woman.

1261. _____. "Which Road, Women Workers?" Christian Science
   Monitor Magazine, 2 February 1946, p. 2. Rep. as a separate by the
   National Woman's Party.

1262. _____. "Why Bar Equality?" Christian Science Monitor
   Magazine, 22 July 1944, p. 3.

1263. Macdonald, Dwight. "Updating the Constitution of the United
   States." Esquire, May 1974, pp. 100-16. Rep. from October 1968 issue.

1264. MacKenzie, Catherine. "Woman Strikes again at this 'Man's World.'"
   New York Times Magazine, 14 November 1937, pp. 7, 22. (N)

1265. Magee, E. S. "What Are Equal Rights for Women?" New Republic,
   29 January 1945, p. 149.

1266. Manning, Alice L. "Congress Upholds Women's Rights: Subcommittees
   in Senate and House Report Favorably on Equal Rights Amendment."
   Independent Woman (National Federation of Business and Professional
   Women's Clubs), September 1941, p. 276. Becomes National Business
   Woman.

1267. _____. "Legislatively Speaking: Senator O'Mahoney's
   Substitute Amendment." Independent Woman (National Federation of
   Business and Professional Women's Clubs), December 1941, p. 372.
   Becomes National Business Woman.

1268. _____. "Legislation." Independent Woman (National Federation
   of Business and Professional Women's Clubs), February 1944, pp. 42-43.
   Becomes National Business Woman.

1269. _____. "May Day Surprise: Senator Lucas' Proposal to Amend
    the Constitution." Independent Woman (National Federation of Business
    and Professional Women's Clubs), June 1941, p. 184. Becomes National
    Business Woman.

1270. _____. "We Buckle on Our Armour and Return to the Fray:
    Unfavorable Vote by the House Judiciary Committee on the Equal Rights
    Amendment." Independent Woman (National Federation of Business and
    Professional Women's Clubs), November 1943, pp. 338, 342-43. Becomes
    National Business Woman. Rep. in entry #2391.

1271. "Many Happy Returns!" National Business Woman (National Federation
    of Business and Professional Women's Clubs), January 1975, p. 5.
    Formerly Independent Woman.

1272. Mares, Frances. "Rallying for the ERA." Cleveland Feminist,
    August 1973, pp. 12-14. (H3, R1)
*
1273. "Martha's Monument." Editorial Research Reports Reminder Service,
    3 September 1970.

1274. Martin, Anne. "Equality Laws vs. Women in Government." Nation,
    16 August 1922, pp. 165-66.

1275. Martin, Edward S. "Aren't These Women Equal Yet?" Colliers,
    29 September 1923, p. 8.

1276. "Maude Strikes Again." Pandora, 27 November 1973, p. 3. (N) (HU,
    S2, R6)

1277. May, Janice. "Equal Rights Amendment." AAUW Journal Newspaper,
    October 1970, p. 3.

1278. "Maximum Effort Needed Now." National Business Woman (National
    Federation of Business and Professional Women's Clubs), January 1972,
    p. 8.2. Formerly Independent Woman.

1279. Maymi, Carmen. "A Step Forward for ERA." Women and Work
    (Women's Bureau), November 1973, p. 14.

1280. McConnell, Nancy Fifield. "Report: The Equal Rights Amendment."
    Christianity and Crisis, 14 October 1974, pp. 229-30.

1281. McLaughlin, Kathleen. "Women's Impact on Public Opinion." Annals
    of the American Academy of Political and Social Science 251 (1947):
    104-12. See entry #492.

1282. McQuatters, Geneva F. "The 80th Congress Gets Under Way."
    Independent Woman (National Federation of Business and Professional
    Women's Clubs), March 1947, pp. 81-82. Becomes National Business
    Woman.

1283. _____. "Elusive Equal Rights." Independent Woman (National
    Federation of Business and Professional Women's Clubs), November 1950,
    pp. 351-52. Becomes National Business Woman.

1284. _____. "Legislative Liaison.: Independent Woman (National Federation of Business and Professional Women's Clubs), July 1951, p. 194. Becomes National Business Woman.

1285. _____. "Victory, with a Halter on It." Independent Woman (National Federation of Business and Professional Women's Clubs), March 1950, pp. 85-86, 93-94. Becomes National Business Woman.

1286. _____. "Voters' Voices on Equal Rights." Independent Woman (National Federation of Business and Professional Women's Clubs), April 1950, pp. 119-20. Becomes National Business Woman.

1287. Meade, Marion. "Alimony for Men--Yes or No?" New Woman, June/July 1972, pp. 54-55, 106, 112.

1288. Mellitz, Marcia B. "Equal Rights Amendment: Far from Dead in Missouri." FOCUS/Midwest 9 (1973): 22.

1289. Melody, Genevieve, and Borchardt, Selma M. "Should Women Teachers Support Equal Rights Amendment?: Pro and Con." Congressional Digest, March 1924, p. 203. See entry #1022.

1290. Meloy, Harriett. Letter to the Editor. AAUW Journal Newspaper, January 1975, p. 2.

1291. "Men and Women Shall Have Equal Rights." Woman's Home Companion, January 1924, p. 2. (Ed)

1292. "Men Put in Their Place." Economist, 4 July 1970, p. 46.

1293. "Men's Law." 51%, August 1972. (N) (WL)

1294. "Men, Women and the Constitution." America, 11 December 1971, p. 501.

1295. Metzger, Sue. "Equal Rights Amendment." Goodbye to All That, 3-24 May 1972, p. 3. (N) (HU, S1, R5) Rep. from San Diego NOW Newsletter.

1296. Meyer, H. N. "Women, 'Big Fourteen' and Equal Rights." New Politics 10 (Fall 1972): 50-60.

1297. Meyers, Eleanor. "ERA." Changing Woman, 31 March 1972, p. 2. (N) (H2, S1, R2)

1298. "Militant Feminists Find a Friend at White House." Human Events, 7 September 1974, pp. 4-5. (N)

1299. "Military Academies: Should They Admit Women?" Congressional Quarterly Weekly Report, 13 July 1974, p. 1821.

1300. Miller, Mrs. Delmas. "The Equal Rights Amendment." Clubwoman (General Federation of Women's Clubs), March 1975, pp. 24-25, 31.

1301. Miller, Emma Guffey, and Kenyon, Dorothy. "Equal Rights: A Debate." New York Times Magazine, 7 May 1944, pp. 14, 36-37. (N)

1302. Miller, Margaret I., and Linker, Helene. "Equal Rights Amendment Campaigns in California and Utah." Society 11 (May/June 1974): 40-53.

1303. Miner, Anne S. "ERA--The Immediate Goal and after Ratification." AAUW Journal, November 1975, pp. 26-27. Unabridged version appears in entry #442.

1304. "Miss Dunshee on 'Equal Rights.'" Woman Citizen, 8 March 1924, pp. 19-20.

1305. "More Boos than Hoorays for ERA." Nation's Business, April 1975, p. 12.

1306. "More Equal Rights." Survey, 1 October 1921, p. 20.

1307. Morgan, A., and McNaughton, F. "Senate's Ladies' Day." Life, 13 February 1950, pp. 16, 18, 21, 22.

1308. "Morse's Statement on Equal Rights Amendment." Changing Woman, 31 March 1972, p. 3. (N) (H2, S1, R2)

1309. Moser, Charles. "ERA: A Threat to Free Society." New Guard (Young Americans for Freedom), July/August 1974, pp. 25-26.

1310. "Much Unfinished Business Faces 'Lame Duck' Session: Equal Rights Amendment." Congressional Quarterly Weekly Report, 23 October 1970, p. 2645.

1311. Natalie, Mary Ann, and Alexander, Dolores. "House Action Set on Forgotten Amendment." New York Woman (Supplement to Manhattan Tribune), 8 August 1970, pp. 1-2. (N) (H, R2)

1312. National Women's Trade Union League of America. "Declaration in Opposition to Proposed Equal Rights Amendment." Proceedings of the National Women's Trade Union League of America 1922: 92-94, 118.

1313. _____. "Endorsement of Women's Status Bill and Opposition to Equal Rights Amendment: Resolution No. 4 by New York League." Proceedings of the National Women's Trade Union League of America 1947: 42.

1314. _____. "Equal Rights Amendment: Resolution No. 5 by Marion Burns, Kansas City League." Proceedings of the National Women's Trade Union League of America 1936: 88.

1315. _____. "Resolution No. 13 by the Madison Committee." Proceedings of the National Women's Trade Union League of America 1926: 88.

1316. "Nebraska Can't Do That to Us! Or, Roll Up Your Sleeve for the E.R.A." Liberator, March 1973, p. 8. (H2, S1, R7)

1317. "Needed--Information about Discrimination." California Woman (California Federation of Business and Professional Women's Clubs), January/February 1973, p. 9.

1318. Nelson, Marilyn. "Uncle Sam Ervin Shows His Colors." Distaff,
November/December 1973, p. 9. (N) (H2, S2, R2)

1319. "A New ERA for ERA?" National Voter (League of Women Voters of
the United States), Summer 1975, pp. 16-17.

1320. Newman, P. M. "The 'Equal Rights' Amendment." American
Federationist (American Federation of Labor and Congress of Industrial
Organizations), August 1938, pp. 815-17.

1321. "News on Equal Rights and Equal Pay Legislation." National
Businss Woman (National Federation of Business and Professional
Women's Clubs), March 1957, p. 30. Formerly Independent Woman.

1322. "New Symbol." Washington Post Parade Magazine, 30 September 1973,
p. 20. (N)

1323. Nickle, Kathy. "Progress Report on the ERA." her-self,
January 1974, p. 9. (N) (H2, S2, R3)

1324. Nigrine, Nita N. "Equal Rights." New York Times Magazine, 21 May
1944, p. 12. (LE) (N)

1325. "The 1972 Platforms: A Real Choice for the Voters: Women's
Rights." Congressional Quarterly Weekly Report, 26 August 1972, p. 2150.

1326. Nixon, Richard M. "Equal Rights for Women." (Letter to Hugh
Scott, 18 March 1972). Weekly Compilation of Presidential Documents,
27 March 1972, p. 630.

1327. "Nixon's Performance: The Voters Will Decide: Women's Rights."
Congressional Quarterly Weekly Report, 12 August 1972, p. 2007.

1328. Norwood, Rose. "Why Bar Equality?" Christian Science Monitor
Magazine, 19 August 1944, p. 10. (LE) (N)

1329. Novack, Cynthia. "Equal Rights Amendment and Protective Laws."
Union W.A.G.E., March/April 1972, p. [4]. (N) (HU, S1, R16)

1330. _____. "The Equal Rights Amendment and Protective Legislation." Union W.A.G.E., December 1971, pp. [5-6]. (N)

1331. _____. "For a Labor E.R.A." Union W.A.G.E., January/
February 1972, p. 3. (N) (HU, S1, R16)

1332. "NOW." Changing Woman, 31 March 1972, p. 3. (N) (H2, S1, R2)

1333. "Now Doorbells for State ERA." Pandora, 25 July 1972, p. 7.
(N) (WL; HU, S1, R13)

1334. "Now Is the Time." Arizona Voter (League of Women Voters of
Arizona), January/February 1975.

1335. "Off Our Asses. . .and on Their Backs." Majority Report, March
1972, p. 5. (N) (HU, S1, R6)

1336. Oliver, Janet. "Federal ERA Scoreboard." Ms., March 1976, p. 94.

1337. Olson, C. T. "U.S. Challenges Discrimination against Women."
Junior College Journal 42 (June/July 1972): 13-16.

1338. Oltman, Ruth. "Opponents of ERA Seek to Obstruct Ratification."
AAUW Journal Newspaper, January 1973, p. 15.

1339. _____. "Passage of ERA Depends upon Vigorous Unified AAUW
Support." AAUW Journal Newspaper, October 1973, pp. 1-2.

1340. "One Giant Leap for Womankind: Proposed Equal Rights Amendment."
Time, 3 April 1972, pp. 16-17.

1341. "One Man's Defense of Equal Rights." AAUW Journal Newspaper,
May 1975, p. 5. Rep. from Hawkeye Gazette (Burlington, Iowa).

1342. "On the E.R.A." Union W.A.G.E., June 1971, p. [2]. (N) (H, R22)

1343. "On the ERA: Do Protective Laws Exist?" What She Wants, May 1973,
p. 4. (N) (H2, S1, R16)

1344. "On the Line." People's World, 19 August 1972. (N) (WL)

1345. "Outsmarting the Ladies." Newsweek, 6 February 1950, pp. 20-21.

1346. Palmer, Hazel. "Here We Stand, We Can Do No Other: Equal Rights
Amendment." Independent Woman (National Federation of Business and
Professional Women's Clubs), December 1953, pp. 433-34, 454. Becomes
National Business Woman.

1347. _____. "The National President Appeals to Every Member."
National Business Woman (National Federation of Business and
Professional Women's Clubs), April 1958, p. 11. Formerly Independent
Woman.

1348. _____. "To All American Citizens: Equal Rights Amendment."
National Business Woman (National Federation of Business and
Professional Women's Clubs), July 1957, inside cover. Formerly
Independent Woman.

1349. _____. "Work for Equal Legal Rights." National Business
Woman (National Federation of Business and Professional Women's Clubs),
April 1957, pp. 2-3. Formerly Independent Woman.

1350. "Passage of Equal Rights Amendment Held Up in Senate." Congressional Quarterly Weekly Report, 23 October 1970, pp. 2618-19.

1350a. "Passage of ERA Depends upon Vigorous, Unified AAUW Support."
AAUW Journal Newspaper, October 1973, pp. 1-2.

1351. Paul, Alice; Gillette, Guy M.; Caraway, Hattie W.; Barbour, W.
      Warren; Chavez, Dennis; Ludlow, Louis; Englebright, H. J.; Norton, Mary
      T.; Smith, Margaret C.; Luce, Clare B.; Stanley, Winifred C.; Phillips,
      Lena Madesin; Wooley, Mary E.; Miller, Emma Guffey; Matthews, Burnita
      Shelton; Schlesinger, Arthur Meier; Swing, Raymond Gram; Buck, Pearl;
      Hepburn, Katharine; Swarthout, Gladys; Banning, Margaret Culkin;
      Maloney, Mollie; O'Donnell, James; Babcock, Caroline Lexow; and
      Oatman, Miriam E. "Should Congress Approve the Proposed Equal Rights
      Amendment to the Constitution?: Pro." Congressional Digest, April
      1943, pp. 107-17. See entry #1371.

1352. Paul, Alice, and Van Kleeck, Mary. "Is Blanket Amendment Best
      Method in Equal Rights Campaign?: Pro and Con." Congressional Digest,
      March 1924, pp. 198, 204. See entry #1022.

1353. Paul, Margaret. "ERA, Abortion Proponents Face Tough Opposition."
      Pandora, 23 January 1973, p. 2. (N) (HU, S1, R13)

1354. _____. "Federal ERA Needs Help." Pandora, 6 February 1973,
      p. 3. (N) (HU, S1, R13)
*
1355. Pellegrino, Victoria Y. "15 Reasons Why We Lost the E.R.A."
      Majority Report, 29 November -13 December 1975, pp. 10, 12. (N)

1356. "People 'Rap' ERA in Bellevue: H.O.W. Joins Them." Pandora,
      25 July 1972, p. 4. (N) (WL; HU, S1, R13)

1357. Perkins, Frances, and Baker, Elizabeth Faulkner. "Do Women in
      Industry Need Special Protection?" Survey, 15 February 1926, pp. 529-
      33, 582-83, 585.

1358. Peteri, Ann. "The Equal Rights Amendment to the U.S. Constitution."
      Dental Assistant 42 (June 1973): 19-21.

1359. Pogrebin, Letty Cottin. "The Working Woman: Equal Rights
      Amendment." Ladies Home Journal, November 1972, pp. 48-50.

1360. "Political Energy--Who's Turning It On?" National Business Woman
      (National Federation of Business and Professional Women's Clubs),
      November 1974, p. 8. Formerly Independent Woman.

1361. "Poll Majority Approves ERA." AAUW Journal Newspaper, January
      1971, p. 3.

1362. Portnow, Billie. "What's Wrong with the Equal Rights Amendment?"
      Jewish Chronicle 25 (July/August 1971): 4-9.

1363. "Position Paper on ERA." Speakout, April 1972, p. 8. (H2, S1, R15)

1364. "Power of a Woman: The Equal Rights Amendment." Ladies Home
      Journal, August 1970, p. 50. (WL)

1365. "Praise, Joy and Hallelujah!" National Business Woman (National
      Federation of Business and Professional Women's Clubs), May 1972,
      p. 8.2. Formerly Independent Woman.

1366. "President Marjorie East's Statement in Support of Equal Rights Amendment." Journal of Home Economics 65 (1973): 73.

1367. Proctor, Pam. "Phyllis Schlafly: She Thinks Women Are Better Off than Men." Washington Post Parade Magazine, 25 May 1975, p. 12. (N)

1368. "Pro-ERA Director Named for Labor Post." Human Events, 14 July 1973, p. 5. (N)

1369. "Progress Report on Equal Rights." National Business Woman (National Federation of Business and Professional Women's Clubs), January/February 1970, p. 8.4. Formerly Independent Woman.

1370. "Proposal Resolutions, #12 and #13." AAUW Journal Newspaper, March 1971, p. 5.

1371. The Proposed Equal-Rights Amendment to the U.S. Constitution: Discussed Pro and Con. Congressional Digest, April 1943, pp. 99-128 (entire issue). See entries #943, 1351.

1371a. Putnam, Frank. "Historical Parallels." Nation, 30 July 1924, p. 123. (LE) Rep. in entry #1705.

1372. "Ratification Is the Target of National Business Women's Week." National Business Woman (National Federation of Business and Professional Women's Clubs), July/August 1972, p. 8.2. Formerly Independent Woman.

1373. "Ratification of ERA." Changing Woman, 29 May 1972, p. 1. (N) (H2, S1, R3) Rep. from Woman Activist.

1374. "Ratification of ERA Predicted by May 1973." National Business Woman (National Federation of Business and Professional Women's Clubs), October 1972, p. 12. Formerly Independent Woman.

1375. "Ratification Scoreboard." Majority Report, May 1972, p. 9. (N) (WL; HU, S1, R6)

1376. "Ratification Update." National Business Woman (National Federation of Business and Professional Women's Clubs), April 1973, pp. 4-5. Formerly Independent Woman.

1377. Raven, Clara. "Testimony in Favor." Woman Physician 26 (1971): 584.

1378. Rawalt, Marguerite. "The Equal Rights Amendment and the Draft." National Business Woman (National Federation of Business and Professional Women's Clubs), November 1972, pp. 6-8. Formerly Independent Woman.

1379. _____. "The Homemaker and the Equal Rights Amendment." Clubwoman (General Federation of Women's Clubs), January 1975, pp. 12, 30.

1380. _____. "Women are Constitutional Outcasts." Woman Physician 26 (1971): 612-20. Rep. in entry #152.

1381. "Reasons for Opposing the Proposed Equal Rights Amendment." AAUW
      Journal, April 1939, pp. 153-57.

1382. "Referenda: Equal Rights." Congressional Quarterly Weekly Report,
      11 November 1972, p. 2987.

1383. Regan, Ronald. "Dynamite Rhetoric." 51%, August 1972. (LE) (N)
      (WL)

1384. "Resolutions Provoke Intense Discussion." AAUW Journal Newspaper,
      August 1971, p. 5.

1385. "Rights for Women." Newsweek, 29 July 1946, p. 17.

1386. Roberts, Sylvia. "Equality of Opportunity in Higher Education:
      Impact of Contract Compliance and the Equal Rights Amendment." Liberal
      Education 59 (1973): 202-16.

1387. Robinson, Helen Ring. "Sex Equality and Brass Tacks." Delineator,
      November 1923, pp. 2, 66, 68.

1388. Romanik, Erma, and Kuhne, Catherine G. "See Your Congressman--
      Now." National Business Woman (National Federation of Business and
      Professional Women's Clubs), November 1957, pp. 4-5. Formerly
      Independent Woman.

1389. "Room at the Top: ERA Ratification Total Climbs." National
      Business Woman (National Federation of Business and Professional
      Women's Clubs), May 1973, pp. 4-5. Formerly Independent Woman.

1390. Root, Chris. "Senator Buckley on the ERA." Speakout, July/
      August 1972, p. 1. (H2, S1, R15)

1391. Rosenberg, Bernard, and Weinman, Saul. "An Interview with Myra
      Wolfgang: Young Women Who Work." Dissent, Winter 1972, pp. 29-36.

1392. Ruckelshaus, Jill. "Is the Press Asleep at the Switch?" National
      Business Woman (National Federation of Business and Professional
      Women's Clubs), December 1975, pp. 6-8. Formerly Independent Woman.

1393.   ; Schlafly, Phyllis; and Alda, Alan. "Forum: Equal
      Rights Amendment." Ladies Home Journal, August 1975, p. 57.

1394. "Rumors of ERA's Demise Have Been Greatly Exaggerated." National
      Business Woman (National Federation of Business and Professional
      Women's Clubs), June 1975, p. 4. Formerly Independent Woman.

1395. Ryan, John A. "Equal Rights for Women--I. Economic Grievances."
      National Catholic Welfare Council Bulletin, March 1926, pp. 12-13, 23.

1396.   . "Equal Rights for Women--II. The Civil Grievances."
      National Catholic Welfare Council Bulletin, April 1926, pp. 14-16.

1397. Safran, Claire. "What You Should Know about the Equal Rights
      Amendment." Redbook, June 1973, pp. 62-76.

1398. Salmans, Sandra, and Whitmore, James. "Women Versus Women."
Newsweek, 3 November 1975, p. 25.

1399. Sanders, Marion K. "Requiem for ERA: Good Causes and Lost
Causes." New Republic, 29 November 1975, pp. 20-21.

1400. Sant Andrea, Alice. "Anti-ERA Flack Comes Home to Ford."
Majority Report, 8 March 1975, p. 13. (N)

1401. "Save Protective Laws!" Union W.A.G.E., November/December 1972,
pp. 1, 8. (N) (HU, S1, R16)

1402. Scheinfeld, Amram. "How 'Equal' Are Women?" Colliers, 18
September 1943, pp. 15, 73-74.

1403. Schlafly, Phyllis. "Are You Paying for Women's Lib and the ERA?:
The Taxpayer Is Footing Much of the Bill, But There Are Ways to Stop
It." Human Events, 23 February 1974, p. 12. (N)

1404. _____. "Let's Stop ERA." New Guard (Young Americans for
Freedom), September 1973, pp. 4-6.

1405. _____. "Men Will Pay Heavy Price for E.R.A." Human Events,
14 June 1975, p. 7. (N)

1406. _____. "Women's Lib and Equal Rights." Human Events, 19
May 1973, p. 12. (N)

1407. "Schlafly Pro and Con." Chicago Tribune Magazine, 24 June 1973,
p. 7. (LE) (N)

1408. Schuler, Nettie R. "Equal Rights Amendment." Jus Suffragii
(International Woman Suffrage News), April 1922, p. 111.

1409. Schwartz, N. "Women and the Amendment." Commonweal, 15 June
1973, pp. 328-31.

1410. Scott, Ann. "The Equal Rights Amendment: What's in It for You?"
Ms., July 1972, pp. 82-86. (H2, S1, R8)

1411. _____. "It's Time for Equal Education." Ms., October 1972,
pp. 122-23. (H2, S1, R8)

1412. Scott, Rachel. "Equal Rights Amendment." Off Our Backs, 27
February 1970, p. 5. (N) (H, R3)

1413. "The Second Women's Industrial Conference and the Assaults upon
It." Life and Labor Bulletin, February 1926, pp. 1-2, 6.

1414. Sedey, Joe. "Stalking the ERA." FOCUS/Midwest 9 (1973): 23.

1415. "Senate Committee Hears Arguments on 'Equal Rights' and Labor
Laws." Life and Labor Bulletin, March 1929, pp. 2-3.

1416. "Senate Hearing." Everywoman, 19 June 1970, p. 4. (N) (H, R1)
Rep. from Off Our Backs.

1417. "Senate Judiciary Committee Hears Arguments against the National Women's [sic] Party Amendment." Life and Labor Bulletin, March 1924, pp. 2-3.

1418. "Senate Scuttles Full Partnership: Equal Rights Amendment." Independent Woman (National Federation of Business and Professional Women's Clubs), August 1953, p. 300. Becomes National Business Woman.

1419. "Senate Subcommittee Amends ERA." National Business Woman (National Federation of Business and Professional Women's Clubs), January 1972, p. 8.4. Formerly Independent Woman.

1420. "Senators for Equal Legal Rights." National Business Woman (National Federation of Business and Professional Women's Clubs), July 1957, pp. 10-11. Formerly Independent Woman.

1421. "Setback for the Feminists." Newsweek, 17 November 1975, p. 53.

1422. "Sex Discrimination: The Last Acceptable Prejudice: The Equal Rights Amendment." Congressional Quarterly Weekly Report, 18 March 1972, p. 597.

1423. Sexton, Patricia Cayo. "Women Debate the Equal Rights Amendment." Dissent, February 1971, pp. 14-17.

1423a. Seydell, Mildred. "Thinking in Type." Think Tank (Atlanta, Georgia), 14 June 1945, p. 1. (Ed) Rep. in entry #2503.

1424. "Shadowed by the Girl She Was." National Business Woman (National Federation of Business and Professional Women's Clubs), July 1957, pp. 4-5, 8. Formerly Independent Woman.

1425. Shaffer, Helen B. "Status of Women." Editorial Research Reports, 5 August 1970, pp. 565-85. Rep. in entry #480.

1426. Shelton, Isabelle. "New Woman Presents the 1972 Presidential 6-Pack: Equal Rights Amendment." New Woman, February 1972, p. 40.

1427. Sherrill, Robert. "That Equal-Rights Amendment: What, Exactly, Does It Mean?" New York Times Magazine, 20 September 1970, pp. 1, 25-27, 98-105. (N) (WL) Rep. in entry #92.

1428. Sherwood, Geraldine. "Labor Opposition Stalls Equal Rights Amendment in the Senate." California Journal, April 1972, pp. 112-15.

1429. "Should the Equal Rights Amendment Be Adopted?" American Forum of the Air 4 (19 July 1942): 1-15 (entire issue).

1430. "Should We Amend the Constitution: Equal Rights Amendment." Senior Scholastic, 21 November 1974, pp. 14-15. Formerly Scholastic Teacher.

1431. Shriver, Lucille. "Testimony Presented on the Part of National Federation of Business and Professional Women's Clubs, Inc." Woman Physician 26 (1971): 372-75.

1432. "Sisters of Abigail Adams." _Time_, 6 February 1950, pp. 12-13.

1433. "Sisters Tell It Like It Is." _Fifth Estate_, 11-24 June 1970, p. 15.
(N) (WL) Rep. from _Off Our Backs_.

1434. "Six States Approve ERA on State Level." _National Business Woman_
(National Federation of Business and Professional Women's Clubs),
January 1973, p. 8.3. Formerly _Independent Woman_.

1435. Smith, Ethel M. "Labor's Position against the Woman's Party
Amendment." _Life and Labor Bulletin_, February 1924, pp. 1-2.

1436. _____. "Labor's Position against the Woman's Party Amendments." _Life and Labor Bulletin_, February 1926, pp. 1-5.

1437. _____. "What Is Sex Equality?" _Century Magazine_ 118 (1929):
96-106.

1438. Smith, Freda. "ERA Demonstration in Capitol." _Lesbian Tide_,
September 1972, pp. 6-7. (HU, S1, R6)

1439. Smith, Harrison. "The Women Are Coming!" _Saturday Review of
Literature_, 17 July 1948, p. 18.

1440. Smith, Jane Norman. "To End Discrimination against Women: A
Blanket Amendment." _Independent Woman_ (National Federation of
Business and Professional Women's Clubs), May 1937, pp. 132, 151.
Becomes _National Business Woman_.

1441. "Sniping at the Equal Rights Amendment: Introduction of H. R.
1972, Calling for Establishment of a Commission on Legal Status of
Women." _Independent Woman_ (National Federation of Business and
Professional Women's Clubs), March 1947, p. 88. Becomes _National
Business Woman_.

1442. "Some Like It Not: Anti-Equal Rights Amendment Forces."
Newsweek, 15 January 1973, p. 17.

1443. Somerville, Rose M. "Searching for Ways to Search for Self."
AAUW Journal, April 1973, pp. 19-23.

1444. "Sponsors in the House." _National Business Woman_ (National
Federation of Business and Professional Women's Clubs), July 1957,
p. 9. Formerly _Independent Woman_.

1445. _Spotlight on the Equal Rights Amendment_. _Hoosier Business Woman_,
November 1974, entire issue.

1446. Stang, Alan. "The Ladies: Those Fascinating Conservative
Women." _American Opinion_, April 1973, pp. 1-14. (N)
*
1447. "Start of an ERA?" _Time_, 6 January 1975, p. 74.

1448. "State ERA Finally Passes; Battle to Get Underway for Federal
Ratification." _Pandora_, 12 December 1972, p. 2. (N) (HU, S1, R13)

1449. "State Official Backs ERA at County Fete." AAUW Journal
Newspaper, May 1974, p. 2.

1450. "State Status Report." National Business Woman (National
Federation of Business and Professional Women's Clubs), January 1974,
p. 8.2. Formerly Independent Woman.

1451. "Status of ERA." AAUW Journal Newspaper, May 1973, p. 11.

1452. Stead, Bette Ann. "The Semantics of Sex Discrimination." Business
Horizons, October 1975, pp. 21-25.

1453. Steffens, Heidi. "Equal Rights Amendment." Off Our Backs, 16 May
1970, p. 6. (N) (H, R3) Rep. in entry #3110.

1454. Stern, Marjorie. "A Big Push for the ERA." American Teacher,
February 1974, p. 30.

1455. Stevens, Doris. "The 'Blanket' Amendment--A Debate: Suffrage Does
Not Give Equality." Forum 72 (1924): 143-52. See entry #1174 for
companion article.

1456. St. George, Katharine, and Bosone, Reva Beck. "Equal Rights
Amendment." AAUW Journal, May 1952, pp. 210-13.

1457. "Still on the Drawing Board: Legislation." National Business
Woman (National Federation of Business and Professional Women's Clubs),
July/August 1975, p. 9. Formerly Independent Woman.

1458. St. John, Jacqueline. "Women's Legislative Issues Today and
Tomorrow." Vital Speeches of the Day 38 (15 June 1972): 528.

1459. "St. Paul Conference: Use ERA as Shield against Societal Stereo-
types." Gold Flower (Minnesota Women's Political Caucus), October
1972, pp. 8-9. (N) (H2, S1, R5)

1460. "Struggle between President and Congress Looms: Women's Rights."
Congressional Quarterly Weekly Report, 15 July 1972, p. 1752.

1461. "Susan B. Anthony Honored." National Business Woman (National
Federation of Business and Professional Women's Clubs), April 1959,
p. 14. Formerly Independent Woman.

1462. Taylor, A. Elizabeth. "Equal Rights for Men and Women." Texas
Outlook, November 1944, p. 32.

1463. Temple, Marjorie L. "Is Your Representative among those Present?"
Independent Woman (National Federation of Business and Professional
Women's Clubs), June 1954, pp. 223-24, 240. Becomes National
Business Woman.

1464. _____. "Pyrrhic Victory: Equal Rights Amendment."
Independent Woman (National Federation of Business and Professional
Women's Clubs), September 1953, pp. 327-28. Becomes National Business
Woman.

1465. _____. "What Do Our Congressmen Think about the Equal Rights Amendment?" Independent Woman (National Federation of Business and Professional Women's Clubs), April 1953, pp. 127-28, 142. Becomes National Business Woman.

1466. _____. "When You Buttonhole Your Congressman on E.R.A." Independent Woman (National Federation of Business and Professional Women's Clubs), November 1953, pp. 399-400. Becomes National Business Woman.

1467. Tennov, Dorothy. "Is the ERA a Joke on Us?" Prime Time, April/May 1973, pp. 8, 11. (LE) (H2, S1, R14)

1468. Terzinc, Nancy R. "Phyllis Schlafly." Chicago Tribune Magazine, 22 July 1973, p. 8. (LE) (N)

1469. "Texas Women Win Equality." Liberator, November 1972, p. 1. (WL; H2, S1, R7)

1470. "Text of Platform Adopted by Democrats at Miami Beach: Rights of Women." Congressional Quarterly Weekly Report, 15 July 1972, p. 1731.

1471. "Text of Platform Adopted by Republicans at Miami Beach: Equal Rights for Women." Congressional Quarterly Weekly Report, 26 August 1972, pp. 2167-68.

1472. Thimmesch, Nick. "Equal Protection." New York Times Magazine, 15 July 1973, p. 21. (LE) (N)

1473. _____. "The Sexual Equality Amendment." New York Times Magazine, 24 June 1973, pp. 8-9, 53. (N)

1474. "33 States Down 5 to Go on ERA." Distaff, March 1974, p. 11. (N) (H2, S2, R2)

1475. Thomas, M. Carey. "Arguments for a Woman's Equal Rights Amendment to the Constitution of the United States." AAUW Journal, March 1925, pp. 23-28. Rep. in entry #463. See entry #1496 for companion article.

1476. _____, and Van Kleeck, Mary. "Second Statement of the Committee Appointed to Present Considerations Affecting an Equal Rights Amendment." AAUW Journal, January 1925, pp. 19-20. Partially rep. in entry #463.

1477. Thyagarajan, Paula Corey. "Opposition Rises to Amendment on Equal Rights." Speakout, April 1973, p. 16. (H2, S1, R16)

1478. "To: Board of Supervisors of San Francisco" and "Resolution for Equal Rights Amendment and Extending Protective Legislation." Union W.A.G.E., 1 August 1971, pp. 2-4. (N) (H, R22)

1479. "Towards Equal Rights." Intellect, December 1973, p. 143.

1480. "Trouble for ERA." Time, 19 February 1973, pp. 22, 25.

1481. Turner, Jennie McMullin. "Women's Rights by Blanket Legislation." _Wisconsin Law Review_ 2 (1923): 103-109.

1482. "'Twas the Night Before Christmas . . . and All Thru the House (and Senate)?" _National Business Woman_ (National Federation of Business and Professional Women's Clubs), December 1974, p. 4. Formerly _Independent Woman_.

1483. "A 20th Amendment Now on the Way." _Literary Digest_, 11 August 1923, p. 17.

1484. "27th Amendment: It's for You, Girls." _Senior Scholastic_, 17 April 1972, p. 19. Formerly _Scholastic Teacher_.

1485. "The 27th Amendment Will Say." _51%_, March 1974, p. 2. (N)

1486. Uda, Joan. "Do You Know What's Happening in Missoula?" _Ms._, April 1974, p. 21. (H2, S2, R5)

1487. "Union Women Rally for E.R.A." _What She Wants_, March 1974, p. 1. (N) (H2, S2, R12)

1488. "United States: Equal Rights and Responsibilities for Women." _International Labour Review_ 103 (1971): 195-96.

1489. Untitled. _Concern_ (United Presbyterian Church of U.S.A.), February 1976, p. 30.

1490. _____. _Everywoman_, 23 October 1970, p. 3. (N) (H, R1) Rep. from _Los Angeles Times_, 16 October 1970 (?).

1491. _____. _51%_, 1 November 1972. (N) (WL)

1492. "Up From Coverture." _Time_, 20 March 1972, pp. 67-68.

1493. U. S. National Women's Agenda. "'We, Women of the United States of America . . .'" _Ms._, December 1975, pp. 109, 112.

1494. Van Bronkhorst, Erin. "ERA Passes Senate." _Pandora_, 23 February 1972, pp. 1-2. (N) (HU, S1, R13)

1495. Van den Haag, Ernest. "Women: How Equal?" _National Review_, 8 September 1970, pp. 945, 963.

1496. Van Kleeck, Mary. "Equal Rights Cannot Be Won by Constitutional Amendment." _AAUW Journal_, March 1925, pp. 21-22. See entry # 1475 for companion article.

1497. _____. "Preliminary Statement for the Committee on the Study of the Relation of the Constitution to Equal Rights for Women." _AAUW Journal_, October 1924, pp. 18-20.

1498. Varda One. "Equality Is Not Enough." _Everywoman_, 10 September 1971, p. 1. (N) (H, R1)

1499. Vida, Ginny. "Feminist Perspective." _Advocate_, 5 November 1975, p. 21. (N)

1500. "Voice of the Month." Feminist Voice 1, no. 10 (1972), pp. 2, 10.
(Ed) (N) (HU, S1, R4)

1500a. Wade, Flo. "Stepping Down from the Pedestal Won't Hurt Too
Much . . . Answers to Operation Wake-Up Scare Stories." New Women's
Times, pt. 1, April 1975, pp. 1, 13; pt. 2, May 1975, p. 2; pt. 3,
June 1975, pp. 2, 3; pt. 4, July 1975, pp. 2,3. (N)

1501. Wahlberg, Rachel Conrad. "Five Fears behind the ERA Battle."
Christian Century, 1 October 1975, pp. 838-40.

1502. "Wait Till Next Year: Equal Rights Amendment." Newsweek, 17
March 1975, p. 23.

1502a. Walzer, Allison. "Who Are They? E.R.A. Opponents." Advocate,
24 March 1976, pp. 11-12. (N)

1503. Warner, J. Margaret. "It Has Happened in New Jersey." Independent
Woman (National Federation of Business and Professional Women's Clubs),
December 1947, pp. 362-63. Becomes National Business Woman.

1504. Warren, Tully E. "Women's Struggle for Equality: The Vote,
Political Office, and the Equal Rights Amendment." Vital Issues
(Center for Information on America) 24, no. 8 (1975).

1505. "Washington--Our Legislative Program and the 81st Congress."
Independent Woman (National Federation of Business and Professional
Women's Clubs), January 1949, pp. 25, 31. Becomes National Business
Woman.

1506. Weber, Jean Jordon. "The County Fair Revisited." Cleveland
Feminist, November 1973, pp. 2-3. (H3, R1)

1507. "Week to Include ERA Rally." Pandora, 22 August 1972, p. 2.
(N) (HU, S1, R13)

1507a. Weiner, L., and Jacobsen, P. "An Exchange on the Equal Rights
Amendment." New Politics 10 (Winter 1973): 84-87.

1508. "We've Been Asked about Equal Rights: Questions and Answers."
U.S. News and World Report, 29 October 1973, p. 89.

1509. "What about 'Equal Rights'?" Public Affairs 2 (March 1924): 22, 27.

1510. "What Equality May Bring." Editorial Research Reports Daily
Service, 3 May 1972.

1510a. "What ERA Can Do." Advocate, 24 March 1976, p. 16. (Ed) (N)

1511. "What ERA Means." National Business Woman (National Federation of
Business and Professional Women's Clubs), November 1973, pp. 8.6-8.7.
Formerly Independent Woman.

1512. "What's Up with ERA?" Sisterlife, January 1974, pp. [13-15].
(H2, S2, R10) Formerly Feminists for Life (Columbus, Ohio).

1513. "What You Should Know about the Equal Rights Amendment." Good Housekeeping, February 1975, p. 164.

1514. Whelan, Charles M. "ERA: A Lawyer's Doubts." America, 17 May 1975, pp. 378-81.

1515. "White House Backing Equal Rights Amendment." Human Events, 24 February 1973, p. 5. (N)

1516. Whittic, Anna Harbottle. "A Defense of the Blanket Amendment." Woman Citizen, 28 June 1924, pp. 17, 29.

1517. "Why the News Blackout on the E.R.A.??" Majority Report, April 1972, p. 7. (N) (HU, S1, R6)

1518. "Why We Support the E.R.A." Women and Revolution, Fall 1973, pp. 24, 20-22. (N) (HU, S2, R7 and 8)

1519. "Why Working Women Oppose the Equal Rip-Off Amendment." her-self, May 1973, p. [8]. (N) (H2, S1, R6) Rep. from Change.

1520. Wiley, Mrs. Harvey W., and Breckinridge, Sophonisba. "Could 'Mothers' Pensions' Operate under Equal Rights Amendment? Pro and Con." Congressional Digest, March 1924, p. 202. See entry #1022.

1521. Wille, Lois. "We Need the Equal Rights Amendment." U.S. Catholic, September 1973, p. 14.

1522. "Will Equality for the Sexes Become Law?" State Government News, October 1974, pp. 6-7.

1523. Williams, Betty. "Another Era or ERA?" AAUW Journal Newspaper, January 1972, p. 4. (Ed)

1524. Withers, Jean. "The ERA: Women in Combat Now Becomes an Issue." Pandora, 25 July 1972, p. 4. (N) (WL; HU, S1, R13)

1525. Wittner, Dale. "'All Women's Liberationists Hate Men and Children.'" Chicago Tribune Magazine, 20 May 1973, pp. 12, 16, 21.

1526. Wohl, Lisa Cronin. "End of an ERA?" New Times, 18 April 1975, p. 68.

1527. _____. "The ERA: What the Hell Happened in New York?" Ms., March 1976, pp. 64-66, 92, 94, 96.

1528. _____. "Phyllis Schlafly: Sweetheart of the Silent Majority." Ms., March 1974, pp. 54-57, 85-89. (H2, S2, R5) Rep. in entry #353.

1529. Wold, Emma; Hill, Elsie; and Smith, Ethel. "Is Federal Amendment Necessary to Accomplish Equal Rights?: Pro and Con." Congressional Digest, March 1924, pp. 199, 206, 207. See entry #1022.

1530. Wolfgang, Myra. "'Don't Talk Theory to Me, Tell Me the Practice.'" People's World, 5 December 1970, p. M-11. (N) (WL)

1531. "Woman Power: Senate Approves Amendment to the Constitution."
Newsweek, 3 April 1972, pp. 28-29.

1532. "A Woman's Block." Nation, 3 September 1924, pp. 230-31.

1533. "'A Woman's Place . . . '" Women in Business (American Business
Women's Association), February 1973, pp. 6-7.

1534. "Women Ask to Be Protected from Their Friends." Literary Digest,
6 February 1926, p. 12.

1535. "Women as Soldiers, Jurors, Prisoners." Women in Business
(American Business Women's Association), June 1973, pp. 14-15.

1536. "Women Eye Movement of Equal Rights Amendment." Women and Work,
March 1973, n.p.

1537. "Women Hand ERA Defeat in Two States." Human Events, 15 November
1975, p. 4.   (N)

1538. "Women's Hour." Economist, 15 August 1970, pp. 39-40.

1539. "Women's Legal Rights in 50 States: Geography of Inequality."
McCall's, February 1971, pp. 90-95.

1540. "Women's Liberation Amendment." Office, October 1970, pp. 46, 48.

1541. "Women's Liberation Testimony." Off Our Backs, 16 May 1970, p. 7.
(N)   (H, R3)

1542. "Women's Rights." American Teacher, September 1974, p. 13.   (N)

1543. "Women's Rights." Congressional Quarterly Almanac 3 (1947):
75, 695.

1544. "Women's Rights: Action in Court and Congress." U.S. News and
World Report, 6 December 1971, p. 86.

1545. "Women's Rights Amendment." Congressional Quarterly Weekly
Report, 29 May 1959, p. 740.

1546. "Women's Rights Amendment." Congressional Quarterly Weekly
Report, 8 July 1960, p. 1191.

1547. "Women's Rights: Senate Approves Equal Rights Amendment."
Scholastic Teacher, 8 February 1950, p. 12.   Becomes Senior Scholastic.

1548. "Women Superiors Back Rights Amendment." National Catholic
Reporter, 9 March 1973, p. 3.   (N)

1549. "Women United Reception." Journal of Home Economics 64 (1972): 60.

1550. "Women Vow Fight for ERA." What She Wants, June 1973, pp. 1, 3.
(N)   (H2, S1, R16)

1551. Wood, Charles W. "Have You a Little Equality in Your Home?"
Colliers, 25 November 1922, pp. 7-8, 29.

1552. "Working Women and the ERA." Women's Press, June 1974, p. 3.
(N) (H3, R5)

1553. Wright, R. M. "Why I Support the ERA: Howard Cosell." Ms.,
October 1975, pp. 78-79.

1554. "A Year for Women." Editorial Research Reports Daily Service,
10 March 1975.

1555. "Yes ERA!" National Voter (League of Women Voters of the United
States), October/November 1973, pp. 1-4.

1556. Younger, Maud, and Schneiderman, Rose. "Will Equal Rights
Amendment Benefit Women in Industry?: Pro and Con." Congressional
Digest, March 1924, pp. 200, 206. See entry #1022.

1557. "Zeroing In!" National Business Woman (National Federation of
Business and Professional Women's Clubs), June 1974, p. 8.8. Formerly
Independent Woman.

C. Equal Rights (National Woman's Party Magazine)

[This magazine is treated much like the Congressional Record:
the listings are in chronological order and within one date by
pagination; the full primary source information is listed here
rather than cited by entry numbers, although cross-reference
is made in other parts of the bibliography to the numbers of
these ER reprints.

The "News from the Field" entries are listed with a subtitle
when there is only one item in the column on the ERA; when
there are two or more items, only the primary heading is used.
The "Press Comments" items are listed separately when there
are more than one ERA article in the column.

Some idea of the nature of the material in an article can be
gathered from its title, length, and authorship. Treatment
varies from legal analyses to reportorial coverage to editorials.]

1558. Fox, Emma. "The Need for a Federal Equality Amendment." ER,
7 July 1923, p. 166.

1559. Bugbee, Emma. "Women Open Compaign [sic] for Equal Rights." ER,
28 July 1923, p. 189. Rep. from New York Tribune, 22 July 1923.

1560. Egan, Lavinia. "The Seneca Falls Conference." ER, 4 August 1923,
pp. 195-99.

1561. "Comments of the Press." ER, 11 August 1923, pp. 207-208.

1562. "Patience." ER, 18 August 1923, p. 212.

1563. "News from the Field." ER, 25 August 1923, p. 223.

1564. "News from the Field." ER, 1 September 1923, pp. 230-31.

1565. "The Function of Law." ER, 8 September 1923, p. 236.

1566. "Comments of the Press." ER, 8 September 1923, p. 240.

1567. "Make the Amendment Mean Something." ER, 15 September 1923, p. 244.

1568. "Preparing for the Campaign on Congress." ER, 22 September 1923, p. 254.

1569. "Lucretia Mott Amendment to Be Introduced December Third." ER, 6 October 1923, p. 266.

1570. "Why the Argument?" ER, 6 October 1923, p. 268.

1571. "Never Put Off till Tomorrow." ER, 20 October 1923, p. 284.

1572. Rehfisch, Carol A. "The Woman's Party--Right or Wrong." ER, 20 October 1923, pp. 285-86.

1573. "Preparedness." ER, 27 October 1923, p. 292.

1574. "Sops." ER, 27 October 1923, p. 292.

1575. "The Lucretia Mott Amendment." ER, 10 November 1923, p. 308.

1576. "Woman's Party Arranges for Deputation to President." ER, 10 November 1923, p. 310.

1577. "Senator Curtis and Representative Anthony to Introduce Amendment." ER, 17 November 1923, p. 315.

1578. "The Insecurity of State Equal Rights Legislation." ER, 17 November 1923, p. 316.

1579. "The Parallel between the Suffrage and the Equal Rights Campaign." ER, 17 November 1923, p. 316.

1580. "News from the Field." ER, 17 November 1923, pp. 319-20.

1581. "Equal Rights Demand Is Taken to President Coolidge." ER, 24 November 1923, pp. 322-23.

1582. "The President's Attitude." ER, 24 November 1923, p. 324.

1583. "Why a Constitutional Amendment." ER, 24 November 1923, p. 324.

1584. Curtis, Charles. "Greetings to the Conference of the National Woman's Party from Senator Charles Curtis of Kansas." ER, 24 November 1923, p. 325.

1585. "Equal Rights in the Nation and States." ER, 1 December 1923, p. 332.

1586. "Comments of the Press." ER, 1 December 1923, p. 336. Rep. from Washington Post, 19 November 1923; New York City Telegram, 5 November 1923.

1587. "Active Lobby of Congress Begins." ER, 8 December 1923, p. 339.

1588. "A Typical Deputation to a Member of Congress." ER, 8 December 1923, pp. 342-43.

1589. "The Equal Rights Amendment Is Introduced." ER, 15 December 1923, p. 347.

1590. "The Introduction of the Equal Rights Amendment in Congress." ER, 15 December 1923, p. 348.

1591. "A National Amendment Is the Permanent Way of Establishing Equal Rights." ER, 15 December 1923, p. 348.

1592. "The President's Message." ER, 15 December 1923, p. 348.

1593. "News from the Field." ER, 15 December 1923, p. 350.

1594. "Comments of the Press." ER, 15 December 1923, p. 352. Rep. from Brooklyn Standard Union, 10 November 1923; Washington (D.C.) Star, 18 November 1923.

1595. Russell, Hortense. "The Amendment Is Introduced." ER, 22 December 1923, p. 355.

1596. "The Opposition." ER, 22 December 1923, p. 356.

1597. "Mrs. Huck Joins Group in Washington." ER, 22 December 1923, p. 357.

1598. "Women Interview National Republican Committee." ER, 22 December 1923, p. 357.

1599. "Lucretia Mott Amendment." ER, 22 December 1923, pp. 358-59.

1600. "An Argument for a Federal Amendment." ER, 29 December 1923, p. 364.

1601. Matthews, Burnita Shelton. "A Federal Amendment Avoids Referendum Campaigns." ER, 29 December 1923, p. 365.

1602. "Comments of the Press." ER, 29 December 1923, p. 368. Rep. from Collier's Weekly, 22 December 1923; Sacramento Union, 20 November 1923.

1603. "Lavinia Dock Appeals to Nurses." ER, 5 January 1924, p. 373.

1604. Wold, Emma. "Equal Rights Bills that Failed in 1923." ER, 5 January 1924, pp. 374-75.

1605. "Maryland Women Rush Equal Rights Work in Congress." ER, 5 January 1924, p. 375.

1606. "News from the Field." ER, 5 January 1924, p. 376.

1607. "Equal Rights and Conscription." ER, 12 January 1924, p. 380.

1608. "News from the Field." ER, 12 January 1924, p. 383.

1609. "Comment of the Press." ER, 12 January 1924, p. 384. Rep. from
      Catholic Citizen (London), 5 December 1923.

1610. "An Objection Destroyed." ER, 19 January 1924, p. 388.

1611. "Another Argument for the Federal Amendment." ER, 19 January
      1924, p. 388.

1612. Marsh, Eleanor Taylor. "Equal Rights and Mothers' Pensions."
      ER, 19 January 1924, p. 390.

1613. "News from the Field: Luncheon of San Diego Members." ER,
      19 January 1924, p. 391.

1614. Russell, Hortense. "With the National Democratic Committee."
      ER, 26 January 1924, p. 395.

1615. "News from the Field." ER, 26 January 1924, pp. 399-400.

1616. "The Judiciary Committee." ER, 2 February 1924, p. 404.

1617. "So Easy." ER, 2 February 1924, p. 404.

1618. Matthews, Burnita Shelton. "Bringing State Laws into Harmony
      with the Federal Amendment." ER, 2 February 1924, p. 405.

1619. "News from the Field." ER, 2 February 1924, p. 407.

1620. "Equal Rights Hearing February 6." ER, 9 February 1924, p. 411.

1621. "Equal Rights Hearing Postponed." ER, 16 February 1924, p. 2.

1622. "Mothers in Industry." ER, 16 February 1924, p. 4.

1623. "Against the Equal Rights Amendment." ER, 23 February 1924, p. 11.

1624. "The Deputation to the President." ER, 23 February 1924, p. 12.

1625. Russell, Hortense. "President Coolidge Receives New England
      Women." ER, 23 February 1924, pp. 13-14.

1626. "News from the Field." ER, 23 February 1924, pp. 14-16.

1627. "Interpretation of the Equal Rights Amendment by the Courts."
      ER, 1 March 1924, p. 20.

1628. "Lawyers and Leaders." ER, 1 March 1924, p. 20.

1629. "News from the Field." ER, 1 March 1924, p. 23.

1630. "A Telegram from Judge Ben B. Lindsey." ER, 8 March 1924, p. 27.

1631. "Virginia Women Interview Their Law Makers." ER, 8 March 1924,
p. 27.

1632. "Congress and the States." ER, 8 March 1924, p. 28.

1633. "Comment of the Press: The Equal Rights Amendment." ER, 8 March
1924, p. 31. Rep. from Oshkosh (Wisconsin) North Western.

1634. "Lobbying in Washington." ER, 15 March 1924, p. 35.

1635. "Industrial Equality." ER, 15 March 1924, p. 36.

1636. "Protective Laws." ER, 15 March 1924, p. 36.

1637. Eastman, Crystal. "Equality or Protection." ER, 15 March 1924,
p. 37. Rep. from Time and Tide, 18 January 1924.

1638. "News from the Field." ER, 15 March 1924, pp. 38-39.

1639. "The Political Conventions." ER, 29 March 1924, p. 51.

1640. "Congress and the Amendment." ER, 29 March 1924, p. 52.

1641. "Daughters of the Morning." ER, 29 March 1924, p. 52.

1642. "Constitutional Amendment Will Meet Situation." ER, 29 March
1924, p. 53.

1643. "News from the Field." ER, 29 March 1924, p. 55.

1644. "Minnesota Progressives Send Message to Congress." ER, 5 April
1924, p. 59.

1645. "The Opposition." ER, 5 April 1924, p. 60.

1646. "The Support of the Progressives." ER, 5 April 1924, p. 60.

1647. Laughlin, Gail. "Why an Equal Rights Amendment?" ER, 5 April
1924, p. 61.

1648. "News from the Field: Mrs. Porter Speaks at Chicago." ER,
5 April 1924, p. 63.

1649. "Congress and the Constitution." ER, 12 April 1924, p. 68.

1650. "Unphysiological Physiology." ER, 12 April 1924, p. 68.

1651. Pittman, Marcy C. "Amendment to Help Women in Government." ER,
12 April 1924, p. 71.

1652. "Campaign on Congress Progresses." ER, 19 April 1924, p. 75.

1653. "From the Minority to the Majority Viewpoint." ER, 19 April 1924,
p. 76.

1654. "Comments of the Press: E.R.A." ER, 19 April 1924, p. 80. Rep. from Catholic Citizen (England), 15 February 1924.

1655. "Carrying Equal Rights to the Constituents of Congress." ER, 26 April 1924, p. 83.

1656. "Maternity Legislation." ER, 26 April 1924, p. 84.

1657. Forbus, Lady Willie. "The Lucretia Mott Amendment." ER, 26 April 1924, pp. 85-86.

1658. "Progressives Continue to Endorse Equal Rights." ER, 3 May 1924, p. 91.

1659. "Mothers' Pensions and the Amendment." ER, 3 May 1924, p. 92.

1660. Sabin, Florence R. "Equal Rights." ER, 3 May 1924, p. 94.

1661. "News from the Field." ER, 3 May 1924, p. 95.

1662. "From the Press: Plea to Support Amendment." ER, 3 May 1924, p. 96. Contains: Florence Garvin, Birth Control Review, April 1924.

1663. "University Women Withdraw Opposition." ER, 10 May 1924, p. 99.

1664. "Which Will Be Next?" ER, 10 May 1924, p. 100.

1665. Byrns, Elinor. "Men and Women Shall Have Equal Rights throughout the United States and Every Place Subject to Its Jurisdiction." ER, 10 May 1924, p. 103.

1666. "In the Field." ER, 10 May 1924, p. 103.

1667. "From the Press: Equal Rights or Special Privileges for Women?" ER, 10 May 1924, p. 104. Rep. from Oakland (California) Examiner, 19 March 1924.

1668. "From the Press: Women and Their Rights." ER, 10 May 1924, p. 104. Rep. from St. Paul Daily News, 15 April 1924.

1669. "The Congressional Campaign." ER, 17 May 1924, p. 107.

1670. "Woman's International League Endorses Equal Rights." ER, 17 May 1924, pp. 109-10.

1671. "In the Field." ER, 17 May 1924, p. 111.

1672. Fraser, Helen. "Equal Rights in U.S.A." ER, 24 May 1924, p. 115. Rep. from Woman's Leader (England), 2 May 1924.

1673. "The Bogey Argument." ER, 24 May 1924, p. 116.

1674. "In the Field." ER, 24 May 1924, p. 119.

1675. Dock, Lavinia. "A Sub-Caste." ER, 31 May 1924, pp. 125-26.

1676. "Preparing for the National Conventions." ER, 7 June 1924, p. 131.

1677. Cobb, Florence Etheridge. "How to Get Equal Rights." ER, 7 June
      1924, p. 133.

1678. "In the Field." ER, 7 June 1924, p. 135.

1679. "With the Political Conventions." ER, 14 June 1924, p. 139.

1680. "Government Discriminations." ER, 14 June 1924, p. 140.

1681. Younger, Maud. "Will the Equal Rights Amendment Benefit Women in
      Industry?" ER, 14 June 1924, p. 141.

1682. "In the Field." ER, 14 June 1924, p. 143.

1683. "Republicans Refuse Equal Rights Plank." ER, 21 June 1924,
      pp. 147, 150.

1684. "The Republicans and Equal Rights." ER, 21 June 1924, p. 148.

1685. "Before the Republican Platform Committee." ER, 21 June 1924,
      pp. 149-50.

1686. Hooker, Edith Houghton. "A Test of Faith." ER, 21 June 1924,
      p. 151.

1687. Colter, Mabel. "Equal Rights and Women Teachers." ER, 28 June
      1924, p. 155.

1688. "A Political Opportunity." ER, 28 June 1924, p. 156.

1689. "Farmer-Labor Party Endorses Equal Rights." ER, 28 June 1924,
      pp. 157-59.

1690. "Farmer-Labor Candidates Support Equal Rights." ER, 28 June
      1924, pp. 159-60.

1691. "Before the Democratic Platform Committee." ER, 5 July 1924,
      p. 163.

1692. "The Woman's Party Election Conference." ER, 5 July 1924, p. 164.

1693. "Democrats Refuse Equal Rights Plank." ER, 5 July 1924, pp. 165-66.

1694. "In the Field." ER, 5 July 1924, p. 167.

1695. "July 4th Convention Endorses Equal Legal Rights." ER, 12 July
      1924, p. 173.

1696. "In the Field: Missouri Members Form State Committees." ER,
      12 July 1924, p. 175.

1697. "Socialists Endorse Equality in Law." ER, 19 July 1924, p. 181.

1698. "Education Association Hears about Equal Rights." ER, 26 July
      1924, p. 189.

1699. "In the Field." ER, 26 July 1924, p. 191.

1700. Worcester, Daisy Lee Worthington. "Welfare Legislation and the Woman's Party." ER, 16 August 1924, pp. 213-14.

1701. "The Women for Congress Conference." ER, 23 August 1924, pp. 221-22.

1702. Paul, Alice. "Women for Congress." ER, 30 August 1924, pp. 229-30.

1703. "Business and Professional Women Endorse Equal Rights." ER, 30 August 1924, p. 232.

1704. "The Campaign Begins." ER, 30 August 1924, p. 237.

1705. "From the Press: Historical Parallels." ER, 30 August 1924, p. 240. Rep. from Nation, 30 July 1924.

1706. Stevens, Doris. "The Equal Rights Amendment." ER, 13 September 1924, pp. 245-46.

1707. "From the Press: Women Only." ER, 13 September 1924, p. 248. Contains a letter from Bertha M. Fowler (Colorado Chapter of Woman's Party) from Colorado Springs Gazette, 21 August 1924.

1708. "The Campaign and the Amendment." ER, 11 October 1924, p. 276.

1709. "From the Press: Women as Governors." ER, 11 October 1924, p. 280. Rep. from Milwaukee Sentinel, 26 September 1924.

1710. "From the Press: Woman's Party." ER, 11 October 1924, p. 280. Rep. from Colorado Springs Telegram, 27 September 1924.

1711. "California Women Endorse Equal Rights." ER, 15 November 1924, p. 315.

1712. "The Opening of Congress." ER, 29 November 1924, p. 332.

1713. "From the Press: Equal Rights Amendment." ER, 29 November 1924, p. 336. Rep. from New Republic, 19 November 1924.

1714. "Deputation to Senator Cummins of the Judiciary Committee." ER, 6 December 1924, p. 339.

1715. "Congress Convenes." ER, 6 December 1924, p. 340.

1716. "Deputation to Congressman Graham." ER, 13 December 1924, p. 347.

1717. "Help Lobby Congress." ER, 13 December 1924, p. 348.

1718. "Hearings on Equal Rights Measure to Be Set This Week." ER, 27 December 1924, p. 363.

1719. "The Frightful Difficulty." ER, 3 January 1925, p. 372.

1720. Putnam, Frank. "Equal Rights Amendment." ER, 3 January 1925, p. 374.

1721. "Hearing on Equal Rights before House Judiciary Committee on February 4." ER, 10 January 1925, p. 379.

1722. "Whose Hearing Is It?" ER, 10 January 1925, p. 380.

1723. "Is Senator Ernst Judicial?" ER, 17 January 1925, p. 388.

1724. "Resolution Sent by the District of Columbia Branch at Its Sunday Meeting to the Senate Judiciary Committee." ER, 17 January 1925, p. 390.

1725. "News from the Field: Woodbury High Holds Debate." ER, 17 January 1925, p. 391.

1726. "From the Press: The Feminist Amendment." ER, 17 January 1925, p. 392. Rep. from Chicago Journal of Commerce and La Salle Street Journal, 17 December 1924.

1727. "Stand Up and Be Counted." ER, 24 January 1925, p. 396.

1728. "From the Press: The Basis of the Demand." ER, 24 January 1925, p. 400. Contains: Kenneth Andrews, New York World, 5 January 1925.

1729. "Senator Wadsworth Receives Deputation." ER, 31 January 1925, p. 403.

1730. "Face to the Dawn." ER, 31 January 1925, p. 404.

1731. "A.A.U.W. Committee Makes Report." ER, 31 January 1925, pp. 406-408.

1732. "News from the Field." ER, 31 January 1925, p. 408.

1733. "Arrangements for Hearings Completed." ER, 7 February 1925, p. 411.

1734. "New York Women Approach Weller." ER, 7 February 1925, p. 411.

1735. "Fixing the Date." ER, 7 February 1925, p. 412.

1736. "Knock and It Shall Be Opened." ER, 14 February 1925, p. 4.

1737. Black, Ruby A. "The Congressional Hearings." ER, 14 February 1925, pp. 5-8.

1738. "News from the Field." ER, 14 February 1925, p. 8.

1739. "California Women Interview Mrs. Kahn." ER, 21 February 1925, p. 11.

1740. "No More, No Less." ER, 21 February 1925, p. 12.

1741. "Representative Perlman Endorses Equal Rights." ER, 21 February 1925, p. 13.

1742. "From the Press: Why They Ask Equal Rights." ER, 21 February 1925, p. 16. Contains: James O'Donnell Bennett, Chicago Tribune 5 February 1925.

1743. "We Do Not Oppose Equal Rights." ER, 28 February 1925, p. 21.

1744. "A Specious Question." ER, 7 March 1925, p. 28.

1745. White, Sue. "Constructive Revolutionists." ER, 7 March 1925, pp. 29-30.

1746. Wheeler, Genevieve Thomas. "Equal Rights by Radio." ER, 21 March 1925, p. 47.

1747. "News from the Field." ER, 21 March 1925, p. 48.

1748. Stevens, Doris. "Industrial Equality." ER, 11 April 1925, pp. 68-69.

1749. Wold, Emma. "Legal Status of American Women." ER, 11 April 1925, pp. 69-72.

1750. Gifford, Elizabeth. "The End of the Road." ER, 18 April 1925, p. 75.

1751. "Is 'Equal Rights' Vague?" ER, 18 April 1925, p. 76.

1752. "The Proof of the Pudding." ER, 18 April 1925, p. 76.

1753. Algeo, Sara M. "The Legal Dependence of Women." ER, 16 May 1925, pp. 110-11.

1754. Dock, Lavinia L. "Concerning Equal Rights." ER, 20 June 1925, p. 147.

1755. "Equal Penalties." ER, 20 June 1925, p. 148.

1756. "Resolutions Passed by Mid-West Conference." ER, 27 June 1925, p. 160.

1757. "News from the Field." ER, 11 July 1925, p. 175.

1758. "News from the Field: Sen. Deneen Deputized on Equal Rights." ER, 18 July 1925, p. 184.

1759. "Have You Interviewed Your Senators and Congressmen?" ER, 25 July 1925, p. 188.

1760. "What Every Member of Congress Ought to Know." ER, 25 July 1925, pp. 189-90.

1761. "News from the Field." ER, 25 July 1925, p. 191.

1762. "News from the Field." ER, 1 August 1925, pp. 198-99.

1763. "News from the Field." ER, 8 August 1925, pp. 207-208.

1764. "Why a Federal Amendment?" ER, 12 September 1925, p. 244.

1765. "Two Sides of the Shield." ER, 19 September 1925, p. 252.

1766. "News from the Field." ER, 19 September 1925, p. 256.

1767. "What Can the Amendment Do?" ER, 26 September 1925, p. 260.

1768. "News from the Field." ER, 26 September 1925, p. 264.

1769. "The Bar Sinister." ER, 3 October 1925, p. 268.

1770. "News from the Field: Kansas Branch to Have Luncheon." ER,
      3 October 1925, p. 272.

1771. Wold, Emma. "Equal Rights in the Legislatures of 1925." ER,
      24 October 1925, pp. 295-96.

1772. "Let the Facts Speak." ER, 14 November 1925, p. 316.

1773. "News from the Field." ER, 21 November 1925, p. 327.

1774. "An Unavoidable Obligation." ER, 28 November 1925, p. 332.

1775. "Council of Catholic Women Opposes Equal Rights." ER, 5 December
      1925, p. 341.

1776. "News from the Field." ER, 12 December 1925, p. 352.

1777. "The Johnson Amendment." ER, 19 December 1925, p. 356.

1778. Black, Ruby A. "Vigorous Congressional Campaign Begins." ER,
      19 December 1925, p. 357.

1779. "News from the Field." ER, 19 December 1925, p. 360.

1780. "Republican Responsibility." ER, 26 December 1925, p. 364.

1781. Levitt, Albert. "Privileges--Or Rights and Duties." ER,
      2 January 1926, pp. 373-75. Rep. from American Bar Association
      Journal, December 1925.

1782. Dorr, Rhita Childe. "Equal Rights for Women." ER, 16 January
      1926, p. 390.

1783. "Press Comment." ER, 16 January 1926, p. 392. Contains: Ann
      Tizia Leitich, "The Woman Question in America," Neve Freie Press
      (Vienna, Austria).

1784. "Women Gather in Washington to Demand Industrial Equality." ER,
      23 January 1926, p. 395.

1785. "Equal Rights and Conscription." ER, 23 January 1926, p. 396.

1786. "President Hears Working Women's Plea for Equality." ER,
      23 January 1926, p. 397-99.

1787. "Press Comment: Feminine Freedom." ER, 23 January 1926, p. 400.
      Rep. from Baltimore Evening Sun.

1788. "Equal Rights Plea Heard by the President." ER, 30 January 1926, pp. 405-406.

1789. "Press Comment: Woman Workers and Protection." ER, 30 January 1926, p. 408. Rep. from Washington (D.C.) Evening Star.

1790. "Press Comment: Equal Rights Again." ER, 6 February 1926, p. 415. Rep. from Buffalo (New York) Sunday Express.

1791. "Press Comment: A Woman's Attack upon State Rights." ER, 13 February 1926, p. 7. Rep. from New York World, 19 January 1926.

1792. "The Way It Goes." ER, 6 March 1926, p. 28.

1793. "The Scope of the Amendment." ER, 3 April 1926, p. 60.

1794. "Whose Creation?" ER, 10 April 1926, p. 68.

1795. "On Being Supported." ER, 17 April 1926, p. 76.

1796. Black, Ruby A. "The Story of the Conference." ER, 15 May 1926, pp. 107, 111-12.

1797. Matthews, Burnita Shelton. "Women Should Have Equal Rights with Men: A Reply." ER, 29 May 1926, pp. 125-27. Rep. from American Bar Association Journal 12 (February 1926): 117-20; also rep. in entry #463.

1798. "Press Comment: Equality." ER, 29 May 1926, p. 127. Rep. from Miami (Florida) Herald.

1799. "News from the Field: Miss Wold Addresses American University Class." ER, 26 June 1926, p. 160.

1800. "Wanted--A Guiding Principle." ER, 7 August 1926, p. 204.

1801. Spencer, Caroline E. "Women for Congress." ER, 7 August 1926, p. 205.

1802. "Press Comment: The Battle for Equal Rights." ER, 25 September 1926, p. 263. Rep. from Milwaukee Journal, 15 August 1926.

1803. "A Case in Point." ER, 30 October 1926, p. 300.

1804. "Putting on the Reverse." ER, 4 December 1926, p. 340.

1805. "Opportunity Knocks Again." ER, 11 December 1926, p. 348.

1806. "News from the Field: Pennsylvania Branch to Give Luncheon." ER, 18 December 1926, p. 360.

1807. "News from the Field: Missouri Branch Broadcasts Equal Rights." ER, 25 December 1926, p. 368.

1808. "News from the Field: Missouri Broadcasts Equal Rights." ER, 15 January 1927, p. 392.

1809. "A Startling Example." ER, 29 January 1927, p. 404.

1810. "President Coolidge Receives Deputation." ER, 26 February 1927, pp. 21-22.

1811. "Cases in Point." ER, 5 March 1927, p. 28.

1812. "News from the Field: Endorses Equal Rights Amendment." ER, 5 March 1927, p. 32.

1813. "A.A.U.W. Concerned with Status of Women." ER, 16 April 1927, p. 77.

1814. "News from the Field." ER, 14 May 1927, p. 112.

1815. "Equal Rights by National Amendment." ER, 11 June 1927, pp. 141-43. Rep. as a separate by the National Woman's Party.

1816. "Equal Rights Caravan to Journey to President Coolidge's Summer Home." ER, 9 July 1927, p. 173.

1817. "News from the Field: New Equal Rights Literature." ER, 9 July 1927, p. 176.

1818. "Delegation to President Coolidge." ER, 16 July 1927, p. 179.

1819. "Equal Rights Resolutions Sent to President." ER, 16 July 1927, pp. 181, 184.

1820. "The President Listens." ER, 23 July 1927, pp. 189-90, 192.

1821. "How Can Support for Equal Rights Be Gained?" ER, 30 July 1927, pp. 197-98.

1822. "Press Comment on Convention: Equal Rights Will Not 'Upset World.'" ER, 30 July 1927, pp. 199-200.

1823. "Every Member an Equal Rights Envoy." ER, 6 August 1927, p. 204.

1824. "One of Many Reasons." ER, 6 August 1927, p. 204.

1825. Laughlin, Gail. "'It Lies within Your Power.'" ER, 6 August 1927, pp. 206-207.

1826. "Washington Women for Equal Rights." ER, 6 August 1927, p. 208.

1827. "News from the Field: Organizing in Montana." ER, 13 August 1927, p. 216.

1828. "Mary Murray Replies Again." ER, 1 October 1927, p. 267.

1829. "Intensive Work for Equal Rights." ER, 22 October 1927, p. 294.

1830. "Another Month of 'Home Work.'" ER, 29 October 1927, p. 300.

1831. "Press Comment: Equal Rights Drive." ER, 29 October 1927, p. 304. Rep. from Washington Herald, 15 October 1927.

1832. "The Folks Back Home." ER, 5 November 1927, p. 308.

1833. "The Winter Campaign." ER, 5 November 1927, p. 309.

1834. "News from the Field." ER, 12 November 1927, pp. 319-20.

1835. "Congressman McLeod and the Equal Rights Amendment." ER, 19 November 1927, p. 325.

1836. "Press Comment: Equal Rights Campaign." ER, 19 November 1927, p. 327. Rep. from Washington (D.C.) Star, 31 October 1927.

1837. "News from the Field." ER, 19 November 1927, p. 328.

1838. "Mrs. Smith at Buffalo." ER, 26 November 1927, p. 331.

1839. "So That's That." ER, 26 November 1927, p. 332.

1840. "News from the Field: Deputation Waits upon Representative Cohen." ER, 26 November 1927, p. 336.

1841. "Campaign Opens with Deputation and Luncheon." ER, 3 December 1927, p. 341.

1842. "News from the Field: Deputation Waits upon Representative Sirovich." ER, 3 December 1927, p. 344.

1843. "Senator Norris Receives Deputation." ER, 17 December 1927, p. 355.

1844. "Press Comment: Intensive Fight for Women's Rights Aim in Winter Session." ER, 17 December 1927, p. 357.

1845. "False Prophets." ER, 21 January 1928, p. 394.

1846. "News from the Field: Organizing in Massachusetts." ER, 28 January 1928, p. 406.

1847. "News from the Field." ER, 4 February 1928, p. 414.

1848. "Think Well, Mr. Congressman." ER, 11 February 1928, p. 4.

1849. "News from the Field: Senator Edwards for Equal Rights." ER, 3 March 1928, p. 32.

1850. "Life Is Too Short." ER, 24 March 1928, p. 52.

1851. "Equal Rights and the Conventions." ER, 2 June 1928, p. 131.

1852. "News from the Field: Equal Rights Amendment Introduced in House." ER, 2 June 1928, pp. 135-36.

1853. "News from the Field." ER, 9 June 1928, pp. 143-44.

1854. "Our Speakers at the Republican Convention." ER, 23 June 1928, p. 155.

1855. "'We Do Hereby Make Covenant.'" ER, 30 June 1928, p. 164.

1856. "The Woman's Party at the Democratic Convention." ER, 7 July
    1928, p. 171.

1857. "We Await Clarification." ER, 14 July 1928, p. 180.

1858. "Party Conference on Presidential Campaign." ER, 14 July 1928,
    p. 181.

1859. "Hopeful Waiting." ER, 28 July 1928, p. 196.

1860. "Appealing to Homemakers." ER, 4 August 1928, p. 204.

1861. "'Boosting Liberty.'" ER, 11 August 1928, p. 212.

1862. "Eastern Women Ask Republicans to Declare for Equal Rights."
    ER, 18 August 1928, p. 221.

1863. "Press Comment: Equal Rights and the Campaign." ER, 18 August
    1928, pp. 223-24. Contains: Rodney Dutcher, Paterson (New Jersey)
    Press-Guardian.

1864. "We Still Seek Clarification." ER, 8 September 1928, p. 244.

1865. "Equal Rights a Campaign Issue." ER, 22 September 1928, p. 258.

1866. "Woman's Party Enters Presidential Campaign." ER, 22 September
    1928, pp. 259-60.

1867. Laughlin, Gail. "The Choice That Lay before Us." ER, 22 September
    1928, p. 261.

1868. "Let's Make Virtue Pay." ER, 29 September 1928, p. 266.

1869. "Equal Rights Amendment and Protective Legislation." ER, 6
    October 1928, pp. 275-76.

1870. "What Governor Smith Said." ER, 6 October 1928, pp. 279-80.

1871. Younger, Maud. "Why the Equal Rights Amendment?" ER,
    13 October 1928, p. 286.

1872. "News from the Field." ER, 13 October 1928, p. 288.

1873. "Herbert Hoover on Industrial Equality." ER, 27 October 1928,
    p. 299.

1874. "Press Comment." ER, 27 October 1928, p. 303. Rep. from Daily
    Palo Alto Times, 14 September 1928.

1875. "Vote for Equal Rights." ER, 3 November 1928, p. 306.

1876. "How Long Will Uncle Sam Wait?" ER, 3 November 1928, pp. 309-10.

1877. "News from the Field." ER, 3 November 1928, p. 312.

1878. "The Old and the New Cerebration." ER, 10 November 1928, p. 314.

1879. "In Striking Contrast." ER, 10 November 1928, pp. 315-16.

1880. "Statement by Vice-President-Elect Curtis." ER, 17 November 1928, p. 323.

1881. "News from the Field: Maryland Branch Presents Program." ER, 24 November 1928, p. 336.

1882. "Press Comment: Chandless and Equal Rights." ER, 1 December 1928, p. 343.

1883. "Amendment Campaign Outlined." ER, 15 December 1928, p. 355.

1884. Kennard, Florence Elizabeth. "Maryland Branch Holds Equal Rights Dinner." ER, 15 December 1928, pp. 355-57.

1885. "News from the Field." ER, 15 December 1928, pp. 359-60.

1886. "News from the Field: Debate Equal Rights Amendment." ER, 22 December 1928, p. 368.

1887. "The Retort Courteous." ER, 29 December 1928, pp. 372-73.

1888. "It Can Be Done." ER, 26 January 1929, p. 402.

1889. "News from the Field: Hearing on Equal Rights Arranged." ER, 2 February 1929, p. 416.

1890. "Senate Hearing on Equal Rights." ER, 9 February 1929, pp. 3-6.

1891. "Press Comment: Women in Industry." ER, 16 February 1929, pp. 14-15. Rep. from Washington Post, 3 February 1929.

1892. "Well Said." ER, 23 February 1929, p. 18.

1893. "Miss Lutz Replies to the Herald." ER, 9 March 1929, pp. 37-38.

1894. "News from the Field: Zonta Hears Debate." ER, 16 March 1929, p. 48.

1895. "Increased Activity in Virginia." ER, 23 March 1929, pp. 53-54.

1896. "News from the Field: Hearings Reported on Air." ER, 23 March 1929, p. 56.

1897. "Methods and Results." ER, 30 March 1929, p. 58.

1898. "New York State Replies." ER, 13 April 1929, p. 74.

1899. "Representative Owen for Equality." ER, 20 April 1929, pp. 83-84.

1900. "The Equal Rights Amendment and Restrictive Labor Legislation." ER, 20 April 1929, p. 87.

1901. "News from the Field: Connecticut Organizes." ER, 20 April 1929,
      p. 88.

1902. "Connecticut Holds Organization Meetings." ER, 4 May 1929,
      pp. 101-102.

1903. "News from the Field: Equal Rights Amendment Introduced." ER,
      4 May 1929, p. 104.

1904. "News from the Field: To Celebrate Suffrage Anniversary."
      ER, 25 May 1929, pp. 127-28.

1905. "Equal Rights Amendment Introduced on Anniversary." ER, 8 June
      1929, pp. 139-40.

1906. Black, Ruby A. "Victory Celebration Demands Action." ER,
      15 June 1929, pp. 147-49.

1907. "Branches Urge Support of Amendment." ER, 22 June 1929, pp. 157-58.

1908. "Florida Woman's Club for Equal Rights." ER, 29 June 1929,
      pp. 165-66.

1909. "News from the Field." ER, 13 July 1929, p. 181.

1910. "News from the Field: Seattle Women Answer Opponents." ER,
      20 July, 1929, p. 192.

1911. "News from the Field: At Workers' Summer School." ER,
      27 July 1929, p. 200.

1912. "Let Them Know." ER, 10 August 1929, p. 210.

1913. "Washington Women for Equal Rights." ER, 10 August 1929, pp. 212-
      13.

1914. "Equal Rights on Radio." ER, 12 October 1929, p. 283.

1915. "Men Attack Equal Rights." ER, 12 October 1929, pp. 284-86.

1916. "The Design of the Equal Rights Amendment." ER, 2 November
      1929, p. 306.

1917. Smith, Jane Norman. "Why an Equal Rights Amendment." ER,
      16 November 1929, pp. 323-25.

1918. "Press Comment: Ancient Fake of the 'Equal Rights' Amendment."
      ER, 16 November 1929, p. 326. Rep. from Labor (Washington, D.C.),
      19 October 1929.

1919. "Help Needed in Preparing Card Index." ER, 28 December 1929,
      p. 371.

1920. "News from the Field." ER, 4 January 1930, p. 384.

1921. "News from the Field: Debate in Milwaukee." ER, 22 March 1930,
      p. 56.

1922. "The Equal Protection of the Laws." ER, 21 June 1930, p. 154.

1923. "News from the Field: Washington Women for Equality." ER, 5 July 1930, pp. 174-75.

1924. "Plans to Push Amendment." ER, 6 September 1930, p. 243.

1925. "Tried and Not Found Wanting." ER, 4 October 1930, p. 274.

1926. "Immediate Action Is Necessary." ER, 1 November 1930, p. 306.

1927. "It Remains to Be Seen." ER, 8 November 1930, p. 314.

1928. "In This Busy World." ER, 22 November 1930, p. 330.

1929. "Feminist Activities Intensified with New Year." ER, 3 January 1931, p. 379.

1930. "Passage of Amendment Demanded." ER, 10 January 1931, pp. 390-91.

1931. "Amendment Needed for Security." ER, 17 January 1931, pp. 395-96.

1932. "Sell the Idea." ER, 24 January 1931, p. 402.

1933. "Excerpts from Equal Rights Testimony." ER, 24 January 1931, p. 404.

1934. "Please Respond." ER, 7 February 1931, p. 2.

1935. "News from the Field: Hawaii Hears Equal Rights Arguments." ER, 18 April 1931, p. 88.

1936. "No Exception." ER, 2 May 1931, p. 98.

1937. Green, Elizabeth. "Equal Rights by Federal Amendment." ER, 2 May 1931, pp. 100-102.

1938. "News from the Field: Mrs. Wiley Addresses Club." ER, 2 May 1931, p. 104.

1939. "Life Is Too Short." ER, 9 May 1931, p. 106.

1940. "News from the Field: For the Amendment." ER, 13 June 1931, p. 152.

1941. "Press Comment: Equal Rights and Protective Legislation for Women." ER, 11 July 1931, pp. 180-81. Contains: L. De Albert, Catholic Citizen (London), 15 June 1931.

1942. "Washington Women Again Support Equality." ER, 18 July 1931, p. 192.

1943. "Press Comment: Legal Equality of Sexes Sought." ER, 1 August 1931, p. 206. Rep. from Buffalo (New York) Evening News, 10 July 1931.

1944. "News from the Field: California Business Women." ER, 19 September 1931, p. 264.

1945. "Plan Your Work." ER, 3 October 1931, p. 274.

1946. "Forward to the Equal Rights Amendment." ER, 24 October 1931,
      p. 298.

1947. "Go and Do Likewise." ER, 31 October 1931, p. 306.

1948. "California Business Women's Program." ER, 7 November 1931, p. 318.

1949. "E Pluribus Unum." ER, 28 November 1931, p. 338.

1950. "News from the Field." ER, 28 November 1931, p. 343.

1951. "It Is Not Enough." ER, 5 December 1931, p. 346.

1952. "Tempus Fugit." ER, 2 January 1932, p. 378.

1953. "News from the Field." ER, 2 January 1932, p. 384.

1954. "News from the Field." ER, 14 January 1932, pp. 399-400.

1955. "The Only Way." ER, 23 January 1932, p. 402.

1956. "Equal Rights Amendment Again Introduced." ER, 23 January 1932,
      p. 403.

1957. "News from the Field." ER, 23 January 1932, pp. 407-408.

1958. "Western Women for Equal Rights." ER, 6 February 1932, p. 6.

1959. "News from the Field." ER, 6 February 1932, p. 8.

1960. "News from the Field: Californians Endorse Amendment." ER,
      20 February 1932, pp. 23-24.

1961. "Join the Chorus." ER, 12 March 1932, p. 42.

1962. "Come to the Hearing." ER, 19 March 1932, p. 50.

1963. "Mrs. Pell Broadcasts Equal Rights." ER, 19 March 1932, pp. 52-53.

1964. "Press Comment: Urges Federal Law for Woman's Rights." ER,
      19 March 1932, p. 55. Contains: Kathryn E. Pickett, Indianapolis Star,
      16 February 1932.

1965. "News from the Field: Amendment Topic at Tea." ER, 26 March
      1932, p. 64.

1966. "A Modern Prophet." ER, 2 April 1932, p. 66.

1967. "Equal Rights Hearing Makes History." ER, 2 April 1932, pp. 67-69.

1968. "Sponsor of Amendment Makes Strong Appeal." ER, 2 April 1932,
      p. 69.

1969. "Press Comment: Equal Rights Battle Begun." ER, 2 April 1932,
      p. 70. Rep. from Los Angeles Times, 24 March 1932.

1970. "Press Comment: Rights for Women Advocated by Ludlow." ER,
    2 April 1932, p. 70. Rep. from New York Times, 24 March 1932.

1971. "News from the Field: Michigan Branch Demands Amendment." ER,
    2 April 1932, p. 72.

1972. "News from the Field: Senator Bulow Honor Guest." ER, 9 April
    1932, p. 80.

1973. "News from the Field: Virginia Hears Report." ER, 16 April 1932,
    p. 88.

1974. "News from the Field: New Leaflet Ready." ER, 23 April 1932,
    p. 95.

1975. "Support the Equal Rights Amendment." ER, 7 May 1932, p. 106.

1976. "The Equal Rights Essay Contest." ER, 14 May 1932, p. 115.

1977. "Press Comment: Demand Equal Rights." ER, 4 June 1932, p. 142.
    Rep. from Washington Herald, 23 May 1932.

1978. "News from the Field." ER, 4 June 1932, p. 144.

1979. "Are Women Persons?" ER, 11 June 1932, p. 146.

1980. "Support the Equal Rights Planks." ER, 11 June 1932, p. 146.

1981. "News from the Field." ER, 11 June 1932, p. 152.

1982. "There Is a Tide." ER, 18 June 1932, p. 154.

1983. "News from the Field." ER, 18 June 1932, p. 160.

1984. "The Way to Victory." ER, 25 June 1932, p. 162.

1985. "The Republican Hearing on the Equal Rights Plank." ER, 25
    June 1932, pp. 163-64.

1986. "Press Comment: 'Brainy Women' in N.W.P. Delegation." ER,
    25 June 1932, p. 166. Rep. from Chicago Herald and Examiner,
    14 June 1932.

1987. "Press Comment: Resist Discrimination in International Law." ER,
    25 June 1932, p. 167.

1988. "The Democratic Hearing on the Equal Rights Plank." ER,
    2 July 1932, pp. 171-72.

1989. "Garfield Opposed to Equal Rights Plank." ER, 2 July 1932,
    pp. 174-75.

1990. "News from the Field." ER, 9 July 1932, p. 184.

1991. "News from the Field." ER, 16 July 1932, pp. 190-91.

1992. "Press Comment." ER, 16 July 1932, p. 192.

1993. "Equal Rights Amendment Is Surest Solution." ER, 27 August
      1932, p. 236.

1994. "Feminist Note: Roosevelt Receives Equal Rights Delegation."
      ER, 17 September 1932, p. 264.

1995. "California Points the Way." ER, 24 September 1932, p. 266.

1996. "Governor Roosevelt Receives Facts on Equal Rights." ER,
      24 September 1932, pp. 267-68.

1997. "Equal Rights Endorsed by California Federation." ER,
      24 September 1932, p. 270.

1998. "Amelia Earhart." ER, 1 October 1932, p. 274.

1999. "The President Receives an Equal Rights Deputation." ER,
      1 October 1932, pp. 275-76.

2000. "News from the Field: California Federation Endorses Equal Rights."
      ER, 1 October 1932, pp. 277-78.

2001. "News from the Field: California Branch Meets." ER,
      8 October 1932, p. 286.

2002. "Isn't It Rather a Pity?" ER, 15 October 1932, p. 290.

2003. "Are Your Eyes Open?" ER, 22 October 1932, p. 298.

2004. "Letters from a Feminist." ER, 22 October 1932, p. 302.

2005. "News from the Field: Illinois Forum Endorses Amendment." ER,
      22 October 1932, p. 304.

2006. Owens, Eloise. "Distinguished Speakers Address California
      Council." ER, 12 November 1932, p. 323.

2007. "News from the Field: An Important Bulletin." ER,
      26 November 1932, p. 344.

2008. "Essay Contest Arouses Interest." ER, 3 December 1932, pp. 347-48.

2009. "News from the Field: California Council Joins Federation."
      ER, 10 December 1932, p. 360.

2010. Wiley, Anna Kelton. "The Equal Rights Amendment." ER,
      31 December 1932, pp. 379-81.

2011. "Arkansas and California Set the Pace." ER, 7 January 1933,
      pp. 387-88.

2012. "Jury Service and the Amendment." ER, 14 January 1933, pp. 395-96.

2013. "News from the Field." ER, 11 March 1933, pp. 47-48.

2014. "Work for Equal Rights Amendment." ER, 18 March 1933, p. 51.

2015. "Advantages of the Equal Rights Amendment." ER, 25 March 1933,
     p. 58.

2016. "News from the Field." ER, 25 March 1933, pp. 61-62.

2017. "What Is Your Record?" ER, 1 April 1933, p. 66.

2018. "News from the Field: Mr. Ludlow Commends Equal Rights." ER,
     8 April 1933, p. 80.

2019. "The Campaign for the Amendment." ER, 15 April 1933, p. 83.

2020. "California Women and the Equal Rights Amendment." ER,
     15 April 1933, p. 86.

2021. "News from the Field." ER, 15 April 1933, pp. 87-88.

2022. "News from the Field: District Club Supports Amendment." ER,
     20 May 1933, p. 128.

2023. "The Hearing on the Equal Rights Amendment." ER, 3 June 1933,
     pp. 139-40.

2024. "Here Is Your Opportunity." ER, 10 June 1933, p. 146.

2025. "Suggestions for a Summer Program." ER, 10 June 1933, p. 146.

2026. "News from the Field: California Women Endorse Amendment."
     ER, 10 June 1933, p. 152.

2027. "The Substance and the Shadow." ER, 17 June 1933, p. 154.

2028. Younger, Maud. "Equal Rights and the 73rd Congress." ER,
     24 June 1933, pp. 163-64.

2029. "Student Essayists Win Notable Award." ER, 8 July 1933,
     pp. 183-84.

2030. "Congressional Committee Wages Home-Town Campaigns." ER,
     29 July 1933, p. 203.

2031. "News from the Field: Bookbinders Endorse Equal Rights
     Amendment." ER, 29 July 1933, pp. 205-206.

2032. "News from the Field: Oppose Legislation Based on Sex." ER,
     12 August 1933, p. 222.

2033. "Press Comments: Advocates Protective Legislation for Women."
     ER, 26 August 1933, p. 240. Rep. from Baltimore Sun, 7 July 1933.

2034. "News from the Field: Endorse Equal Rights Amendment." ER,
     16 September 1933, p. 261.

2035. "Students Receive Essay Contest Awards." ER, 23 September 1933,
     pp. 267-68.

2036. "Student Council Meets." ER, 23 September 1933, p. 269.

2037. "Let's Go!" ER, 7 October 1933, pp. 282, 288.

2038. "Have You Seen Your Representative?" ER, 14 October 1933, p. 293.

2039. "The N.R.A. Points the Way." ER, 21 October 1933, pp. 292-93 [sic].

2040. "Discuss Inequalities in N.R.A. Codes." ER, 21 October 1933,
      pp. 293-94 [sic].

2041. "News from the Field: Michigan Clubwomen for Equal Rights." ER,
      18 November 1933, p. 327.

2042. Wiley, Anna Kelton. "Equal Rights Debate in the District of
      Columbia Federation of Women's Clubs." ER, 17 March 1934, pp. 51-52.

2043. Greathouse, Rebekah S. "The Necessity of an Equal Rights
      Amendment." ER, 17 March 1934, pp. 52-53.

2044. Friedman, Mrs. William S. "The Viewpoint of the Opposition." ER,
      17 March 1934, pp. 53-54.

2045. "Federated Club to Study Equal Rights Amendment." ER, 2 June
      1934, pp. 142-43.

2046. "News from the Field: Jane Norman Smith Speaks at Larchmont."
      ER, 2 June 1934, p. 144.

2047. "News from the Field: Farmer-Labor Women's Club Urges Equal
      Rights." ER, 9 June 1934, p. 152.

2048. "Ohio Feminists Welcome Mrs. Hilles." ER, 14 July 1934, pp. 188-89.

2049. "Press Comment: Mrs. Hilles Addresses Columbus Branch." ER,
      14 July 1934, pp. 191-92. Contains: Mary Jose, Columbus Citizen,
      21 June 1934.

2050. West, Helen Hunt. "Mobilizing for the Equal Rights Amendment."
      ER, 21 July 1934, p. 198.

2051. "Press Comment: Ohio Law Unfair to Women." ER, 21 July 1934,
      pp. 199-200. Rep. from Columbus Dispatch, 21 June 1934.

2052. "Press Comment: Equal Rights Fight Pushed." ER, 21 July 1934,
      p. 200. Rep. from Detroit Press, 16 June 1934.

2053. Farrell, E. Eva. "Equal Rights and Individuality." ER,
      4 August 1934, p. 212.

2054. "Pro and Con." ER, 4 August 1934, pp. 214-15.

2055. Matthews, Burnita Shelton. "The Equal Rights Amendment." ER,
      18 August 1934, pp. 228-31.

2056. "Tell Lawyers Need of Equal Rights Amendment." ER, 22 September
      1934, pp. 269-70.

2057. "News from the Field: Slides of 'Suffrage Days' Shown." ER,
      29 September 1934, p. 280.

2058. "Press Comment: Demand Equal Rights in Law." ER, 6 October 1934,
      p. 287. Rep. from Milwaukee Sentinel, 30 August 1934.

2059. "Minnesota Nurses' Association Endorses Equal Rights Amendment."
      ER, 13 October 1934, pp. 293-94.

2060. "Alma Whitaker Interviews Alberta Gude Lynch on Equal Rights." ER,
      20 October 1934, pp. 300-301.

2061. "News from the Field: Debate Equal Rights Amendment." ER,
      20 October 1934, p. 304.

2062. "Ohio Welcomes Mrs. Hilles." ER, 10 November 1934, p. 324.

2063. "The Woman's Party Convention." ER, 17 November 1934, pp. 331-32.

2064. "News from the Field." ER, 17 November 1934, p. 336.

2065. Wiley, Mrs. Harvey W. "Why the Equal Rights Amendment?" ER,
      1 December 1934, pp. 347-49.

2066. "Michigan Club Women Endorse Equal Rights Amendment." ER,
      1 December 1934, pp. 351-52.

2067. "News from the Field." ER, 1 December 1934, p. 352.

2068. "Press Comment: Sees Equal Rights Amendment within Year." ER,
      8 December 1934, pp. 359-60. Rep. from Baltimore Sun, 18 November
      1934.

2069. "Endorses Amendment." ER, 15 February 1935, p. 1.

2070. "Object." ER, 15 February 1935, p. 1.

2071. "Representative Ludlow on the Equal Rights Amendment." ER,
      15 February 1935, p. 2.

2072. Smith, Jane Norman. "Support and Alimony Laws under the Amend-
      ment." ER, 15 February 1935, p. 2.

2073. Pollitzer, Anita. "Make the Amendment Move." ER, 1 March 1935,
      pp. 1-2.

2074. "Endorsing the Equal Rights Amendment." ER, 1 March 1935, p. 2.

2075. "Protective Legislation." ER, 1 March 1935, p. 3.

2076. "Amendment Literature." ER, 1 March 1935, p. 4.

2077. Smith, Jane Norman. "The Woman Worker and the Equal Rights
      Amendment." ER, 1 March 1935, p. 4.

2078. Wiley, Mrs. Harvey. "Equal Rights Amendment Endorsed by District of Columbia Federation of Women's Clubs." ER, 15 March 1935, pp. 1-2.

2079. "Letters Favoring Amendment Read at District of Columbia Federation Meeting." ER, 15 March 1935, pp. 3-4.

2080. "Object." ER, 1 April 1935, p. 1.

2081. "Progress." ER, 15 April 1935, p. 1.

2082. "Who Is Labor?" ER, 1 April 1935, p. 2.

2083. "The Press." ER, 1 April 1935, p. 3.

2084. "Amendment Advances Politically." ER, 1 May 1935, p. 1.

2085. "Amendment Endorsed." ER, 1 May 1935, p. 4.

2086. "Need for Amendment Grows." ER, 15 May 1935, p. 1.

2087. "Immediate Action Necessary." ER, 15 May 1935, pp. 1-2.

2088. "Important Endorsement." ER, 15 May 1935, p. 2.

2089. "The Amendment and War." ER, 15 May 1935, p. 3.

2090. "Amendment Endorsed by Maine Federation of Women's Clubs." ER, 1 June 1935, p. 1.

2091. "Have Women Equal Rights Now?" ER, 1 June 1935, p. 1. Introduces following article.

2091a. Greathouse, Rebekah S. "Constitutional Rights of Women." ER, 1 June 1935, pp. 1-3.

2092. "Iowa Discusses Amendment." ER, 1 June 1935, pp. 3-4.

2093. "Mrs. Wiley Presents Amendment." ER, 1 June 1935, p. 4.

2094. "Zonta Discusses Equal Rights." ER, 1 June 1935, p. 4.

2095. "Country Awakening to Need for Equal Rights." ER, 15 June 1935, p. 1. Introduces following article.

2095a. Lutz, Alma. "Women Citizens' Rights." ER, 15 June 1935, p. 1. Rep. from Christian Science Monitor, 21 April 1935.

2096. "Bindery Local Endorses Amendment." ER, 15 July 1935, p. 1.

2097. "Business and Professional Women Vote to Study Equal Rights Amendment." ER, 1 August 1935, p. 1.

2098. "Osteopaths Endorse Amendment." ER, 15 August 1935, p. 1.

2099. "Women Lawyers Support Equality Campaign." ER, 1 August 1935, p.1.

2100. "The Amendment." ER, 1 September 1935, p. 1.

2101. "Lawyers Press for Early Passage of Equal Rights Amendment." ER, 1 September 1935, pp. 1-2.

2102. "Osteopaths Press for Amendment." ER, 1 September 1935, p. 2.

2103. "Ladies of Grand Army Support Amendment." ER, 15 September 1935, p. 3.

2104. "Council of Women Will Study Amendment." ER, 15 October 1935, p. 1.

2105. "More Endorsements of the Amendment." ER, 1 November 1935, p. 2.

2106. "Women Dentists Endorse Amendment." ER, 1 December 1935, p. 1.

2107. Bobst, Sue. "California Business Women Endorse Amendment." ER, 1 December 1935, p. 3.

2108. Pollitzer, Anita. "Congressional." ER, 15 December 1935, pp. 3-4.

2109. "Congressional Campaign Opens." ER, 1 January 1936, p. 1.

2110. "Civil Service Women Endorse Amendment." ER, 15 January 1936, p. 1.

2111. "Congressional Outlook Encouraging." ER, 15 January 1936, p. 1.

2112. Swing, Betty Gram. "Report of the Congressional Committee." ER, 1 February 1936, pp. 1-2.

2113. "Eight National Associations Endorse Amendment." ER, 1 February 1936, p. 3.

2114. "Idaho Women Endorse Amendment." ER, 15 February 1936, pp. 1-2.

2115. Swing, Betty Gram. "Report of the Congressional Committee." ER, 1 March 1936, p. 1.

2116. _____. "Report of Congressional Committee." ER, 15 March 1936, p. 4.

2117. "Medical Women's Association Has Endorsed Amendment." ER, 1 April 1936, p. 2.

2118. "Creation of a Committee for Endorsements." ER, 1 April 1936, p. 3.

2119. "There Is Still Time for Action." ER, 1 May 1936, p. 2.

2120. "Ohio Democrat Club Endorses Amendment." ER, 1 May 1936, pp. 3-4.

2121. "Plans for Party Conventions." ER, 15 May 1936, p. 1.

2122. "Senator Borah's Reply." ER, 15 May 1936, p. 1.

2123. "Ohio Labor Clubs Endorse Amendment." ER, 15 May 1936, p. 2.

2124. "The Equal Rights Amendment: What It Is and Why Its Adoption Is Imperative." ER, 1 June 1936, pp. 1-3.

2125. "One of the Planks in the Platform Adopted by State Democrats of Delaware at the State Convention, May 12, 1936." ER, 1 June 1936, p. 4.

2126. Swing, Betty Gram. "Amendment Receives Favorable Action." ER, 15 June 1936, p. 1.

2127. "The Democratic Convention." ER, 1 July 1936, pp. 1-3.

2128. "A Discussion on the Equal Rights Amendment." ER, 1 July 1936, pp. 3-4; part II, 15 July 1936, pp. 2, 5. Contains a broadcast and discussion by Betty Gram Swing and Senator Carl A. Hatch, 1 June 1936.

2129. "Soroptimists Endorse Amendment." ER, 15 July 1936, p. 4.

2130. "National Women's Real Estate Association Endorses Amendment." ER, 1 August 1936, p. 2.

2131. "Progress Registered in Campaign for Equal Rights Amendment." ER, 1 August 1936, p. 3. Contains portions of extension of remarks of Louis Ludlow in House, 8 June 1936.

2132. "Put the Constitution Back of Women." ER, 1 August 1936, p. 4.

2133. "Soroptimists Endorse Amendment." ER, 1 September 1936, pp. 3-4.

2134. Pollitzer, Anita. "Make Your Demand for Equality Now." ER, 15 September 1936, p. 1.

2135. "Cheers for Accomplishment." ER, 15 September 1936, p. 3.

2136. "Help the Amendment" and "Help Complete Congressional Poll." ER, 1 November 1936, p. 2.

2137. "Biennial Convention National Woman's Party: A Plea for the Amendment." ER, 1 December 1936, p. 2.

2138. "Greatest Obstacle." ER, 15 January 1937, p. 2.

2139. "No Compromise with Right." ER, 15 January 1937, p. 2.

2140. Pollitzer, Anita. "Lobbyists Demand Prompt Passage of Amendment." ER, 15 January 1937, p. 3.

2141. "Here Is the Yard Stick." ER, 1 February 1937, p. 10.

2142. "Equal Rights Amendment Gains Powerful Advocate." ER, 1 February 1937, p. 11.

2143. "Why Discriminate against Citizens?" ER, 1 February 1937, p. 13.

2144. "Judiciary Committees." ER, 1 February 1937, p. 14.

2145. "Women's Biennial Fight for Freedom." ER, 1 February 1937, p. 14.

2146. "Is This Citizenship?" ER, 15 February 1937, p. 18.

2147. Copeland, Royal S. "Adoption of Equal Rights Amendment Vital."
ER, 15 February 1937, p. 19.

2148. "Correct Diagnosis." ER, 15 March 1937, p. 34.

2149. "Pros and Cons of the Equal Rights Amendment." ER, 1 April 1937,
pp. 46-47.

2150. "Congressman Bigelow Endorses Equal Rights." ER, 15 April 1937,
pp. 51, 55.

2151. "Amendment an Emergency." ER, 1 May 1937, p. 58.

2152. "Magna Carta for Women." ER, 15 May 1937, p. 66.

2153. Pollitzer, Anita. "Pass the Equal Rights Amendment Now." ER,
15 May 1937, p. 68.

2154. Walker, Amelia Himes. "Go Forward with Us." ER, 15 May 1937,
pp. 70-71.

2155. "News from the Field." ER, 1 June 1937, p. 79.

2156. "Simple Statement of Principle." ER, 15 June 1937, p. 82.

2157. "Minnesota Federation Endorses." ER, 15 June 1937, p. 85.

2158. "Speakers of Note Urge Equal Rights." ER, 15 June 1937, p. 85.

2159. "For Equal Rights." ER, 15 June 1937, p. 87.

2160. "Two Legislative Hurdles." ER, 1 July 1937, p. 90.

2161. "Women Fight on Two Fronts." ER, 1 July 1937, p. 90.

2162. Pollitzer, Anita. "Two Victories for Equal Rights Amendment."
ER, 1 July 1937, pp. 92-93, 96.

2163. "Another Amendment Endorsement." ER, 1 July 1937, p. 94.

2164. "Business Women Act." ER, 1 July 1937, p. 94.

2165. Weed, Helena Hill. "National News for Women." ER, 1 July 1937,
p. 95.

2166. "The Practical Solution." ER, 15 July 1937, p. 98.

2167. Burdick, Usher L. "This Congress Should Pass Equal Rights
Amendment." ER, 15 July 1937, p. 104.

2168. "The March of Women." ER, 1 August 1937, p. 106.

2169. "Business and Professional Women for Equal Rights." ER,
1 August 1937, pp. 110-11, 112.

2170. "Do Women Desire More Proof?" ER, 15 August 1937, p. 114.

2171. "Now Is the Opportune Time." ER, 15 August 1937, p. 114.

2172. "Threatened with Freedom." ER, 1 September 1937, p. 122.

2173. "Women Take Stock." ER, 1 September 1937, p. 122.

2174. "Support for Equal Rights Comes from Maryland Clubs." ER, 1 September 1937, p. 128.

2175. "The Immediate Task." ER, 15 September 1937, p. 130.

2176. Hughs, Sarah. "The Equal Rights Amendment!" ER, 15 September 1937, p. 136.

2177. "Government Workers Council to Remain Active." ER, 1 October 1937, p. 144.

2178. "Significance of Equal Rights Amendment." ER, 15 October 1937, pp. 149, 152.

2179. Moss, Margaret C. "Trade Unionist Wants Equal Rights Amendment." ER, 15 November 1937, pp. 164-65, 167.

2180. "Judiciary Committees." ER, 15 November 1937, p. 167.

2181. "Labor Organizations Endorse Amendment." ER, 1 December 1937, p. 176.

2182. Miller, Emma Guffey. "Constitutional Amendment the Solution." ER, 15 December 1937, pp. 179, 184.

2183. "Equal Rights Campaign." ER, 15 December 1937, p. 182.

2184. "Democracy for Women." ER, 1 January 1938, p. 186.

2185. "Brilliant Banquet Features National Conference." ER, 1 January 1938, pp. 187, 189.

2186. "Reunion Links Past and Present." ER, 1 January 1938, pp. 188-89.

2187. "A Fundamental Principle." ER, 1 February 1938, p. 202.

2188. "Trade Unionists for Equal Rights." ER, 1 February 1938, p. 207.

2189. "When They Understand It." ER, 15 February 1938, p. 210.

2190. "Senate Committee Defers Vote to Study Record." ER, 15 February 1938, pp. 211-13.

2191. "Emma Guffey Miller Addresses Senate Committee." ER, 15 February 1938, p. 214-16.

2192. "Equal Rights Amendment." ER, 1 March 1938, p. 218.

2193. "Mrs. Pell Asks Victory for Democracy." ER, 1 March 1938, p. 220.

2194. "Illinois Women for Amendment." ER, 1 March 1938, p. 222.

2195. "Guaranteeing Basic Rights." ER, 15 March 1938, p. 226.

2196. "Statement of Mary Murray before Senate Committee." ER, 15 March 1938, pp. 227, 231.

2197. "'Failure Is Impossible.'" ER, 1 April 1938, p. 234.

2198. "Equal Rights Amendment Now before Senate." ER, 1 April 1938, pp. 235-36.

2199. "Equal Rights Versus Prejudice." ER, 15 April 1938, p. 242.

2200. Sabin, Florence Rena. "Why I Favor the Equal Rights Amendment." ER, 15 April 1938, p. 244.

2201. "And in the Meantime." ER, 1 May 1938, p. 250.

2202. "Resolutions Urging Amendment." ER, 1 May 1938, p. 252.

2203. "What Every Woman Ought to Know." ER, 15 May 1938, pp. 260-61.

2204. "Labor Unions Endorse Amendment." ER, 15 May 1938, p. 263.

2205. "Study the Amendment." ER, 1 June 1938, p. 266.

2206. "Georgia B. and P. W. Unanimously Endorses Equal Rights." ER, 1 June 1938, p. 268.

2207. "Michigan Branch Holds Annual Meet." ER, 1 June 1938, p. 271.

2208. "The Amendment Moves." ER, 15 June 1938, p. 274.

2209. "New Jersey Bar Studies Status of Women." ER, 15 June 1938, pp. 275, 280.

2210. Avery, Edwina A. "Regional Meeting Held in Atlantic City." ER, 15 June 1938, p. 278.

2211. "Women on Every News Front: For Equal Rights for Women." ER, 1 July 1938, p. 287. Contains a letter by Frank Putnam from St. Louis Post-Dispatch.

2212. "Convention Important to Amendment Campaign." ER, 15 September 1938, pp. 323, 327.

2213. "The Next Step Forward." ER, 1 October 1938, pp. 332, 339.

2214. "Another National for Equal Rights." ER, 1 November 1938, p. 351.

2215. "National Council of Women Urges Its Members to Study Amendment." ER, 1 November 1938, p. 354.

2216. "Equality under Law." ER, 15 November 1938, p. 363.

2217. "Inter-Club Council of Buffalo Hears Equal Rights Discussion." ER, 15 November 1938, p. 368.

2218. "Safeguard Democracy!" ER, 1 December 1938, p. 370.

2219. "News from the Field." ER, 1 December 1938, p. 373.

2220. "On the Eve of a New Congress." ER, 15 December 1938, p. 380.

2221. "Equal Rights Plank." ER, 1 January 1939, p. 4.

2222. "Equal Rights Amendment Re-introduced in Congress." ER,
      15 January 1939, p. 11.

2223. "Gertrude Atherton for Amendment." ER, 15 January 1939, p. 14.

2224. "Time for Action." ER, 1 February 1939, p. 18.

2225. Whitney, Josepha. "I Appeal to Women for United Support." ER,
      1 February 1939, pp. 20, 24.

2226. "Help Pass the Amendment." ER, 1 February 1939, p. 23.

2227. Lutz, Alma. "A Feminist Thinks It Over." ER, 1 February 1939,
      p. 23.

2228. "Mrs. Pell Asks President to Receive Miss Anthony's Birthday
      Deputation." ER, 1 February 1939, p. 24.

2229. "An Authority Is Mistaken." ER, 15 February 1939, p. 26.

2230. Matthews, Burnita Shelton. "Glimpse of Laws Shows Need for Equal
      Rights." ER, 15 March 1939, p. 43.

2231. "Laura Berrien in New England." ER, 15 March 1939, p. 47.

2232. "An Ill Wind." ER, 1 April 1939, p. 50.

2233. "Amendment in Judiciary Committees." ER, 1 April 1939, p. 56.

2234. "Tell Them the Truth." ER, 15 April 1939, p. 58.

2235. "Georgia Branch of Party Reorganizes for Campaign." ER,
      15 April 1939, p. 61.

2236. Lutz, Alma. "A Feminist Thinks It Over: The Dead Letter of the
      Law." ER, 15 April 1939, p. 64.

2237. "History's Measure." ER, 1 May 1939, p. 66.

2238. "Impetus Given Equal Rights Amendment." ER, 1 May 1939, p. 67.

2239. Lutz, Alma. "A Feminist Thinks It Over: A Lesson in Contrasts."
      ER, 1 May 1939, p. 69.

2240. "From a Bryn Mawr Graduate." ER, 1 May 1939, p. 70.

2241. "Lucretia Mott Federation." ER, 1 May 1939, p. 72.

2242. "Finance Committee Raising Funds." ER, June 1939, p. 84.

2243. "An Amendment Will Stop the Leak." ER, July 1939, p. 87.

2244. "Business and Professional Women." ER, July 1939, p. 88.

2245. "North Carolina Alive to Equal Rights." ER, July 1939, p. 89.

2246. "The Equal Rights Amendment: Questions and Answers." ER, July 1939, pp. 90-92.

2247. "Equal Rights Amendment Support Strengthened." ER, August 1939, p. 99.

2248. "Equal Rights at the New York World's Fair." ER, September 1939, p. 109.

2249. Palmer, Mildred. "Booth at Fair Spreads Cause of Equal Rights." ER, October 1939, p. 115.

2250. "Equal Rights Amendment." ER, November 1939, p. 126.

2251. "School Women for Amendment." ER, November 1939, p. 128.

2252. "Says a Woman Executive." ER, November 1939, p. 132.

2253. "Now Is Time." ER, December 1939, p. 134.

2254. "Senator Burke to Speak." ER, December 1939, p. 137.

2255. "Truly a Democracy." ER, December 1939, p. 138.

2256. "Biennial Conference Held in Nation's Capitol." ER, January 1940, pp. 141, 143.

2257. "'As Simple Justice.'" ER, January 1940, p. 142.

2258. "National President Writes." ER, January 1940, p. 144.

2259. "Representative Norton for Amendment Resolution." ER, February 1940, p. 6.

2260. "You and the Amendment Campaign." ER, February 1940, p. 8.

2261. "Maryland Women Lobby Congress." ER, March 1940, p. 10.

2262. "Women, We Warn You!" ER, April 1940, p. 14.

2263. "Pearl Buck on the Equal Rights Amendment." ER, April 1940, p. 16.

2264. "Amendment on Study Program." ER, May 1940, p. 18.

2265. "The Parties and Women." ER, May 1940, p. 18.

2266. Brown, Helen Elizabeth. "Woman Lawyer Defends 'Equal Rights' Amendment." ER, May 1940, pp. 20-21.

2267. Lutz, Alma. "A Feminist Thinks It Over: Strange Reasoning." ER, May 1940, p. 24.

2268. Babcock, Caroline. "Challenge." ER, October 1940, p. 26.

2269. "The Democratic Convention." ER, October 1940, p. 27.

2270. "The Republican Convention." ER, October 1940, p. 27.

2271. "Two Years." ER, November 1940, p. 30.

2272. "Equal Rights Amendment Introduction." ER, January 1941, p. 41.

2273. Battle, George Gordon. "The Equal Rights Amendment." ER,
      February 1941, p. 10.

2274. "Resolution of Medical Women." ER, February 1941, p. 16.

2275. "Men Advocates." ER, March 1941, p. 18.

2276. "Men Advocates." ER, April 1941, p. 30.

2277. "Ohio Republicans Endorsed the Amendment." ER, May 1941, p. 43.

2278. "Unity." ER, May 1941, p. 48.

2279. Wolfe, Clara Snell. "American Association of University Women's
      Convention." ER, June 1941, p. 54.

2280. Lutz, Alma. "A Feminist Thinks It Over: That Word, Equality."
      ER, June 1941, p. 56.

2281. Moncure, Dorothy Ashby. "Relation of Fair Labor Standards Act
      to Status of Equal Rights Amendment." ER, July 1941, pp. 60, 63.

2282. Lutz, Alma. "A Feminist Thinks It Over: 'Of Men and Women.'"
      ER, July 1941, p. 64.

2283. "Sub-Judiciary Committees of Congress Make History." ER, August
      1941, p. 65.

2284. Capewell, Edna. "Business and Professional Women Re-endorse
      Equal Rights Amendment." ER, August 1941, p. 67.

2285. Murrell, Ethel Ernest. "Senate Joint Resolution No. 72." ER,
      August 1941, pp. 68-69.

2286. "Women, Arise!" ER, August 1941, p. 71.

2287. Lutz, Alma. "A Feminist Thinks It Over: There Is a Tide in the
      Affairs of Women." ER, September 1941, p. 80.

2288. "Ripples from the Radio." ER, October 1941, pp. 81, 86. (Emma
      Guffey Miller and Senator Guy M. Gillette)

2289. Mesta, Perle S. "Present Status." ER, December 1941, p. 102.

2290. "Another Man Advocate." ER, December 1941, p. 105.

2291. "Proclamation: Equal Rights Amendment." ER, December 1941, p. 109.

2292. Mesta, Perle S. "Present Status of the Amendment." ER,
   January 1942, p. 2.

2293. "Present Status." ER, March 1942, p. 18.

2294. "Katharine Hepburn Endorses Equal Rights Amendment." ER,
   April 1942, p. 25.

2295. "Status of Amendment." ER, April 1942, p. 26.

2296. "A School Man Speaks for Equal Rights." ER, April 1942, p. 30.

2297. Lutz, Alma. "A Feminist Thinks It Over: Women and the Bill of
   Rights." ER, April 1942, p. 32.

2298. Mesta, Perle. S. "Equal Rights Amendment Reported Favorably by
   Senate Judiciary Committee 9-3." ER, May 1942, p. 33.

2299. "Equal Rights and Security." ER, May 1942, p. 38.

2300. "California Equal Opportunity Committee, Pennsylvania Teachers
   and Ohio Nurses Endorse Equal Rights Amendment." ER, May 1942, p. 39.

2301. "Men Physicians of New York and New Jersey Support Women's Fight
   for Equal Rank and Pay in Medical Reserve Corps." ER, June 1942, p. 43.

2302. "Women's Declaration of Independence." ER, July 1942, p. 49.

2303. "National Education Association Endorses Equal Legal Status."
   ER, July 1942, p. 50.

2304. "Status of the Amendment in the House Judiciary Committee." ER,
   July 1942, pp. 50, 54.

2305. "National Education Association Endorses Equal Rights." ER,
   August 1942, p. 59.

2306. "Hope of the World." ER, August 1942, p. 60.

2307. "Women's Independence Day, July 19, 1942." ER, August 1942,
   pp. 60-61.

2308. "'Should the Equal Rights Amendment Be Adopted?'" ER,
   August 1942, p. 61.

2309. "Re-endorses the Equal Rights Amendment." ER, August 1942, p. 62.

2310. Brown, Helen Elizabeth. "Unequal Justice under Law." ER,
   August 1942, pp. 63-67. Rep. as a separate by National Woman's Party.

2311. "Advocates for the Equal Rights Amendment." ER, September 1942,
   p. 71.

2312. Crocker, Gertrude. "Democracy or Totalitarianism--Which?" ER,
   September 1942, pp. 72, 75.

2313. "Jeanette Marks Endorses the Equal Rights Amendment." ER, October 1942, p. 78.

2314. "Congressional Advocates of Equal Rights Amendment." ER, October 1942, p. 79.

2315. "Harrisburg (Pa.) Women Endorse Equal Rights." ER, November 1942, p. 86.

2316. "Equal Rights Amendment Advocates." ER, November 1942, p. 91.

2317. Phillips, Lena Madesin. "'Praise the Lord and Pass the Ammunition.'" ER, November 1942, p. 93.

2318. Wiley, Anna Kelton. "This Too Shall Pass!" ER, December 1942, p. 97.

2319. Rhoads, May Frank. "On Our Way." ER, December 1942, p. 99.

2320. Wiley, Anna Kelton. "Introduction of Equal Rights Amendment in House of Representatives, January 6, 1943." ER, January 1943, pp. 2, 7.

2321. "Address by Representative Louis Ludlow of Indiana at Lucretia Mott Sesquicentennial." ER, January 1943, p. 3.

2322. "Endorses the Equal Rights Amendment." ER, January 1943, p. 6.

2323. "Speeches Made on Woman's Day in the Senate." ER, February, 1943, pp. 11-13.

2324. Rhoads, May Frank. "Woman's Day in the Senate, January 21, 1943." ER, February 1943, pp. 9, 14.

2325. Babcock, Caroline Lexow. "Judiciary Committees in 78th Congress." ER, February 1943, p. 15.

2326. Lutz, Alma. "A Feminist Thinks It Over: The Equal Rights Amendment." ER, February 1943, p. 16.

2327. "Amendment Receives Unanimous Favorable Report from Both Judiciary Subcommittees of Congress." ER, March 1943, p. 17.

2328. Craig, Elisabeth May. "Mme. Chiang Kai-Shek Approves the Equal Rights Amendment." ER, March 1943, p. 18.

2329. "Women Members of Congress Endorse Amendment." ER, March 1943, p. 19.

2330. "News from the Branches." ER, March 1943, p. 24.

2331. "Debate on Equal Rights Amendment." ER, March 1943, p. 25.

2332. Matthews, Burnita Shelton. "The Freedom of Women." ER, March 1943, p. 26.

2333. "Appeal from Laura M. Berrien, Treasurer." ER, March 1943, p. 28.

2334. "Equal Rights Amendment on Senate Judiciary Committee Agenda for Monday, April 12, 1943." ER, April 1943, p. 29.

2335. Buck, Pearl. "'Equal Rights' by Amendment?" ER, April 1943, p. 32. Rep. from New York Times, 28 March 1943 and as a separate by the National Woman's Party.

2336. "Petition to Senate Judiciary Committee." ER, April 1943, p. 32.

2337. Greathouse, Rebekah Scandrett. "Argument for the Amendment." ER, April 1943, p. 33.

2338. "Letter to the Editor." ER, April 1943, p. 33. Contains a letter by Elizabeth B. Schlesinger to the New York Herald-Tribune, 19 February 1943.

2339. "News from the Branches: White Plains." ER, April 1943, p. 34.

2340. Lutz, Alma. "A Feminist Thinks It Over: The Protection of the Equal Rights Amendment." ER, April 1943, p. 36. Rep. as a separate by the National Woman's Party.

2341. Wiley, Anna Kelton. "Appeal for 'Equal Rights.'" ER, April 1943, p. 36.

2342. "The Amendment Advances in Senate." ER, May 1943, pp. 37, 44.

2343. Weed, Helena Hill. "History Repeats Itself." ER, May 1943, pp. 38, 43.

2344. "Strong Sentiment in the Senate for Equal Rights Amendment." ER, May 1943, p. 39.

2345. Rhoads, May Frank. "Formation of Women's Joint Legislative Committee for Equal Rights." ER, May 1943, p. 40.

2346. "Sentiment Growing for the Amendment." ER, May 1943, p. 40.

2347. "Married Women in Florida." ER, May 1943, p. 41.

2348. "Welcome, Mrs. Kitchelt." ER, May 1943, p. 41.

2349. "Rising Tide for Equal Rights Breaks on University Women." ER, May 1943, p. 42.

2350. Berrien, Laura M. "Treasurer's Appeal and Report." ER, May 1943, p. 43.

2351. Wiley, Anna Kelton. "Another Milestone Passed." ER, June 1943, pp. 45, 46, 50.

2352. "Distinguished Citizens Endorse the Amendment." ER, June 1943, p. 47.

2353. "Women's Press Club Endorses Amendment." ER, June 1943, p. 49.

2354. Norris, Katharine A. "We Ask Action by the House Judiciary."
ER, June 1943, p. 50.

2355. "More Tributes to Mothers' Day." ER, June 1943, p. 51.

2356. Lutz, Alma. "A Feminist Thinks It Over: To The Nation." ER,
June 1943, p. 52.

2357. "Board of Directors of the General Federation of Women's Clubs
Endorses the Equal Rights Amendment, July 1, 1943." ER, July/August
1943, p. 53.

2358. Wiley, Anna Kelton. "Directors of General Federation of Women's
Clubs Endorse Amendment." ER, July/August 1943, pp. 54, 57.

2359. "Distinguished Citizens Endorse the Amendment." ER, July/August
1943, p. 55.

2360. Bray, Cecil Norton. "The Equal Rights Amendment Moves Forward."
ER, July/August 1943, p. 56.

2361. Allen, Ella Vollstedt. "National Education Association and Equal
Rights." ER, July/August 1943, p. 57.

2362. "Rupert Hughes--Equal Rights Advocates." ER, September/October
1943, p. 61.

2363. "Radio Talk by Laura M. Berrien." ER, September/October 1943,
pp. 62, 71.

2364. "Los Angeles County Federation for Amendment." ER, September/
October 1943, p. 63.

2365. "New York Herald Tribue Comes Out Unqualifiedly for the Amendment."
ER, September/October 1943, p. 63. Contains editorial of 20 September
1943.

2366. "Pennsylvania Federation of Democratic Women." ER, September/
October 1943, p. 63.

2367. "Colorado Springs City Federation Resolution." ER, September/
October 1943, p. 64.

2368. "Connecticut State Federation." ER, September/October 1943, p. 64.

2369. Pollitzer, Anita. "Congress Opens." ER, September/October 1943,
p. 64.

2370. "Quota Club of Binghamton, N.Y." ER, September/October 1943, p. 64.

2371. "Resolution Adopted by Broome County (N.Y.) Republican Woman's Club,
June 3, 1943." ER, September/October 1943, p. 64.

2372. "Equal Rights Radio Committee." ER, September/October 1943, p. 66.

2373. Kitchelt, Florence L.C. "An Open Letter to Miss Anderson." ER,
September/October 1943, p. 67.

2374. "Radio Address of Florence Bayard Hilles." ER, September/
     October 1943, pp. 68, 71.

2375. "Seneca Falls Day." ER, September/October 1943, p. 69.

2376. "Roll Call of the States." ER, September/October 1943, pp. 70, 71.

2377. Downey, Mary Elizabeth. "Florence Bayard Hilles Library." ER,
     September/October 1943, p. 72.

2378. Lutz, Alma. "A Feminist Thinks It Over: The Equal Rights
     Amendment--A Requirement of Democratic Government." ER, September/
     October 1943, p. 72.

2379. Daniels, John. "The Equal Rights Amendment." ER, November
     1943, p. 75.

2380. "Editorials on House Judiciary Committee's Action." ER,
     November 1943, pp. 77-79. Contains: "A Matter of Justice," New
     York Herald Tribune, 7 October 1943; "Pigeonhole Decision," White
     Plains (New York) Reporter Dispatch, 12 October 1943; "Equal Rights
     Amendment Defeated But Not Killed," New Haven Connecticut Journal
     Courier, 11 October 1943; "Equal Rights for Women," Christian Science
     Monitor (Boston), 30 October 1943; Henry George III, "Government for
     the People--Equal Rights Amendment," Wilmington (Delaware) Sunday
     Morning Star, 26 September 1943; "Women's 'Equal Rights,'" Hartford
     (Connecticut) Courant, 8 October 1943; Frank Putnam, Houston Press,
     27 October 1943; "Bring It to Debate," Miami Herald, 9 November 1943.

2381. "Further Endorsements." ER, November 1943, p. 79.

2382. "National Council of Women Urges Amendment Be Submitted." ER,
     November 1943, p. 82.

2383. "Resolution of Indiana Society for Equal Rights Amendment." ER,
     November 1943, pp. 82, 83.

2384. "The Vote in House Judiciary Committee." ER, November 1943,
     pp. 74-75.

2385. "Deputation to Congress." ER, November 1943, pp. 81, 83.

2386. Boyer, Gaeta Wold. "Congressmen Act to Bring Amendment Out of
     Committee." ER, December 1943, pp. 85, 86.

2387. "More Endorsements." ER, December 1943, pp. 87, 90.

2388. "Virginia Women Approve Equal Rights Amendment." ER,
     December 1943, p. 87.

2389. "Elizabeth Cady Stanton Memorial Meeting." ER, December 1943,
     pp. 88-90. Contains addresses by Emma Guffey Miller and Chauncey W.
     Reed.

2390. "Charleston City (S.C.) Federation Endorses Amendment." ER,
     December 1943, p. 90.

2391. Manning, Alice L. "We Buckle on Our Armour and Return to the Fray." ER, December 1943, p. 91. Rep. from Independent Woman, November 1943.

2392. "Statement from Edwina Austin Avery." ER, December 1943, p. 91. Rep. from Think Tank (Atlanta, Georgia), 23 September 1943.

2393. "Resolution Sent to Women's Clubs." ER, December 1943, p. 92.

2394. Boyer, Gaeta Wold. "The Opening of the New Session, 78th Congress." ER, January 1944, pp. 1-2.

2395. "Letter to the President." ER, January 1944, p. 2.

2396. "Editorial Support and Nationwide Publicity for the Equal Rights Amendment." ER, January 1944, p. 3.

2397. "Southern California Rallies to Support of Amendment." ER, January/February 1944, pp. 4-6.

2398. "Analysis of Vote of October 5th, 1943, of the Judiciary Committee of the House of Representatives." ER, January 1944, p. 6.

2399. "Prominent Citizens Support the Amendment." ER, January 1944, pp. 8-9.

2400. Boyer, Gaeta Wold. "Report of Progress." ER, February 1944, pp. 13, 14, 15.

2401. "Governor Henry F. Schricker of Indiana Supports Equal Rights Amendment." ER, February 1944, p. 14.

2402. "Resolution." ER, February 1944, p. 15.

2403. Barney, Nora Stanton. "Answer to the Opposition." ER, February 1944, p. 16.

2404. Armstrong, Florence A. "An Appeal." ER, February 1944, p. 18.

2405. Hovnanian, Beryl R. "Report of Tennessee Branch, 1943." ER, February 1944, p. 18.

2406. "General Federation of Women's Clubs Poll on the Equal Rights Amendment." ER, February 1944, p. 19.

2407. "Rupert Hughes Champions Cause." ER, February 1944, p. 19.

2408. Wolfe, Clara Snell. "Report of Ohio Branch." ER, February 1944, p. 19.

2409. Boyer, Gaeta Wold. "Discharge Petition on Its Way." ER, March 1944, pp. 21, 22, 25.

2410. Miller, Emma Guffey, and Guyer, Alice D. "Letter Sent to All Members of Congress in Reply to Opposition of the C.I.O." ER, March 1944, p. 23.

2411. "Some Endorsements of the Amendment." <u>ER</u>, March 1944, p. 23.

2412. "Virginia Federation Sends Resolution to Congress." <u>ER</u>, March 1944, p. 24.

2413. Smith, Jane Norman. "Answer to the Opposition." <u>ER</u>, March 1944, p. 26.

2414. "Help the Equal Rights Amendment Now." <u>ER</u>, March 1944, p. 27.

2415. "The Third Governor to Endorse." <u>ER</u>, April 1944, p. 30.

2416. Carroll, Madalene. "The Equal Rights Amendment." <u>ER</u>, April 1944, p. 31.

2417. Eggleston, Marge. "Equal Rights for Women." <u>ER</u>, April 1944, p. 33.

2418. "Senator Joseph H. Ball of Minnesota, Former Senator Robert L. Owen of Oklahoma, Ada Davenport Kendall, and Dade County (Fla.) Federation Endorse the Amendment." <u>ER</u>, April 1944, p. 33.

2419. Kefauver, C. R. "Women Not Free?" <u>ER</u>, April 1944, p. 34. Contains a letter to <u>New York Herald Tribune</u>, 10 February 1944.

2420. Lutz, Alma. "A Feminist Thinks It Over: Women's Economic Freedom Is at Stake." <u>ER</u>, April 1944, p. 36.

2421. Wiley, Anna Kelton. "Clubs of the General Federation Endorse Equal Rights Amendment." <u>ER</u>, May 1944, pp. 37-38.

2422. "The Fourth Governor to Endorse." <u>ER</u>, May 1944, p. 38.

2423. "Endorsements and Announcements." <u>ER</u>, May 1944, p. 39.

2424. "Outlook for 1944." <u>ER</u>, May 1944, p. 39.

2425. "'Epic News' Approves Equal Rights Amendment." <u>ER</u>, May 1944, p. 41. Rep. from <u>Oakland (California) Epic News</u>.

2426. Lockwood, Marie T. "Is Catholic Church Opposed to Equal Rights Amendment?" <u>ER</u>, May 1944, p. 41. Contains a letter to <u>Sunday Visitor</u>, 11 April 1944.

2427. Wright, Alice Morgan. "Important Message to the American Association of University Women." <u>ER</u>, May 1944, p. 42.

2428. "Judge Harry O. Chamberlin, Indianapolis, Indiana, Speaks for Equal Rights Amendment." <u>ER</u>, June/July 1944, p. 45.

2429. "Delaware Democrats Endorse Equal Rights." <u>ER</u>, June/July 1944, p. 46.

2430. "Pennsylvania Democratic State Committee." <u>ER</u>, June/July 1944, p. 46.

2431. Ferguson, Mrs. Walter. "Women Fight Equal Rights!" <u>ER</u>, June/July 1944, p. 47. Rep. from <u>New York World-Telegram</u>.

2432. "Rupert Hughes Returns to Equal Rights Amendment." ER,
      June/July 1944, p. 47.

2433. "Statements by George Gordon Battle, Sheridan Downey, and Scott
      Nearing." ER, June/July 1944, p. 47.

2434. Greathouse, Rebekah S. "The Effect of Constitutional Equality
      on Working Women." ER, June/July 1944, p. 48. Contains an address
      in Washington, 23 January 1944, printed by American Economic Review,
      March 1944 Supplement.

2435. O'Neal, Cecelia. "Equal Rights Is a Basic Principle." ER,
      June/July 1944, p. 50.

2436. "N.E.A. Supports Equal Rights Amendment." ER, August/September
      1944, p. 54.

2437. "Women Seek Mrs. Roosevelt's Support for Equal Rights Amendment."
      ER, August/September 1944, p. 54.

2438. "Democratic Governors Endorse Amendment." ER, August/September
      1944, p. 55.

2439. "Republican Governors Endorse Equal Rights Amendment." ER,
      August/September 1944, p. 55.

2440. Putnam, Mabel Raef. "Equal Rights Victory at G.O.P. Convention."
      ER, August/September 1944, pp. 56-58.

2441. Pollitzer, Anita. "Democrats Adopt Equal Rights Amendment Plank."
      ER, August/September 1944, pp. 58-60.

2442. "'Signer's Day' in Campaign to Pass Amendment in this Session."
      ER, August/September 1944, p. 62.

2443. "Endorses Equal Rights Amendment: Essex County Democratic
      Committee." ER, August/September 1944, p. 64.

2444. "Coming in on a Pledge and a Prayer." ER, October/November 1944,
      pp. 65-67.

2445. Kitchelt, Florence L. C. "Answer to Editorial in the Washington
      Post." ER, October/November 1944, p. 67. (24 July 1944)

2446. Pollock, Channing. "Telegram." ER, October/November 1944, p. 67.

2447. "Senators Pledge Support of Amendment." ER, October/November
      1944, p. 68.

2448. Maloney, Mollie. "Opposition's Temporary Victory." ER,
      October/November 1944, p. 69.

2449. "A Press Comment: GOP Senators Blame CIO for Equal Rights Delay."
      ER, October/November 1944, p. 69. Rep. from Washington Daily News,
      16 September 1944.

2450. "Statements by Nora Stanton Barney and Margaret A. Hickey." ER, October/November 1944, p. 70. Contains Barney's letter of 4 September 1944 to New York Times and Herald Tribune.

2451. Wright, Alice Morgan. "League of Women Voters and the Amendment." ER, October/November 1944, pp. 71-72.

2452. "More Governors Endorse Amendment." ER, October/November 1944, p. 75.

2453. Downey, Mary Elizabeth. "Florence Bayard Hilles Library." ER, October/November 1944, p. 76.

2454. Gates, Gertrude. "Present Situation Regarding the Amendment." ER, December 1944, pp. 77-78.

2455. "More Endorsements." ER, December 1944, pp. 79, 82.

2456. "Asks Senate to Pass Amendment: Industrial Women's League for Equality." ER, December 1944, p. 83.

2457. Maloney, Mollie. "Trade Union Women Support Equal Rights Amendment." ER, December 1944, p. 83.

2458. "Arizona Women Back Equal Rights Amendment." ER, December 1944, p. 84.

2459. "Brilliant Meeting at 'Pickfair.'" ER, December 1944, p. 84.

2460. "Baltimore, Maryland." ER, December 1944, p. 88.

2461. Lutz, Alma. "A Feminist Thinks It Over: Equal Rights under Law Not a Swindle." ER, December 1944, p. 88.

2462. Babcock, Caroline Lexow. "Equal Rights Amendment Leads Concurrent Resolutions in the House in 79th Congress." ER, January/February 1945, p. 2.

2463. "Speech by Representative Louis Ludlow of Indiana." ER, January/February 1945, p. 3.

2464. Sherwin, Ella M. "How Amendment Affects Working Men and Women." ER, January/February 1945, p. 7.

2465. Chodorov, Frank. "Equal Rights for Women." ER, January/February 1945, p. 10. Rep. from Analysis 1 (January 1945): 4.

2466. Hine, Elizabeth M. "An Appeal to Business and Professional Women." ER, January/February 1945, p. 10.

2467. "Endorsements." ER, January/February 1945, p. 11.

2468. Lutz, Alma. "A Feminist Thinks It Over: A National Issue with International Influence." ER, January/February 1945, p. 12.

2469. Forbes, Elizabeth. "Amendment Introduced in Senate." ER, March/April 1945, p. 13.

2470. Babcock, Caroline Lexow. "Sub-Judiciary Committee of the House Considers Equal Rights Amendment." ER, March/April 1945, pp. 14, 20.

2471. "Speech of Judge John M. Robison on Equal Rights Amendment." ER, March/April 1945, pp. 15-17. (Speech to House, 29 January 1945)

2472. "Resolution Passes." ER, March/April 1945, p. 17.

2473. "Radio Talk by Rupert Hughes." ER, March/April 1945, pp. 18-19. (3 March 1945)

2474. Barney, Nora Stanton. "Why I Am for the Equal Rights Amendment." ER, March/April 1945, pp. 21-22.

2475. "Endorsements." ER, March/April 1945, p. 23.

2476. "Recent Broadcasts." ER, March/April 1945, pp. 24, 26.

2477. Conway, Edith Bartlett. "Massachusetts Branch." ER, March/April 1945, p. 25.

2478. Owen, Robert L. "From a Champion of the Cause." ER, March/April 1945, p. 25.

2479. Bray, Cecil Norton. "The Amendment in the Senate." ER, May/June 1945, pp. 30-31.

2480. Pollitzer, Anita. "House Committee Favorably Reports the Amendment." ER, May/June 1945, pp. 32-33.

2481. Marks, Jeannette. "The Story of the Brees Resolution (1943-45)." ER, May/June 1945, pp. 34-35.

2482. "James A. Farley and State of North Dakota Endorse Amendment." ER, May/June 1945, p. 35.

2483. Snyder, Ruth M. "Nora Stanton Barney Visits Los Angeles." ER, May/June 1945, p. 36.

2484. "Endorsements." ER, May/June 1945, p. 37.

2485. "Endorsement by Dr. Frank P. Graves." ER, May/June 1945, p. 38.

2486. Lutz, Alma. "A Feminist Thinks It Over: Biological Difference Not an Obstacle to Justice." ER, May/June 1945, p. 40.

2487. Walker, Amelia Himes. "House Judiciary Committee Reports Equal Rights Amendment First Time in History of Amendment." ER, July/August 1945, pp. 41, 50.

2488. "The Equal Rights Amendment in the Senate." ER, July/August 1945, p. 42.

2489. "A Proclamation by the Governor of the State of Utah." ER, July/August 1945, p. 47.

2490. "Governors Continue to Support the Equal Rights Amendment." ER,
July/August 1945, p. 48.

2491. "97th Anniversary Seneca Falls Convention." ER, July/August,
1945, p. 48.

2492. "Address of Ella M. Sherwin." ER, July/August 1945, pp. 49-50.

2493. Lutz, Alma. "A Feminist Thinks It Over: Retooling Our Thinking."
ER, July/August 1945, p. 52.

2494. Wiley, Anna Kelton. "President Reaffirms Stand on Amendment."
ER, September/October 1945, p. 53.

2495. Bray, Cecil Norton. "Cardinal Agrees with the President." ER,
September/October 1945, p. 54.

2496. Wood, Helena Hill. "Hearing on the Equal Rights Amendment before
the Sub-committee of the Senate Judiciary Committee--September 28,
1945." ER, September/October 1945, pp. 55-58.

2497. "Some Endorsements." ER, September/October 1945, p. 58.

2498. "Rupert Hughes on the Equal Rights Amendment." ER, September/
October 1945, p. 60. Contains a radio talk (Los Angeles) 18 August
1945.

2499. Pollitzer, Anita. "Campaigning during the Congressional Recess."
ER, September/October 1945, pp. 61-62.

2500. Lutz, Alma. "A Feminist Thinks It Over: Where Do We Go from
Here?" ER, September/October 1945, p. 64.

2501. "Important Endorsement." ER, November/December 1945, p. 66.

2502. "Senate Judiciary Sub-Committee Reports Amendment." ER,
November/December 1945, p. 66.

2503. Seydell, Mildred. "Thinking in Type." ER, November/December
1945, p. 69. Rep. from Think Tank (Atlanta, Georgia), 14 June 1945.

2504. "Hearing on Equal Rights Amendment before Sub-Committee of Senate
Judiciary Committee." ER, November/December 1945, p. 70.

2505. "Endorsements." ER, November/December 1945, p. 72.

2506. Lutz, Alma. "A Feminist Thinks It Over: Equal Pay Laws Need
Backing of Equal Rights Amendment." ER, November/December 1945, p. 72.

2507. "Senate Judiciary Committee Victory." ER, January/February 1946,
pp. 1, 3.

2508. Avery, Nina Horton. "Equal Rights Amendment." ER, January/
February 1946, p. 2.

2509. "Important Endorsements." ER, January/February 1946, p. 2.

2510. Miller, Emma Guffey. "Increasing Support for Amendment." ER,
      January/February 1946, p. 4.

2511. Wells, Agnes E. "Statement Presented to Judiciary Committee of
      the House of Representatives in Support of E. R. Amendment, March 31,
      1945." ER, January/February 1946, p. 5.

2512. "Campaign Notes." ER, January/February 1946, p. 6.

2513. "An Episcopal Bishop Endorses Amendment." ER, January/February
      1946, p. 6.

2514. "Resolutions." ER, January/February 1946, p. 7.

2515. Lutz, Alma. "A Feminist Thinks It Over: To Bring Us Up-to-Date."
      ER, January/February 1946, p. 8.

2516. "Timely Aid from Soroptimists." ER, January/February 1946, p. 8.

2517. "Yonkers Churches Endorse Amendment." ER, March/April 1946, p. 11.

2518. Pollitzer, Anita. "Equal Rights Amendment on Senate Calendar."
      ER, March/April 1946, pp. 13, 16.

2519. "Walter M. Nelson Champions Equal Rights Amendment." ER, March/
      April 1946, p. 15.

2520. "Campaign Notes." ER, March/April 1946, p. 16.

2521. "Judge Harold D. Achor Proclaims Constitutional Amendment Necessary
      for the Protection of Women." ER, March/April 1946, p. 17.

2522. "Resolutions." ER, March/April 1946, pp. 18-19.

2523. Lutz, Alma. "A Feminist Thinks It Over: Civil Liberties for
      Women." ER, March/April 1946, p. 20.

2524. Pollitzer, Anita. "What You Can Do for the Amendment." ER,
      May/June 1946, p. 22.

2525. "Resolution Voted at Biennial Meeting National Council of Women
      of the United States, May 8, 1946." ER, May/June 1946, p. 22.

2526. "Democrats and Republicans Reaffirm Support of Equal Rights
      Amendment through Chairmen of Their National Committees." ER,
      May/June 1946, p. 23.

2527. Norris, Katharine A. "Senate Majority Leader Barkley Receives
      Women's Joint Legislative Committee for Equal Rights." ER,
      May/June 1946, pp. 24, 30.

2528. Vanderburg, Helen. "Iowa Endorses Equality." ER, May/June 1946,
      p. 29.

2529. "'Before God and the Law We Are Equal.'" ER, May/June 1946, p. 32.

2530. "Equal Rights Amendment Reaches Vote in Senate, July 19, 1946."
ER, July/August 1946, pp. 33, 35, 40.

2531. "The Next Step." ER, July/August 1946, p. 34.

2532. "Unfinished Business." ER, July/August 1946, p. 34. Contains an
editorial from New York Herald Tribune, 20 July 1946.

2533. "Excerpts from the Debate." ER, July/August 1946, pp. 36-40.
Rep. from Congressional Record, 17-19 July 1946.

2534. "A Message to American Women on the Eve of the November Elections."
ER, September/October 1946, pp. 41-43.

2535. "The Amendment in the Election Campaign." ER, September/October
1946, pp. 44-45.

2536. "Biennial Convention of National Woman's Party." ER, September/
October 1946, p. 47.

2537. Oatman, Miriam. "Eastern Regional Conference." ER, September/
October 1946, p. 48.

2538. Wells, Agnes E. "Message from the Convention Chairman." ER,
January/February 1947, p. 2.

2539. "Equal Rights Amendment Introduced in 80th Congress." ER,
January/February 1947, pp. 4-5.

2541. "Equal Rights Amendment Introduced in Senate." ER, March/April
1947, pp. 9-10.

2542. "Congressional Digest Devoted to Equal Rights." ER, March/April
1947, p. 10.

2543. "North Dakota Backs Equal Rights Amendment." ER, March/April
1947, p. 10.

2544. "Anti-Equality Bill in Congress." ER, March/April 1947, p. 13.

2545. "Governor of Wisconsin Endorses Equal Rights Amendment." ER,
March/April 1947, p. 15.

2546. "Meetings at Alva Belmont House." ER, March/April 1947, p. 16.

2547. "Campaign in Congress Increases in Strength." ER, May/June
1947, p. 1.

2548. Bray, Cecil Norton. "Garden Party for Congressional Sponsors at
Alva Belmont House." ER, May/June 1947, p. 2.

2549. "Republicans, Opportunity Knocks!" ER, May/June 1947, p. 2.

2550. Ackley, Fannie. "'One's Right to . . . Equality Not Based on
Physical Strength.'" ER, May/June 1947, p. 3.

2551. Lemke, William. "Statement on Equal Rights Amendment." ER, May/June 1947, p. 3.

2552. "News from the States." ER, May/June 1947, pp. 7-8.

2553. "A Word to the Republicans." ER, July/August 1947, p. 10.

2554. Russell, Dorothy M. "Prospects for Victory in the 80th Congress." ER, July/August 1947, p. 11.

2555. "Congressional Sponsors of Equal Rights Amendment Honored at Garden Party." ER, July/August 1947, pp. 12-13.

2556. "National Chairman Visits Cities in Middle West." ER, July/August 1947, p. 15.

2557. "Appeal for Funds." ER, July/August 1947, p. 16.

2558. "News from the States." ER, July/August 1947, p. 16.

2559. "Another Governor Endorses the Equal Rights Amendment." ER, September/December 1947, p. 17.

2560. "A Call to Action on Equal Rights Amendment." ER, September/December 1947, pp. 17, 20.

2561. Walker, Amelia Himes. "Our Own Pilgrim's Progress." ER, September/December 1947, p. 19.

2562. "Endorses Amendment." ER, September/December 1947, p. 31.

2563. "New Jersey Branch." ER, September/December 1947, p. 31.

2564. "Organization of 147 Thousand Women Endorses Equal Rights Amendments." ER, September/December 1947, p. 31.

2565. Walker, Amelia Himes. "The Senate Sub-Committee Reports." ER, January/February 1948, p. 1.

2566. "Equal Rights Amendment on Agenda of Senate Judiciary Committee." ER, January/February 1948, p. 2.

2567. Vickers, Mrs. George T. "New Jersey Leads the Way toward Equality." ER, January/February 1948, p. 2.

2568. Pollitzer, Anita. "John Marshall . . . Friend and Leader." ER, January/February 1948, p. 3.

2569. "Governor of Hawaii Endorses." ER, January/February 1948, p. 10.

2570. "News from the States." ER, January/February 1948, p. 12.

2571. Pollitzer, Anita. "Victory in Senate Judiciary Committee." ER, March/April 1948, pp. 13, 15.

2572. _____. "Victory in House Judiciary Committee As We Go to Press." ER, March/April 1948, p. 14.

2573. "The Tide Is High." ER, March/April 1948, p. 14.

2574. Carter, Anne. "Hearing before Sub-Committee of the House Judiciary on the Equal Rights Amendment." ER, March/April 1948, pp. 18-19, 26.

2575. "Brief Memorandum . . . In Opposition to S. J. Res. 67, H. R. 2007." ER, March/April 1948, p. 20.

2576. "Help from Women's Clubs." ER, March/April 1948, p. 22.

2577. "Ending an Anachronism." ER, March/April 1948, p. 28. Rep. from New York Herald Tribune, 5 April 1948.

2578. "Of Historic Significance: Report to the United States Senate on the Equal Rights Amendment." ER, March/April 1948, p. 28.

2579. Pollitzer, Anita. "All Major Political Parties Declare for Equal Rights Amendment." ER, May/August 1948, pp. 29-30.

2580. Mizen, Mamie Sydney. "Statement to Members." ER, May/August 1948, pp. 31, 33.

2581. Brown, Helen Elizabeth. "By Their Fruits . . . " ER, May/August 1948, pp. 32-33.

2582. Lee, Berniece M. "The Democratic Party . . . Champion of Human Rights." ER, May/August 1948, pp. 34-35.

2583. Phillips, Lena Madesin. "Progressive Party Declares for the E. R. Amendment." ER, May/August 1948, p. 36.

2584. "Convention of National Woman's Party April 1, 2, 3, 1949-- Washington, D.C." ER, September/December 1948, p. 45.

2585. Miller, Emma Guffey. "Now Is the Hour for Victory." ER, September/December 1948, p. 47.

2586. Ratterman, Helena T. "Women Physicians and Equality for Women." ER, September/December 1948, p. 49.

2587. Sayre, Pearl M. "Join Hands for Victory Now." ER, September/ December 1948, p. 49.

2588. Swing, Betty Gram. "Women Will Never Forget the Year 1949." ER, January/March 1949, p. 3.

2589. Russell, Dorothy M. "The Opening of Congress: January 3, 1949." ER, January/March 1949, p. 5.

2590. Ogle, Dora G. "History of the Equal Rights Amendment." ER, January/March 1949, pp. 6-7, 18.

2591. Master, Anne S. "The American Women's Medical Association Learns That Women Are Not Persons." ER, January/February 1949, p. 7.

2592. "Congresswomen Support Equal Rights Amendment." ER, January/March 1949, pp. 12-13.

2593. "National Committeewomen of Both Parties Support the Equal Rights Amendment." ER, January/March 1949, p. 14.

2594. O'Riordan, Margaret M. "The Democratic Party Supports the Amendment." ER, January/March 1949, p. 14.

2595. Avery, Nina B. Horton. "Joint Legislative Committee for Equal Rights." ER, January/March 1949, p. 20.

2596. "California; Illinois; South Dakota." ER, January/March 1949, p. 23.

2597. Wells, Agnes E. "Greetings to Members of National Woman's Party." ER, April/June 1949, p. 25.

2598. "Needed: Word from the Grassroots." ER, April/June 1949, p. 26.

2599. "Highlights of the 1949 Convention of the National Woman's Party." ER, April/June 1949, p. 27.

2600. Mizen, Mamie Sydney. "Seneca Falls Day Meeting Urges President and Congress to Act on Equal Rights Amendment." ER, July/August 1949, p. 33.

2601. "Urgent." ER, July/August 1949, p. 34.

2602. Wells, Agnes E. "The Trip West." ER, July/August 1949, p. 35.

2603. Armstrong, Florence A. "Eight Points on the Equal Rights Amendment." ER, July/August 1949, p. 38. Rep. as a separate by the National Woman's Party.

2604. Gillette, Guy M. "Senate Advance of Equal Rights Amendment in First Session of Eighty-First Congress." ER, September/October 1949, pp. 41, 42.

2605. "It Pays to Organize." ER, September/October 1949, p. 42.

2606. "From the Airways." ER, September/October 1949, p. 44.

2607. "News from the States." ER, September/October 1949, p. 46.

2608. "The Epic You Will Write." ER, November/December 1949, p. 50.

2609. "The Honorable Katharine St. George of New York." ER, November/December 1949, p. 50.

2610. Pollitzer, Anita. "Position of the Amendment as Congress Reconvenes." ER, November/December 1949, p. 51.

2611. "News from the States." ER, November/December 1949, p. 53.

2612. Wells, Agnes E. "Senate Passes Equal Rights Amendment 63 to 19." ER, January/February 1950, p. 1.

2613. Paul, Alice. "Vote on Equal Rights Amendment." ER, January/February 1950, p. 2.

2614. "Stalwart Friends." ER, January/February 1950, p. 2.

2615. Pollitzer, Anita. "Equal Rights Amendment Passes the Senate with Contradictory Rider Attached." ER, January/February 1950, pp. 3-6.

2616. Wolfe, Clara Snell. "Ohio Labor Leaders Want Law for Men and Women." ER, January/February 1950, p. 7.

2617. "Democratic Women Call for Amendment in Original Form." ER, March/April 1950, p. 9.

2618. "House Action on Equal Rights Amendment Begins." ER, March/April 1950, p. 9.

2619. "Honorable Katharine St. George Launches Discharge Petition." ER, March/April 1950, pp. 11-12.

2620. "A Friend on Another Front." ER, March/April 1950, p. 12.

2621. "Important National Committeewomen of Both Parties Back Equal Rights Amendment." ER, March/April 1950, p. 13.

2622. "News from the States: New York City Committee." ER, March/April 1950, p. 15.

2623. "The Harvest of Our Sowing." ER, May/June 1950, p. 18.

2624. "News from the States." ER, May/June 1950, p. 19.

2625. "A Resolution." ER, May/June 1950, p. 22.

2626. "Status of the Amendment." ER, July/August 1950, p. 26.

2627. Mizen, Mamie Sydney. "Sponsors of Amendment Speakers at Observance of Seneca Falls Day." ER, July/August 1950, p. 28.

2628. "National Federation of Business and Professional Women's Clubs Endorses Equal Rights." ER, July/August 1950, p. 29.

2629. "Pledge Congressional Candidates for the Equal Rights Amendment without the Hayden Rider: Support Senate Friends Who Voted Equality Straight." ER, September/October 1950, p. 33.

2630. "New York State Conventions Re-Affirm Equal Rights Amendment Planks." ER, September/October 1950, p. 35.

2631. Walker, Amelia Himes. "The Little Caravan." ER, September/October 1950, p. 36.

2632. "Equal Rights Amendment Retains Old Friends, Finds New in Eighty-Second Congress." ER, November/December 1950, p. 41.

2633. "Equal Rights-in-Wonderland." ER, November/December 1950, p. 42.

2634. "Equal Rights Amendment Introduced in Eighty-Second Congress." ER, January/February 1951, p. 1.

2635. "On Its Way . . . " ER, January/February 1951, p. 2.

2636. "American Association of University Women in Los Angeles Support Equal Rights Amendment." ER, January/February 1951, p. 6.

2637. "News from the States." ER, January/February 1951, p. 7.

2638. Crawford, Mary Sinclair. "The AAUW Convention." ER, March/April 1951, p. 13.

2639. Dock, Lavina. "A Nurse's Appeal for the Equal Rights Amendment." ER, March/April 1951, p. 15.

2640. "Status of the Amendment." ER, May/June 1951, p. 18.

2641. "News from NWP Branches . . . " ER, May/June 1951, p. 22.

2642. "Connecticut AAUW Supports the Equal Rights Amendment." ER, July/August 1951, p. 30.

2643. "Santa Monica, California Committee." ER, September/October 1951, p. 36.

2644. "Senator Herbert O'Connor Speaks." ER, September/October 1951, p. 36.

2645. "A Staunch Supporter." ER, September/October 1951, p. 36.

2646. "Activities of National Chairman." ER, November/December 1951, p. 43.

2647. "Bar Unit to Study Equal Rights Law." ER, November/December 1951, p. 45.

2648. "Thank You Senator O'Conor." ER, November/December 1951, p. 46.

2649. Brown, Helen Elizabeth. "What Is the Constitution of the United States Worth to American Women?" ER, January/February 1952, p. 6. Originally an address before Lawyers Civic Association of Maryland, printed in the Baltimore Daily Recorder and as a separate by the National Woman's Party.

2650. "History of 'Questions and Answers' Pamphlets." ER, January/February 1952, p. 7.

2651. "The Honorable Katharine St. George." ER, March/April 1952, p. 9.

2652. Murrell, Ethel Ernest. "Full Citizenship for Women: An Equal Rights Amendment." ER, March/April 1952, p. 12; May/June 1952, p. 3; July/August 1952, p. 10. Rep. from American Bar Association Journal, January 1952.

2653. "The Equal Rights Amendment." ER, March/April 1952, p. 13. Contains an editorial from American Bar Association Journal, January 1952.

2654. "World Report on Woman's Rights: Los Angeles, California." ER, May/June 1952, p. 4.

2655. "Success in Chicago." ER, July/August 1952, p. 9.

2656. "The National Election of November 4." ER, November/December 1952, p. 2.

2657. "News from N.W.P. Branches . . . Wyoming." ER, September/October 1952, p. 2.

2658. "Judge Helen Elizabeth Brown, of the Baltimore Housing Court Said, in Her Talk before the American Society of Women Accountants on 'Women and the American Constitution.'" ER, November/December 1952, p. 4.

2659. Editorial. ER, January/February 1953, pp. 1, 2.

2660. "Excerpts from Speech of Honorable Katharine St. George on Sponsor Day." ER, March/April 1953, pp. 1, 4.

2661. "Over the Top." ER, March/April 1953, p. 2.

2662. "Sponsors of the Equal Rights Amendment." ER, March/April 1953, p. 3.

2663. "New York; Wisconsin." ER, May/June 1953, pp. 2, 3, 4.

2664. "U.S. Senate Passes Equal Rights Amendment with Nullifying Rider." ER, September/December 1953, pp. 1-4.

2665. "Now You Know." ER, September/December 1953, p. 2.

2666. "National Woman's Party Opposes the Hunt Amendment." ER, September/December 1953, p. 5.

2667. Paul, Alice. "Equality Not Superiority Nor Inferiority." ER, September/December 1953, p. 6.

2668. Lutz, Alma. "Is the Hayden Rider a Practical Joke on the Women of the United States." ER, September/December 1953, p. 7. Contains a letter to New York Herald Tribune, 28 July 1953.

2669. Brucker, Herbert. "A Wise Editor Speaks." ER, September/December 1953, p. 8. Contains "The Rocky Path of Equal Rights," Hartford (Connecticut) Courant, 21 July 1953.

2670. "Women Band Together for Equal Rights." ER, October 1954, pp. 1, 4.

2671. "To All American Women." ER, October 1954, p. 2.

2672. "Woman's Bureau Withdraws Opposition." ER, October 1954, pp. 4-5.

2673. Phillips, Lena Madesin. "Business and Professional Women Again Endorse." ER, October 1954, p. 5.

2674. "Women Lawyers Renew Endorsement." ER, October 1954, p. 5.

2675. "Women Ministers Endorse." ER, October 1954, p. 5.

2676. "A.F. of L. Will Study Equal Rights Amendment." ER, October 1954, p. 6.

2677. Brown, Helen Elizabeth. "Broken Pledges Damage Nation's Prestige." ER, October 1954, p. 7.

2678. "The Equal Rights Amendment." ER, November 1954, p. 2.

2679. Mizen, Mamie Sydney. "The Time of Harvest." ER, November 1954, p. 2.

2680. "Celler Has Opposed Granting Women Their Rights in the U. S. Constitution." ER, November 1954, p. 6.

2681. Griswold, Mabel E. "Endorsement by Women Ministers." ER, November 1954, p. 7.

2682. "Endorsement by Women Lawyers." ER, November 1954, pp. 7-8.

2683. "Endorsement by Women Accountants." ER, November 1954, p. 8.

D. Newsletters

[Most of the references in this group are from the Herstory microfilms. There are no subject indexes to Herstory at the present time, and this is the first bibliography to comprehensively treat it in terms of any topic. However, the organization of newsletters and other periodical material on Herstory leaves much to be desired. Consequently, an attempt is made here to be more methodical. A word about arrangement is therefore in order.

The newsletters are listed alphabetically by title and within each title, chronologically. When a newsletter does not have a distinctive title of its own, e.g., NOW Newsletter, its location or the name of the chapter is added. Other than this emendation, all titles are given exactly as they appear on the newsletter.

Titles change quite often and this can be confusing. Since all the newsletters of a single organization are listed in one place, despite a title change, certain steps have been taken for the sake of clarity. The primary title listing is the one from which the most references come; any other titles, either previous or subsequent to that one, are given in the heading and are, of course, maintained in the citation. In addition, a cross reference is made to such "secondary" titles where they might have appeared alphabetically (except in such cases where they would obviously appear right next to the primary one anyway).

The organization and its location is indicated in all the
headings where appropriate. No attempt has been made to cross-
reference newsletter and organization because the mixture of
city, county, and state titles provides little help to the
researcher looking for a newsletter from a specific place.
If one is well enough acquainted with a publication to know
the correct city, county, or state title, the chances are that
the newsletter title would also be known. Only in the case
of an actual newsletter title change has cross-referencing been
deemed helpful. The index lists NOW entries by chapter title.

While not generally of high-quality writing or scholarship,
these newsletters can be helpful to someone interested in the
history of ERA passage and ratification on a local level.]

ACLU Newsletter (American Civil Liberties Union, New York)

2684. "Equal Rights Amendment Approved by Legislature." ACLU Newsletter,
    17 November 1972. (WL)

Action N.O.W. (North Orange County N.O.W., Fullerton, California;
    formerly N.O.W. News and Orange County N.O.W. Newsletter)

2685. "Equal Rights Amendment." N.O.W. News, June 1970, p. [2].
    (H, R19)

2686. "Support the Equal Rights Amendment." N.O.W. News, [September
    1970], pp. 1-2. (H, R19)

2687. "Equal Rights Amendment." Orange County N.O.W. Newsletter, July
    1971, p. 3. (H, R19)

2688. "Equal Rights for Women Crippled by Wiggin's Rider." Orange
    County N.O.W. Newsletter, August 1971, p. [8-10]. (H, R19)

2689. "The Hanging of Charles Wiggins." Orange County N.O.W. Newsletter,
    September 1971, pp. 2-3. (H, R19)

2690. "Equal Rights Amendment." Orange County N.O.W. Newsletter,
    December 1971, p. 4. (HU, S1, R10)

2691. Schwartz, Joanne. "The ERA and Alimony and Child Support Laws."
    Action N.O.W., April 1972, p. 7. (HU, S1, R10)

2692. "Status of Equal Rights Amendment." Action N.O.W., May 1972,
    pp. 6-7. (HU, S1, R10)

2693. "American Bar Association--House of Delegates Resolution--February
    8, 1972." Action N.O.W., June 1972, p. 6. (HU, S1, R10)

2694. "Equal Rights Amendment." Action N.O.W., June 1972, p. 7. (WL;
    HU, S1, R10)

2695. "Latest News on the ERA." Action N.O.W., July 1972, p. 6. (HU,
    S1, R10)

2696. Voss, Deb. "Legislative Workshop." Action N.O.W., July 1972, p. 4.
(WL; HU, S1, R10)

2697. "Legislation." Action N.O.W., July 1972, p. 6. (WL; HU, S1, R10)

2698. "ERA." Action N.O.W., November 1972, p. 6. (HU, S1, R10)

2699. "In the Law." Action N.O.W., December 1972, p. 3. (WL; HU, S1,
R10)

2700. Thomas, Helen Barrios. "The ERA Is Dying . . . " Action N.O.W.,
February 1973, p. 9. (HU, S1, R10)

2701. "Have Women Achieved Equality? You Decide." Action N.O.W. 4,
no. 2 (February [1973]), p. 10. (WL; HU, S1, R10)

2702. "E.R.A." Action N.O.W., April 1974, p. 2. (HU, S2, R4)

Action NOW (Snohomish County N.O.W., Seattle, Washington)

2703. "Supports ERA." Action NOW, October 1971, p. 1. (HU, S1, R11)

2704. "ERA Passes." Action NOW, 16 February 1972, pp. 1-2. (HU, S1, R11)

2705. "Statement on the ERA." Action NOW, 16 March 1972, p. 5. (HU,
S1, R11)

2706. "ERA Meeting." Action NOW, 11 June 1972, p. 1. (HU, S1, R11)

2707. Fitzgerald-Hansen, Colleen. "Why an Equal Rights Amendment?"
Action NOW, 11 June 1972, pp. 1, 3. Submitted to Everett Herald for
17 June 1972 guest editorial. (HU, S1, R11)

2708. "Kick Off for ERA Campaign." Action NOW, 11 June 1972, pp. 2, 3.
(HU, S1, R11)

2709. Koontz, Elizabeth D. "Poor Women and the Equal Rights Amendment."
Action NOW, 14 August 1972, p. 3. (WL; HU, S1, R12)

2710. "Labor News." Action NOW, 14 August 1972, p. 4. (WL; HU, S1, R12)

2711. "ERA Moneymakers NOW Available." Action NOW, 14 August 1972, p. 5.
(HU, S1, R12)

2712. Oak. "The ERA--The Time Is Here to Work Hard for It!!" Action
NOW, 13 September 1972, p. 5. (HU, S1, R12)

2713. Temcov, Joanne. "Union Labor News." Action NOW, 13 September
1972, p. 6. (HU, S1, R12)

2714. Swanson, Jan. "Vote Yes on November 7!!--The ERA Campaign."
Action NOW, 12 October 1972, p. 3. (HU, S1, R12)

2715. Clausen, Win. "Past Action: ERA Blues." Action NOW, 15 November
1972, pp. 1,4, 5. (HU, S1, R12)

2716. Fitzgerald-Hansen, Colleen. "Status of the Equal Rights Amendment."
Action NOW, 12 February 1973, pp. 1, 3. (HU, S1, R12)

2717. "Sexist-Biased Reporting." Action NOW, 12 February 1973, p. 3.
(HU, S1, R12)

2718. Fitzgerald-Hansen, Colleen. "Equality Wins 29-19." Action NOW,
10 April 1973, p. 1. (HU, S1, R12)

2719. Fraser, Karen. "Status of Equal Rights Amendment Nationally."
Action NOW, 10 April 1973, p. 1. (HU, S1, R12)

2720. "ERA--Five to Go." Action NOW, May 1974, p. 7. (HU, S2, R5)

Act NOW (Chicago N.O.W., Illinois)

2721. "Equal Rights Amendment NOW" and "National Action on Child Care
and Equal Rights Amendment." Act NOW, 15 April 1969, p. 1. (H, R17)

2722. "Senate Victory on ERA Predictable." Act NOW, 14 August 1969,
p. 5. (H, R17)

2723. "NOW Urges Vote on Equal Rights Amendment." Act NOW, 14 November
1969, p. [4]. (H, R17)

2724. "Equal Rights Amendment." Act NOW, 16 April 1970, p. 5. (H, R17)

2725. "ERA." Act NOW, 13 July 1970, p. [4]. (H, R17)

2726. "ERA . . . Pass/Fail." Act NOW, 12 October 1970, p. 1. (H, R17)

2728. "ERA--S. J. 61 in '70." Act NOW, 16 November 1970, p. 1. (H, R17)

2729. "Deceptive Vote on ERA?" Act NOW, 16 November 1970, p. [6].
(H, R17)

2730. "Equal Rights Amendment." Act NOW, 13 March 1971, p. [6]. (H,
R17)

2731. "ERA Report." Act NOW, June 1971, p. [4]. (H, R17)

2732. "ERA Report." Act NOW, July 1971, p. [6]. (H, R17)

2733. "ERA Report." Act NOW, August 1971, p. [5]. (H, R17)

2734. Horowitz, JoAnn Rose. "ERA Report." Act NOW, October 1971, p. 4.
(HU, S1, R8)

2735. _____. "Equal Rights Amendment." Act NOW, December 1971,
p. 1. (HU, S1, R8)

2736. "Bloody Marys for the Equal Rights Amendment." Act NOW, February
1973, p. 1. (HU, S1, R8)

2737. Untitled. Act NOW, March 1973, pp. 1-2. (HU, S1, R8)

2738. "ERA News." Act NOW, April 1973, p. [4]. (HU, S1, R8)

2739. "Equal Rights Amendment--A Defeat and a Victory." Act NOW, May
1973, p. [6]. (HU, S1, R8)

2740. "ERA Fundraising Photographs Still Available." Act NOW, June
1973, p. [6]. (HU, S1, R8)

2741. "ERA." Act NOW, August 1973, p. 5. (HU, S2, R3)

2742. "Who's against Women's Equality? 1776-1973." Act NOW, October
1973, pp. 1, 7. (HU, S2, R3)

2743. "ERA Committee." Act NOW, October 1973, p. 9. (HU, S2, R3)

Akamai Sister (Hawaii Women's Liberation, Honolulu)

2744. "Women's ERA Is Stalled by Congress." Akamai Sister, July 1970,
p. 3. (H, R13)

2745. "Woman as Nigger." Akamai Sister, August 1970, p. 1. (H, Add)

ALA/SRRT Task Force Status of Women in Librarianship Newsletter
(American Library Association Social Responsibilities Round Table,
Chapel Hill, North Carolina)

2746. "Equal Rights Amendment." ALA/SRRT Task Force Status of Women in
Librarianship Newsletter, August 1970, pp. 4-5. (H, R13)

2747. "Equal Rights Amendment." ALA/SRRT Task Force Status of Women
in Librarianship Newsletter, November 1970, p. 3. (H, R13)

Albuquerque NOW Newsletter (New Mexico): See La Voz de la Mujer

Alert (Federation of Organizations for Professional Women, Washington,
D.C.)

2748. "Equal Rights Amendment." Alert, Fall 1973, p. 6. (H3, R1)

2749. "Current Status of ERA." Alert, Spring 1974, pp. 1-2. (WL;
H3, R1)

Alert (Women's Legislative Review, Middletown, Connecticut)

2750. "Lawyer Probes ERA Defeat in Connecticut Legislature" and "Whither
the ERA . . . and Why?" Alert, [November] 1972, p. 2. (H2, S1, R1)

2751. "Who Needs the Equal Rights Amendment?" Alert, [November] 1972,
p. 3. (H2, S1, R1)

2752. "Women and the ERA." Alert, February 1973, pp. 1-4 (entire issue).
(H2, S1, R1)

2753. "Can a State Rescind Ratification of the ERA? Noted Lawyer Says
'No.'" Alert, June 1973, p. [2]. (H2, S1, R1)

2754. "It's Not Just Money, Honey."   _Alert_, June 1973, p. [3].
(H2, S1, R1)

2755. "Women's Coalition to Focus on State ERA." _Alert_, December/
January 1973/74, p. 1. (H2, S2, R1)

2756. "Schaffer Discusses ERA." _Alert_, March 1974, p. 2.   (H2, S2, R1)

2757. "CSW Commissioner against ERA." _Alert_, May 1974, p. 3.
(H2, S2, R1)

Alliance Link (Downers Grove, Illinois): See _Link_

American Association of University Women News (California Division)

2758. "ERA Affair Is Planned." _American Association of University
Women News_, January 1972, p. 3. (H2, S1, R2)

2759. "ERA Needs AAUW Support." _American Association of University
Women News_, January 1972, p. 4. (H2, S1, R2)

2760. Mahnke, Kit. "CSD Members Active in ERA Project." _American
Association of University Women News_, January 1976, p. 1.

American Negro Woman (Cleveland, Ohio)

2761. "The Equal Rights Amendment." _American Negro Woman_, March 1974,
p. 1. (H3, R1)

And Ain't I a Woman? (Seattle Women's Liberation, Washington)

2762. "WL--S on ERA." _And Ain't I a Woman?_ 1, no. 4. [November 1970],
p. 4. (H, R13)

". . . & Nothing Less" (St. Louis N.O.W., Missouri; formerly _St. Louis
NOW Newsletter_)

2763. "Ratification of the ERA in Missouri." _St. Louis NOW Newsletter_,
[May 1972], p. [2]. (HU, S1, R11)

2764. "Equal Rights Amendment Ratification Committee." _St. Louis NOW
Newsletter_, October 1972, p. [2]. (HU, S1, R11)

2765. "ERA." _St. Louis NOW Newsletter_, December 1972, p. [3]. (HU, S1,
R11)

2766. Sedey, Mary Anne. "ERA Ratification Committee." _St. Louis NOW
Newsletter_, April 1973, p. [4]. (HU, S1, R11)

2767. "Blood for ERA Successful." _St. Louis NOW Newsletter_, May 1973,
p. 1. (HU, S1, R11)

2768. Krauska, Pat. "Blood and Breakfast for ERA." _St. Louis NOW
Newsletter_, May 1973, p. 5. (HU, S1, R11)

2769. "Research Your Rep." _". . . & Nothing Less_," July 1973, pp. 1, 2.
(HU, S2, R5)

2770. "400 March on August 25." "<u>. . . & Nothing Less</u>," September 1973,
   p. 1. (HU, S2, R5)

2771. McCuskey, Sharon. "ERA Task Force Report." "<u>. . . & Nothing Less</u>,"
   February 1974, p. 5. (HU, S2, R5)

2772. _____. "ERA Task Force Report." "<u>. . . & Nothing Less</u>,"
   March 1974, p. 5. (HU, S2, R5)

2773. _____. "ERA Task Force Report." "<u>. . . & Nothing Less</u>,"
   April 1974, p. 4. (HU, S2, R5)

2774. _____. "ERA Task Force Report." "<u>. . . & Nothing Less</u>,"
   May 1974, p. 6. (HU, S2, R5)

2775. "ERA Task Force Report." "<u>. . . & Nothing Less</u>," June 1974, p. 6.
   (HU, S2, R5)

<u>Androgyny</u> (N.O.W., Sparks, Nevada)

2776. "The ERA Center." <u>Androgyny</u>, January 1974, p. 6.
   (H3, R3)

<u>Ann Arbor NOW Newsletter</u> (Michigan)

2777. "ERA Alert." <u>Ann Arbor NOW Newsletter</u>, May 1974, p. 2. (H3, R2)

<u>Anne Arundel N.O.W. News</u> (N.O.W., Annapolis, Maryland)

2778. "The Equal Rights Amendment--What Will It Do to Us?" <u>Anne Arundel
   County N.O.W.</u>, September 1972, pp. 3-4. (H2, S1, R9)

2779. "The Equal Rights Amendment to the Maryland Constitution." <u>Anne
   Arundel N.O.W. News</u>, October 1972, pp. 1-2. (H2, S1, R9)

2780. "Women Give Their Blood for the ERA." <u>Anne Arundel N.O.W. News</u>,
   January 1973, p. 1. (H2, S1, R9)

2781. "ERA." <u>Anne Arundel N.O.W. News</u>, 8 March 1974, p. 2. (H2, S2, R6)

<u>anNOWncements</u> (Midland N.O.W., Michigan)

2782. "ERA." <u>anNOWncements</u>, January 1974, p. 6. (H2, S2, R7)

<u>Applecart</u> (Central Savannah River Area N.O.W., Augusta, Georgia)

2783. "Last Minute Flash on the ERA!" <u>Applecart</u>, March 1973, p. 6.
   (H2, S1, R9)

2784. "Equal Rights Amendment." <u>Applecart</u>, May 1973, p. 2. (H2, S1, R9)

2785. "Action Committee on the ERA." <u>Applecart</u>, October 1973, p. [2].
   (H2, S2, R6)

2786. "E.R.A. News." <u>Applecart</u>, February 1974, p. 1. (H2, S2, R6)

2787. "Club Opposes ERA." Applecart, February 1974, p. 3. (H2, S2, R6)

2788. "E.R.A. News." Applecart, [March (?) 1974], pp. 1-2. (H2, S2, R6)

2789. "ERA Issues." Applecart, [March (?) 1974], p. [3]. (H2, S2, R6)

2790. "Women's Concerns in 1974." Applecart, [March (?) 1974], p. [5].
(H2, S2, R6)

Arizona Women's Political Caucus (Phoenix)

2791. "The Equal Rights Amendment--What It Means to You!" Arizona
Women's Political Caucus, May 1972, p. [4]. (H2, S1, R12)

2792. "The Equal Rights Amendment." Arizona Women's Political Caucus,
September 1972, p. [7]. (H2, S1, R12)

2793. "Letter from the Editor." Arizona Women's Political Caucus,
November 1972, pp. 1, [5]. (H2, S1, R12)

2794. "Thoughts from a Feminist . . . " Arizona Women's Political
Caucus, November 1972, p. [8]. (WL; H2, S1, R12)

2795. "AWPC Asks Support: Equal Rights Amendment." Arizona Women's
Political Caucus, January 1973, pp. [1-3]. (H2, S1, R12)

2796. "Equal Rights" and "Influential Legislators." Arizona Women's
Political Caucus, March 1973, p. 1. (H2, S1, R12)

2797. "Progress of the ERA in the Arizona Legislature." Arizona Women's
Political Caucus, March 1973, p. 2. (H2, S1, R12)

2798. "We Are Coming Back." Arizona Women's Political Caucus, July 1973,
pp. 1-2.   (H2, S2, R9)

2799. "Arizona Legislature Has Yet to Vote on ERA. Arizona Women's
Political Caucus, April 1974, p. [2]. (H2, S2, R9)

Around and About NOW (Great Falls N.O.W., Montana)

2800. "ERA I.Q." Around and About NOW, November 1973, p. 3. (H3, R3)

2801. "Missoula Editorial." Around and About NOW, December 1973, p. 3.
(H3, R3)

2802. "ERA and Facts: Why the Equal Rights Amendment?" Around and
About NOW, December 1973, pp. 5-6. (H3, R3)

2803. Hewitt, Gloria. "ERA Ratified." Around and About NOW, January
1974, pp. 2-3. (H3, R3)

Association of American Colleges Project on the Status and Education of
Women (Washington, D.C.)

2804. "How the Equal Rights Amendment to the Constitution Affects
Educational Institutions." Association of American Colleges Project on
the Status and Education of Women, June 1972, p. 1. (H2, S1, R1)

As We See It NOW (Detroit N.O.W., Michigan; formerly Michigan NOW
 Newsletter)

2805. Aries. "Equal Rights Amendment." Michigan NOW Newsletter,
 September 1970, pp. 1-3. (H, R18)

2806. _____. "Equal Rights Amendment." Michigan NOW Newsletter,
 October 1970, pp. 1-2. (H, R18)

2807. Calvin, Bonnie. "Equal Rights Amendment--Deliberately Weakened!"
 Michigan NOW Newsletter, November 1970, pp. 1-2. (H, R18)

2808. Rugenstein, Lisa. "Equal Rights Amendment Coalition with Labor
 Formed." Michigan NOW Newsletter, December 1970, pp. [5-6]. (H, R18)

2809. Horowitz, JoAnn. "Equal Rights Amendment." As We See It NOW,
 May/June 1971, p. 9. (H, R18)

2810. "Lobby and Legislation Workshop." As We See It NOW, October 1971,
 p. 4. (HU, S1, R9)

2811. "Equal Rights Amendment Soon in House!!!" As We See It NOW,
 October 1971, p. 10. (HU, S1, R9)

2812. "ERA in Mich. House." As We See It NOW, March 1972, p. 2.
 (HU, S1, R9)

2813. Smith, Mary Jo. "ERA." As We See It NOW, May 1972, p. 6.
 (HU, S1, R9)

2814. "ERA Triumphs in Michigan." As We See It NOW, June 1972, p. 3.
 (HU, S1, R9)

2815. "Ratification of the ERA in Michigan Is History Now, But the
 Voting Records Are Not to Be Forgotten." As We See It NOW, July 1972,
 p. 4. (WL; HU, S1, R9)

2816. "ERA Blood Money." As We See It NOW, February/March 1973, p. 4.
 (HU, S1, R9)

2817. Alpern, Harriet. "Myths vs Facts." As We See It NOW, November/
 December 1973, p. 7. (HU, S2, R3)

Berkeley NOW Newsletter (California)

2818. "A Brief History of Two Constitutional Amendments: Suffrage and
 Equal Rights." Berkeley NOW Newsletter, 22 August 1970, p. [2].
 (H, R17)

2819. "Equal Rights Amendment Threatened?" Berkeley NOW Newsletter,
 19 September 1970, pp. 8-9. (H, R17) Rep. from entry #3826.

2820. Witter, Jean. "The ERA: There's Still Hope!" Berkeley NOW
 Newsletter, November 1970, p. 12. (H, R17)

2821. "The E.R.A. Again." Berkeley NOW Newsletter, March 1971, p. 10.
 (H, R17)

2822. "The Equal Rights Amendment." _Berkeley NOW Newsletter_, April 1971,
      p. 9. (H, R17)

2823. "ERA Needs Your Help!" _Berkeley NOW Newsletter_, June 1971, p. 10.
      (H, R17)

2824. Hernandez, Aileen. "E.R.A." _Berkeley NOW Newsletter_, July 1971,
      p. 7. (H, R17)

2825. "Congress Recesses without Action on E.R.A." _Berkeley NOW
      Newsletter_, August 1971, p. 7. (H, R17)

2826. "We Have Come a Long Way, Sisters! (But Not Far Enough!)."
      Berkeley NOW Newsletter, July 1972, p. 1. (WL; HU, S1, R7)

2827. "Unfinished Business: ERA Recall Mills." _Berkeley NOW Newsletter_,
      July 1972, p. 3. (WL; HU, S1, R7)

2828. "ERA." _Berkeley NOW Newsletter_, August 1972, p. 5. (HU, S1, R7)

2829. "Troika Confronts Mills." _Berkeley NOW Newsletter_, September 1972,
      p. 2. (HU, S1, R7)

2830. "Blood for the E.R.A." _Berkeley NOW Newsletter_, January 1973, p. 4.
      (HU, S1, R7)

2831. "ERA in Big Trouble." _Berkeley NOW Newsletter_, February 1973,
      p. 1. (HU, S1, R7)

2832. "ERA Will Not Be Ratified in 1973." _Berkeley NOW Newsletter_,
      May 1973, p. 4. (WL; HU, S1, R8)

Boston NOW Newsletter (N.O.W., Massachusetts)

2833. "The Equal Rights Amendment." _Boston NOW Newsletter_, April 1970,
      p. 3. (H, Add)

2834. "The Saga of the Equal Rights Amendment." _Boston NOW Newsletter_,
      June 1970, pp. 6-8. (H, Add)

2835. "A Walk for Equality." _Boston NOW Newsletter_, September 1970, p. 3.
      (H, Add)

Boulder NOW (N.O.W., Colorado)

2836. "Colorado Equal Rights Amendment." _Boulder NOW_, August 1972, p. 3.
      (H2, S1, R9)

Breakthrough (Interstate Association of Commissions on the Status of
      Women, Washington, D.C.)

2837. _Breakthrough_, February 1973, passim.

Bridge (Unitarian Universalist Women's Federation, Boston, Massachusetts;
      formerly _Unitarian Universalist Women's Federation Newsletter_;
      newsletter becomes _SpeakOut_; _Bridge_ becomes a journal)

2838. "Action Needed on Equal Rights Amendment." <u>Unitarian Universalist Women's Federation Newsletter</u>, [March 1971], p. [2]. (H, R22)

2839. "On the Equal Rights Amendment." <u>Bridge</u>, September/October 1971, p. 7. (HU, S1, R15)

2840. "Equal Rights Amendment." <u>Bridge</u>, March 1972, p. [2]. (HU, S1, R15)

2841. "Equal Rights Amendment Passed; State Action Needed." <u>Bridge</u>, May/June 1972, p. 5. (HU, S1, R15)

2842. "Has Your State Ratified the Equal Rights Amendment?" <u>Bridge</u>, September/October 1972, p. 7. (HU, S1, R15)

2843. "Help Needed on Equal Rights Amendment." <u>SpeakOut</u>, 1 March 1973, p. 3. (HU, S1, R15)

<u>Broadside</u> (Houston N.O.W., Texas)

2844. "Here We Go Again . . . ERA--Washington, ELRA--Austin." <u>Broadside</u>, March 1971, pp. 5-6. (H, R18)

2845. "Legislature Passes ELRA." <u>Broadside</u>, May 1971, p. 7. (H, R18)

<u>Brooklyn NOW Newsletter</u> (N.O.W., New York)

2846. "What Is Emmanuel Celler to You?" <u>Brooklyn NOW Newsletter</u>, [1971], p. 4. (H, R17; H, Add)

2847. "Equal Rights Amendment: Victory in the House! On to the Senate!" <u>Brooklyn NOW Newsletter</u>, October 1971 (?), p. 9. (HU, S1, R8)

<u>California NOW Newsletter</u> (Los Angeles)

2848. "E.R.A. Funds" and "38 State Ratification Needed for the E.R.A." <u>California NOW Newsletter</u>, May 1973, pp. 1, 2. (H2, S1, R9)

<u>Call to Action</u>: See <u>Jacksonville Women's Movement</u> (N.O.W., Florida)

<u>Capitol Alert</u> (Sacramento N.O.W. Legislative Committee, California)

2849. "Equal Rights Amendment." <u>Capitol Alert</u>, 10 May 1971, p. 1. (H, R19)

2850. "Equal Rights Amendment." <u>Capitol Alert</u>, 23 June 1971, p. 1. (H, R19)

2851. "Equal Rights Amendment." <u>Capitol Alert</u>, 2 August 1971, p. 2. (H, R19)

2852. "ERA Passes House." <u>Capitol Alert</u>, 30 October 1971, p. 2. (HU, S1, R2)

2853. "The ERA Needs Support." <u>Capitol Alert</u>, 23 November 1971, p. 1. (HU, S1, R2)

2854. "Nixon and the ERA." Capitol Alert, 20 December 1971, p. 2.
(HU, S1, R2)

2855. "ERA Has Been Amended." Capitol Alert, 21 January 1972, p. 1.
(HU, S1, R2)

2856. "State Equal Rights Amendment Introduced." Capitol Alert,
21 February 1972, p. 1. (HU, S1, R2)

2857. "51 Lawmakers Agree to Co-Author State ERA." Capitol Alert,
17 March 1972, p. 1. (HU, S1, R2)

2858. "Floor Vote Scheduled for Federal ERA." Capitol Alert,
17 March 1972, p. 3. (HU, S1, R2)

2859. "Congress Passes Equal Rights Amendment--Ratification by California
Expected in April." Capitol Alert, 31 March 1972, p. 1. (HU, S1, R2)

2860. "Assembly Committee OKs ERA Ratification--Sends Resolution to
Floor for Vote." Capitol Alert, 18 April 1972, pp. 1-2. (HU, S1, R2)

2861. "Equal Rights Ratification Stalled in Senate." Capitol Alert,
30 April 1972, pp. 1-2. (HU, S1, R2)

2862. "Mills Calls for Plebiscite on ERA Ratification." Capitol Alert,
16 May 1972, p. 1. (HU, S1, R2)

2863. "ERA Ratification Effectively Halted by Mills." Capitol Alert,
5 June 1972, p. 1. (HU, S1, R2)

2864. "'Day of Dissent' for E.R.A." Capitol Alert, 19 June 1972, p. 1.
(HU, S1, R2)

2865. "E.R.A. Opponent Given Award." Capitol Alert, 19 June 1972, p. 3.
(HU, S1, R2)

2866. "ERA Supporters Launch Recall Drive against Senator Mills" and
"11 Senators Have Signed Karabian's Letter on ERA." Capitol Alert,
5 July 1972, p. 1.

2867. "Recorded E.R.A. Debate Available." Capitol Alert, 5 July 1972,
p. 4.

2868. "Attempted Removal of E.R.A. Resolution from Committee Fails."
Capitol Alert, 24 July 1972, p. 1. (WL; HU, S1, R2)

2869. "Mills' Response to Recall Effort." Capitol Alert, 24 July 1972,
p. 2. (WL; HU, S1, R2)

2870. "Poll of Senators on ERA Made Public." Capitol Alert, 10 August
1972, p. 1. (HU, S1, R2)

2871. "Mills Recall Petitions Begin Circulating." Capitol Alert,
10 August 1972, pp. 1-2. (HU, S1, R2)

2872. "Mills Reverses Stand on Equal Rights Amendment." Capitol Alert,
      8 September 1972, p. 1.   (WL; HU, S1, R2)   Rep. in entry #3329.

2873. "The AFL-CIO and the Equal Rights Amendment: A Continuing
      Propaganda Campaign." Capitol Alert, 4 October 1972, pp. 1, 4.
      (HU, S1, R2) Rep. in entry #3761.

2874. "Mills Will Still Vote against E.R.A." Capitol Alert, 4 October
      1972, p. 2.   (WL; HU, S1, R2)

2875. "Further Attempts to Block E.R.A. Ratification." Capitol Alert,
      3 November 1972, p. 1.   (HU, S1, R2)

2876. "California is 22nd State to Ratify the E.R.A.--But It Took 8
      Months!!!" Capitol Alert, 22 November 1972, p. 1.   (HU, S1, R2)

2877. "Status of ERA Ratification Nationwide." Capitol Alert,
      22 November 1972, pp. 1-2.   (HU, S1, R2)

2878. "AB 1710 Passed by Senate . . . AFL-CIO Condemns E.R.A.
      Ratification." Captiol Alert, 22 November 1972, p. 2.   (HU, S1, R2)

2879. "Assembly Leadership Kills Proposal for E.R.A. Conformance
      Committee" and "Last Developments on E.R.A. Ratification for 1972--
      Nationwide." Capitol Alert, 21 December 1972, p. 2.   (HU, S1, R2)

2880. "Anti-E.R.A. Coalitions Form across U.S." and "Emergency ERA
      Blood Money Action February 5th." Capitol Alert, 20 January 1973, p. 1.
      (WL; HU, S1, R2)

2881. "Four More States Ratify Rights Amendment." Capitol Alert,
      12 February 1973, p. 1.   (HU, S1, R2)

2882. "ERA Ratification Status Nationwide." Capitol Alert, 6 March
      1973, p. 2.   (HU, S1, R2)

2883. "Griffiths Introduces Resolution for ERA-related Study."
      Capitol Alert, 6 March 1973, p. 5.   (HU, S1, R2)

2884. "Controversy over ERA Recission." Capitol Alert, 24 March 1973,
      p. 1.   (WL; HU, S1, R2)

2885. "E.R.A. Will Not Be Ratified in 1973." Capitol Alert, 20 April
      1973, p. 1.   (HU, S1, R2)

2886. "E.R.A. Recission Attempt Fails." Capitol Alert, 31 May 1973,
      p. 3.   (HU, S1, R2)

2887. "Alabama is 13th State to Reject E.R.A." Capitol Alert,
      19 June 1973, p. 2.   (HU, S1, R2)

2888. "Assembly Approves 'ERA Conformance' Vehicle." Capitol Alert,
      10 July 1973, p. 3.   (HU, S2, R1)

2889. "E.R.A. Bracelets Available." Capitol Alert, 10 October 1973,
      p. 5.   (HU, S2, R1)

2890. "State Bar Forms ERA Conformance Committee." Capitol Alert,
16 November 1973, p. 3.

2891. "E.R.A.--Only Five States to Go." Capitol Alert, 25 February
1974, p. 1.   (HU, S2, R1)   Rep. in entry #1107.

2892. "Wakefield Proposes ERA Referendum." Capitol Alert, 25 February
1974, p. 2.   (HU, S2, R1)

2893. "Update of National ERA Status" and "Women's Commission Receives
National Funding." Capitol Alert, 25 March 1974, p. 2.   (HU, S2, R1)

Caucus for Women in Statistics Newsletter (Philadelphia, Pennsylvania)

2894. "The Equal Rights Amendment: An Impossible Dream?" Caucus for
Women in Statistics Newsletter, March 1973, p. 1.   (H2, S1, R2)

CCLC Legislative Newsletter

2895. Waller, Carleen. "The Shame of Tennessee . . . Rescinding the
Equal Rights Amendment." CCLC Legislative Newsletter, May 1974,
pp. 5-6.

2896. "Senate Rescinds ERA." CCLC Legislative Newsletter, 25 March
1974, p. [1].

CCSW Newsletter (California Commission on the Status of Women, Sacramento)

2897. "ERA Conformance." CCSW Newsletter, July 1973, p. 2.   (H3, R1)

2898. "Rockefeller Foundation Makes Quarter-Million Dollar Grant to
Commission." CCSW Newsletter, March 1974, p. 1.   (H3, R1)

2899. "ERA Ratifications Increase." CCSW Newsletter, March 1974, p. 4.
(H3, R1)

2900. "Anti-ERA." CCSW Newsletter, April 1974, p. 4.   (H3, R1)

2901. "ERA Project." CCSW Newsletter, June 1974, p. 6.

2902. "The ERA and You." CCSW Newsletter, August 1974, p. 3.

2903. "President Ford Urges ERA Ratification." CCSW Newsletter,
September 1974, p. 2.

2904. "Meet Anita Miller." CCSW Newsletter, September 1974, p. 3.

2905. "The ERA and You." CCSW Newsletter, September 1974, p. 5.

2906. "The ERA and You." CCSW Newsletter, October 1974, p. 2.

2907. "ERA and You." CCSW Newsletter, November 1974, p. 4.

2908. "The ERA and You." CCSW Newsletter, December 1974, p. 4.

2909. "The ERA and You." CCSW Newsletter, January 1975, p. 4.

2910. "The ERA and You." CCSW Newsletter, February 1975, p. 4.

2911. "The ERA Prayer." CCSW Newsletter, February 1975, p. 6.

2912. "ERA and You." CCSW Newsletter, March 1975, p. 2.

2913. "ERA Reaches 34 Ratifications." CCSW Newsletter, March 1975, p. 3.

2914. "ERA and You." CCSW Newsletter, April 1975, p. 4.

2915. "Women Wake Up!" CCSW Newsletter, May 1975, p. 4.

2916. "ERA '76 Telethon." CCSW Newsletter, July 1975, p. 8.

2917. "ERA Update." CCSW Newsletter, August 1975, p. 4.

Center for Women's Studies and Services Newsletter (San Diego, California)

2918. "ERA: How Can Anything So Simple, Be So Complex?" Center for Women's Studies and Services Newsletter, December 1973, pp. 20-21. (HU, S2, R1)

Central Connecticut NOW Newsletter (N.O.W., Hartford)

2919. Untitled. Central Connecticut NOW Newsletter, May 1972, p. 1. (HU, S1, R8)

2920. "ERA, Where Are You??" Central Connecticut NOW Newsletter, (HU, S1, R8)

2921. "E.R.A. Hearing." Central Connecticut NOW Newsletter, February 1973, p. 4. (HU, S1, R8)

Central New Jersey NOW Newsletter (N.O.W., Princeton)

2922. "Plan on Equal Rights." Central New Jersey NOW Newsletter, March 1970, p. 6. (H, R19)

2923. "Equal Rights NOW." Central New Jersey NOW Newsletter, March 1970, p. 8. (Newsclip) (H, R19)

2924. "Equal Rights Amendment Rally." Central New Jersey NOW Newsletter, April 1970, p. 6. (H, R19)

2925. Amick, Donna. "Campaign for Women's Equal Rights Arrives in Trenton." Central New Jersey NOW Newsletter, May 1970, p. 7. Rep. in entry #5642.

2926. "Women Fill Hearing on Rights Equality." Central New Jersey NOW Newsletter, May 1970, p. 7. (H, R19) Rep. from entry #5159.

2927. "Congress Is Warned of Feminist Strike." Central New Jersey NOW Newsletter, May 1970, p. 7. (H, R19) Rep. from entry #5160.

2928. Cassell, Kay. "You Can Help! Write for Equal Rights." Central New Jersey NOW Newsletter, June 1970, p. 3. (H, R19)

2929. "Memo from Flora Crater, 13 August 1970." Central New Jersey NOW
     Newsletter, August 1970, p. 3.   (H, R19)

2930. "ACLU Comes Out in Support of E.R.A." Central New Jersey NOW
     Newsletter, December 1970, p. 2.   (H, R19)

2931. "Equal Rights Amendment Reintroduced." Central New Jersey NOW
     Newsletter, March 1971, pp. 1, 3.   (H, R19)

2932. "Thompson Promises to Support ERA." Central New Jersey NOW
     Newsletter, May 1971, p. 3.

2933. "ERA Passes First Hurdle." Central New Jersey NOW Newsletter,
     May 1971, p. 4.   (H, R19)

2934. Women United for the ERA. "Position Memorandum as to the Draft
     Equal Rights Amendment." Central New Jersey NOW Newsletter, July
     1971, pp. 6-7.   (H, R19)

2935. "Common Cause" and "House Debates Amendment to End Sex
     Discrimination." Central New Jersey NOW Newsletter, October 1971, p.
     12.   (HU, S1, R8)

2936. "Equal Rights Amendment Passed in the House of Representatives."
     Central New Jersey NOW Newsletter, November 1971, p. 13.   (HU, S1, R8)

2937. "ERA Passes House 354 to 23!!!" Central New Jersey NOW Newsletter,
     December 1971, p. 7.   (HU, S1, R8)

2938. "Abernethy with an E Is as Wrong as He Can Be." Central New Jersey
     NOW Newsletter, December 1971, pp. 7-8.   (HU, S1, R8)

2939. "Equal Rights Amendment and the Draft." Central New Jersey NOW
     Newsletter, December 1971, pp. 9-10.   (HU, S1, R8)

2940. "Equal Rights Amendment to the N.J. State Constitution." Central
     New Jersey NOW Newsletter, February 1972, pp. 3-4.   (HU, S1, R8)

2941. "The Equal Rights Amendment." Central New Jersey NOW Newsletter,
     February 1972, p. 5.   (HU, S1, R8)

2942. "Women's Rights 'Phony,' Says Mills." Central New Jersey NOW
     Newsletter, April 1972, p. 9.   (WL; HU, S1, R8)

2943. "ERA Implementation Committee." Central New Jersey NOW Newsletter,
     May 1972, p. 6.   (HU, S1, R8)

2944. "ERA Tally: Legislation." Central New Jersey NOW Newsletter,
     June 1972, p. 11.   (WL; HU, S1, R8)

2945. "Our National Priority: Equal Rights Amendment." Central New
     Jersey NOW Newsletter, February 1973, pp. 2-4.   (HU, S1, R8)

2946. "Rights Amendment Snagged in Maine Senate, 16-16." Central New
     Jersey NOW Newsletter, March 1973, p. 11.   (HU, S1, R8)

2947. "Women's Rights Amendment Wins Connecticut Ratification." Central New Jersey NOW Newsletter, April 1973, p. 10. (HU, S1, R8)

2948. "AFL-CIO Endorses ERA." Central New Jersey NOW Newsletter, November 1973, p. 8. (HU, S2, R3)

Central New York NOW Newsletter (New York State N.O.W., Liverpool)

2949. "ERA." Central New York NOW Newsletter, June 1973, p. 1. (HU, S1, R8)

Cincinnati NOW Newsletter (N.O.W., Ohio; becomes Cincinnati NOW News)

2950. "Legislative Committee." Cincinnati NOW Newsletter, 14 June 1972. (WL)

2951. "Latest on the E.R.A." Cincinnati NOW Newsletter, 19 June 1972, pp. [4-5]. (H2, S1, R9)

2952. "Legislative Committee." Cincinnati NOW Newsletter, 19 June 1972, p. [4]. (WL; H2, S1, R9)

2953. "Women's ERA Booth--Ohio State Fair" and "Ratification of ERA." Cincinnati NOW Newsletter, 20 July 1972, p. 3. (WL; H2, S1, R9)

2954. "Women's Day Celebration." Cincinnati NOW Newsletter, 17 August 1972, pp. 1-4. (H2, S1, R9)

2955. "Where Do You Stand as a Feminist?" Cincinnati NOW Newsletter, 19 September 1972, p. 1. (WL; H2, S1, R9)

2956. "NOW ERA Action" and "State Fair." Cincinnati NOW Newsletter, 19 September 1972, p. [6]. (H2, S1, R9)

2957. "Information Workshop on ERA." Cincinnati NOW Newsletter, 18 December 1972, p. 2. (H2, S1, R9)

2958. "Give Blood for the ERA!" Cincinnati NOW Newsletter, 17 January 1973, p. 1. (H2, S1, R9)

2959. "Latest on ERA." Cincinnati NOW Newsletter, February/March 1973, p. 1. (H2, S1, R9)

2960. "The ERA Is Not Dead Yet!" Cincinnati NOW Newsletter, 17 April 1973, pp. 1-2. (H2, S1, R9)

2961. "ERA Needs Your Help. We Must Not Be Over-Confident!" Cincinnati NOW News, January 1974, p. 3. (H2, S2, R6)

2962. "At Long, Long Last, the ERA Is Ratified in Ohio." Cincinnati NOW News, February 1974, pp. 1-2. (H2, S2, R6)

Civil Liberties (American Civil Liberties Union, New York City, N.Y.)

2963. "Union Supports Sex Amendment." Civil Liberties, December 1970. (WL)

Cleveland NOW Newsletter (N.O.W., Ohio; becomes Women Unite NOW)

2964. "Equal Rights Amendment." Cleveland NOW Newsletter, July 1971,
   p. 7. (H, R17)

2965. "The Equal Rights Amendment." Cleveland NOW Newsletter, May
   1972, p. 4. (HU, S1, R8)

2966. Tussey, Jean Y. "Equal Rights Amendment." Women Unite NOW,
   June/July 1972, p. 3. (HU, S1, R8)

2967. Carroll, Betty. "Committee Report: Legislation." Women Unite
   NOW, June/July 1972, p. 5. (WL; HU, S1, R8)

2968. "Ratification of E.R.A.--The Right to Be a Person!" Women
   Unite NOW, June/July 1972, p. 7. (WL; HU, S1, R8)

2969. "Gilligan Endorses Ratification of E.R.A." Women Unite NOW,
   August 1972, p. 8. (HU, S1, R8)

2970. Baker, Jayne. "Support Ratification of the Equal Rights
   Amendment." Women Unite NOW, January/February 1973, p. 5. (WL; HU,
   S1, R8)

2971. "ERA Coalition Formed." Women Unite NOW, April 1973, pp. 4-5.
   (WL; HU, S1, R8)

2972. "Save a Life and Give Your Blood for the ERA" and "A Special ERA
   Meeting." Women Unite NOW, April 1973, p. 1. (WL; HU, S1, R8)

2973. "ERA Coalition Formed." Women Unite NOW, May 1973, pp. 1-5.
   (HU, S1, R8)

2974. "The Equal Rights Amendment." Women Unite NOW, June 1973, pp. 2-3.
   (HU, S1, R8)

2975. "ERA Quotables." Women Unite NOW, June 1973, pp. 4, 6, 8.
   (HU, S1, R8)

2976. Johnson, Susan Mallula. "Rally for Ratification of ERA." Women
   Unite NOW, August 1973, pp. 1-2. (HU, S2, R3)

2977. _____. "ERA Opposition." Women Unite NOW, August 1973, p. 5.
   (HU, S2, R3)

2978. "ERA and Strange Bedfellows." Woman Unite NOW, [December 1973],
   p. 5. (HU, S2, R3)

2979. "ERA." Woman Unite NOW, January 1974, pp. 1-8. (Various articles).
   (HU, S2, R3)

2980. "Equality of Rights under the Law Shall Not Be Denied or Abridged
   by the United States or Any State on Account of Sex." Woman Unite NOW,
   February 1974, pp. 1-2. (HU, S2, R3)

2981. "Ohio Ratifies ERA." Woman Unite NOW, March 1974, pp. 1-2.
   (HU, S2, R3)

Coalition of St. Louis Women (Missouri)

2982. "International Women's Day" and "Vermont Royster in the Wall Street Journal." Coalition of St. Louis Women, Winter/Spring 1976.

Cold Day in August (Baltimore Women's Liberation, Maryland)

2983. "Equality of Rights under the Law Shall Not Be Abridged or Denied Because of Sex." A Cold Day in August, October [1972], pp. 5-6. (H2, S1, R3)

2984. "Equal Rights Amendment." A Cold Day in August, February [1973], p. 14. (WL; H2, S1, R3)

2985. "Repeal of ERA Approval." A Cold Day in August, April [1973], pp. 14-15. (H2, S1, R3)

2986. "Missouri Kills = Rights Amendment." A Cold Day in August, June [1973], p. 18. (H2, S1, R3)

Common Cause Report from Washington (D.C.)

2987. "Equal Rights Amendment." Common Cause Report from Washington, March 1972, pp. 1-4. Extra edition.

Common Sense (Women's Advisory Group, Portland, Oregon)

2988. Citizens' Advisory Council on the Status of Women. "The Equal Rights Amendment--What It Will and Won't Do." Common Sense, June 1973, pp. 4-7. (H2, S1, R3) Rep. from entry #372; also rep. in entries #306, 4074.

Connect (United Presbyterian Church in the U.S.A., New York, New York)

2989. Titles Unknown. Connect, January 1974, p. 6; February 1974, p. 4; August 1974, p. 2; January 1975, p. 6; February 1975, p. 5; March 1975, p. 6.

Continuing Currents (Continuing Education for Women, University of Hawaii)

2990. Saunders, Marion. "Women Unite to Celebrate ERA." Continuing Currents, March/April 1972, pp. 1-2. (H2, S1, R4)

2991. Gething, Judith R. "Does Hawaii Need an Equal Rights Amendment?" Continuing Currents, September 1972, pp. 3-4. (H2, S1, R4)

2992. "ERA Ratification: The Way It Stands State by State" and "ERA Supporters Swing into Action--Again!" Continuing Currents, September 1972, p. 5. (H2, S1, R4)

2993. Putman, Pat. "Equal Rights, Hawaii's Laws, and the Next Legislative Session." Continuing Currents, November/December 1972, pp. 4-6. (H2, S1, R4)

Contra Costa N.O.W. Newsletter (N.O.W., Walnut Creek, California)

2994. "Continue to Pummel Nejedley with Letters." Contra Costa N.O.W. Newsletter 1, no. 5 [July 1972], pp. 1-2. (H2, S1, R10)

2995. "E.R.A. Petition" and "E.R.A. Update." Contra Costa N.O.W. Newsletter, August 1972, p. 1. (WL; H2, S1, R10)

2996. "Equal Rights Amendment." Contra Costa N.O.W. Newsletter, August 1972, insert. (WL; H2, S1, R10)

2997. "The Equal Rights Amendment Confirms the Principle of Equal Rights under the Law for Men and Women and for Women by Requiring That They Be Treated as Individuals." Contra Costa N.O.W. Newsletter, August 1972, p. [4?]. (H2, S1, R10)

2998. "E.R.A. Update." Contra Costa N.O.W. Newsletter, September 1972, p. 1. (WL; H2, S1, R10)

2999. "ERA Still in Trouble in Eight States." Contra Costa N.O.W. Newsletter, March 1973, p. 3. (H2, S1, R10)

3000. Coordinating Council for the Equal Rights Amendment Newsletter (North Dakota Women's Coalition, Fargo; continuing coverage from 11 May 1974)

Cry Out (Roanoke Valley Women's Coalition, Virginia)

3001. Chan, Sandy. "The ERA and the Virginia Assembly, or Why Justice Wears a Blindfold." Cry Out, 7 March 1973, p. 2. (H2, S1, R4)

3002. McDiarmid, Dorothy S. "More about the ERA." Cry Out, 7 March 1973, p. 3. (LE) (H2, S1, R4)

3003. "Status of the ERA." Cry Out, 7 March 1973, p. 3. (H2, S1, R4)

CSW News (Commission on the Status of Women, Harrisburg, Pennsylvania; also includes press releases and CSW Report)

3004. Press Release. CSW News, 9 June [1972]. (H2, S1, R3)

3005. "Equal Rights Amendment." CSW News, July 1972, p. 1. (WL; H2, S1, R3)

3006. "Governor Proclaims August 26 Equal Rights Day: Calls on Senate to Pass ERA." CSW News, August 1972, p. 1. (H2, S1, R3)

3007. "Governor Shapp Declares Equal Rights Day--Urges Senate to Ratify ERA." CSW News, 17 August 1972. (Press Release) (H2, S1, R3)

3008. Press Release. CSW News, 21 September 1972. (H2, S1, R3)

3009. "Equal Rights Day." CSW Report, 21 August 1972. (H2, S1, R3)

3010. "Equal Rights Amendment Ratified." CSW News, September/October 1972, pp. 4-5. (H2, S1, R3)

3011. "Equal Rights Amendment." CSW News, April 1973, p. 5. (H2, S1, R3)

3012. Series of articles exploring the implications of the Pennsylvania State ERA. CSW Report, 14, 21, 28 May and 4 June 1973.

3013. Press Release. CSW News, 18 June [1973]. (H2, S1, R3)

3014. "Governor Shapp Announces Review of Existing Law under ERA." CSW News, August 1973, p. 1. (H2, S2, R2)

Dade County NOW Newsletter (N.O.W., Coconut Grove, Florida)

3015. "Call to Action!" Dade County NOW Newsletter, [August ?], p. [2]. (H, R17)

Daughters of Sarah (Peoples Christian Coalition, Chicago, Illinois)

3016. Gundry, Patricia. "The inERAnt Facts." Daughters of Sarah, September 1975, pp. 9-10.

Denver NOW Newsletter (N.O.W., Colorado)

3017. "Help Equality-for-Sexes Amendment." Denver NOW Newsletter, July 1971, p. 1. Includes excerpt from Denver Post. (H, R17)

3018. "Equal Rights Amendment." Denver NOW Newsletter, September 1971, p. 1. (H, R17)

3019. "ERA Forever." Denver NOW Newsletter, October 1971, p. 1. (HU, S1, R8)

3020. "Equal Rights Amendment Out of Committee!" and "Equality Debate Should End." Denver NOW Newsletter, April 1972, pp. 1, 2. (HU, S1, R8)

3021. "Constitutional Equality for Women." Denver NOW Newsletter, June 1972, p. 2. (HU, S1, R8)

3022. "Lack of Funds Limits Newsletter." Denver NOW Newsletter, September 1972, p. 1. (HU, S1, R8)

3023. "Women Give Blood for Equal Rights." Denver NOW Newsletter, February 1973, p. 1. (HU, S1, R8)

3024. "ERA--What's Happening." Denver NOW Newsletter, March 1973, p. 1. (HU, S1, R8)

3025. "Where Anti-ERA Funds Come From." Denver NOW Newsletter, March 1973, p. 3. (HU, S1, R8)

3026. "ERA Bracelets Available." Denver NOW Newsletter, February 1974, p. 1. (HU, S2, R3)

Do It NOW (Chicago, Illinois): See NOW Acts

Do It NOW (Madison N.O.W., Wisconsin)

3027. "Equal Rights Coalition--Status Report." Do It NOW, April 1973,
   p. 1. (H2, S1, R11)

Durham NOWletter (N.O.W., North Carolina)

3028. "ERA Coalition Formed." Durham NOWletter, [May 1974], p. [2].
   (H3, R3)

D.W.L. Newsletter (Dayton Women's Liberation, Ohio)

3029. "Why E.R.A." D.W.L Newsletter, March/April 1973, pp. 2-3.
   (HU, S1, R3)

3030. Rosenthal, Pam. "In the Name of Equality . . . Women Lose Rights."
   D.W.L. Newsletter, March/April 1973, pp. 4-5. (HU, S1, R3)

East Bay NOW Newsletter (N.O.W., California)

3031. "ERA Countdown." East Bay NOW Newsletter, March 1974, p. 2.
   (HU, S2, R4)

Eastern Massachusetts NOW Newsletter (N.O.W., Boston)

3032. "Women Unite to Work for E.R.A." Eastern Massachusetts NOW
   Newsletter, 15 April 1971, pp. 1, 5. (H, R18)

3033. "Mass. Congressmen Need Letters about Equal Rights Amendment."
   Eastern Massachusetts NOW Newsletter, 2 August 1971, p. 4. (H, R18)

3034. "Equal Rights Amendment Passes House--Senate Vote Will Be
   Delayed." Eastern Massachusetts NOW Newsletter, 18 October 1971, p. 1.
   (HU, S1, R9)

3035. "Brook and Kennedy Making Up Their Minds on Equal Rights
   Amendment." Eastern Massachusetts NOW Newsletter, 18 October 1971,
   p. 4. (HU, S1, R9)

3036. Hogan, Betsy. "The Advocates." Eastern Massachusetts NOW
   Newsletter, 14 January 1972, pp. 13-14. (HU, S1, R9)

3037. "Flaherty Supports State ERA"; "ERA Hearings Held at McAD"; and
   "Legislative." Eastern Massachusetts NOW Newsletter, 15 February
   1972, p. 8. (WL; HU, S1, R9)

3038. "Judiciary Committee Approves ERA." Eastern Massachusetts NOW
   Newsletter, 14 March 1972, pp. 1-2. (HU, S1, R9)

3039. "Kennedy Supports ERA--At Last!" Eastern Massachusetts NOW
   Newsletter, 14 March 1972, p. 2. (HU, S1, R9)

3040. Caplan, Pat. "State House Hearings." Eastern Massachusetts NOW
   Newsletter, 14 March 1972, pp. 2, 5. (HU, S1, R9)

3041. "ERA Passes Senate." Eastern Massachusetts NOW Newsletter,
   14 April 1972, pp. 1, 12. (WL; HU, S1, R9)

3042. "ERA Stalled in Massachusetts." Eastern Massachusetts NOW Newsletter, 15 May 1972, pp. 1, 7. (WL; HU, S1, R9)

3043. Wan, Julia. "Message from the President." Eastern Massachusetts NOW Newsletter, 15 May 1972, p. 2. (WL; HU, S1, R9)

3044. "California Is 22nd State to Ratify the Equal Rights Amendment." Eastern Massachusetts NOW Newsletter, 1 December 1972, p. 2. (HU, S1, R9)

3045. Ferber, Betty. "Trouble Ahead for the E.R.A.?" Eastern Massachusetts NOW Newsletter, 1 February 1973, pp. 7-8. (HU, S1, R9)

3046. "E.R.A. S.O.S." Eastern Massachusetts NOW Newsletter, 1 February 1973, p. 9. (HU, S1, R9)

3047. "State Equal Rights Amendment." Eastern Massachusetts NOW Newsletter, 1 February 1973, p. [29]. (HU, S1, R9)

3048. "$$$ ERA $$$." Eastern Massachusetts NOW Newsletter, 1 March 1973, p. 1. (HU, S1, R9)

3049. "April Is E.R.A. Month in Massachusetts." Eastern Massachusetts NOW Newsletter, 1 April 1973, p. 3. (HU, S1, R9)

3050. "The ERA in Maine." Eastern Massachusetts NOW Newsletter, 1 May 1973, p. 10. (HU, S1, R9)

3051. "Update on the ERA." Eastern Massachusetts NOW Newsletter, 1 May 1973, p. 16. (HU, S1, R9)

3052. "State Equal Rights Amendment--115313." Eastern Massachusetts NOW Newsletter, 1 June 1973, p. 15. (HU, S1, R9)

3053. Cunningham, Tom. "The ERA in Maine." Eastern Massachusetts NOW Newsletter, 1 November 1973, p. 4. (HU, S2, R4)

El Paso County N.O.W. Newsletter (N.O.W., Colorado Springs, Colorado)

3054. "ERA Meeting Opposition." El Paso County N.O.W. Newsletter, [April 1973], p. 2. (H2, S1, R10)

3055. Webb, Patricia Kueck. "Fed Up with Lib." El Paso County N.O.W. Newsletter, May 1973, p. 3. (H2, S1, R10)

3056. "ERA Still in Trouble." El Paso County N.O.W. Newsletter, June 1973, p. 9. (H2, S1, R10)

3057. E.R.A. Central Newsletter (Chicago, Illinois; continuing coverage from Spring 1972)

ERA Law Project (Ohio Attorney General's Office, Columbus)

3058. "ERA Task Force Submits Report on Change in Law." ERA Law Project, 31 December 1975, p. 3.

3059. ERA Missouri (Missouri E.R.A. Coalition, Jefferson City;
continuing coverage from December 1975)

3060. ERA Monitor (Equal Rights Amendment Project of the California
Commission on the Status of Women, Sacramento; bi-weekly coverage from
26 November 1975; now monthly Equal Rights Monitor, April 1976)

3061. ERA United Newsletter (Raleigh, North Carolina; continuing monthly
coverage from 21 April 1974 to 22 May 1975; not available to public)

3061a. ERA Update (Idaho ERA Task Force, Boise; continuing coverage from
9 January 1976)

3062. ERA--Yes (League of Women Voters of the United States, Washington,
D.C.; continuing coverage from December 1973 every 3 or 4 months;
not available to general public)

3063. ERA--Yes! (League of Women Voters of Georgia, Atlanta)

3064. ERA--Yes! (League of Women Voters of Indiana, Indianapolis)

Essecond Sex (North Shore N.O.W., Essex County, Rockport, Massachusetts)

3065. "Equal Rights Amendment." Essecondsex, November 1971, p. 5.
(HU, S1, R11)

3066. "Equal Rights Amendment." Essecondsex, March 1972, p. 6.
(HU, S1, R11)

3067. "Equal Rights Amendment." Essecondsex, May 1972, pp. 11-13.
(WL; HU, S1, R11)

3068. "ERA Passage in Doubt." Essecondsex, September 1972, pp. 2-4.
(HU, S1, R11)

Essex County NOW Newsletter (N.O.W., South Orange, New Jersey)

3069. "Equal Rights Amendment." Essex County NOW Newsletter, March
1972, p. [3]. (H2, S1, R10)

3070. "Equal Rights Amendment Passed the Senate on March 22nd."
Essex County NOW Newsletter, April 1972, p. 2. (H2, S1, R10)

3071. Untitled. Essex County NOW Newsletter, May 1972, p. 4. (WL;
H2, S1, R10)

3072. "ERA." Essex County NOW News, March 1973, p. 6. (H2, S1, R10)

3073. "ERA." Essex County NOW News, April 1973, p. 6. (H2, S1, R10)

3074. "ERA." Essex County NOW News, May 1973, p. 4. (H2, S1, R10)

Every Woman's Center Newsletter (Amherst, Massachusetts)

3075. "Equal Rights Amendment." Every Woman's Center Newsletter,
October 1973, p. 1. (H2, S2, R3)

Executive Woman (Sandra Brown Publishing Company, New York, New York)

3076. "ERA Strategies Are Soaring: 'Eight More in '74.'" Executive Woman, 15 December 1973, p. 4. (H3, R1)

Facts and Issues (League of Women Voters of Maryland, Baltimore)

3077. "The Maryland Experience: ERA." Facts and Issues, June 1974.

Fair Employment Report (Business Publishers, Inc., Silver Springs, Maryland)

3078. "Discrimination against Women Documented at Senate Hearings on Constitutional Amendment." Fair Employment Report, 11 May 1970, p. 57. (WL)

Female Liberation Newsletter (Boston, Massachusetts; later Cambridge)

3079. "Equal Rights." Female Liberation Newsletter, 1 November 1971, p. 5. (HU, S1, R4) Rep. from entry #5700a.

3080. "Equal Rights Amendment." Female Liberation Newsletter, 24 April 1972, p. [6]. (HU, S1, R4)

3081. "Now Pushes for Passage of the ERA." Female Liberation Newsletter, 19 June 1972, p. [3]. (HU, S1, R4)

3082. "N.O.W. Marches for E.R.A." Female Liberation Newsletter, 17 December 1973, p. 6. (HU, S2, R2)

Female Liberation Newsletter (Twin Cities Female Liberation, Minneapolis, Minnesota)

3083. Elizabeth, Ann. "Commentary: The Equal Rights Amendment." Female Liberation Newsletter, August/September [1970], pp. 16-17. (H, R15) Rep. in entry #1007.

Feminine Focus (Intercollegiate Association of Women Students, Lansing, Michigan)

3084. "Equal Rights Amendment Passes the House!" Feminine Focus, November 1971, p. 3. (HU, S1, R4)

3085. "Forthcoming Action on the Equal Rights Amendment." Feminine Focus, December/January 1971/72, pp. 1-2. (HU, S1, R4)

Feminist Party (San Francisco, California)

3086. Davall, Irene. "The Liberated Woman: ERA." Feminist Party, Fall 1973, p. [5]. (H3, R2)

F.E.W.'s News and Views (Federally Employed Women, New Port Richey, Florida)

3087. "Progress (?) on Equal Rights." F.E.W.'s News and Views, July 1970, pp. 2,5. (H, Add)

3088. "Equal Rights Amendment in Danger." F.E.W.'s News and Views, September 1970, p. [4]. (H, Add)

3089. "Equal Rights Amendment Reintroduced." F.E.W.'s News and Views, April 1971, p. 1. (H, Add)

3090. "Equal Rights--Hearing Reports Available." F.E.W.'s News and Views, April 1971, p. [2]. (H, Add)

3091. Fields, Daisy. "ERA Advances." F.E.W.'s News and Views, November 1971, p. 1. (HU, S1, R4)

3092. _____. "ERA Victory in Sight but Not Yet Won." F.E.W.'s News and Views, April 1972, p. [3]. (HU, S1, R4)

3093. "Drive for E.R.A. Ratification Begun." F.E.W.'s News and Views, June 1972, p. 2. (HU, S1, R4)

3094. Ransohoff, Pricilla B. "Let's Work for the E.R.A.!" F.E.W.'s News and Views, January 1973, p. 2. (HU, S1, R4)

3095. "The Equal Rights Amendment (ERA)--'Eight More in '74.'" F.E.W.'s News and Views, December 1973, p. 3. (HU, S2, R2)

3096. "ERA Progress" and "American Society for Public Administration Endorses the E.R.A." F.E.W.'s News and Views, February 1974, p. 2. (HU, S2, R2)

3097. Florida State '76-'77 Coalition Newsletter (Delray Beach; continuing coverage from August 1975)

Focus on Women (YWCA Women's Center, Orange, New Jersey)

3098. "The YWCA and the ERA." Focus on Women, November 1972, p. 3. (H2, S1, R5)

3099. "Keeping Up with the ERA." Focus on Women, April/May 1973, p. 1. (H2, S1, R5)

Fox Valley/Elgin NOW Newsletter (N.O.W., Illinois)

3100. "ERA." Fox Valley/Elgin NOW Newsletter, October 1973, p. 5. (H3, R3)

Fresno NOW Newsletter (N.O.W., California)

3101. "Give Blood for the E.R.A." Fresno NOW Newsletter, February 1973, p. [4]. (H2, S1, R10)

From NOW On (Montgomery N.O.W., Alabama)

3102. "ERA Conference." From NOW On, 28 November 1973, p. 4. (H3, R3)

3103. "Only 6 to Go." From NOW On, January 1974, p. 5. (H3, R3)

3104. "Alabama Citizens for ERA." From NOW On, January 1974, p. [7]. (H3, R3)

3105. "ACERA Conference." From NOW On, 14 February 1974, pp. 1, 3.
(H3, R3)

From NOW On (Montgomery County N.O.W., Rockville, Maryland)

3106. "Citizens' Coalition for Equal Rights Amendment." From NOW On,
September 1972, p. 5. (H2, S1, R11)

3107. "President's Message." From NOW On, March 1973, p. 1. (H2, S1,
R11)

3108. "Equal Rights Amendment." From NOW On, April 1973, p. 4.
(H2, S1, R11)

3109. "8 More in '74." From NOW On, December 1973, p. [5]. (H2, S2, R7)

Front Page (Bloomington Women's Liberation, Indiana)

3110. Steffens, Heidi. "Equal Rights Amendment." Front Page, 25 May
1970, p. 5. (H, R13) Rep. from entry #1453.

Genesis III (Philadelphia Task Force on Women in Religion, Pennsylvania)

3111. "Judaism and the E.R.A." Genesis, May/June 1972, p. 1.
(HU, S1, R5)

3112. "Lutheran Church in America Approves Consulting Committee on
Women, Asks Synods and Congregations to Work for ERA Ratification."
Genesis III, July/August 1972, p. 2. (WL)

3113. "ERAction." Genesis III, September/October 1973, p. [10].
(HU, S2, R2)

3114. "E.R.A." Genesis III, March/April 1974, p. 10. (HU, S2, R2)

Georgia Voter (League of Women Voters of Georgia, Atlanta)

3115. "ERA: Alive and Well Maybe Living in Georgia." Georgia Voter,
July/August 1973, pp. [1-2].

Greater Kansas City NOW Newsletter (Missouri): See Here and NOW

Greater Pittsburgh NOW Newsletter (Pennsylvania): See NOW Hear This!

The Hand That Rocks the Rock (Slippery Rock Women's Liberation,
Pennsylvania; formerly Lysistrata)

3116. "Call to Action." The Hand That Rocks the Rock, May 1972, p. 1.
(HU, S1, R5)

3117. Curry, Elizabeth. "The Equal Rights Amendment: The Parent of a
Son Comments." The Hand That Rocks the Rock, September 1972, pp. 4-5.
(HU, S1, R5)

3118. "Pennsylvania Becomes Twenty-First State to Pass the Equal Rights
Amendment to the United States Constitution." The Hand That Rocks
the Rock, October 1972, p. 6. (HU, S1, R5)

Harbor-South Bay NOW Newsletter (N.O.W., San Pedro, California)

3119. "Legislative Action." Harbor-South Bay NOW Newsletter, November
1972, p. 2. (H2, S1, R10)

3120. "California Is 22nd State to Ratify the E.R.A.--But It Took 8
Months!!!" Harbor-South Bay NOW Newsletter, December 1972, p. 1.
(H2, S1, R10)

3121. "Urgent--The E.R.A. Is Dying." Harbor-South Bay NOW Newsletter,
February 1973, p. 1. (H2, S1, R10)

Harrisburg Women's Rights Newsletter (Pennsylvania)

3122. Riznyk, Louise. "ERA in Trouble." Harrisburg Women's Rights
Newsletter, March 1973, p. [11]. (H2, S1, R5)

Here and NOW (Greater Kansas City N.O.W., Missouri; formerly Greater
Kansas City NOW Newsletter)

3123. "Equal Rights Amendment." Greater Kansas City NOW Newsletter,
[April 1971], p. 1. (H, R18)

3124. "Equal Rights Amendment Workshop." Greater Kansas NOW Newsletter,
[May 1971], pp. 2-3. (H, R18)

3125. Untitled. Here and NOW, April 1972, p. 1. (HU, S1, R9)

3126. "Ratification of the ERA in Missouri." Here and NOW, June 1972,
p. 1. (HU, S1, R9)

3127. Untitled. Here and NOW, October 1972, p. 3. (HU, S1, R9)

3128. "The Equal Rights Amendment." Here and NOW, January 1973, p. 1.
(HU, S1, R9)

3129. "ERA Hearing--Missouri Style." Here and NOW, February 1973,
pp. 2-3. (HU, S1, R9)

3130. "The Equal Rights Amendment Is Not Dead." Here and NOW, April
1973, pp. 1-2. (HU, S1, R9)

3131. "Blood Money for the ERA." Here and NOW, April 1973, p. 3.
(HU, S1, R9)

3132. "How to Succeed at Lobbying without Really Trying!" Here and
NOW, May 1973, pp. 1-2. (HU, S1, R9)

3133. "ERA--The Way They Voted." Here and NOW, May 1973, p. 5.
(HU, S1, R9)

3134. "Know the Opposition!" Here and NOW, July 1973, pp. 1-3.
(HU, S2, R4)

3135. "Autumn and the ERA." Here and NOW, October 1973, pp. 1-3.
(HU, S2, R4)

3136. "ERA Flash." Here and NOW, October 1973, p. 9. (HU, S2, R4)

3137. "The Legislators Speak . . . But Not for Us." Here and NOW,
January 1974, pp. 1-2. (HU, S2, R4)

3138. "ERA Briefing--Questions and Answers." Here and NOW, January
1974, pp. 2-3. (HU, S2, R4)

3139. "Missouri Hearing on ERA." Here and NOW, January 1974, pp. 4-5.
(HU, S2, R4)

3140. "The ERA and Older Women: No Age Limit to Equal Rights." Here
and NOW, March/April 1974, pp. 1-3. (HU, S2, R4)

3141. "Why Can't Missouri Be Counted on Equal Rights?" Here and NOW,
March/April 1974, p. [11]. Rep. from entry #5765. (HU, S2, R4)

Here and NOW (New Orleans N.O.W., Louisiana)

3142. "E.R.A." Here and NOW, [November 1972], p. [3]. (H2, S1, R11)

3143. "E.R.A." Here and NOW, [January 1973], p. 3. (H2, S1, R11)

3144. "ERA." Here and NOW, March 1973, p. 5. (H2, S1, R11)

3145. "E.R.A. Report." Here and NOW, April 1973, pp. 3-4. (H2, S1, R11)

3146. "Blood Money." Here and NOW, April 1973, p. 5. (H2, S1, R11)

3147. Parker, Mrs. John D. Letter Opposing ERA, 28 June 1973. New
Orleans NOW Newsletter, 10 August 1973, p. 2. (H2, S2, R7)

3148. Latimer, Clay. "ERA Report Coalition Organizing in New Orleans."
Here and NOW, October 1973, p. 8. (H2, S2, R7)

3149. "In Case You Didn't Know." Here and NOW, December 1973, pp. 1-3.
(H2, S2, R7)

3150. "Louisiana ERA Workshop." Here and NOW, [March 1974], pp. [5-6].
(H2, S2, R7)

3151. "The ERA." Here and NOW, April 1974, p. [7]. (H2, S2, R7)

3152. "ERA Luncheon Nets One Million $." Here and NOW, May 1974, p. 2.
(H2, S2, R7)

3153. "The ERA." Here and NOW, June 1974, pp. [11-12]. (H2, S2, R7)

Here and NOW (Santa Cruz N.O.W., California)

3154. "Equal Rights Amendment." Here and NOW, May 1972, p. 1.
(H2, S1, R12)

3155. "Equal Rights Amendment--The Continuing Saga." Here and NOW,
June 1972, p. 1. (WL; H2, S1, R12)

3156. "Questions and Answers about the Equal Rights Amendment." Here and NOW, July/August 1972, pp. 2-3. (WL; H2, S1, R12)

3157. "The Draft and the Equal Rights Amendment." Here and NOW, April 1973, p. [6]. (H2, S1, R12)

3158. "Second Anti-ERA Measure Proposed." Here and NOW, May 1974, p. 5. (H2, S2, R8)

Homefront (Institute for American Democracy, Washington, D.C.)

3159. "The Rightists Step In." Homefront, February 1973, pp. 5-8.

Human Equality (Ann Snyder Moser, Honolulu, Hawaii)

3160. "Equal Rights Amendment." Human Equality, 1 January 1972, p. 3. (H2, S1, R6)

3161. Women's Equity Action League. "Equal Rights Amendment." Human Equality, 1 February 1972, pp. [5-6]. (H2, S1, R6)

3162. "Equal Rights Amendment Again?--Yes, Again." Human Equality, 6 May 1972, p. 2. (H2, S1, R6)

Human Rights for Women (Washington, D.C.)

3163. "House Passes Equal Rights Amendment." Human Rights for Women, [August 1970], p. [3]. (H, R15)

Indianapolis NOW Newsletter (N.O.W., Indiana; becomes NOW Knows and Indianapolis Woman)

3164. "16 More to Go." Indianapolis NOW Newsletter, 20 December 1972, pp. 2, 7. (WL)

3165. "Support the E.R.A." Indianapolis NOW Newsletter, January 1973, pp. 1-4. (H2, S1, R10)

3166. "Support the E.R.A." Indianapolis NOW Newsletter, February 1973, pp. 1-2. (H2, S1, R10)

3167. "ERA Info." Indianapolis NOW Newsletter, March 1973, pp. 1-2. (H2, S1, R10)

3168. "ERA Opponent Strategy." NOW Knows, August 1973, p. 6. (H2, S2, R6)

3169. "Primary Results and ERA Chances" and "HERA." Indianapolis Woman, June 1974, p. 3. (H2, S2, R6)

Indianapolis Women's Liberation Newsletter (Indiana)

3170. Campbell, Norma, and Tracey, Maggie. "In Support of the Equal Rights Amendment." Indianapolis Women's Liberation Newsletter, December 1970, pp. 1, 6, 10. (H, R16)

3171. "Legal Equality." Indianapolis Women's Liberation Newsletter,
May 1972, p. 9. (HU, S1, R5)

Jacksonville Women's Movement (N.O.W., Florida; formerly Call to Action)

3172. "Equal Rights Amendment." Call to Action, 1 December 1972, p. 1.
(H2, S1, R10)

3173. "Equal Rights Amendment." Jacksonville Women's Movement, 5 March
1973, p. 1. (H2, S1, R10)

3174. "Birthday Party for ERA." Jacksonville Women's Movement,
5 March 1973, p. 3. (H2, S1, R10)

3175. "ERA." Jacksonville Women's Movement, 5 April 1973, p. 1.
(H2, S1, R10)

3176. "ERA." Jacksonville Women's Movement, October 1973, p. 4.
(H2, S2, R6)

3177. "Legislation--ERA." Jacksonville Women's Movement, January 1974,
p. 2. (H2, S2, R6)

3178. "Men for ERA of Duval County." Jacksonville Women's Movement,
February 1974, p. 6. (H2, S2, R6)

3179. "State ERA Funds." Jacksonville Women's Movement, March 1974, p. 5.
(H2, S2, R7)

3180. "Urgent! Write Letters! The E.R.A. Is in Trouble in Florida!"
Jacksonville Women's Movement, March 1974, p. 7. (H2, S2, R7)

John Birch Society Bulletin (Belmont, Massachusetts)

3181. "The Equal Rights Amendment." John Birch Society Bulletin,
February 1973, pp. 24-25.

Joyous Struggle (Albuquerque Women's Center Newsletter, University of
New Mexico)

3182. "Ratification of the ERA." Joyous Struggle, June 1973, p. 6.
(H2, S1, R6)

3183. Ahern, Virginia H. "The League of Women Voters of New Mexico
Summarizes New Mexico Statute Revisions under ERA." Joyous Struggle,
January 1976, pp. 4-5.

3184. Frakes, Jean. "Report on ERA." Joyous Struggle, 15 February
1975, p. 3.

Kansas City Women's Liberation Newsletter (Missouri)

3185. "ERA Rally; ERA Scoreboard." Kansas City Women's Liberation
Newsletter, December 1972, pp. 10-11. (HU, S1, R18)

3186. "ERA Status." Kansas City Women's Liberation Newsletter, April/
May 1973, p. 16. (HU, S1, R18)

KNOW News (Pittsburgh, Pennsylvania)

3187. "Skullduggery against the Equal Rights Amendment or Male
Chauvinism Makes Strange Bedfellows." KNOW News, [August 1970].
(Press Release) (H, R16)

3188. Women United Release. KNOW News, 31 July 1971, pp. 5-6. (H, R16)

3189. "Statement by the Vice President (Nixon) on the Equal Rights
Amendment, 2 September 1960." KNOW News, 31 July 1971, p. 13.
(H, R16)

Lakeworth NOW Newsletter (N.O.W., Florida)

3190. "Update on the Equal Rights Amendment, from Our Task Force Leader,
Ann Ayers." Lakeworth NOW Newsletter, March 1973, pp. 1-2. (H2, S1,
R10)

3191. Excerpt from the Congressional Record, Senate, 22 March 1972.
Lakeworth NOW Newsletter, March 1973. (H2, S1, R10) Rep. from
entry #152.

3192. "A Debate on the Equal Rights Amendment." Lakeworth NOW Newsletter,
April 1973, p. [2]. (H2, S1, R10)

3193. "The Score Is 31-19." Lakeworth NOW Newsletter, April 1973, p. 4.
(H2, S1, R10)

Lancaster Women's Liberation Newsletter (Pennsylvania)

3194. Untitled. Lancaster Women's Liberation Newsletter, 19 March 1972,
p. 5. (H2, S1, R6)

3195. "ERA--The Time to Act Is Now." Lancaster Women's Liberation
Newsletter, 19 March 1972, p. 7. (H2, S1, R6)

3196. "The ERA." Lancaster Women's Liberation Newsletter, 14 May 1972,
p. 12. (H2, S1, R6)

3197. "ERA--PA.'s Procrastination." Lancaster Women's Liberation
Newsletter, 28 May 1972, p. 8. (H2, S1, R6)

3198. "The Equal Rights Debate in Pa. Goes On." Lancaster Women's
Liberation Newsletter, 18 June 1972, pp. 2-3. (H2, S1, R6)

3199. "Gentlemen: . . . And, Sister." Lancaster Women's Liberation
Newsletter, 30 July 1972, pp. 4-7. (H2, S1, R6)

3200. "Women's Rights." Lancaster Women's Liberation Newsletter,
27 August 1972, pp. 3-4. (H2, S1, R6)

3201. "The ERA--Where It Stands." Lancaster Women's Liberation
Newsletter, 7 January 1973, p. 6. (H2, S1, R6)

3202. "ERA--In Trouble!" Lancaster Women's Liberation Newsletter,
18 February 1973, p. 1. (H2, S1, R6)

3203. "ERA." Lancaster Women's Liberation Newsletter, November 1973,
p. 5. (H2, S2, R4)

La Voz de la Mujer (Albuquerque N.O.W., New Mexico; becomes Albuquerque
NOW Newsletter)

3204. "Current Status of the Equal Rights Amendment." La Voz de la
Mujer, September 1970, p. 1. (H, R19)

3205. "Status of the Equal Rights Amendment." La Voz de la Mujer,
October 1970, p. 1. (H, R19)

3206. Kanowitz, Leo. "The Equal Rights Amendment and the Overtime
Illusion." La Voz de la Mujer, October 1970, pp. 2-4; November 1970,
pp. 3-7. (H, R19) Rep. from entry #88.

3207. "Status of the Equal Rights Amendment." La Voz de la Mujer,
November 1970, p. 1. (H, R19)

3208. National Committee for Equal Rights Amendment. "Equal Rights
Amendment for Women." La Voz de la Mujer, March 1971, p. 2. (H, R19)

3209. George Washington University Women's Liberation. "The Equal Rights
Amendment and the Draft." La Voz de la Mujer, May 1971, p. 1. (H,
R19) Rep. from entry #580; also rep. in entries #141, 1161, 3939.

3210. Berger, Carthuers Gholson. "The Equal Rights Amendment."
La Voz de la Mujer, May 1971, pp. 7-8. (H, R19) Rep. from entry #580.

3211. Hernandez, Aileen C. "Statements from the Testimony to Subcommittee
#4 of House Committee on the Judiciary, March 31, 1971." La Voz de la
Mujer, June 1971, pp. 1-2, 4. (H, R19) Rep. from entry #364.

3212. "ERA." La Voz de la Mujer, August 1971, p. 4. (H, R19)

3213. Levine, Marcy. Excerpts from "Chivalry Is to Sexism as the
'White Man's Burden' Is to Racism: An Open Letter to Robert Sherrill."
La Voz de la Mujer, November 1971, pp. 1-5. (HU, S1, R7)

3214. "ERA and KGGM." Albuquerque NOW Newsletter, August 1972, p. 8.
(HU, S1, R7)

3215. "ERA Spots." Albuquerque NOW Newsletter, November 1972, p. 1.
(HU, S1, R7)

3216. "Equal Rights Amendment Passes Committee!!" Albuquerque NOW
Newsletter, February 1973, p. 5. (HU, S1, R7)

3217. "ERA!" Albuquerque NOW Newsletter, February 1973, p. 1.
(HU, S1, R7)

3218. Windsor, Janet, and Soule, Chris. Untitled. Albuquerque NOW
Newsletter, March 1973, pp. 1-2. (HU, S1, R7)

3219. "State ERA." Albuquerque NOW Newsletter, September 1973, p. 1.
(HU, S2, R3)

3220. "ERA Bracelets" and "AFL-CIO Position on ERA." Albuquerque NOW
Newsletter, November 1973, p. 2. (HU, S2, R3)

L.A. Women's Liberation Newsletter (Los Angeles, California; becomes
Women's Center Newsletter)

3221. "The Equal Rights Controversy." L.A. Women's Liberation Newsletter,
2 October 1970, p. [8]. (H, R16)

3222. "Equal Rights Controversy." L.A. Women's Liberation Newsletter,
December 1970, p. 7. (H, R16)

3223. "The ERA." Women's Center Newsletter, November 1972, p. 6.
(HU, S1, R15)

Legislative Lookout (American Association of University Women,
Washington, D.C.; not available to the public)

3224. "ERA and Coalition Politics" and "ERA Ratification Status."
Legislative Lookout, November 1974, p. 5.

3225. "ERA." Legislative Lookout, October 1975, p. 2.

Liberator (North Palm Beach County N.O.W., Lake Worth, Florida)

3226. "Phyllis Schlafly, ERA Opponent, Is Hired as CBS Commentator."
Liberator, August 1973, p. 2. (H2, S2, R7)

3227. "ERA Recrudesces." Liberator, August 1973, pp. [4-6]. (H2, S2, R7)

3228. "Beare Predicts ERA Passage in '74." Liberator, September 1973,
p. 2. (H2, S2, R7)

3229. "Lawmaker Predicts ERA Passage at NOW Suffrage Day Picnic."
Liberator, September 1973, p. 4. (H2, S2, R7)

3230. "Silent Vigil Silenced by ERA '74 Panel but May Be Revived."
Liberator, October 1973, pp. 1-2. (H2, S2, R7)

Lincoln NOWsletter (N.O.W., Nebraska)

3231. "The Battle for the E.R.A. Goes On." Lincoln NOWsletter, August
1972, p. 1. (H2, S1, R10)

3232. "ERA--Equal Rights Amendment." Lincoln NOWsletter, 12 February
1973, p. [2-4]. (H2, S1, R10)

3233. Shore, Ellie. "Some Thoughts on the ERA." Lincoln NOWsletter,
31 March 1973, p. 1. (H2, S1, R10)

3234. "We're Not Broken Yet." Lincoln NOWsletter, 31 March 1973, p. [3].
(H2, S1, R10)

3235. "Equal Rights Amendment." <u>Lincoln NOWsletter</u>, 11 June 1973, p. 6.
(H2, S1, R10)

<u>Link</u> (Chicago, Illinois; formerly <u>Alliance Link</u>, Downers Grove, Illinois)

3236. "Senate Presently Debating Equal Rights Amendment." <u>Alliance
Link</u>, October 1970, p. 1. (H2, S2, R4)

3237. "ERA Up to States" and "Situation in Illinois." <u>Link</u>, April
1972, pp. 1-2. (H2, S2, R4)

3238. "House Defeats ERA--Again." <u>Link</u>, June 1972, pp. 1-2. (H2, S2, R4)

<u>Live NOW</u> (Lehigh Valley N.O.W., Pennsylvania)

3239. "Equal Rights Amendment." <u>Live NOW</u>, June 1973, p. 2. (H2, S1, R10)

<u>Long Island NOW Newsletter</u> (Nassau N.O.W., Great Neck, New York)

3240. "Javits and the Equal Rights Amendment." <u>Long Island NOW News-
letter</u>, [November 1970], p. [2]. (H, R18)

3241. "Equal Rights Amendment." <u>Long Island NOW Newsletter</u>, [January/
February 1971], p. 8. (H, R18)

3242. "Equal Rights Amendment." <u>Long Island NOW Newsletter</u>, [March/
April 1971], p. 4. (H, R18)

3243. "Illinois Women First in Nation with Equal Rights." <u>Long Island
NOW Newsletter</u>, [Summer 1971], p. 4. (H, R18)

3244. "ERA Passage Could Ease Swamped Court Calendars." <u>Long Island
NOW Newsletter</u>, [September/October 1971], p. 6. (H, R18)

3245. "All about the Equal Rights Amendment." <u>Long Island NOW Newsletter</u>,
[February 1972], p. 3. (HU, S1, R9)

3246. "Questions and Answers about the ERA." <u>Long Island NOW Newsletter</u>,
[February 1972], pp. 5-6. (HU, S1, R9)

3247. "Victory for the ERA." <u>Long Island NOW Newsletter</u>, [April 1972],
p. 3. (HU, S1, R9)

3248. "Status of ERA." <u>Long Island NOW Newsletter</u>, [16 July 1972], p. 5.
(WL; HU, S1, R9)

3249. "N.Y. Ratifies ERA." <u>Long Island NOW Newsletter</u>, [June 1972],
p. 6. (WL; HU, S1, R9)

3250. "ERA Status Report." <u>Long Island NOW Newsletter</u>, [February 1973],
p. 6. (HU, S1, R9)

3251. "ERA Fight." <u>Long Island NOW Newsletter</u>, [March 1973], p. 7.
(HU, S1, R9)

3252. "ERA: Only Five More to Go." <u>Long Island NOW Newsletter</u>,
[April 1974], p. 3.

Los Angeles NOW Newsletter (California): See NOW News (Los Angeles)

Mainely NOW (Portland N.O.W., Maine)

3253. "Coalition Builds for ERA." Mainely NOW, August 1973, p. 1.
   (H3, R3)

3254. Carey-Harriman, Frances. "Way ERA Died in the Senate." Mainely
   NOW, August 1973, p. [3]. (H3, R3)

3255. "Housewives for ERA." Mainely NOW, November 1973, p. [4]. (H3, R3)

3256. "Where the States Stand--June 10, 1973." Mainely NOW, November
   1973, p. [6]. (H3, R3)

3257. "Sample of Organizations." Mainely NOW, November 1973, p. [7].
   (H3, R3)

Maine Women's Newsletter (Brunswick)

3258. Lucas, Sandra. "History Repeats Herself: ERA and Maine Suffrage."
   Maine Women's Newsletter, April/May 1974, pp. 2-3. (H3, R2)

3259. "The Same Old Line." Maine Women's Newsletter, April/May 1974,
   p. 7. (H3, R2)

Majority Report (Springfield N.O.W., Illinois; formerly Springfield
NOW Newsletter)

3260. "The E.R.A.: An Historical Perspective." Springfield NOW
   Newsletter, February 1974, pp. 1-3. (H3, R3)

3261. "ERA--Up to the Minute News." The Majority Report, May 1974,
   pp. 1-2. (H3, R3)

3262. "E.R.A. News." The Majority Report, June 1974, p. 1. (H3, R3)

Marin County NOW Newsletter (N.O.W., San Rafael, California)

3263. "Equal Rights Amendment." Marin County NOW Newsletter, March
   1972, p. 1. (HU, S1, R9)

3264. "ERA." Marin County NOW Newsletter, June 1972, p. 1. (HU, S1, R9)

3265. "ERA." Marin County NOW Newsletter, September 1972, p. 1.
   (HU, S1, R9)

3266. "Blood Money for the E.R.A." Marin County NOW Newsletter,
   February 1973, p. [2]. (WL; HU, S1, R9)

3267. "ERA." Marin County NOW Newsletter, March 1973, p. 2. (HU, S1, R9)

Marin Women's Newsletter (Marin Women's Publishing Cooperative, San
   Rafael, California)

3268. "What Makes 'Equal Rights' Controversial." Marin Women's Newsletter,
   June 1972, p. 3. (H2, S1, R7)

3269. "Rules Committee Blocks Equal Rights Amendment." Marin Women's
Newsletter, June 1972, p. 4. (H2, S1, R7)

3270. "E.R.A. We Win." Marin Women's Newsletter, December/January
1972/73, p. 10. (H2, S1, R7)

Martha's Vineyard Image of Women Task Force (Eastern Massachusetts N.O.W.,
Martha's Vineyard)

3271. "Common Cause Endorses Women's Rights." Martha's Vineyard Image
of Women Task Force, November 1971, p. 1. (HU, S1, R9)

Michigan NOW Newsletter (Detroit): See As We See It NOW

Monmouth County NOW Newsletter (N.O.W., Red Bank, New Jersey)

3272. "How Now." Monmouth County NOW Newsletter, May 1973, p. 4.
(H2, S1, R11)

3273. "Only Five to Go." Monmouth County NOW Newsletter, June 1974,
p. 6. (H2, S2, R7) Rep. from Parade, 31 March 1973.

3274. Montana ERA Ratification Council Newsletter (Helena; continuing
coverage from Spring 1973 to January 1975)

Monterey Peninsula NOW Newsletter (N.O.W., California)

3275. "ERA Contributions." Monterey Peninsula NOW Newsletter, April
[1973], p. 2. (H2, S1, R11)

3276. "The Equal Rights Amendment." Monterey Peninsula NOW Newsletter,
November 1973, p. [11]. (H2, S2, R7)

Moving (Roanoke Valley N.O.W., Virginia)

3277. "ERA Central." Moving, January 1974, pp. 3-4. (H3, R3)

3278. "ERA." Moving, February 1974, p. 1. (H3, R3)

3279. "Editorial." Moving, February 1974, pp. [8-9]. (H3, R3)

3280. "ERA: Post-Mortem." Moving, March 1974, p. 1. (H3, R3)

Ms. Archivist (Society of American Archivists, Women's Caucus, Columbus,
Ohio)

3281. Mellquist, Bronwyn M. "Equality of Rights Shall Not Be Denied."
Ms. Archivist, Summer 1973, pp. 1-3. (H2, S1, R9)

Ms. On Scene (Alliance of Media Women, Marion, Ohio)

3282. "Common Cause." Ms. on Scene, Fall 1973, p. 5.

3283. "Sisterhood Happenings." Ms. on Scene, Summer 1974, p. 4.

Muliebrity Majority (Rockford N.O.W., Illinois; formerly Rockford NOW
   Newsletter)

3284. Cevene, Jan. "Feminist Attorney Speaks for ERA" and "What You Can
   Do for the ERA." Rockford NOW Newsletter, 24 March 1973, p. 3.
   (H2, S1, R11)

3285. "Status of ERA across USA." Rockford NOW Newsletter, 24 March
   1973, p. 4. (H2, S1, R11)

3286. "Guidelines for Action on the ERA." Rockford NOW Newsletter,
   24 March 1973, p. 5. (H2, S1, R11)

3287. Cevene, Jan. "Illinois Senate E.R.A. Status as of May 15, 1973."
   Rockford NOW Newsletter, 25 May 1973, pp. 4-5. (H2, S1, R11)

3288. Witte, Sue. "Lets Have Some ERA Action." Muliebrity Majority,
   13 February 1974, p. 3. (H2, S2, R8)

3289. Feldman, Clare. "Wilma Scott Heide Speaks in Rockford."
   Muliebrity Majority, 13 February 1974, p. 3. (H2, S2, R8)

3290. Deuth, Dixie. "Some Dare Call It Treason." Muliebrity Majority,
   13 February 1974, pp. 4-5. (H2, S2, R8)

3291. "Your Legislators Discuss the ERA." Muliebrity Majority,
   13 April 1973, p. 3. (H2, S2, R8)

3292. "Equal Rights Amendment Week Proclaimed." Muliebrity Majority,
   May 1974, p. 7. (H2, S2, R8)

Muncie Delaware NOW Newsletter (N.O.W., Muncie, Indiana)

3293. "Equal Rights Amendment." Muncie Delaware NOW Newsletter,
   [May 1970], p. 1. (H, R18)

3294. "Equal Rights Amendment." Muncie Delaware NOW Newsletter,
   [November 1970], pp. 2-3. (H, R18)

National Ad Hoc Committee for ERA Memos (Falls Church, Virginia)

3295. "To Women and Organizations for the Equal Rights Amendment."
   National Ad Hoc Committee for ERA, 1 July 1970; 8 July 1970; 17 July
   1970; 23 June 1970; 27 July 1970; 13 August 1970; 3 September 1970;
   25 September 1970; 2 October 1970; 19 October 1970; [November 1970];
   30 November 1970. (H, R16)

3296. "Equal Rights Amendment for Women." National Ad Hoc Committee
   for ERA, [Summer 1970]. (H, R16)

3297. "Statement Re: Equal Rights Amendment Vote, August 10."
   National Ad Hoc Committee for ERA, 9 August 1970. (H, R16)

3298. "Women Want Equal Rights Now!!!" National Ad Hoc Committee for
   ERA, 26 August 1970. (H, R16)

3299. Press Packet of 13 November 1970. See entry #580. (H, R16)

National Women's Political Caucus Newsletter (Washington, D.C.; becomes
   NWPC; formerly National Women's Political Caucus Legislative Alert)

3300. "Equal Rights Amendment." National Women's Political Caucus
   Legislative Alert, 1 September 1971, p. 1. (H2, S1, R13)

3301. "Equal Rights Amendment." National Women's Political Caucus
   Legislative Alert, February 1972, p. 3. (H2, S1, R13)

3302. Untitled. National Women's Political Caucus Newsletter, March
   1972, pp. 1-4 (entire issue). (H2, S1, R13)

3303. "Legislative Alert!," 8 March 1972. National Women's Political
   Caucus Newsletter, March 1972, insert (?). (H2, S1, R13)

3304. "The ERA . . . Time's Running Out!" National Women's Political
   Caucus Newsletter, December 1972, pp. 3-4. (H2, S1, R13)

3305. "NWPC Number One: We've Got to Try Harder." National Women's
   Political Caucus Newsletter, April 1973, pp. 3-4. (H2, S1, R13)

3306. "The ERA . . . Off to a Glorious Start." NWPC, January/February
   1974, p. 4. (H2, S2, R9)

3307. "ERA Success Stories." NWPC, March 1974, p. 6. (H2, S2, R9)

National Women's Political Caucus of Northern California Newsletter
   (Alameda County N.W.P.C., Berkeley, California)

3308. "The Equal Rights Amendment Confirms the Principle of Equal Rights
   under the Law for Men and Women by Requiring That They Be Treated as
   Individuals." National Women's Political Caucus of Northern California
   Newsletter, July 1972, insert. (H2, S1, R12)

3309. "The ERA . . . Time's Running Out!" National Women's Political
   Caucus of Northern California Newsletter, December 1972, pp. 3-4.
   (H2, S1, R12)

3310. "ERA Referendum Proposal, AB 3216." National Women's Political
   Caucus of Northern California Newsletter, March 1974, p. 3. (H2, S2,
   R8)

NCAWE News (National Council of Administrative Women in Education,
   National Education Association, Washington, D.C.)

3311. "Equal Rights Amendment." NCAWE News, January 1974, p. [2].
   (H2, S2, R6)

3312. Nevadans for ERA Newsletter (Carson City; continuing coverage from
   summer 1975)

New Broom (Legislative Newsletter, Boston, Massachusetts)

3313. "The Equal Rights Amendment." New Broom, June 1971, pp. 1-4
   (entire issue). (H, R16)

New Deborah (St. Louis, Missouri)

3314. "ERA." New Deborah, February 1973, pp. 1-2.

New Directions for Women (Newark, Delaware)

3315. "Council Elaborates on Proposed ERA." New Directions for Women,
Summer 1972, pp. 1-2. (H3, R3)

3316. Elle. "What about Equal Rights?" New Directions for Women,
Fall 1973, p. 6. (H3, R3)

3317. "AFL-CIO Supports Rights Amendment." New Directions for Women,
Winter 1973, p. 11. (H3, R3) Rep. from entry #4138.

New Directions for Women in New Jersey (Dover)

3318. "Pending State Legislation." New Directions for Women in New
Jersey, Fall 1972, p. 7.

3319. "ERA Bracelets." New Directions for Women in New Jersey, Fall
1973, p. 13.

3320. "New Jersey Legislation." New Directions for Women in New Jersey,
Winter 1973, p. 10.

3321. "ERA Bracelets." New Directions for Women in New Jersey, Winter
1974, p. 1.

3322. "Stop ERA Head Challenged by Brenda Fasteau." New Directions for
Women in New Jersey, Spring 1974, p. 3. (H2, S2, R9)

3323. "Equal Rights--No Nonsense." New Directions for Women in New
Jersey, Fall 1975, p. 2. (Ed)

3324. Sheldrick, Pamela. "ERA Fight Nears Climax." New Directions for
Women in New Jersey, Winter 1975, p. 16.

New Jersey WEAL (Women's Equity Action League, Old Bridge)

3325. "Equal Rights Amendment." New Jersey WEAL, March 1972, p. 4.
(H2, S1, R19)

News and Opinions of Women (San Francisco N.O.W., California; becomes
San Francisco NOW Newsletter)

3326. "U.S. Senate Clobbers Equal Rights Amendment." News and Opinions
of Women, November 1970, p. 3. (H, R20)

3327. "The Equal Rights Amendment." News and Opinions of Women, June
1971, p. 2. (H, R20)

3328. "ERA Tally." San Francisco NOW Newsletter, June 1972, p. 1.
(HU, S1, R11)

3329. "Sen. Mills Reverses Position on ERA; Will Vote It Out of
     Committee." San Francisco NOW Newsletter, October 1972, p. 1.
     (HU, S1, R11)   Rep. from entry #2872.

3330. Lahr, Lorraine. "ERA Ratified." San Francisco NOW Newsletter,
     December 1972, p. 1. (HU, S1, R11)

3331. "The ERA Is Alive and Well (?)." San Francisco NOW Newsletter,
     [May 1973], p. [2]. (HU, S1, R11)

3332. "ERA--Five to Go." San Francisco NOW Newsletter, March 1974, p. 1.
     (HU, S2, R5)

News and Views (Willamette Valley N.O.W., Salem, Oregon)

3333. "ERA." News and Views, December 1971, p. 2. (H2, S1, R12)

3334. "E.R.A. Passes! 38 States Must Ratify." News and Views,
     April 1972, p. 1. (H2, S1, R12)

3335. News for and from Housewives for E.R.A. (Chicago, Illinois;
     continuing coverage from summer 1973 in connection with E.R.A. Central)

News from the National Organization for Women (Fullerton N.O.W.,
     California)

3336. "Equal Rights Amendment Passed by Senate." News from the National
     Organization for Women, Special Bulletin, 30 March 1972, p. 1.
     (H2, S1, R10)

A Newsletter about Women's Issues (Olympia, Washington): See NOW Is the
     Time

New York State Voter (League of Women Voters of New York State, New
     York City)

3337. "Speak Out for ERA!" New York State Voter, September 1975,
     pp. 1-4 (entire issue).

Northern New Jersey NOW Newsletter (Westwood and Ho Ho Kus): See N.O.W.--
     NOW

Northern Virginia NOW Newsletter (N.O.W., Falls Church; later Alexandria)

3338. "Equal Rights Amendment Hearings." Northern Virginia NOW
     Newsletter, May 1970, p. 1. (H, R20)

3339. "Next N.O.W. Action." Northern Virginia NOW Newsletter, May
     1970, p. 2. (H, R20)

3340. "Virginia Chapter of N.O.W. Asks Virginia Congressmen to Push
     Constitutional Amendment for Women." Press Release, 1 May 1970.
     Northern Virginia NOW Newsletter, May 1970, p. [4].   (H, R20)

3341. "The Equal Rights Amendment." Northern Virginia NOW Newsletter,
     July 1970, p. 1. (H, R20)

3342. "Equal Rights Amendment to Be Voted on Soon." Northern Virginia
NOW Newsletter, September 1970, p. 1. (H, R20)

3343. "Women Lobby for Senate Passage of ERA." Press Release,
8 September 1970. Northern Virginia NOW Newsletter, September 1970,
p. [4]. (H, R20)

3344. "Women Continue to Press for Equal Rights; ERA Will Be Revived."
Northern Virginia NOW Newsletter, October 1970, p. 2. (H, R20)

3345. "Women Persist toward Elusive ERA." Northern Virginia NOW
Newsletter, January 1971, p. 6. (H, R20)

3346. "ERA Faces Uphill Fight--As in 1923, Ad Infinitum."   Northern
Virginia NOW Newsletter, February 1971, p. 2. (H, R20)

3347. "ERA Hearings Set for March 24." Northern Virginia NOW Newsletter,
March 1971, p. 1. (H, R20)

3348. "ERA Gets Boost in House Hearings." Northern Virginia NOW
Newsletter, 26 April 1971, pp. 1, 2, 3. (H, R20)

3349. "Spectre of Sam Ervin Hovers over ERA in Senate." Northern
Virginia Newsletter, 23 May 1971, pp. 1, 4. (H, R20)

3350. "Equal Rights Amendment Faces Precarious Future; Women Will
Persist." Northern Virginia NOW Newsletter, 13 August 1971, p. 3.
(H, R20)

3351. "Vote on ERA Set for Wed., September 22; Women Must Work to Win."
Northern Virginia NOW Newsletter, 17 September 1971, pp. 1, 2. (H, R20)

3352. "ERA Success in House; Senate Action in Nov." Northern Virginia
NOW Newsletter, 22 October 1971, p. 8. (HU, S1, R10)

3353. "NOW to Advertise for Equal Rights." Northern Virginia NOW
Newsletter, January 1972, p. 1. (HU, S1, R10)

3354. "Equal Rights Amendment Needs You Right Now." Northern Virginia
NOW Newsletter, 15 March 1972, p. [6]. (HU, S1, R10)

3355. Shelton, Isabelle. "How Equal Rights Passed Senate." Northern
Virginia NOW Newsletter, 17 April 1972, n.p. (HU, S1, R10)
Rep. from entry #5738.

3356. "At Last!! ERA Passed!!" Northern Virginia NOW Newsletter,
17 April 1972, p. 9. (HU, S1, R10)

3357. "ERA News." Northern Virginia NOW Newsletter, 20 July 1972, p. 3.
(WL; HU, S1, R10)

3358. "ERA News." Northern Virginia NOW Newsletter, 17 October 1972,
p. 8. (HU, S1, R10)

3359. "For More Information on ERA." Northern Virginia NOW Newsletter,
23 November 1972, p. 2. (WL; HU, S1, R10)

3360. Robinson, Lora. "ERA News." <u>Northern Virginia NOW Newsletter</u>, 23 November 1972, p. 7. (WL; HU, S1, R10)

3361. Crossley, Melanie. "President's Message." <u>Northern Virginia NOW Newsletter</u>, 17 January 1973, p. 3. (WL; HU, S1, R10)

3362. "ERA News." <u>Northern Virginia NOW Newsletter</u>, 17 January 1973, p. [7]. (WL; HU, S1, R10)

3363. "ERA News." <u>Northern Virginia NOW Newsletter</u>, 15 February 1973, p. 4. (HU, S1, R10)

3364. "ERA News." <u>Northern Virginia NOW Newsletter</u>, 14 March 1973, p. 3. (HU, S1, R10)

3365. "Virginia ERA Central." <u>Northern Virginia NOW Newsletter</u>, May 1973, pp. 1, 2. (HU, S1, R10)

3366. Heinz, Elise. "Va. Supreme Court Gives State ERA the Ax." <u>Northern Virginia NOW Newsletter</u>, May 1973, p. 3. (HU, S1, R10)

3367. "ERA Developments." <u>Northern Virginia NOW Newsletter</u>, May 1973, p. 5. (HU, S1, R10)

3368. "ERA Bake Sale." <u>Northern Virginia NOW Newsletter</u>, 18 June 1973, p. 11. (HU, S1, R10)

3369. Robinson, Lora. "ERA Activities Revisited." <u>Northern Virginia NOW Newsletter</u>, 18 June 1973, p. 8. (HU, S1, R10)

3370. "ERA Task Force Hearing." <u>Northern Virginia NOW Newsletter</u>, September 1973, pp. 1, 12. (HU, S2, R4)

3371. "ERA Task Force." <u>Northern Virginia NOW Newsletter</u>, September 1973, p. 4. (HU, S2, R4)

3372. "Equal Rights Amendment." <u>Northern Virginia NOW Newsletter</u>, May 1974, pp. 4-5. (HU, S2, R4)

<u>North Suburban Chicago NOW</u> (Illinois): See <u>NOW North</u>

<u>NOW</u> (New York State N.O.W.): See <u>NOW News and Notes</u>

<u>NOW Acts</u> (National N.O.W., Los Angeles, California; later Chicago, Illinois; also <u>Do It NOW</u>)

3373. "Equality Amendment to Constitution Needs Push." <u>NOW Acts</u>, Fall 1968, pp. 2, 4. (H, R17)

3374. "As We Go to Press" and "Celler Promises Hearings at New York ERA Rally." <u>NOW Acts</u>, July 1970, p. 1. (H, R17)

3375. "When Chips Are Down Will Senators Fink Out?" <u>NOW Acts</u>, September 1970, pp. 3-4. (H, R17)

3376. "ERA Killed by Senate Cop-Out." <u>NOW Acts</u>, December 1970, pp. 1, 3-4. (H, R17)

3377. "ERA Clobbered." NOW Acts, Spring 1971, pp. 1, 8. (H, R17)

3378. "ERA Passed by Congress: 'Failure WAS Impossible.'" NOW Acts 5,
no. 1 [1972], pp. 1-3. (HU, S1, R10)

3379. "Equal Rights Amendment Update." Do It NOW, September 1972. (WL)

3380. "League of Women Votes and ERA Ratification." Do It NOW,
October/November 1972, p. 5. (WL)

3381. "Ratification of the Equal Rights Amendment." Do It NOW,
December 1972. (WL)

NOW Bakersfield (N.O.W., California)

3382. "Actions for the Passage of the ERA." NOW Bakersfield, November
1972, p. 2. (H2, S1, R9)

3383. "Blood for the E.R.A." NOW Bakersfield 2, no. 2 (n.d.), p. 3.
(H2, S1, R9)

NOW Hear This! (Greater Pittsburgh N.O.W., Pennsylvania; formerly
Greater Pittsburgh NOW Newsletter)

3384. Witter, Jean. Untitled. Greater Pittsburgh NOW Newsletter,
September 1969, p. [3]. (H, R19)

3385. "Pennsylvania Equal Rights Amendment." NOW Hear This!, December
1969, p. 8. (H, R19)

3386. "Pennsylvania Equal Rights Amendment." NOW Hear This!, January
1970, p. 1. (H, R19)

3387. "ERA Activities Planned." NOW Hear This!, January 1970, p. 4.
(H, R19)

3388. "Constitutional Equality Day." NOW Hear This!, February 1970,
p. 10. (H, R19)

3389. Bowdler, Nancy. "Pennsylvania Legislation." NOW Hear This!,
March 1970, p. 2. (H, R19)

3390. "Equal Rights Amendment." NOW Hear This!, March 1970, p. 11.
(H, R19)

3391. "Pennsylvania Legislation." NOW Hear This!, April 1970, pp. 2-4.
Includes Senator Jack E. McGregor, Press Release, 10 March 1970. (H, R19)

3392. "Equal Rights for Women." NOW Hear This!, May 1970, p. 2. (H, R19)

3393. "Equal Rights Amendment Hearings." NOW Hear This!, May 1970, p. 4.
(H, R19)

3394. Witter, Jean. "Equal Rights Amendment." NOW Hear This!,
June 1970, pp. 1-2. (H, R19)

N.O.W. Hear This (Portland N.O.W., Oregon)

3395. "Equal Rights Amendment Passes U.S. House." N.O.W. Hear This,
    20 October 1971, p. 1.   (H, R19; HU, S1, R11)

3396. "Current Status of ERA and Senate Bill 2515." N.O.W. Hear This,
    17 November 1971, p. 1. (HU, S1, R11)

3397. "Extracts from Do It NOW." N.O.W. Hear This, 15 December 1971,
    p. 1. (HU, S1, R11)

3398. "Feminist Alert on ERA." N.O.W. Hear This, 22 March 1972, p. 1.
    (WL; HU, S1, R11)

3399. "Equal Rights Amendment Passes." N.O.W. Hear This, 19 April 1972,
    p. 1. (HU, S1, R11)

3400. "League of Women Voters Takes Stand on ERA." N.O.W. Hear This,
    15 October 1972, p. 4. (HU, S1, R11)

3401. "The Equal Rights Anthem" and "The E.R.A. Victory March." N.O.W.
    Hear This, November 1972, p. 1. (HU, S1, R11)

3402. "Chapter Joins Equal Rights Alliance." N.O.W. Hear This, January
    1973, p. [5]. (HU, S1, R11)

3403. "National Status of the ERA--Not as Bad as Some Think." N.O.W.
    Hear This, February 1973, p. 2. (HU, S1, R11)

3404. "The Look of the ERA." N.O.W. Hear This!, January 1974, p. 4.
    (HU, S2, R5)

3405. "ERA" and "Religion: Catholic Organizations Supporting the ERA."
    N.O.W. Hear This!, February 1974, p. 3. (HU, S2, R5)

3406. "Rights Amendment Ratification Forecast." N.O.W. Hear This!,
    May 1974, p. 2. (HU, S2, R5)

NOW Is the Time (N.O.W., Evansville, Indiana)

3407. "The ERA and Older Women: No Age Limit on Equal Rights." NOW
    Is the Time, May 1974, p. 4. (H3, R3)

NOW Is the Time (Thurston County N.O.W., Olympia, Washington; becomes
A Newsletter about Women's Issues)

3408. "Support ERA Ratification in Other States." NOW Is the Time,
    April 1973, p. 3. (H2, S1, R12)

3409. "How Is the ERA?" Newsletter about Women's Issues, June 1973,
    p. 5. (H2, S1, R12)

NOW Knows (Indianapolis, Indiana): See Indianapolis NOW Newsletter

NOWletter (Baton Rouge N.O.W., Louisiana)

3410. "Equal Rights Amendment Supported by Unitarian Church." NOWletter,
    May/June 1971, p. 6.   (H, R17)

3411. "Equal Rights Amendment Killed in Congress." NOWletter, July
    1971, p. 2.   (H, R17)

3412. "Washington Post Urges Equal Rights Amendment Be Passed."
    NOWletter, January 1972, p. 8.   (HU, S1, R7)

3413. "Bar Association Supports Sex Equality." NOWletter, 15 February
    1972, p. [3].   (WL; HU, S1, R7)

3414. "Blood for the ERA." NOWletter, March 1972, p. 8.   (HU, S1, R7)

3415. "Women's Equal Rights Proposal Is Approved." NOWletter, April
    1972, pp. 1-2.   (HU, S1, R7)

3416. "Oh . . . That Mine Adversary Had Written a Book." NOWletter,
    April 1972, p. 2.   (HU, S1, R7)

3417. Martin, Linda.   "Rep. Johnston Vows to Head Floor Fight against
    ERA Ratification." NOWletter, May 1972, pp. 3-4.   (HU, S1, R7)

3418. "Unitarian Fellowship of Baton Rouge Supports the Equal Rights
    Amendment." NOWletter, May 1972, p. 5.   (HU, S1, R7)

3419. Untitled (discussion of fiction and fact about ERA). NOWletter,
    June 1972, pp. 2-4.   (WL; HU, S1, R7)

3420. Fife, Darlene; Chifici, Diane; and Scott, Barbara.   "Who's Taking
    Care of Ms Johnson?" NOWletter, June 1972, p. 6.   (WL; HU, S1, R7)

3421. "Speakers for the ERA." NOWletter, October 1972, p. 8.   (HU, S1,
    R7)

3422. "NOW News." NOWletter, December 1972, p. 2.   (HU, S1, R7)

3423. "ERA Status." NOWletter, September/October 1973, p. 5.   (HU, S2,
    R3)

NOWletter (Temple Hills N.O.W., Maryland)

3424. "Equal Rights Amendment." NOWletter, December 1973, p. 2.
    (H3, R3)

NOW News (Caddo-Bossier City N.O.W., Shreveport, Louisiana; formerly
NOW Press)

3425. "Blood Money for ERA." NOW Press, March 1973, p. 1.   (H2, S1, R9)

3426. "ERA Coalition." NOW News, December 1973, p. 1.   (H3, R6)

3427. "ERA Coalition." NOW News, January 1974, p. 1.   (H2, S2, R6)

3428. "ERA Coalition." NOW News, March 1974, p. 9.   (H2, S2, R6)

3429. "Governor Sees ERA Passage." NOW News, June 1974, p. 1. (H2, S2, R6)

3430. "Schlafly Starts Swatting." NOW News, June 1974, pp. 1-2. (H2, S2, R6)

3431. "Tennessee Rescinds." NOW News, June 1974, p. 7. (H2, S2, R6)

3432. "ERA--United Lobbies." NOW News, June/July 1974, p. 1. (HU, S2, R6)

NOW News (Los Angeles N.O.W., California; formerly Southern California NOW Newsletter and Los Angeles NOW Newsletter)

3433. Longwell, Marjorie. "Statement of the Equal Rights Amendment to the Constitution." Southern California NOW Newsletter, April 1969, pp. 13-14. (H, R18)

3434. Crawford, Clare. "Sens. McCarthy, Tower Sponsor Ladies." Southern California NOW Newsletter, April 1969, p. 14. (H, R18) Rep. from entry #5663.

3435. "Why the Equal Rights for Women Amendment?" Los Angeles NOW Newsletter, July/August 1969, pp. 30-31. (H, R18)

3436. "Support the ERA." NOW News, September 1970, p. 3. (H, R18)

3437. "Legislation Proposed." NOW News, December 1970, p. 3. (H, R18)

3438. Troy, Fran. Letter to Editor. NOW News, December 1970, p. 3. (H, R18)

3439. "Equal Rights Amendment." NOW News, April 1971, p. 3. (H, R18)

3440. "Federal Action." NOW News, May 1971, p. 6. (H, R18)

3441. Carter, Jean D. "ERA and the Draft." NOW News, July 1971, p. 2. (H, R18)

3442. "ERA Needs Help." NOW News, July 1971, p. 4. Includes text of KNBC Editorial, 5 July 1971. (H, R18)

3443. Kennedy, Edward M. "There Is Something You Can Do about the ERA!!!" NOW News, August 1971, pp. 2-3. (H, R18)

3444. "ERA Now in Senate." NOW News, November 1971, p. 1. (HU, S1, R9)

3445. "Giant ERA Rally." NOW News, January 1972, p. 1. (HU, S1, R9)

3446. "ERA Rally." NOW News, February 1972, p. 3. (HU, S1, R9)

3447. "Last Chance on ERA." NOW News, March 1972, p. 1. (HU, S1, R9)

3448. "Speakers to Make ERA Effort." NOW News, May 1972, p. 1. (HU, S1, R9)

3449. "ERA Ratification." NOW News, May 1972, p. 5. (HU, S1, R9)

3450. "Double Play against Women on Equal Rights Amendment." NOW News, July 1972, p. 1. (WL; HU, S1, R9)

3451. "Equal Rights Amendment Threatened Again." NOW News, October 1972, p. 1. (HU, S1, R9)

3452. "California Becomes 22 State to Ratify ERA Nov. 13." NOW News, November 1972, p. 1. (HU, S1, R9)

3453. "E.R.A. Drive Goes On." NOW News, March 1973, p. 1. (HU, S1, R9)

N.O.W. News (North Orange County, Fullerton, California): See Action N.O.W.

N.O.W. News (Passaic County N.O.W., Wayne, New Jersey)

3454. Untitled. N.O.W. News, April 1973, pp. 4-5. (H2, S1, R11)

3455. "ERA: State by State." N.O.W. News, September 1973, pp. 4-5. (H2, S2, R8)

NOW News (Sacramento, California): See Sacramento NOW Newsletter

NOW News and Notes (New York State N.O.W., Skaneateles; formerly NOW)

3456. "Equal Rights Amendment." NOW News and Notes, [July 1971], p. [2]. (H, R19)

NOW New York (New York City N.O.W.)

3457. "National." NOW New York, [Fall 1969], p. [7]. (H, R19)

NOW North (North Suburban Chicago N.O.W., Skokie, Illinois; formerly North Suburban Chicago NOW and NOWsletter)

3458. "The ERA." North Suburban Chicago NOW, [30 June 1971]. (H2, S1, R11)

3459. "Legislation Committee." NOW North, November 1971, p. [2]. (H2, S1, R11)

3460. "NOW Members Discuss Women's Rights with Senatorial Aides." NOW North, January 1972, p. 3. (H2, S1, R11)

3461. "ERA Action." NOW North, February 1972, p. 1. (H2, S1, R11)

3462. "Victory in the 49th Year." NOW North, March 1972, p. 1. (H2, S1, R11)

3463. "ERA Status." NOW North, April 1972, p. 3. (H2, S1, R11)

3464. "Illinois and the ERA." NOW North, April 1972, pp. 3-4. (H2, S1, R11)

3465. "ERA Ammunition." NOW North, April 1972, pp. 4-5. (H2, S1, R11)

3466. "Ratify ERA (Ill.)." NOW North Bulletin, 4 May 1972, pp. 1-2.
(H2, S1, R11)

3467. "ERA Fails House Again." NOW North, May/June 1972, p. 3.
(H2, S1, R11)

3468. "Will You Vote for the Equal Rights Amendment?" NOW North,
October 1972, p. 1. (H2, S1, R11)

3469. "E.R.A.--Round Three!" NOW North, November 1972, pp. 5-7.
(H2, S1, R11)

3470. "Will Illinois Ratify the ERA?" NOW North, February 1973, p. 1.
(H2, S1, R11)

3471. "ERA Program New Meeting Place." NOW North, February 1973, pp. 1-
2. (H2, S1, R11)

3472. "More on ERA . . . From Our Legislative Coordinator." NOW
North, February 1973, pp. 3-4. (H2, S1, R11)

3473. "Friedan Appears at ERA Fund-Raising." NOW North, February 1973,
p. 4. (H2, S1, R11)

3474. "Important ERA Strategy Meeting." NOW North, March 1973, p. 4.
(H2, S1, R11)

3475. "ERA Brought Up-to-Date." NOW North, March 1973, p. 5. (H2, S1, R11)

3476. "Feminist Homework." NOW North, March 1973, p. 9. (H2, S1, R11)

3477. "You Are on an ERA Alert!" NOW North, April 1973, p. 1.
(H2, S1, R11)

3478. "Chapter ERA Action"; "ERA Outlook"; and "ERA Fund-Raising." NOW
North, April 1973, p. 2. (H2, S1, R11)

3479. "Feminist Homework." NOW North, April 1973, p. 7. (H2, S1, R11)

3480. "ERA Is Not on the Shelf--It's in Your Hands!!" NOW North, May
1973, pp. 1-2. (H2, S1, R11)

3481. "The Truth Comes Out" and "ERA in Court." NOW North, June 1973,
p. 4. (H2, S1, R11)

3482. "In the General Assembly." NOW North, June 1973, pp. 4-5.
(H2, S1, R11)

3483. "Wondering Whatever Happened to the ERA." NOW North, October
1973, p. 4. (H2, S2, R7)

3484. "ERA Education Day." NOW North, February 1974, p. 4. (H2, S2, R7)

3485. "The ERA." NOW North, May 1974, p. 7. (H2, S2, R7)

NOW NOTES (Atlanta N.O.W., Georgia)

3486. "Push for the Equal Rights Amendment." NOW Notes, February 1970, p. [2]. (H, R17)

3487. "Equal Rights Amendment." NOW Notes, April 1970, p. [2]. (H, R17)

3488. "Equal Rights Amendment." NOW Notes, Summer 1970, pp. 4-5. (H, R17)

3489. Griffiths, Martha. Letter on the ERA, 2 September 1970. NOW Notes, Summer 1970, p. [8]. (H, R17)

3490. "ERA Petition." NOW Notes, February 1972, p. 7. (HU, S1, R7)

3491. "Victory!!" NOW Notes, March 1972, p. 1. (HU, S1, R7)

3492. "ERA Ratification Strategy Meeting." NOW Notes, July 1972, p. 2. (HU, S1, R7)

3493. "Equal Rights Amendment." NOW Notes, August 1972, pp. 1-8 (entire issue). (WL; HU, S1, R7)

3494. "ERA--Now!" NOW Notes, November 1972, pp. 4-5. (HU, S1, R7)

3495. "ERA--Political Action!" NOW Notes, March 1973, p. 2. (HU, S1, R7)

3496. Smith, Pat. "Political Action." NOW Notes, [April 1973], p. [4]. (WL; HU, S1, R7)

3497. "Feminist News Digest." NOW Notes, November 1973, pp. 10-11. (HU, S2, R3)

NOW Notes (Erie County N.O.W., New York)

3498. "E.R.A. Update." NOW Notes, February 1974, p. 5. (H3, R3)

NOW Notes (Tacoma N.O.W., Washington)

3499. "June 26 Meeting Notes." NOW Notes, 10 July 1972, p. 1. (WL; H2, S1, R12)

3500. Untitled. NOW Notes, 13 August 1972, p. 1. (WL; H2, S1, R12)

N.O.W.-NOW (Northern New Jersey N.O.W., Westwood; later Ho Ho Kus; formerly Northern New Jersey NOW Newsletter)

3501. "Work for Passage of the ERA" and "House Hearings on Equal Rights Amendment Four Days Beginning March 24, 1971." Northern New Jersey NOW Newsletter, April [1971], pp. 6-7. (H, R18; H, Add)

3502. "Current Status of the Equal Rights Amendment." Northern New Jersey NOW Newsletter, May 1971, p. 3. (H, R18)

3503. "ERA Support Increases." Northern New Jersey NOW Newsletter, October 1971, p. 9. (HU, S1, R10)

3504. "Facts You Should Know about the Equal Rights Amendment."
Northern New Jersey NOW Newsletter, November 1971, p. 9. (HU, S1, R10)

3505. "'Gathering of Forces' for the ERA." N.O.W.-NOW, February 1972,
p. 8. (HU, S1, R10)

3506. "Good News from Trenton--Grab Those Pens!!!" N.O.W.-NOW,
February 1972, p. 11. (HU, S1, R10)

3507. "Equal Rights Amendment." N.O.W.-NOW, April 1972, p. 7.
(HU, S1, R10)

3508. "'Privileged Women' and the E.R.A." N.O.W.-NOW, February 1973,
p. 9. (HU, S1, R10)

NOW . . . or Never (Southwest Cook County N.O.W., Chicago, Illinois;
formerly Southwest Cook County NOW Newsletter)

3509. "Equal Rights Amendment." Southwest Cook County NOW Newsletter,
February 1973, p. [2]. (H2, S1, R12)

3510. "ERA Defeated in Illinois House." Southwest Cook County NOW
Newsletter, April 1973, p. 1. (H2, S1, R12)

3511. "ERA Up-date Report." NOW . . . or Never, July 1973, p. 3.
(H2, S2, R8)

3512. "ERA Up-date." NOW . . . or Never, August 1973, p. 4. (H2, S2, R8)

3513. "On the Offensive for ERA." NOW . . . or Never, November/December
1973, p. 4. (H2, S2, R8)

3514. "ERA Notes: 35 Down, 5 to Go." NOW . . . or Never, February
1974, pp. 6-8. (H2, S2, R8)

NOW Press (Shreveport-Bossier City, Louisiana): See NOW News (Caddo-
Bossier City)

NOW Press (Solano N.O.W., Fairfield, California)

3515. "E.R.A. and the Draft." NOW Press, August 1973, p. [2]. (H2, S2,
R8)

NOWsletter (Kitsap County N.O.W., Poulsbo, Washington)

3516. Untitled. NOWsletter, 30 November 1971, p. 2. (H2, S1, R10)

3517. Untitled. NOWsletter, 13 January 1972, pp. 2-3. (H2, S1, R10)

3518. "More on the National Equal Rights Amendment." NOWsletter,
13 January 1972, pp. 6-7. (H2, S1, R10)

3519. Untitled. NOWsletter, 25 February 1972, p. 1. (H2, S1, R10)

3520. "ERA." NOWsletter, 27 May 1972, p. 1. (H2, S1, R10)

3521. "ERA Campaign Needs." NOWsletter, 30 June 1972, p. 2. (H2, S1, R10)

3522. "ERA Office." NOWsletter, 28 July 1972, p. 1. (H2, S1, R10)

3523. "Late Bulletin!!!" NOW Newsletter, 28 July 1972, p. 3. (WL; H2, S1, R10)

3524. "Questions and Answers about the Equal Rights Amendment for the State of Washington." NOWsletter, 28 September 1972, pp. [3-4]. (H2, S1, R10)

3525. "ERA--The Way It Stands State by State." NOWsletter, 29 November 1972, p. 5. (H2, S1, R10) Rep. from entry #3844.

3526. "Note from NOW Legislative Office." NOWsletter, January 1973, p. 1. (H2, S1, R10)

3527. "Equal Rights Amendment Ratification." NOWsletter, February 1973, pp. 1-2. (H2, S1, R10)

3528. "ERA Passes!!!" NOWsletter, March 1973, p. 1. (H2, S1, R10)

3529. "Counsel on Constitutional Amendments Expresses Opinion on Rescinding Ratification." NOWsletter, April 1973, p. 2. (H2, S1, R10) Rep. from entry #4130.

3530. "ERA Opposition." NOWsletter, May 1973, p. 4. (H2, S1, R10) Rep. from entry #4131.

NOWsletter (North Suburban Chicago): See NOW North

NOWsletter (Sherman Oaks, California): See San Fernando Valley NOW News

NOW What? (Conejo Valley N.O.W., Thousand Oaks, California)

3531. "ERA." NOW What?, September 1972, p. 4. (H2, S1, R10)

NWPC: See National Women's Political Caucus Newsletter

Ohio Woman (Ohio Bureau of Employment Services, Columbus, Ohio)

3532. "What Is the 'Equal Rights Amendment'?" Ohio Woman, July 1972, p. [4]. (H2, S1, R13)

On Our Way (Women's Center, Waterbury, Connecticut)

3533. "Conn. Ratifies ERA!" On Our Way, July 1973, p. 1. (H3, R4)

On the Way (Anchorage Women's Liberation, Alaska)

3534. "Equal Rights Amendment Now in Senate." On the Way, February 1972, p. 2. (HU, S1, R13)

3535. Haaland, Dorothy. "Why We Need the ERA!!!" On the Way, February 1972, p. 3. (HU, S1, R13)

3536. "Martha Griffiths Speaks." On the Way, February 1972, pp. 3-4.
(HU, S1, R13)

3537. "More about the ERA." On the Way, May 1972, p. 1. (HU, S1, R13)

3538. "Celebrating a Small Victory." On the Way, June 1972, pp. 2-3.
(WL; HU, S1, R13)

3539. "E.R.A. Loses in California?" On the Way, June 1972, p. 3.
(HU, S1, R13)

3540. "Many Women Are Thinking about Their Rights: But There Are Some?"
On the Way, July 1972, p. 3 [sic]. (WL; HU, S1, R13)

3541. Haaland, Dorothy. "Zonta Favors Equal Rights." Anchorage Women's
Liberation, July 1972, p. 2. (WL; HU, S1, R13)

3542. Kidd, Sylvia; Cousins, Joan; and Bollenbach, Amy. "The Equal
Rights Amendment." On the Way, March 1973, pp. 3,5. (HU, S1, R13)

3543. Bollenbach, Amy. "The E.R.A.? Why Support It!" On the Way,
April 1973, pp. 9-11. (HU, S1, R13)

3544. "'Union Group Does Turnabout.'" On the Way, November 1973, p. 4.
(HU, S2, R6)

3545. "What Does the Equal Rights Amendment Mean?" On the Way!,
December 1973, pp. 1-2. (HU, S2, R6)

3546. "What Does the Equal Rights Amendment Mean?" On the Way!,
January 1974, p. 11. (HU, S2, R6)

3547. "What Does the Equal Rights Amendment Mean?" On the Way!,
February 1974, p. 6. (HU, S2, R6)

Orange County N.O.W. Newsletter (Fullerton, California): See Action
N.O.W.

Oregon Council for Women's Equality (Portland)

3548. "Equal Rights Amendment in U.S. Congress." Oregon Council for
Women's Equality, 25 June 1971, Legislative Supplement p. 2.
(H, R14)

3549. "Equal Rights Amendment (ERA) Passes House." Oregon Council for
Women's Equality, 15 October 1971, p. 1. (HU, S1, R13)

3550. "Equal Rights Amendment (ERA)." Oregon Council for Women's
Equality, 15 October 1971, Supplement p. 4. (HU, S1, R13)

3551. "Equal Rights Amendment (ERA)." Oregon Council for Women's
Equality, 15 January 1972, Supplement p. 3. (HU, S1, R13)

3552. "Congressional Dialogue on the Equal Rights Amendment." Oregon
Council for Women's Equality, 10 April 1972, p. 8. (HU, S1, R13)

3553. "Equal Rights Amendment Passes Senate." Oregon Council for
   Women's Equality, 10 April 1972, Supplement p. 3. (HU, S1, R13)

3554. "The Equal Rights Amendment." Oregon Council for Women's Equality,
   [July (?) 1972], Supplement p. 1. (HU, S1, R13)

3555. Greenspan, Carol M. "Ratification of the Equal Rights Amendment
   Next Big Thrust." Oregon Council for Women's Equality, Fall 1972,
   pp. 1, 2. (HU, S1, R13)

Page One (Atlanta, Georgia)

3556. "E.R.A." Page One, June 1973, p. 3. (H2, S1, R13)

Palo Alto NOW Newsletter (N.O.W., California)

3557. "ERA." Palo Alto NOW Newsletter, June 1973, p. 5. (H2, S1, R11)

Palo Alto/Stanford Women's Center Newsletter (California)

3558. "The Paradox of the Equal Rights Amendment." Palo Alto/Stanford
   Women's Center Newsletter, 27 October 1972, p. 1. (H2, S1, R19)

Pennsylvania Commission for Women News (Philadelphia)

3559. "Commission Schedules ERA Hearings December 8 in Philadelphia"
   and "ERA Defeats: What Went Wrong?" Pennsylvania Commission for
   Women News, [December 1975], pp. [1-2].

Peoria NOW Newsletter (N.O.W., Illinois)

3560. "Chapters Asked to Give E.R.A. Top Priority." Peoria NOW
   Newsletter, January 1974, p. 6. (H3, R3)

3561. "ERA Lobby Workshop Set for February 2." Peoria NOW Newsletter,
   February 1974, p. 4. (H3, R3)

3562. "At State Workshop: 'It's Going to Pass . . .'" Peoria NOW
   Newsletter, February 1974, pp. 4-5. (H3, R3)

3563. "Human Relations Unit Delays Stand on ERA." Peoria NOW Newsletter,
   February 1974, p. 4. (H3, R3)

3564. "32 Down and Six to Go." Peoria NOW Newsletter, February 1974,
   p. 6. (H3, R3)

3565. "Following Up on ERA." Peoria NOW Newsletter, March 1974, pp. 2-4.
   (H3, R3)

3566. "The Battle for the Equal Rights Amendment Continues." Peoria
   NOW Newsletter, April 1974, pp. 1-3. (H3, R3)

3567. "State Senate Rejects Equal Rights Amendment: Defeat or Mini-
   Victory?" Peoria NOW Newsletter, June 1974, p. 1. (H3, R3)

Philadelphia N.O.W. Newsletter (N.O.W., Pennsylvania)

3568. "Equal Rights Amendment." Philadelphia N.O.W. Newsletter,
November/December 1970, pp. 2-3. (H, R19)

3569. "More about Politics and Legislation." Philadelphia N.O.W.
Newsletter, April 1971, p. 9. (H, R19)

3570. "Pennsylvania Equal Rights Amendment." Philadelphia N.O.W.
Newsletter, May 1971, pp. 2-3. (H, R19)

3571. "Equal Rights for Women." Philadelphia N.O.W. Newsletter,
August 1971, p. 3. (H, R19)

3572. "Equal Rights Amendment." Philadelphia N.O.W. Newsletter,
October 1971, p. 1. (HU, S1, R11)

3573. Cummings, Joan. "Martha Griffiths Speaks at Villanova."
Philadelphia N.O.W. Newsletter, February 1972, pp. 5-6. (HU, S1, R11)

3574. "Sept. 11 and 12--ERA." Philadelphia N.O.W. Newsletter, August
1972, p. 11. (WL; HU, S1, R11)

Philadelphia Women's Political Caucus Newsletter (Pennsylvania)

3575. Brunswick, Joan. "Help Wanted: For Equal Rights Amendment."
Philadelphia Women's Political Caucus Newsletter, May 1972, p. 4.
(H2, S1, R12)

3576. _____. "The Equal Rights Amendment: Exercise in Futility.
Philadelphia Women's Political Caucus Newsletter, June 1972, p. 6.
(H2, S1, R12)

3577. "The Fight for ERA." Philadelphia Women's Political Caucus
Newsletter, July/August 1972, p. 5. (H2, S1, R12)

3578. "Equal Rights Amendment." Philadelphia Women's Political Caucus
Newsletter, September 1972, p. 2. (H2, S1, R12)

3579. "Report on Senate Visits." Philadelphia Women's Political Caucus
Newsletter, October 1972, p. 4. (H2, S1, R12)

3580. Davidson, Ann. "State Ratifies ERA." Philadelphia Women's
Political Caucus Newsletter, October 1972, p. 6. (H2, S1, R12)

3581. "I Gave My Blood for the Equal Rights Amendment." Philadelphia
Women's Political Caucus Newsletter, February 1973, p. 6. (H2, S1, R12)

Phoenix NOW Newsletter (N.O.W., Arizona; becomes Phoenix NOW News)

3582. "Equal Rights Amendment." Phoenix NOW Newsletter, August 1972,
pp. 5-6. (WL; HU, S1, R11)

3583. "The Equal Rights Amendment Ratification Bill." Phoenix NOW
Newsletter, October 1972, p. 5. (WL; HU, S1, R11)

3584. "Equal Rights Amendment." Phoenix NOW News, January 1973, p. 1.
(HU, S1, R11)

3585. "Equal Rights Amendment." Phoenix NOW News, February 1973, p. 1.
(HU, S1, R11)

3586. "ERA." Phoenix NOW Newsletter, June 1973, p. 1. (HU, S1, R11)

3587. "ERA." Phoenix NOW Newsletter, July 1973, p. 1. (HU, S2, R5)

3588. "ERA." Phoenix NOW Newsletter, May 1974, p. 5. (HU, S2, R5)

Phyllis Schlafly Report (Alton, Illinois)

3589. "What's Wrong with 'Equal Rights' for Women?" Phyllis Schlafly
Report, February 1972, pp. [1-4].

3590. "The Fraud Called the Equal Rights Amendment." Phyllis Schlafly
Report, May 1972, sec. 2, pp. [1-4] (entire issue).

3591. "The Right to Be a Woman." Phyllis Schlafly Report, November
1972, pp. [1-4].

3592. "ERA Backfires at Bank of America." Phyllis Schlafly Report,
January 1973, sec. 2, p. [1].

3593. "2-Minute Editorial against ERA for TV 'Equal Time' Response."
Phyllis Schlafly Report, January 1973, sec. 2, p. [2].

3594. "What the Equal Rights Amendment Means." Phyllis Schlafly Report,
January 1973, sec. 2, p. [3].

3595. "No ERA-Style Draft of Women in Israel" and "Quotable Quotes."
Phyllis Schlafly Report, January 1973, sec. 2, p. [4].

3596. "Dear State Legislator: The Buck Stops with You." Phyllis
Schlafly Report, February 1973, sec. 2, pp. [1-4].

3597. "Should Women Be Drafted?" Phyllis Schlafly Report, March 1973,
sec. 2, pp. [1-4].

3598. "How Will ERA Change State Laws?" Phyllis Schlafly Report,
April 1973, sec. 2, pp. [1-4].

3599. "Section 2 of the Equal Rights Amendment." Phyllis Schlafly
Report, May 1973, pp. [1-4].

3600. "Can a State Rescind Ratification of ERA?" Phyllis Schlafly
Report, June 1973, sec. 2, pp. [1-4].

3601. "Women in Industry Oppose Equal Rights Amendment." Phyllis
Schlafly Report, July 1973, sec. 2, pp. [1, 4].

3602. Testimony of Myra K. Wolfgang before Michigan Senate Committee on
the Judiciary, 18 April 1972. Phyllis Schlafly Report, July 1973,
sec. 2, pp. [2-4].

3603. "The Precious Rights ERA Will Take Away from Wives." Phyllis Schlafly Report, August 1973, pp. [1-4].

3604. "ERA Won't Help Women in Education." Phyllis Schlafly Report, September 1973, sec. 2, pp. [1-4].

3605. "Pennsylvania and Colorado Courts Prove ERA Takes Away Rights from Wives." Phyllis Schlafly Report, November 1973, sec. 2, pp. [1-4].

3606. "Effect of ERA on Family Property Rights." Phyllis Schlafly Report, January 1974, sec. 2, pp. [1-2].

3607. Harwood, Senator Madeline. "What's Wrong with That?" (Speech in Vermont Legislature) Phyllis Schlafly Report, January 1974, sec. 2, p. [3].

3608. "Catholic Women Vote No on ERA." Phyllis Schlafly Report, January 1974, sec. 2, p. [4].

3609. "Are You Financing Women's Lib and ERA?" Phyllis Schlafly Report, February 1974, sec. 2, pp. [1-4].

3610. "What Section 2 Really Means." Phyllis Schlafly Report, February 1974, sec. 2, p. [4].

3611. "Playboy and Rockefeller Foundations Finance ERA." Phyllis Schlafly Report, April 1974, sec. 2, pp. [1-3].

3612. "How ERA Changes State Support Laws." Phyllis Schlafly Report, April 1974, sec. 2, p. [4].

3613. "How ERA Will Hurt Divorced Women." Phyllis Schlafly Report, May 1974, sec. 2, pp. [1-3].

3614. "Women of Industry, Inc." Phyllis Schlafly Report, May 1974, sec. 2. p. [4].

3615. "Why Virginia Rejected ERA." Phyllis Schlafly Report, June 1974, pp. [1-3].

3616. "Who Opposes the Equal Rights Amendment?" Phyllis Schlafly Report, July 1974, sec. 2, pp. [1-4].

3617. "HEW Regulations about 'Sexism' in the Schools." Phyllis Schlafly Report, August 1974, sec. 2, pp. [1-4].

3618. "E.R.A. and Homosexual 'Marriages.'" Phyllis Schlafly Report, September 1974, sec. 2, pp. [1-4].

3619. "How ERA Will Affect Social Security." Phyllis Schlafly Report, October 1974, sec. 2, pp. [1,3].

3620. Moore, Mack A. "Economics of the Equal Rights Amendment." Phyllis Schlafly Report, October 1974, sec. 2, pp. [2-3].

3621. "The Arkansas Study on E.R.A." Phyllis Schlafly Report, November
      1974, sec. 2, pp. [1-4].

3622. "E.R.A. Means Abortion and Population Shrinkage." Phyllis Schlafly
      Report, December 1974, sec. 2, pp. [1-3].

3623. "The Money Connection." Phyllis Schlafly Report, December 1974,
      sec. 2, p. [4].

3624. "How E.R.A. Will Affect Churches and Private Schools." Phyllis
      Schlafly Report, March 1975, sec. 2, pp. [1-4].

3625. "NBC Portrays the E.R.A. Society." Phyllis Schlafly Report,
      March 1975, sec. 2, p. [3].

Planner (Minnesota Planning and Counseling Center for Women, Minneapolis)

3626. Rose, Caroline B. "Some Effects of the Passage of the Equal
      Rights Amendment." Planner, October 1970, p. [3]. (H, R20)

Pomona Valley NOW Newsletter (N.O.W., Claremont, California)

3627. "Proposed 26th [sic] Amendment Passes House." Pomona Valley NOW
      Newsletter, [September 1970], p. 3. (H, R19)

3628. "Flash." Pomona Valley NOW Newsletter, 10 September 1972, p. [2].
      (WL; HU, S1, R11)

3629. "Movement to Recall California State Senator James Mills."
      Pomona Valley NOW Newsletter, 10 September 1972, p. [3]. (WL; HU, S1,
      R11)

3630. "Equality of Rights under the Law Shall Not Be Denied or Abridged
      by the United States or Any State of [sic] Account of Sex." Pomona
      Valley NOW Newsletter, 10 September 1972, p. [3]. (WL; HU, S1, R11)

3631. "James Whetmore and the ERA." Pomona Valley NOW Newsletter,
      October 1972, p. [3]. (HU, S1, R11)

3632. "Senator Whetmore." Pomona Valley NOW Newsletter, November 1972,
      p. [2]. (HU, S1, R11)

3633. "E.R.A." Pomona Valley NOW Newsletter, December 1972, p. 3.
      (HU, S1, R11)

3634. "Status of ERA." Pomona Valley NOW Newsletter, March 1973, p. 3.
      (HU, S1, R11)

3635. "E.R.A. Bracelets Available." Pomona Valley NOW Newsletter,
      November/December 1973, p. 1. (HU, S2, R5)

Puce Mongoose (United Sisters, Garwood, New Jersey)

3636. Jinx. "Newview." Puce Mongoose, September 1975, pp. 1, 2, 3, 4.

Quad Cities NOW Newsletter (N.O.W., Moline, Illinois; formerly
   Quad Cities NOW)

3637. "Report on E.R.A." Quad Cities NOW, July 1972, p. 3. (H2, S1, R11)

3638. "Equal Rights Amendment." Quad Cities NOW, December 1972, p. [3].
   Rep. from entry #895. (WL; H2, S1, R11)

3639. "Feminist Homework." Quad Cities NOW, January 1973, p. [3].
   (WL; H2, S1, R11)

3640. "A Plea, I.E. Help!" Quad Cities NOW, February 1973, p. 3.
   (H2, S1, R11)

3641. "Potpourri from the President." Quad Cities NOW, March 1973, p. 1.
   (H2, S1, R11)

3642. "The House Vote and ERA Lobbying"; Daughters of ERA Lobbying";
   Potpourri from the President"; and "ERA Revisited Yet Again Once More."
   Quad Cities NOW, April 1973, pp. 1-2. (H2, S1, R11)

3643. "E.R.A. Suit Filed." Quad Cities NOW Newsletter, July 1973, p. 7.
   (H2, S2, R8)

3644. "Statewide ERA Meeting." Quad Cities NOW Newsletter, February
   1974, p. 2. (H2, S2, R8)

3645. "ERA Letter Writing." Quad Cities NOW Newsletter, March 1974, p.
   4. (H2, S2, R8)

3646. "ERA Report." Quad Cities NOW Newsletter, June 1974, p. 3.
   (H2, S2, R8)

Rhode Island NOW Newsletter (N.O.W., Providence)

3647. "Support." Rhode Island NOW Newsletter, April 1973, p. 2.
   (H2, S1, R11)

Right NOW (Columbus N.O.W., Ohio)

3648. Schwart, Karen. "You've Come a Long Way ERA (?)." Right NOW,
   February 1972, p. 2. (H2, S1, R9)

3649. "Divorce, Alimony, and the ERA." Right NOW, March 1972, p. 7.
   (H2, S1, R9) Rep. from entry #3838.

3650. "Updating the ERA." Right NOW, June 1972, p. 1. (H2, S1, R10)

3651. Malis, Mary. "Updating the ERA." Right NOW, July 1972, p. 1.
   (H2, S1, R10)

3652. "Citizens' Progress." Right NOW, August 1972, p. 2. (H2, S1, R10)

3653. "ERA Congress." Right NOW, September 1972, pp. 1-2. (H2, S1, R10)

3654. Harris, Phyllis. "State Dems Support ERA." Right NOW, October
   1972, p. 3. (H2, S1, R10)

3655. "Winners Support ERA." Right NOW, November/December 1972, p. 3.
(WL; H2, S1, R10)

3656. "Too Good to Write??" Right NOW, January 1973, p. 2. (H2, S1,
R10)

3657. "Homemakers for Equality." Right NOW, January 1973, p. 3.
(H2, S1, R10)

3658. "Students for ERA." Right NOW, January 1973, p. 4. (H2, S1, R10)

3659. "Here We Go Again." Right NOW, January 1973, p. 10. (H2, S1,
R10)

3660. "Women, the Law, and the ERA." Right NOW, January 1973, p. 11.
(H2, S1, R10)

3661. "Be My Equal Valentine." Right NOW, February 1973, p. 1.
(H2, S1, R10)

3662. "ERA Prognosis." Right NOW, February 1973, p. 2. (H2, S1, R10)

3663. "Homemakers for ERA." Right NOW, February 1973, pp. 2-3.
(H2, S1, R10)

3664. Havens, Mary R. "Action NOW." Right NOW, March 1973, p. 3.
(H2, S1, R10)

3665. "ERA Benefit--A Real Upper!" Right NOW, March 1973, p. 4.
(H2, S1, R10)

3666. "Educator for ERA." Right NOW, March 1973, p. 7. (H2, S1, R10)

3667. "Opponent Assaults Reporter." Right NOW, March 1973, p. 8.
(H2, S1, R10)

3668. "Klan Is Anti." Right NOW, March 1973, p. 10. (H2, S1, R10)

3669. "Are You Bored with ERA?" Right NOW, April 1973, p. 1.
(H2, S1, R10)

3670. "Equal Rights Amendment Passes House." Right NOW, April 1973,
p. 2. (H2, S1, R10)

3671. "States That Have/Have Not Ratified the ERA." Right NOW, April
1973, p. 4. (H2, S1, R10)

3672. Munday, Mildred B. "State Council Meeting." Right NOW, April
1973, pp. 4-5. (H2, S1, R10)

3673. Untitled. Right NOW, May 1973, p. 1. (H2, S1, R10)

3674. Connelly, Kathleen. "One More Reason for ERA." Right NOW, May
1973, p. 3. (H2, S1, R10)

3675. "ERA." Right NOW, October 1973, p. 4. (H2, S2, R6)

3676. "ERA." Right NOW, November 1973, p. 4. (H2, S2, R6)

3677. "Gov. at ERA Meeting" and "ERA Lives!" Right NOW, December 1973, p. 1. (H2, S2, R6)

3678. "ERA Needs Help!" Right NOW, January 1974, p. 1. (H2, S2, R6)

3679. Teegardin, Pat. "ERA." Right NOW, January 1974, p. 4. (H2, S2, R6)

3680. "Roll Call on E.R.A." Right NOW, February/March 1974, p. 2. (H2, S2, R6)

3681. "Survey of Registered Voters of the 15th Senatorial District, State of Ohio, Conducted during December, 1973 on Behalf of the Columbus Chapter of NOW." Right NOW, February/March 1974, pp. 5-6. (H2, S2, R6)

Right NOW (Virginia Beach N.O.W., Virginia; formerly Virginia Beach NOW Newsletter)

3682. "ERA Task Force." Virginia Beach NOW Newsletter, [10 July 1973], p. [3]. (H2, S1, R12)

3683. "ERA Task Force News." Right NOW, July 1973, p. 2. (H2, S2, R8)

3684. "From ERA Task Force." Right NOW, [September 1973], p. 1. (H2, S2, R8)

3685. "ERA Task Force." Right NOW, [October 1973], pp. 2-3. (H2, S2, R8)

3686. "ERA Task Force." Right NOW, December 1973, pp. 4-5. (H2, S2, R8)

3687. "ERA News." Right NOW, January 1974, p. 5. (H2, S2, R8)

3688. Henderson, Vera. "ERA--An Overview of the Last Year." Right NOW, February 1974, pp. 2-4. (H2, S2, R8)

Rockford NOW Newsletter (Illinois): See Muliebrity Majority

Sacramento NOW Newsletter (N.O.W., California; formerly NOW News; Legislative Committee puts out Capitol Alert)

3689. "Equal Rights Amendment Modified--Nullified?" NOW News, [October 1970], p. 1. (H, R19)

3690. "Victory after 49 Years: Congress Passes the Equal Rights Amendment." Sacramento NOW Newsletter, April 1972, p. 1. (HU, S1, R11)

3691. "Equal Rights Amendment." Sacramento NOW Newsletter, April 1972, pp. [2-3]. (HU, S1, R11)

3692. Green, Kathy. "Legislation." Sacramento NOW Newsletter, May 1972, p. 4. (WL; HU, S1, R11)

3693. _____. "Legislation." Sacramento NOW Newsletter, June 1972, p. 6. (HU, S1, R11)

3694. _____. "Still No Equal Rights Amendment." Sacramento NOW Newsletter, July 1972, p. 3. (HU, S1, R11)

3695. "Mills Agrees to Release ERA from Committee." Sacramento NOW Newsletter, October 1972, p. 2. (HU, S1, R11) Rep. from Capitol Alert.

3696. "Legislative Task Force." Sacramento NOW Newsletter, November 1972, p. [7]. (HU, S1, R11)

3697. "Are We People Now?" Sacramento NOW Newsletter, December 1972, p. 1. (WL; HU, S1, R11)

3698. "E.R.A. Bracelets." Sacramento NOW Newsletter, October 1973, p. 2. (HU, S2, R5)

Saint Joan's International Alliance Newsletter (Milwaukee, Wisconsin; formerly Saint Joan's Alliance Newsletter)

3699. "Equal Rights Amendment." Saint Joan's Alliance Newsletter, 26 January 1970, p. 2. (H, R20)

3700. "Equal Rights Amendment." Saint Joan's International Alliance Newsletter, March 1971, p. 2. (H, Add)

3701. Finn, C. Virginia. "Equal Rights Amendment Is Needed by Americans of Both Sexes." Saint Joan's International Alliance Newsletter, July 1971, p. 11. (H, Add)

3702. "The Equal Rights Amendment." Saint Joan's International Alliance Newsletter, August 1972, p. 4. (HU, S1, R14)

3703. "ERA Score Card." Saint Joan's International Alliance Newsletter, December 1972, p. 19. (HU, S1, R14)

3704. "The Equal Rights Amendment: Where, Oh Where, Did It Go?" Saint Joan's International Alliance Newsletter, June 1973, pp. 2-6. (HU, S1, R14) Reprints entries #5678, 5708, 5712.

San Diego County NOW News (N.O.W., California)

3705. "Equal Rights Amendment for Women." San Diego County NOW News, April 1971, p. [3]. (H, R19)

3706. "Equal Rights Amendment." San Diego County NOW News, September 1971, p. 3. (H, R19)

3707. "Women's Equal Rights Bill Cooled." San Diego County NOW News, October 1971, p. 1. (H, R19) Rep. from entry #5782.

3708. "ERA Now in Senate." San Diego County NOW News, November 1971, p. [5]. (HU, S1, R11)

3709. "Nixon Endorses Amendment to Aid Women." San Diego County NOW
News, March 1972, p. 3. (HU, S1, R11). Rep. from entry #5716.

3710. "Equal Rights Amendment." San Diego NOW County News, April 1972,
p. 1. (HU, S1, R11)

3711. Metzger, Sue. "Equal Rights Amendment (ERA)." San Diego County
NOW News, April 1972, p. [2A]. (HU, S1, R11)

3712. "Ratification of the E.R.A.--Progress Report." San Diego County
NOW News, April 1972, p. 4. (HU, S1, R11)

3713. "The Equal Rights Amendment." San Diego County NOW News, 15 May
1972, pp. 1-2. (HU, S1, R11)

3714. "ERA Half Way Home!" San Diego County NOW News, 16 June 1972, p. 2.
(HU, S1, R11)

3715. "Drive to Recall Senator Mills." San Diego County NOW News,
15 July 1972, p. 1. (WL; HU, S1, R11)

3716. Dymally, Mervyn M. Letter, 6 July 1972. San Diego County NOW
News, 15 July 1972, p. [3]. (WL; HU, S1, R11)

3717. "One Law at a Time." San Diego County NOW News, 15 July 1972,
p. [3]. (HU, S1, R11)

3718. Perret, Norma. "Dear Ms. Mills." San Diego County NOW News,
15 July 1972, p. [4]. (WL; HU, S1, R11)

3719. Banowsky, Bill. "What's Right with 'Equal Rights.'" San Diego
County NOW News, 15 August 1972, p. 3. (WL; HU, S1, R11) Rep. from
entry #5648.

3720. "Equal Rights Amendment--Progress!!!" San Diego County NOW News,
18 September 1972, p. 1. (HU, S1, R11)

3721. "Crisis with the E.R.A.--Again!!!" San Diego County NOW News,
16 October 1972, p. 1. (HU, S1, R11)

3722. Stanley, Margaret. "California Ratified the ERA!!!" San Diego
County NOW News, 20 November 1972, p. 1. (HU, S1, R11)

3723. _____. "President's Message." San Diego County NOW News,
15 January 1973, p. 1. (HU, S1, R11)

3724. _____. "Legislative Taskforce." San Diego County NOW News,
15 January 1973, p. 2. (HU, S1, R11)

3725. _____. "ERA Ratification Moves Along." San Diego County
NOW News, 18 February 1973, p. 2. (HU, S1, R11)

3726. "Wall Street Journal Supports Women's Rights Movement." San Diego
County NOW News, 15 July 1973, p. [2]. (HU, S2, R5)

3727. "Local Program Set on Legal/Social Effects of Equal Rights
Amendment." San Diego County NOW News, 15 August 1973, p. 2.
(HU, S2, R5)

3728. "SD NOW Taskforce Pushes for ERA Passage." San Diego County NOW
News, 15 October 1973, p. 3. (HU, S2, R5)

3729. "AFL-CIO Announces Its Support of the Equal Rights Amendment."
San Diego County NOW News, 15 November 1973, p. 1. (HU, S2, R5)

3730. "Equal Rights Amendment Moves Closer to Adoption." San Diego
County NOW News, 15 February 1974, p. 3. (HU, S2, R5)

San Fernando Valley NOW News (N.O.W., Sherman Oaks, California; formerly
NOWsletter)

3731. "Top Priority." NOWsletter, May 1970, p. [3]. (H, R19)

3732. "NOW and the ERA." NOWsletter, December 1972, p. [2]. (HU, S1,
R11)

3733. "Arguments to Use in Favor of Ratification." San Fernando Valley
NOW News, May 1973, p. [4]. (HU, S1, R11)

3734. "The Bible and the ERA." San Fernando Valley NOW News, September
1973, p. 5. (HU, S2, R5)

San Fernando Valley N.W.P.C. Newsletter (National Women's Political
Caucus, North Hollywood, California)

3735. "Cusanovich Declares for ERA" and "May 24 Deadline for ERA."
San Fernando Valley N.W.P.C. Newsletter, 18 May 1972, p. 1. (H2, S1,
R12)

3736. "Rebuttals to Common Arguments against Equal Rights Amendment."
San Fernando Valley N.W.P.C. Newsletter, 15 June 1972, p. 1.
(WL; H2, S1, R12)

3737. "New Strategy for E.R.A." San Fernando Valley N.W.P.C. Newsletter,
15 June 1972, p. 4. (WL; H2, S1, R12)

3738. Untitled. San Fernando Valley N.W.P.C. Newsletter, 25 July 1972,
pp. 4-5. (H2, S1, R12)

3739. "ERA." San Fernando Valley N.W.P.C. Newsletter, 5 September
[1972], p. 3. (H2, S1, R12)

3740. "State Senate Mail Running against ERA?" and "ERA and the
Protective Labor Laws." San Fernando Valley N.W.P.C. Newsletter,
5 October 1972, p. 4. (H2, S1, R12)

3741. "Equal Rights Amendment." San Fernando Valley N.W.P.C. Newsletter,
27 February 1973, p. [5]. (H2, S1, R12)

3742. "The Current Status of ERA." San Fernando Valley N.W.P.C.
Newsletter, 29 March 1973, p. 3. (WL; H2, S1, R12)

3743. "Alabama Is 13th State to Reject ERA." San Fernando Valley
N.W.P.C. Newsletter, 29 June 1973, p. 3. (H2, S1, R12)

3744. "ERA Referendum." San Fernando Valley N.W.P.C. Newsletter,
28 March 1974, p. [4]. (H2, S2, R9)

San Francisco NOW Newsletter (California): See News and Opinions of
Women

San Joaquin N.O.W. Newsletter (N.O.W., Stockton, California)

3745. Untitled. San Joaquin N.O.W. Newsletter, 1 March 1972, p. 4.
(H2, S1, R11)

3746. "From Women United, We Offer the Following Discussion of the
Federal Equal Rights Amendment." San Joaquin N.O.W. Newsletter,
1 March 1972, pp. 6-10. (H2, S1, R11)

3747. Untitled. San Joaquin N.O.W. Newsletter, 1 April 1972, p. 6.
(H2, S1, R11)

3748. "Legislative Task Force." San Joaquin N.O.W. Newsletter,
6 May 1972, pp. 2-6. (H2, S1, R11)

3749. Untitled. San Joaquin N.O.W. Newsletter, [June 1972], n.p.
(H2, S1, R11)

3750. "(Non) Progress on the Equal Rights Amendment." San Joaquin N.O.W.
Newsletter, 1 July 1972, pp. 2-3. (WL; H2, S1, R11)

3751. Letters to the Editor of the San Francisco Chronicle. San Joaquin
N.O.W. Newsletter, 1 August 1972, p. 4. (WL; H2, S1, R11)

3752. "The Equal Rights Amendment Is a Dead Issue for This Year."
San Joaquin N.O.W. Newsletter, 1 August 1972, pp. 11-13. (WL; H2, S1,
R11)

3753. "Help Recall Senator James ('Mickey Mouse') Mills." San Joaquin
N.O.W. Newsletter, 1 September 1972, pp. 2-3. (WL; H2, S1, R11)

3754. "On August 16th a Panel Discussion Was Held in San Francisco
Concerning the Legal Ramifications of the E.R.A." San Joaquin N.O.W.
Newsletter, 1 September 1972, p. 3. (H2, S1, R11)

3755. "Assemblywoman March Fong Ejected from the Sutter Club."
San Joaquin N.O.W. Newsletter, 1 September 1972, pp. 3-4. (H2, S1, R11)

3756. "Poll of Senators on E.R.A. Made Public." San Joaquin N.O.W.
Newsletter, 1 September 1972, p. 4. (WL; H2, S1, R11)

3757. "The National Board of Directors of N.O.W. Has Declared California
a State of Emergency with Regard to the Equal Rights Amendment."
San Joaquin N.O.W. Newsletter, 1 September 1972, pp. 4-5. (H2, S1, R11)

3758. "Other NOW Activities: First, Some Good News!" San Joaquin N.O.W.
Newsletter, 1 October 1972, pp. 6-7. (H2, S1, R11)

3759. "Some Other Good News." San Joaquin N.O.W. Newsletter, 1 October 1972, p. 9. (H2, S1, R11)

3760. "ERA Opponents Fight Dirty." San Joaquin N.O.W. Newsletter, 1 October 1972, p. 12. (H2, S1, R11)

3761. Untitled. San Joaquin N.O.W. Newsletter, 1 November 1972, pp. 3-4. (H2, S1, R11) Rep. from entry #2873.

3762. Benson, Carol. Untitled. San Joaquin N.O.W. Newsletter, December/ January 1972/73, p. 20. (WL; H2, S1, R11)

3763. "Legislation." San Joaquin N.O.W. Newsletter, December/January 1972/73, pp. 8-10. (H2, S1, R11)

3764. "Legislation." San Joaquin N.O.W. Newsletter, February 1973, pp. 13-14. (H2, S1, R11)

3765. Untitled. San Joaquin N.O.W. Newsletter, March 1973, pp. 1-3. (H2, S1, R11)

3766. "Equal Rights Amendment at a Standstill." San Joaquin N.O.W. Newsletter, April/May 1973, p. 11. (H2, S1, R11)

San Mateo County N.O.W. Newsletter (N.O.W., Burlingame, California)

3767. "National News." San Mateo County N.O.W. Newsletter, April/May 1973, p. 3. (HU, S1, R11)

Santa Barbara NOW Newsletter (N.O.W., California)

3768. "Equal Rights for Women??" Santa Barbara NOW Newsletter, April 1972, p. 1. (H2, S1, R12)

3769. "ERA-ERA-ERA-." Santa Barbara NOW Newsletter, May 1972, pp. [1-3]. (H2, S1, R12)

3770. "ERA." Santa Barbara NOW Newsletter, June/July 1972, p. [2]. (H2, S1, R12)

3771. "ERA and California." Santa Barbara NOW Newsletter, December 1972, p. [2]. (H2, S1, R12)

3772. "Urgent . . . The E.R.A. Is Dying!" Santa Barbara NOW Newsletter, February 1973, p. [2]. (H2, S1, R12)

3773. "E.R.A." Santa Barbara NOW Newsletter, May 1973, p. 3. (H2, S1, R12)

Sisters in Solidarity Newsletter (Women's Liberation, Denver, Colorado)

3774. "The Equal Rights Amendment." Sisters in Solidarity Newsletter, May 1972, pp. 5-6. (HU, S1, R15)

Sisters in Struggle (Merritt College Women's Collective, Oakland, California)

3775. "Equal Rights Amendment." Sisters in Struggle, [November 1972], pp. [3-4]. (H2, S1, R15)

Sisters Stand (Women's Liberation groups of Salt Lake City, Utah)

3776. Curtis (Combs), Rita. "Not Separate but Equal." Sisters Stand, [December 1971], p. [9]. (H2, S1, R15)

Skirting the Capitol (Marian Ash, Sacramento, California)

3777. "Do We Really Want Equality?" Skirting the Capitol, 12 February 1968, pp. 1-4 (entire issue). (H, R21)

3778. "The Equal Rights Amendment." Skirting the Capitol, 17 June 1968, p. 1. (H, R21)

3779. "A Review of the Equal Rights Amendment." Skirting the Capitol, 16 June 1969, pp. 1-2. (H, R21)

3780. "The Equal Rights Amendment Gets Top Level Support." Skirting the Capitol, 16 March 1970, p. 4. (H, R21)

3781. "At the National Level." Skirting the Capitol, 27 April 1970, pp. 3-4. (H, R21)

3782. "The Equal Rights Amendment." Skirting the Capitol, 8 June 1970, p. 4. (H, R21)

3783. "Equal Rights Amendment in Trouble." Skirting the Capitol, 7 September 1970, pp. 2-3. (H, Add)

3784. "U.S. Senate Clobbers Equal Rights Amendment." Skirting the Capitol, 19 October 1970, pp. 1-2. (H, R21)

3785. "The Equal Rights Amendment." Skirting the Capitol, 16 November 1970, p. 4. (H, R21)

3786. "The Equal Rights Amendment." Skirting the Capitol, 14 December 1970, p. 3. (H, R21)

3787. "Death to the E.R.A.--1970." Skirting the Capitol, 29 December 1970, p. 1. (H, R21)

3788. "The Equal Rights Amendment for 1971." Skirting the Capitol, 11 March 1971, p. 1. (H, R21)

3789. "At the National Level." Skirting the Capitol, 21 June 1971, pp. 3-4. (H, R21)

3790. "Equal Rights Amendment Suffers Serious Blow." Skirting the Capitol, 12 July 1971, pp. 2-3. (H, R21)

3791. "The Equal Rights Amendment." Skirting the Capitol, 7 September 1971, pp. 3-4. (H, R21)

3792. "Pure Equal Rights Amendment Passes House." Skirting the Capitol, 15 October 1971, pp. 1-4 (entire issue). (HU, S1, R15)

3793. "Cold Reception to the E.R.A. in California." Skirting the Capitol, 10 April 1972, pp. 1-5. (HU, S1, R15)

3794. "Monday Night--April 17, 1972--7:30 P.M." Skirting the Capitol, 12 April 1972, pp. 1-4 (entire issue--includes editorial).

3795. "'Darn' the Torpedoes--Full Speed Ahead!" Skirting the Capitol, 9 May 1972, pp. 1-4 (entire issue). (HU, S1, R15)

3796. "Skirmish Lost--The Battle Begins!" Skirting the Capitol, 30 May 1972, pp. 1-4 (entire issue). (HU, S1, R15)

3797. "The E.R.A. Picture Today." Skirting the Capitol, 28 August 1972, pp. 1-4 (entire issue). (HU, S1, R15)

3798. "E.R.A. Campaign Strategy." Skirting the Capitol, 11 September 1972, pp. 1-4 (entire issue). (HU, S1, R15)

3799. "A Warning on the E.R.A." Skirting the Capitol, 23 October 1972, pp. 1-2. (HU, S1, R15)

3800. "Senator Mills Creates an E.R.A. Stalemate!" Skirting the Capitol, 10 November 1972, pp. 1-4. (HU, S1, R15)

3801. "The 27th Amendment Ratified by California." Skirting the Capitol, 27 November 1972, pp. 1-4. (HU, S1, R15)

3802. "Opposition to E.R.A. Grows." Skirting the Capitol, 20 February 1973, pp. 1-2. (HU, S1, R15)

3803. "E.R.A. Report." Skirting the Capitol, 12 March 1973, pp. 1-2. (HU, S1, R15)

3804. "Can Ratification Action Be Rescinded?" Skirting the Capitol, 17 April 1973, pp. 1-3. (HU, S1, R15)

3805. "BPW Pledges Money for ERA Ratification." Skirting the Capitol, 13 August 1973, p. 1. (HU, S2, R7)

South Bay NOW Newsletter (N.O.W., Sunnyvale, California; becomes Sunnyvale-South Bay Newsletter)

3806. "Equal Rights Amendment." South Bay NOW Newsletter, September 1970, p. 2. (H, R20)

3807. "The Equal Rights Amendment Has Been Defeated for this Session of Congress." South Bay NOW Newsletter, [10 January 1971], p. 1. (H, R20)

3808. "The Amendment on the Equal Rights Amendment or Aye, There's the Rub." South Bay NOW Newsletter, [August 1971], p. 8. (H, R20)

3809. "The E.R.A. (Latest News)." South Bay NOW Newsletter, June/July 1972, p. 8. (HU, S1, R12)

3810. "ERA . . . Back to the Assembly." South Bay NOW Newsletter,
November/December 1972, p. 3.   (HU, S1, R12)

3811. "Legislation." South Bay NOW Newsletter, December/January 1972/73,
pp. 2-3.   (WL; HU, S1, R12)

3812. "ERA Needs Your Blood." South Bay NOW Newsletter, February 1973,
p. 3.   (HU, S1, R12)

3813. "Second Resolution to Rescind ERA Introduced." South Bay NOW
Newsletter, May/June 1973, p. 3.   (HU, S1, R12)

3814. "ERA Referendum?" Sunnyvale-South Bay Newsletter, March 1974, p. 4.
(HU, S2, R5)

Southeastern Connecticut N.O.W. News/Notes (N.O.W., Stonington)

3815. "More on the ERA." Southeastern Connecticut N.O.W. News/Notes,
24 February 1973, p. [3].   (H2, S1, R12)

3816. "Connecticut Women Become Citizens: ERA Passes House and Senate."
Southeastern Connecticut N.O.W. News/Notes, [14 March 1973], p. 1.
(H2, S1, R12)

3817. "ERA First--Then a Union." Southeastern Connecticut N.O.W. News/
Notes, 7 April 1973, p. 1.   (H2, S1, R12)

Southern California National Women's Political Caucus Newsletter
(Los Angeles)

3818. "Equal Rights Amendment Goes to Senate Soon." Southern California
National Women's Political Caucus Newsletter, January 1972, p. 4.
(H2, S1, R13)

3819. "More on Equal Rights Amendment." Southern California National
Women's Political Caucus Newsletter, January 1972, p. 8.   (H2, S1, R13)

3820. "NWPC Calls for Prompt Ratification of ERA" and "The Next Step."
Southern California National Women's Political Caucus Newsletter,
April 1972, p. 2.   (H2, S1, R13)

3821. "Call in the Big Guns on ERA." Southern California National
Women's Political Caucus Newsletter, April 1972, p. 3.   (H2, S1, R13)

3822. "Equal Rights Amendment." Southern California National Women's
Political Caucus Newsletter, July 1972, p. 3.   (H2, S1, R13)

Southern California NOW Newsletter (Los Angeles): See NOW News
(Los Angeles)

Southwest Cook County NOW Newsletter (Illinois): See NOW . . . or Never

SpeakOut (Unitarian Universalist Women's Federation Newsletter): See
Bridge

Spokeswoman (Urban Research Corporation, Chicago, Illinois)

3823. "Women Testify for the Equal Rights Amendment." Spokeswoman,
5 June 1970, p. [3]. (H, R21)

3824. "Griffith Circulates Discharge Petition for Equal Rights Amendment."
Spokeswoman, 30 June 1970, p. 3. (H, R21)

3825. "Push to Pass ERA." Spokeswoman, 30 July 1970, p. 3. (H, R21)

3826. "House Victory on ERA Swallowed by Senate Threat." Spokeswoman,
28 August 1970, p. 1. (H, R21) Rep. in entry #2819.

3827. "ERA." Spokeswoman, 30 September [1970], p. 7. (H, R21)

3828. "Equal Rights Amendment." Spokeswoman, 30 September [1970],
p. 6. (H, R21)

3829. "Equal Rights Amendment." Spokeswoman, 30 October [1970], p. 5.
(H, R21)

3830. "Equal Rights Amendment." Spokeswoman, 1 January 1971, p. 6.
(H, R21)

3831. "Equal Rights Amendment." Spokeswoman, 1 March 1971, p. 4. (H,
R21)

3832. "Equal Rights." Spokeswoman, 1 June 1971, p. 6. (H, R21)

3833. "ERA." Spokeswoman, 1 July 1971, p. 6. (H, R21)

3834. "A.A.U.W." Spokeswoman, 1 August 1971, p. 7. (H, R21)

3835. "ERA Is Half Way Home." Spokeswoman, 1 November 1971, p. 3.
(HU, S1, R16)

3836. "ERA Si." Spokeswoman, December 1971, p. 6. (HU, S1, R16)

3837. "Legislation: Reed vs Reed." Spokeswoman, 1 January 1972, p. 5.
(HU, S1, R16)

3838. "Alimony and Testimony." Spokeswoman, 1 February 1972, p. 1.
(HU, S1, R16) Rep. in entry #3649.

3839. "Note from Washington: ERA Si." Spokeswoman, 1 February 1972,
p. 6. (HU, S1, R16)

3840. Untitled. Spokeswoman, 1 April 1972, p. 1. (HU, S1, R16)

3841. "Go to the Mattresses State by State; Crater's Raiders Can Claim
Coup." Spokeswoman, 1 May 1972, p. 2. (WL; HU, S1, R16)

3842. "Make ERA a Campaign Issue." Spokeswoman, 1 August 1972, p. 8.
(HU, S1, R16)

3843. "ERA Breakthrough in California." Spokeswoman, 1 October 1972,
    p. 5. (WL; HU, S1, R16) Rep. in entry #1086.

3844. "ERA--The Way It Stands State by State." Spokeswoman, 1 October
    1972, p. 5. (HU, S1, R16) Rep. in entry #3525.

3845. "16 States to Go for ERA Victory." Spokeswoman, 15 January 1973,
    p. 4. (HU, S1, R16)

3846. "Where Does Anti-ERA Money Come From?" Spokeswoman, 15 February
    1973, pp. 1, 8. (HU, S1, R16)

3847. "NOW and Ms. Hypo ERA." Spokeswoman, 15 April 1973, p. 3.
    (WL; HU, S1, R16)

3848. "Redbook Polls Leaders on ERA." Spokeswoman, 15 June 1973, p. 4.
    (HU, S1, R16)

3849. "AFL-CIO Endorses ERA." Spokeswoman, 15 November 1973, p. 2.
    (HU, S2, R7)

3850. "ERA: Only Five More to Go." Spokeswoman, 15 March 1974, p. 1.
    (HU, S2, R7)

3851. "Catholic Women Organize to Support the ERA." Spokeswoman,
    15 June 1974, p. 5. (HU, S2, R7)

Springfield NOW Newsletter (Illinois): See Majority Report

St. John's County NOW (N.O.W., St. Augustine, Florida)

3852. "Equal Rights Amendment." St. John's County NOW, 15 January 1973,
    p. [2]. (H2, S1, R11)

St. Louis NOW Newsletter (Missouri): See ". . . & Nothing Less"

Sunnyvale-South Bay Newsletter (California): See South Bay NOW Newsletter

Tell-a-Woman (Women's Center, Philadelphia, Pennsylvania)

3853. "Equal Rights Amendment." Tell-a-Woman, June 1972, p. 1.
    (H2, S1, R16)

3854. "Equal Rights Amendment." Tell-a-Woman, September 1972, p. 2.
    (WL; H2, S1, R16)

3855. "The Equal Rights Amendment." Tell-a-Woman, March 1973, p. 5.
    (H2, S1, R16)

Texas WEAL Newsletter (Women's Equity Action League, Dallas)

3856. "Equal Legal Rights." Texas WEAL Newsletter, April 1972, p. 3.
    (H2, S1, R19)

3857. "New York Approves Women's Amendment." Texas WEAL Newsletter,
    June 1972, p. 2. (H2, S1, R19)

3858. "Equal Rights Amendment Would Bear on Finances." Texas WEAL
    Newsletter, June 1972, pp. 5-6. (H2, S1, R19)

3859. "Under Texas Laws You're Not Equal" and "Why Not the Equal Legal
    Rights Amendment?" Texas WEAL Newsletter, September 1972, p. 5.
    (H2, S1, R19)

3860. "ERA Voted Down in Oklahoma." Texas WEAL Newsletter, February
    1973, p. 8. (H2, S1, R19)

3861. "Texas ERA." Texas WEAL Newsletter, March 1973, p. 7. (H2, S1,
    R19)

3862. "Push to Repeal ERA Underway." Texas WEAL Newsletter, April 1973,
    p. 5. (H2, S1, R19)

Time to Unite (Women United, Washington, D.C.; press releases)

3863. Release No. 1, 7 April 1971. (H2, S1, R18)

3864. Release No. 2, 23 April 1971. (H2, S1, R18)

3865. Release No. 3, 19 May 1971. (H2, S1, R18)

3866. Release No. 4, 1 June 1971. (H2, S1, R18)

3867. Release No. 5, 3 June 1971. (H2, S1, R18)

3868. Release No. 6, 17 June 1971. (H2, S1, R18)

3869. Release No. 7, 18 June 1971. (H2, S1, R18)

3870. Release No. 8, 13 July 1971. (H2, S1, R18)

3871. Release No. 9, 17 August 1971. (H2, S1, R18)

3872. "Report on State of Equal Rights Amendment." Release No. 15,
    25 October 1971. (H2, S1, R18) Reprints entries #5432, 5788.

3873. Release No. 16, 12 November 1971. (H2, S1, R18)

3874. Release No. 17, 14 December 1971. (H2, S1, R18)

3875. Release No. 18, 2 March 1972. (H2, S1, R18)

3876. Release No. 19, 3 April 1972. (H2, S1, R18)

Tippecanoe NOW News (N.O.W., West Lafayette, Indiana)

3877. "ERA." Tippecanoe NOW News, November 1973, p. 1. (H3, R3)

Title VII Report (New York, New York)

3878. "Equal Rights Bill." Title VII Report, 24 August 1970, p. 1.
    (H, R21)

3879. "Getting the Message Across." Title VII Report, 21 September 1970, pp. 1-3. (H, R21)

3880. "ERA Gets Bi-Partisan Support." Title VII Report, 21 September 1970, p. 4. (H, R21)

Together (ASUC L.A. Communications Board, Los Angeles, California)

3881. "Equal Rights for Whom?" Together, 19 November 1973, p. 8. (N) (H2, R2, R11)

Torch (DuPage N.O.W., Glen Ellyn, Illinois)

3882. "E.R.A." Torch, November 1972, p. [2]. (H2, S1, R10)

3883. "ERA Status." Torch, December 1972, p. 3. (H2, S1, R10)

3884. "E.R.A." Torch, February 1973, pp. [2-3]. (H2, S1, R10)

3885. "Minutes from February 14th." Torch, March 1973, pp. [1-2].

3886. "Political News." Torch, March 1973, p. [2]. (H2, S1, R10)

3887. "ERA Vote"; "ERA Wine and Cheese Party"; and "Bus-In." Torch, April 1973, p. [3]. (H2, S1, R10)

3888. "E.R.A." Torch, May 1973, p. [2]. (H2, S1, R10)

3889. "ERA News." Torch, June 1973, p. [3]. (H2, S1, R10)

3890. "ERA News: Calling All Housewives." Torch, July 1973, pp. [3-4]. (H2, S2, R6)

3891. "ERA News." Torch, January 1974, p. [2]. (H2, S2, R6)

3892. "ERA News." Torch, February 1974, p. [2]. (H2, S2, R6)

3893. "ERA News." Torch, March 1974, p. [2]. (H2, S2, R6)

3894. "ERA News." Torch, April 1974, p. [4]. (H2, S2, R6)

3895. "ERA News." Torch, May 1974, p. [2]. (H2, S2, R6)

3896. "ERA News." Torch, June 1974, pp. [3-4]. (H2, S2, R6)

Traffic Jam (Women at A.T. & T., Seattle, Washington)

3897. "Forum on the Equal Rights Amendment and Protective Legislation." Traffic Jam, 1 February 1971, p. [2]. (H, R21)

3898. "Protective Laws." Traffic Jam, 22 February 1971, p. [2]. (H, R21)

Tucson NOW Newsletter (N.O.W., Arizona)

3899. "ERA on Its Way." Tucson NOW Newsletter, November 1972, p. 1. (H2, S1, R12)

3900. "The Arizona Constitution." Tucson NOW Newsletter, December 1972, p. 2. (H2, S1, R12)

3901. "ERA Report: Resolution for 1973." Tucson NOW Newsletter, January 1973, p. 1. (H2, S1, R12)

3902. "ERA Report: Busier Month Ahead." Tucson NOW Newsletter, February 1973, pp. [1-2]. (H2, S1, R12)

3903. "ERA Report: Work Continues." Tucson NOW Newsletter, March 1973, p. 1. (H2, S1, R12)

3904. "ERA--It Lives!" Tucson NOW Newsletter, April 1973, p. 1. (H2, S1, R12)

3905. "ERA Memorial--City Council Tie." Tucson NOW Newsletter, May 1973, p. 1. (H2, S1, R12)

3906. "State Bill Is OK, But . . ." Tucson NOW Newsletter, June 1973, p. 1. (H2, S1, R12)

3907. "Star Supports ERA." Tucson NOW Newsletter, September 1973, p. 1. (H2, S2, R8)

3908. "AFL-CIO Supports ERA" and "ERA Moving." Tucson NOW Newsletter, November 1973, p. 1. (H2, S2, R8)

3909. "ERA--Here We Come." Tucson NOW Newsletter, January 1974, p. 1. (H2, S2, R8)

3910. "ERA Victory." Tucson NOW Newsletter, February 1974, p. 1. (H2, S2, R8)

3911. "Fayhee Packs 'Em in on the ERA!" Tucson NOW Newsletter, February 1974, p. [3]. (H2, S2, R8)

3912. "ERA--Out and Onward." Tucson NOW Newsletter, March 1974, p. 1. (H2, S2, R8)

3913. "e.r.a. letdown--an editorial." Tucson NOW Newsletter, April 1974, p. [2]. (H2, S2, R8)

3914. "Pro ERA Effort by Legislature." Tucson NOW Newsletter, June 1974, p. 1. (H2, S2, R8)

Twin Cities NOW Newsletter (N.O.W., Minneapolis, Minnesota)

3915. "Rally for Rights." Twin Cities NOW Newsletter, August 1972, pp. [1-2]. (H2, S1, R12)

Union County NOW Newsletter (N.O.W., Westfield, New Jersey)

3916. "Equal Rights Amendment." Union County NOW Newsletter, June 1971, p. [2]. (H2, S1, R12)

3917. "Last Chance for the ERA?" Union County NOW Newsletter, Summer
1971, p. 3. (H2, S1, R12)

3918. "Equal Rights Amendment." Union County NOW Newsletter, September
1971, p. 3. (H2, S1, R12)

3919. "Equal Rights Amendment." Union County NOW Newsletter, November
1971, p. 5. (H2, S1, R12)

3920. "Equal Rights Amendment." Union County NOW Newsletter, December
1971, p. 4. (H2, S1, R12)

3921. "ERA in Danger." Union County NOW Newsletter, February 1972, p. 1.
(H2, S1, R12)

3922. "Hooray Hooray for the ERA." Union County NOW Newsletter,
April 1972, p. 1. (H2, S1, R12)

3923. "N. J. Ratifies ERA." Union County NOW Newsletter, May 1972, p. 7.
(H2, S1, R12)

Unitarian Universalist Women's Federation Newsletter: See Bridge

United Sisters (Women's Center Newsletter, Tampa, Florida)

3924. "ERA Hearings Held." United Sisters, March 1973, p. 13.
(H2, S1, R16)

3925. Genevieve, Bonnie. "What Will Happen to the ERA?" United Sisters,
April 1973, p. 4. (H2, S1, R16)

3926. Morgan, Julie. "The E.R.A. And US." (Poem) United Sisters,
May 1973, pp. 8-9. (H2, S1, R16)

3927. "ERA Vote Preceded by Ceremony Honoring Junior Miss." United
Sisters, September 1973, p. 4. (H2, S2, R11)

University of Virginia News Letter (Charlottesville)

3928. Joyner, Nancy D. "The Commonwealth's [Virginia's] Approach to
the Equal Rights Amendment." University of Virginia News Letter,
15 May 1974, pp. 33-36.

Up to NOW (Fairfield N.O.W., Ohio)

3929. Cargill, Jennie. "Report from ERA Coordinator." Up to NOW,
January 1974, p. [4]. (H3, R2)

3930. _____. "Report from ERA Coordinator." Up to NOW, February
1974, p. 2. (H3, R2)

Ventura NOW (N.O.W., California)

3931. "State of the ERA." Ventura NOW, April 1973, p. 2. (H2, S1, R12)

3932. "Resolution to Rescind ERA Ratification." Ventura NOW, April
  1973, p. 3. (H2, S1, R12)

Virginia Beach NOW Newsletter: See Right NOW (Virginia Beach)

3933. Virginia ERA Ratification Council Newsletter (Charlottesville;
  continuing coverage)

Vocal Majority (Washington, D.C. N.O.W.; formerly Washington D.C. NOW
  Newsletter)

3934. "Equal Rights Amendment." Washington, D.C. NOW Newsletter, May/
  June 1970, p. 1. (H, Add)

3935. "A Council for the ERA." Vocal Majority, January 1971, p. 4.
  (H, R20)

3936. "ERA Hearings." Vocal Majority, March 1971, p. 5. (H, R20)

3937. "ERA Hearings." Vocal Majority, May 1971, p. 6. (H, R20)

3938. "Kicking the Traces: 'Do Union Women Want the ERA?'" Vocal
  Majority, May 1971, p. 16. (H, R20)

3939. George Washington University Women's Liberation. "The Equal Rights
  Amendment and the Draft." Vocal Majority, May 1971, p. 24. (H, R20)
  Rep. from entry #580; also rep. in entries #141, 1161, 3209.

3940. "ERA Needs Help." Vocal Majority, June 1971, pp. 15-16. (H, R20)

3941. Burris, Carol. "The E.R.A. on June 22, 1971." Vocal Majority,
  July 1971, p. 6. (H, R20)

3942. "Blood for the ERA." The Vocal Majority, March 1973, p. 4.
  (HU, S1, R12)

3943. "Equal Rights Amendment Push" and "CBS Hires ERA Opponent."
  Vocal Majority, July 1973, p. 11. (HU, S2, R5)

3944. "U.S. Commission on Civil Rights Endorses Equal Rights Amendment."
  Vocal Majority, September 1973, p. 6. (HU, S2, R5)

Vocational Center for Women (Nassau County Department of General
  Services, Carle Place, New York)

3945. "What Every Woman Should Know about the Equal Rights Amendment."
  Vocational Center for Women 3, no. 1 (n.d.), p. [4]. (H2, S1, R16)

Washington D.C. NOW Newsletter: See Vocal Majority

Washington Newsletter for Women (Barrer and Associates, Inc.,
  Washington, D.C.)

3946. "Equal Rights Amendment." Washington Newsletter for Women,
  July 1970, p. 3. (H, Add)

3947. "Equal Rights Amendment." Washington Newsletter for Women,
    August 1970, p. 3. (H, R22)

3948. Washington Newsletter for Women, 18 August 1970, entire issue.

WEAL Washington Report (Women's Equity Action League, Washington, D.C.)

3949. "Equal Rights Amendment." Congressional and Court Action of
    Interest to Women as of 9/31/71. Published by National Capitol
    Chapter, Women's Equity Action League.

3950. "Equal Rights Amendment." WEAL Washington Report, October 1971,
    p. 1. (HU, S1, R18)

3951. "Equal Rights Amendment." WEAL Washington Report, 15 November
    1971, p. 1. (HU, S1, R18)

3952. "Equal Rights Amendment." WEAL Washington Report, 14 January
    1972, p. 1. (HU, S1, R18)

3953. "Equal Rights Amendment." WEAL Washington Report, 8 March 1972,
    p. 1. (HU, S1, R18)

3954. "Equal Rights Amendment." WEAL Washington Report, 1 May 1972,
    p. 1. (HU, S1, R18)

3955. "Equal Rights Amendment." WEAL Washington Report, 1 December
    1972, p. 1. (HU, S1, R18)

3956. "Report from ERA Committee Head Marguerite Rawalt." WEAL
    Washington Report, June 1974, p. 6. (HU, S2, R8)

Western Connecticut NOW Newsletter (N.O.W., Stratford)

3957. "Urgent! Action Needed for Equal Rights Amendment!" Western
    Connecticut NOW Newsletter, [September 1970], p. 1. (H, R17)

3958. "Equal Rights Amendment." Western Connecticut NOW Newsletter,
    [March 1971], p. 2. (H, R17)

3959. "ERA." Western Connecticut NOW Newsletter, May 1971, p. 1.
    (H, R17)

3960. "Illinois ERA." Western Connecticut NOW Newsletter, June 1971,
    p. [2]. (H, R17)

3961. "ERA." Western Connecticut NOW Newsletter, July 1971, p. 2.
    (H, R17)

3962. "ERA." Western Connecticut NOW Newsletter, October 1971, p. 2.
    (HU, S1, R12)

3963. "Disgraced and Disappointed." Western Connecticut NOW Newsletter,
    April 1972, p. 1. (HU, S1, R12)

3964. "Connecticut Ratifies the ERA." Western Connecticut NOW Newsletter, March 1973, p. 2. (HU, S1, R12)

What NOW (Milwaukee N.O.W., Wisconsin)

3965. "Senators Go Home without Action on Equal Rights Amendment." What NOW, November 1970, p. 1. (H, R18)

3966. "Step Up Pressure for E.R.A." What NOW, December 1970, p. 3. (H, R18)

3967. "ERA Fight Not Dead!" What NOW, April 1971, p. [2]. (H, R18)

3968. "Support ERA, Write" and "If They Amend the ERA." What NOW, July 1971, p. 7. (H, R18)

3969. "ERA Needs Boost." What NOW, August 1971, p. 7. (H, R18)

3970. "ERA on Brink of Decision." What NOW, October 1971, p. 1. (WL)

3971. "New Year's Resolution Urge ERA." What NOW, January 1972, p. 4. (HU, S1, R9)

3972. Guiseppi, Meg. "ERA." What NOW, April 1973, pp. 9-10. (HU, S1, R10)

Wisconsin Women Newsletter (Center for Women's and Family Living Education, University of Wisconsin, Madison; formerly Women's Education Newsletter)

3973. "Equal Rights Amendment." Women's Education Newsletter, October 1970, pp. 1-2. (H, R22)

3974. "Equal Rights Amendment." Wisconsin Women Newsletter, February 1971, pp. 7-8. (H, R22)

3975. "Wisconsin Equal Rights Amendment." Wisconsin Women Newsletter, February 1972, pp. 5-6. (HU, S1, R16)

3976. "Wisconsin Ratifies U.S. Equal Rights Amendment." Wisconsin Women Newsletter, June 1972, p. 1. (WL; HU, S1, R16)

3977. "Passage of Equal Rights Implementation Package Heads Priority List of Wisconsin Women." Wisconsin Women Newsletter, January 1973, pp. 3-4. (HU, S1, R16)

3978. "Why Women Need the ERA." Wisconsin Women Newsletter, July 1975, p. 4. Reprint of a 1930s newspaper article.

Witchita NOW Newsletter (N.O.W., Kansas)

3979. "Ratification of ERA Crucial Issue." Witchita NOW Newsletter, August 1972, p. 2. (HU, S1, R12)

3980. "More on the Equal Rights Amendment." Witchita NOW Newsletter, December 1972, p. 2. (HU, S1, R12)

3981. "ERA in Trouble." Witchita NOW Newsletter, February 1973, pp. 2-5. (HU, S1, R12)

3982. "ERA Count Uncertain." Witchita NOW Newsletter, 31 March 1973, p. 3. (HU, S1, R12)

Woman (Davis Women's Center, California)

3983. "Equal Rights?" Woman, May/June 1972, p. 4. (H2, S1, R16)

Woman Activist (Falls Church, Virginia)

3984. Untitled. Woman Activist, 14 January 1970, pp. 1-3 (entire issue). (H, R22)

3985. "Senate Joint Resolution 8 and 9; House Joint Resolution 208"; "Senate Sponsors This Session"; "These Senators Record in 91st Session"; and "The Filibuster Rule." Woman Activist, 14 February 1971, p. 1. (H, R22)

3986. "Equal Rights Amendment for Women." Woman Activist, 14 February 1971, p. [2]. (H, R22)

3987. "Senator Stennis (D. Miss.) Meets George Washington University Women's Liberation February 10." Woman Activist, 14 February 1971, p. [3]. (H, R22)

3988. "House Hearings on Equal Rights Amendment Four Days Beginning March 24, 1971" and "Workshop for Women." Woman Activist, 15 March 1971, p. 1. (H, R22)

3989. "House Members Sponsoring the Equal Rights Amendment." Woman Activist, 15 March 1971, p. [4]. (H, R22)

3990. "House Hearings on Equal Rights"; "First Decision Must Be for ERA"; and "Excerpts from Testimony at Equal Rights Hearing before House Judiciary Committee #4." Woman Activist, 15 April 1971, pp. 1-3. (H, R22)

3991. "House Acts for ERA"; "The Woman's Lobby"; "Visit Senators May 19"; and "Senator Vance Hartke, S. J. Res. 79." Woman Activist, 15 May 1971, p. 1. (H, R22)

3992. "Texts of the Equal Rights Amendment--A Comparison." Woman Activist, 15 May 1971, p. [3]. (H, R22)

3993. "House Judiciary Committee Met June 14 on ERA," etc. Woman Activist, 15 June 1971, p. 1. (H, R22)

3994. "Events and Information for Virginia Women Who Believe in Equal Treatment under Law for All Women." Woman Activist (Virginia edition), 15 June 1971, p. [2]. (H, R22)

3995. "House Judiciary Committee Votes Crippling Wiggins Amendment to ERA." Woman Activist, 1 July 1971, pp. 1-2. (H, R22)

3996. "Floor Fight on ERA Assured" and "Harris Asks Senate to Act on ERA." Woman Activist, 15 July 1971, pp. 1, 2. (H, R22)

3997. "Texts of the Equal Rights Amendment--Comparison #2." Woman Activist, 15 July 1971, p. [3]. (H, R22)

3998. "House Vote to Be Close on ERA." Woman Activist, 15 August 1971, pp. 1, 2. (H, R22)

3999. Crater, Flora. Letter to Congress. Woman Activist, 15 August 1971, p. [5]. (H, R22)

4000. "Support of the Proposed Equal Rights Amendment to the United States Constitution." Woman Activist, 15 August 1971, p. [6]. (H, R22)

4001. "Senator Sam Ervin (D.N.C.) Prepares to Filibuster ERA in the Senate." Woman Activist, 15 August 1971, p. [7]. (H, R22)

4002. "Coming Votes on EEOC and ERA to Test House on Women's Rights." Woman Activist, 15 September 1971, p. 1. (H, R22)

4003. "House Votes Equal Rights for Women--Senate Action in November Probable." Woman Activist, 15 October 1971, pp. [1-3]. (HU, S1, R16)

4004. "Heide Testifies with Clarity and Clout before Senate Judiciary Committee." Woman Activist, 15 November 1971, p. 1. (HU, S1, R16)

4005. "Senator Ervin Amends Amends Amends Amends." Woman Activist, 15 November 1971, p. [6]. (HU, S1, R16)

4006. "Need for Equal Rights Amendment Confirmed by Supreme Court Decision and Senate Action." Woman Activist, 15 December 1971, p. 1. (HU, S1, R16)

4007. "Sex and the Single Administratrix." Woman Activist, 15 December 1971, p. [2]. (HU, S1, R16) Rep. from entry #5433.

4008. "Five Winning Steps for Senate Passage of Equal Rights Amendment." Woman Activist, 15 December 1971, p. [4-5]. (HU, S1, R16)

4009. "Senate Judiciary Committee to Act on ERA February 29." Woman Activist, February 1972, p. 1. (HU, S1, R16)

4010. "Current Position of Senators on the Equal Rights Amendment." Woman Activist, February 1972, p. [2]. (HU, S1, R16)

4011. "Senators to Debate Women's Equality Next Week." Woman Activist, March 1972, p. 1. (HU, S1, R16)

4012. "To: Women Lobbyists," etc. Woman Activist, March 1972, p. [2]. (HU, S1, R16)

4013. "Spong Still Uncommitted to Vote for Equal Rights Amendment." Woman Activist (Virginia edition), March 1972, p. 1. (HU, S1, R16)

4014. "ERA Passage Signals New Political Woman Constituency." Woman
Activist, April 1972, p. 1. (HU, S1, R16)

4015. "Plan for State Ratification of ERA and the Woman Constituency."
Woman Activist, April 1972, pp. [4-5]. (HU, S1, R16)

4016. "Crater's Raiders." Woman Activist, April 1972, p. [6].
(HU, S1, R16)

4017. "Why the Equal Rights Amendment?" Woman Activist, April 1972,
p. [7]. Flyer reprint. (HU, S1, R16)

4018. Shelton, Isabelle. "How Equal Rights Passed Senate." Woman
Activist, April 1972, p. [8]. (HU, S1, R16) Rep. from entry #5738.

4019. "Ratification of ERA." Woman Activist, May 1972, p. 1.
(HU, S1, R16)

4020. "Ratification of ERA." Woman Activist (Virginia edition), June
1972, p. [6]. (HU, S1, R16)

4021. "Ratification of ERA Crucial Issue Now." Woman Activist
(Virginia edition), July 1972, p. [6]. (WL; HU, S1, R16)

4022. "Plan for the Woman Constituency and State Ratification of ERA."
Woman Activist, 26 August 1972, p. 19. (WL; HU, S1, R16)

4023. "Equal Rights Amendment for Women." Woman Activist, 26 August
1972, p. 20. (WL; HU, S1, R16)

4024. "California Ratifies ERA." Woman Activist (Virginia edition),
November 1972, p. [5]. (HU, S1, R16)

4025. "ERA Ratification." Woman Activist, January 1973, p. 1.
(HU, S1, R16)

4026. "Status of ERA to Date: Crater to Chair NWPC Ratification
Committee." Woman Activist, February 1973, p. 11. (HU, S1, R16)

4027. "Congresswomen Martha Griffiths and Margaret Heckler Attack
Misinformation of ERA Opponents." Woman Activist, March 1973, p. 1.
(HU, S1, R16)

4028. "NWPC Adopts Elective Strategy for ERA." Woman Activist, April
1973, p. 1. (HU, S1, R16)

4029. "Chronology of U.S. Congressional Action on the Equal Rights
Amendment." Woman Activist, April 1973, p. 4. (HU, S1, R16)

4030. "ERA Ratification Must Wait until 1974." Woman Activist, April
1973, p. 5. (HU, S1, R16)

4031. "The Equal Rights Amendment--Review and Strategy." Woman
Activist, October/November 1973, pp. 5-6. (HU, S2, R7)

4032. "ERA Countdown." Woman Activist, February 1974, p. 5. (HU, S2,
R7)

4033. "So Near, and Yet . . ." Woman Activist, 15 March 1974, p. 4.
(HU, S2, R7) Rep. from entry #5741.

4034. "Democracy in Virginia--For Men Only." Woman Activist, 15 March
1974, p. 1. (HU, S2, R7)

4035. "ERA Skewered in Secrecy by Thomson and Miller: Virginia Women's
Political Caucus Leads Protest." Woman Activist (Virginia edition),
15 March 1974, p. 1. (HU, S2, R7)

4036. "Resolution in Protest of Action of Assembly on ERA." Woman
Activist (Virginia edition), 15 March 1974, p. 2. (HU, S2, R7)

4037. Dewar, Helen. "Women's Rights Bill Loses in Va.: Confidential
Memo Held to Blame." Woman Activist, 15 March 1974, p. 7. (HU, S2,
R7) Rep. from entry #5463.

4038. "ERA Status." The Woman Activist, May 1974, p. 7. (HU, S2, R7)

4039. "State Elections Help ERA Ratification in '75." Woman Activist,
November 1974, p. 3.

4040. "Illinois Women for ERA File New Lawsuit." Woman Activist,
November 1974, p. 5.

4041. "Strategies for ERA Ratification 1975." Woman Activist, November
1974, p. 6.

4042. "ERA Status and Strategies." Woman Activist, July 1975, p. 6.

4043. "Status and Strategies for ERA Ratification." The Woman Activist,
26 August 1975, entire issue.

4044. "ERA Status Strategies." Woman Activist, September 1975.

4045. "Political Right Makes Anti-ERA Major Issue." Woman Activist
(Virginia edition), November 1975, p. [1].

4046. "ERA Status and Strategies." Woman Activist (Virginia edition),
November 1975, p. 11.

4047. Brickey, Carolyn. "Virginia Election Improves ERA Chances:
Fewer Women Run, More Elected." Woman Activist (Virginia edition),
November 1975, insert.

4047a. "Precinct Issue Politics." Woman Activist, December 1975, p. 7.

4047b. "ERA Election Day Precinct Survey." Woman Activist, December
1975, p. 8.

Woman Lobbyist (Woman Activists in New York State)

4048. "ERA Alert." Woman Lobbyist, 5 May 1975, pp. 1-2 (entire issue).

Womanpower (Brookline, Massachusetts)

4049. "The Equal Rights Amendment for Women Will Probably Come to a
Vote in the House in Mid-October." Womanpower, October 1971, p. 2.
(H, R22)

Women (Berkshire Women's Liberation Newsletter, Lenox, Massachusetts)

4050. "Equal Rights." Women, 28 February 1972, p. [3]. (H2, S1, R17)

4051. Vivi. "Equal Rights Amendment: Not Yet." Women, 21 April 1973,
p. 11. (H2, S1, R17)

4052. "Update on the E.R.A." Women, March 1974, p. 24. (H2, S2, R12)

Women and Work (U.S. Department of Labor, Washington, D.C.)

4053. "Women Eye Movement of Equal Rights Amendment." Women and Work,
March 1973, pp. [13-14]. (H2, S1, R17)

Women Are Human (Ohio State University Library, Columbus)

4054. Fennessy, K. "The Proposed 27th Amendment--The Equal Rights
Amendment." Women Are Human, 2 June 1972, pp. [3-5]. (H2, S1, R17)

4055. "The Proposed 27th Amendment--The Equal Rights Amendment."
Women Are Human, 9 June 1972, pp. 3-4. (H2, S1, R17)

4056. "Citizens for the ERA." Women Are Human, 25 April 1972, p. 3.
(H2, S1, R17)

4057. "Citizens for the ERA." Women Are Human, 25 August 1972, p. 3.
(WL; H2, S1, R17)

4058. "Citizens for the Equal Rights Amendment." Women Are Human,
6 October 1972, p. 4. (H2, S1, R17)

4059. "ERA Bumper Stickers." Women Are Human, 3 November 1972, p. 4.
(H2, S1, R17)

4060. "The Equal Rights Amendment." Women Are Human, 10 November 1972,
pp. 3-4. (H2, S1, R17)

4061. "Equal Rights Amendment." Women Are Human, 9 February 1973,
pp. 3-4. (H2, S1, R17)

4062. "Equal Rights Amendment." Women Are Human, 2 March 1973, p. 4.
(H2, S1, R17)

4063. "Equal Rights Amendment." Women Are Human, 7 March 1973, p. 3.
(H2, S1, R17)

4064. "Equal Rights Amendment." Women Are Human, 16 March 1973, p. 3.
(H2, S1, R17)

4065. "The Equal Rights Amendment." Women Are Human, 6 April 1973, p. 4.
(H2, S1, R17)

4066. "Equal Rights Amendment." Women Are Human, 13 April 1973, p. 6.
(H2, S1, R17)

4067. "Equal Rights Amendment." Women Are Human, 27 April 1973, p. 4.
(H2, S1, R17)

4068. "State Equal Rights Amendment." Women Are Human, 4 May 1973,
pp. 3-4. (H2, S1, R17)

Women for Change Center Newsletter (Dallas, Texas)

4069. "Equal Legal Rights Issue." Women for Change Center Newsletter,
[January 1972], p. [2]. (H2, S1, R17)

4070. "Equal Rights Legislation Coming Up Soon." Women for Change
Center Newsletter, [February 1972], p. [8]. (H2, S1, R17)

4071. "Senate Passes Equal Rights Amendment: 88-4 March 1972."
Women for Change Center Newsletter, April 1972, p. 9. (H2, S1, R17)

4072. "ERA." Women for Change Center Newsletter, April 1973, p. [2].
(H2, S1, R17) Associated Press item and a reprint from Dallas
Morning News, 9 February 1973.

4073. "ERA." Women for Change Center Newsletter, June/July 1973, p.
[2]. (H2, S1, R17) Rep. from entry #4132.

4074. Citizens' Advisory Council on the Status of Women. "Equal Rights
Amendment--What It Will and Won't Do." Women for Change Center
Newsletter, June/July 1973, p. [4]. (H2, S1, R17) Rep. from entry
#372; also rep. in entries #306, 2983.

4075. "ERA." Women for Change Center Newsletter, August 1973, p. 2.
(H2, S2, R12) Rep. from entry #5677.

Women in Struggle (Winneconne, Wisconsin)

4076. "End of an E.R.A." Women in Struggle, January/February 1971,
p. [6]. (H, R22)

4077. "E.R.A. Lives." Women in Struggle, October 1971, supplement
p. [2]. (HU, S1, R17)

4078. "Uphill Again." Women in Struggle, January/February 1972, p. 4.
(WL; HU, S1, R17)

4079. "Unaccommodating." Women in Struggle, March/April 1972, pp. [2,
3]. (HU, S1, R17)

4080. "E.R.A. on the Way." Women in Struggle, May/June 1972, p. 1.
(WL; HU, S1, R17)

4081. "More on E.R.A." Women in Struggle, May/June 1972, p. [2].
(WL; HU, S1, R17)

4082. Untitled. Women in Struggle, July/August 1972, pp. 3, 7, 8.
(WL; HU, S1, R17)

Women New York (Women's Division, State of New York, New York City)

4083. Women New York, November 1975, pp. 1-8 (entire issue).

Women's Caucus for Political Science Newsletter (Gainesville, Florida)

4084. "The Equal Rights Amendment." Women's Caucus for Political
Science Newsletter, Summer 1970, p. 13. (H, R22)

Women's Center Newsletter (Los Angeles, California): See L.A. Women's
Liberation Newsletter

Women's Center Newsletter (Storrs, Connecticut)

4085. "Equal Rights Amendment." Women's Center Newsletter, [13 February
1973], p. 4. (H2, S1, R15)

4086. "ERA Panel Discussion." Women's Center Newsletter, [13 February
1973], p. 8. (H2, S1, R15)

Women's Education Newsletter (Madison, Wisconsin): See Wisconsin
Women Newsletter

Women's Liberation Center of Nassau County Newsletter (New York)

4087. "ERA." Women's Liberation Center of Nassau County Newsletter,
April 1973, p. 10. (H2, S1, R7)

Women's Pages (Women's Center, Richmond, Virginia)

4088. "ERA Central." Women's Pages, February 1974, p. 1. (H3, R5)

Women's Rights Newsletter (State Women's Caucus, California Democratic
Council, Los Angeles)

4089. "Women Besiege Washington February 17 for Equal Rights Amendment."
Women's Rights Newsletter, February 1970, p. 1. (H, Add)

4090. "Equal Rights Amendment." Women's Rights Newsletter, May 1970,
p. 2. (H, R23)

4091. "What Happened to the Equal Rights Amendment?" Women's Rights
Newsletter, March 1972, p. 2. (H, Add)

4092. "Speaking of Removing Legal Barriers . . ." Women's Rights
Newsletter, June 1971, p. 2. (H, R23)

Women's Work and Education (Institute of Women's Professional Relations,
Connecticut College, New London)

4093. "Equal Rights." Women's Work and Education 8 (April 1937): 11.

4094. "Equal Rights." Women's Work and Education 14 (October 1943): 8.

Women Today (Washington, D.C.)

4095. "ERA--An Idea Whose Time Has Come?" Women Today, 15 February
1971, p. 1. (H, R23)

4096. "ERA Finally Gets Hearing." Women Today, 19 March 1971, p. 1.
(H, R23)

4097. "House Subcommittee Hearings on ERA Ended after Six Days."
Women Today, 16 April 1971, p. 1. (H, R23)

4098. "Women United to Fight for ERA." Women Today, 16 April 1971,
p. 4. (H, R23)

4099. "ERA Is on Its Way." Women Today, 17 May 1971, p. 1. (H, R23)

4100. "ERA Passage Could Ease Swamped Court Calendars." Women Today,
26 July 1971, p. 2. (H, R23)

4101. "ERA: Keep Those Cards and Letters Coming." Women Today,
26 July 1971, p. [6]. (H, R23)

4102. "G.O.P. Urges Passage of E.R.A." Women Today, 14 August 1971,
p. 1. (H, R23; H, Add)

4103. "Home Economists Support E.R.A., Abortion Repeal." Women Today,
14 August 1971, p. [3]. (H, R23)

4104. "Ervin Strikes Again." Women Today, 6 September 1971, p. 1.
(H, Add)

4105. "E.R.A. Still in Limbo." Women Today, 20 September 1971, p. 1.
(H, Add)

4106. "Action on Equal Rights Amendment Postponed Again." Women Today,
4 October 1971, p. 1. (HU, S1, R17)

4107. "American Jewish Congress Supports the Equal Rights Amendment."
Women Today, 18 October 1971, p. 1. (HU, S1, R17)

4108. "E.R.A. Passes House." Women Today, 18 October 1971, p. [6].
(HU, S1, R17)

4109. "Women Will Have to Wait until Next Year for Senate Action on
E.R.A." Women Today, 31 October 1971, p. 1. (HU, S1, R17)

4110. "Does Reed Decision Affect Fight for Equality?" Women Today,
13 December 1971, pp. [2-3]. (HU, S1, R17)

4111. "Rep. Martha Griffiths Issues Appeal to Supporters of the E.R.A."
Women Today, 27 December 1971, p. [5]. (HU, S1, R17)

4112. "No Rest Yet for Weary E.R.A. Supporters." Women Today,
10 January 1972, p. 1. (HU, S1, R17)

4113. "C.A.C.S.W. Memorandum Explores the E.R.A. and Alimony and
Child Support Laws." Women Today, 7 February 1972, p. [2].
(HU, S1, R18)

4114. "L.A. Women Successfully Organize Male Support for the E.R.A."
Women Today, 21 February 1972, p. 1. (HU, S1, R18)

4115. "E.R.A. Clears Senate Committee." Women Today, 6 March 1972,
p. 1. (HU, S1, R18)

4116. "A Mandate for Sex Equality: E.R.A. Is Approved by Overwhelming
Majority." Women Today, 3 April 1972, p. 1. (HU, S1, R18)

4117. "Don't Delay Getting on the E.R.A. Ratification Bandwagon."
Women Today, 1 May 1972, p. 1. (HU, S1, R18)

4118. "They've Just Begun to Fight." Women Today, 15 May 1972, p. 4.
(WL; HU, S1, R18)

4119. "California N.W.P.C. and N.O.W. Promise No Campaign Work until
ERA Is Ratified." Women Today, 12 June 1972, p. 2. (HU, S1, R18)

4120. "Massachusetts Becomes 20th State to Ratify ERA; 18 More Needed;
District of Columbia City Council Endorses ERA; and ABA Journal
Scoffs at 'Legal Chaos' Predictions by ERA Opponents." Women Today,
24 July 1972, p. 7. (WL; HU, S1, R18)

4121. "Citizens Coalition for ERA Formed in Maryland." Women Today,
21 August 1972, p. 5. (HU, S1, R18)

4122. "Ratification of the Equal Rights Amendment Is First on BPW
Platform" and "California Senator James R. Mills Reverses Stand on
Ratification of ERA." Women Today, 2 October 1972, p. 1. (HU, S1,
R18)

4123. "Communist Party Opposes Equal Rights Amendment; American Party
Does Too." Women Today, 30 October 1972, p. 1. (HU, S1, R18)

4124. "Texas, Colorado and Hawaii Pass State Equal Rights Amendment."
Women Today, 11 December 1972, p. 2. (HU, S1, R18)

4125. "NOW Predictions--ERA State-by-State." Women Today, 8 January
1973, p. 2. (HU, S1, R18)

4126. "January a Good Month to Watch for ERA." Women Today, 22 January
1973, p. 1. (HU, S1, R18)

4127. "NOW Launches Blood Drive for ERA." Women Today, 5 February
1973, p. [6]. (HU, S1, R18)

4128. "ERA Ratification in Jeopardy after Recent Defeats in Five States."
Women Today, 19 February 1973, p. 2. (HU, S1, R18)

4129. "Support for ERA Mounting among Religious Leaders in the U.S."
and "President Nixon Voices Support of ERA." Women Today, 5 March
1973, p. 1. (HU, S1, R18)

4130. "Counsel on Constitutional Amendments Expresses Opinion on
Rescinding Ratification." Women Today, 16 April 1973, p. 1.
(WL; HU, S1, R18) Rep. in entry #3529.

4131. "ERA Opposition Is Attempt to Organize Women for Conservative
Political Purposes." Women Today, 30 April 1973, p. 1. (HU, S1, R18)
Rep. in entry #3530.

4132. "It's Time to Think about Next Year for Ratification of the ERA."
Women Today, 14 May 1973, p. 1. (HU, S1, R18) Rep. in entry #4073.

4133. "'Redbook' Encourages Support for ERA Ratification with Campaign."
Women Today, 28 May 1973, p. 5. (HU, S1, R18)

4134. "NOW Announces Formation of Two-Year National Strategy Plan for
ERA Ratification." Women Today, 11 June 1973, p. 1. (HU, S1, R18)

4135. "BPW Pledges Money for ERA Ratification." Women Today,
23 July 1973, p. 1. (HU, S2, R8)

4136. "League of Women Voters Launch ERA Ratification Campaign with
Sale of Bracelet." Women Today, 15 October 1973, p. 1. (HU, S2, R8)

4137. "League of Women Voters Announces ERA Campaign." Women Today,
29 October 1973, p. 1. (HU, S2, R8)

4138. "NOW & BPW Rejoice over AFL-CIO Commitment to ERA" and "BPW
Prexy Tours 14 States." Women Today, 12 November 1973, p. 1.
(HU, S2, R8) Rep. in entry #3317.

4139. "ERA: Countdown--Maine, Montana." Women Today, 21 January 1974,
p. 8. (HU, S2, R8)

4140. "Only Six More States Needed for ERA." Women Today, 4 February
1974, p. 15. (HU, S2, R8)

4141. "WEAL Poll in Ohio Showed 90 Percent of Random Population Sample
Supported ERA." Women Today, 4 February 1974, pp. 15-16. (HU, S2, R8)

4142. "BPW Announces Financial Boost to ERA Campaign." Women Today,
4 February 1974, p. 16. (HU, S2, R8)

4143. "'Beautiful Ohio' Is Number 33 in Ratification Race." Women Today,
18 February 1974, p. 21. (HU, S2, R8)

4144. "California Legislator Will Meet Legislators in Unratified States
to Discuss ERA." Women Today, 4 March 1974, p. 31. (HU, S2, R8)

4145. "Attempts to Rescind Tennessee ERA Vote Fail" and "Virginia ERA
Ratification Killed by State Senate Committee for This Year."
Women Today, 1 April 1974, p. 39. (HU, S2, R8)

4146. "California Commission on Status of Women Will Study Impact of
ERA." Women Today, 1 April 1974, p. 43. (HU, S2, R8)

4147. "ERA a Lost Cause in Missouri for This year." Women Today,
15 April 1974, p. 45. (HU, S2, R8)

4148. "Florida Senate Rejects Equality for Women" and "ERA Proponents
Will Ask the Voters." Women Today, 29 April 1974, p. 53. (HU, S2, R8)

4149. "ERA Rescission Move Stopped in House Committee in Michigan."
Women Today, 27 May 1974, p. 65. (HU, S2, R8)

4150. "Chicago Legislator Keeps ERA Alive in Illinois." Women Today,
10 June 1974, p. 71. (HU, S2, R8)

4151. "ERA Vote Due in Louisiana and Illinois." Women Today, 24 June
1974, p. 79. (HU, S2, R8)

4152. "ERA Campaign Planned by BPW." Women Today, 6 January 1975, p. 3.

4153. "ERA Dead This Year in Virginia and Oklahoma." Women Today,
3 February 1975, p. 13.

4154. "ERA Is on Its Way with Help from Betty Ford." Women Today,
17 February 1975, p. 1.

4155. "Now, Men for ERA, Democrat and Republican Leaders Support the
ERA." Women Today, 3 March 1975, p. 25.

4156. "Prospects for Ratification of ERA This Year Have Dimmed."
Women Today, 17 March 1975, p. 31.

4157. "No Chance for ERA Ratification in 1975." Women Today, 14 April
1975, p. 43.

4158. "Plans Made for National Focus of ERA Ratification in 76."
Women Today, 26 May 1975, p. 65.

4159. "ERA Loses in North Carolina, No Chance for Passage in 1975" and
"President Gives ERA His Strong Support." Women Today, 28 April
1975, p. 51.

4160. "ERA Nixed in Florida Despite Support from Betty Ford and Governor
Askew." Women Today, 12 May 1975, p. 57.

4161. "ERA Dead in Missouri." Women Today, 9 June 1975, p. 69.

4162. "ERA Rejected in Louisiana." Women Today, 23 June 1975, p. 76.

4163. "ERA '76 Telethon Committee Opens Office in Los Angeles."
Women Today, 18 August 1975, p. 100.

4164. "President Ford Calls for Commitment to Remove Barriers to Women's
Equality" and "LWV President Calls for 'Doubling of Efforts' for ERA
Ratification." Women Today, 24 November 1975, p. 143.

4165. "Pennsylvania Reports State ERA Effects Have Been 'Overwhelmingly
Positive.'" Women Today, 22 December 1975, p. 161.

Women Unite NOW (Ohio): See Cleveland NOW Newsletter

Yellow Ribbon (United Methodist Women's Caucus, Evanston, Illinois)

4166. "Resolution on Equal Rights of Women—Adopted by the 1972 General
Conference." Yellow Ribbon, March 1973, p. 5. (H2, S1, R20)

Your Cue from CCEW (Council for the Continuing Education of Women,
Miami–Dade Community College, Miami, Florida)

4167. "ERA in Florida." Your Cue from CCEW, Fall 1972, p. [4]. (WL;
H2, S1, R20)

YWCA News from Atlanta (Georgia)

4168. "Midtown Hosts ERA Workers." YWCA News from Atlanta, October
1973, p. 4. (H3, R5)

4168a. "Equal Rights Amendment" and "The Forum for Ratification of the
Equal Rights Amendment." YWCA News of Atlanta, Fall 1973, p. 4.
(H3, R5)

Zero Population Growth (ZPG, Washington, D.C.)

4169. "Women's Rights." Zero Population Growth, September 1972. (WL)

E. Newspapers

[The only newspapers covered are those which are formally
indexed or which are widely available in references such as
Editorials on File, Herstory, and Women and the Law. They
appear alphabetically by newspaper; the citations are arranged
chronologically within each paper. Only the miscellaneous
group is arranged alphabetically by author and title.

When the citation is to the first section of a paper, no
section number is indicated.

Letters to the editor are cited by their author and the heading
given in the paper. More than one author almost always indicates
more than one letter.]

1. *Chicago Tribune*

4170. Bennett, O'Donnell. "Why They Ask Equal Rights." CT,
5 February 1925. Rep. in entry #1742.

4171. Claessens, Marilyn. "An Amendment Mainly for Women." CT,
23 January 1972, sec. 5, p. 2, col. 2.

4172. Edwards, Willard. "Senate Faces Women's Rights Clash." CT,
17 February 1972, p. 26, col. 3.

4173. Siddon, Arthur. "Reject Ban on Drafting of Women." CT,
22 March 1972, sec. 2, p. 8, col. 1.

4174. _____. "Equal Rights Plan Up to States." CT, 23 March 1972, p. 7, col. 4.

4175. "Four Rabbi Groups Hit Proposed Bid for Women's Rights." CT, 4 April 1972, sec. 1A, p. 13, col. 7.

4176. "Tennessee 10th State to Back Women's Lib." CT, 5 April 1972, p. 13, col. 1.

4177. "Rights Bill Ratification Delay Seen." CT, 6 April 1972, sec. N4A, p. 8, col. 5.

4178. Philbrick, Richard. "Catholic Bishops Weigh Women's Rights Issue." CT, 13 April 1972, sec. 2, p. 15, col. 3.

4179. "House Unit OKs Women's Rights." CT, 4 May 1972, sec. 1A, p. 4, col. 5.

4180. "Illinois Rejects Women's Rights OK." CT, 17 May 1972, p. 1, col. 5.

4181. "Women Scorned." CT, 20 May 1972, p. 8, col. 2. (Ed)

4182. Rubinstein, Helen Cotta. "Defeat of the E.R.A." CT, 20 May 1972, p. 8, col. 6. (LE)

4183. Elmer, John. "Ogilvie Urges Women's Rights Amendment OK." CT, 20 May 1972, sec. N1B, p. 20, col. 6.

4184. "Amendment Endorsed." CT, 24 May 1972, p. 7, col. 1.

4185. Toll, Carolyn. "Women Back, Fight Rights Amendment." CT, 24 May 1972, sec. 1A, p. 6, col. 1.

4186. Elmer, John. "Equal Rights Gets Senate OK." CT, 25 May 1972, p. 6, col. 2.

4187. Fahey, Rose Mary. "Danger in 'Equal Rights.'" CT, 26 May 1972, p. 16, col. 3. (LE)

4188. Dyer, Representative Giddy. "Common Sense and Equal Rights." CT, 27 May 1972, p. 12, col. 2.

4189. Kilian, Michael. "Marching Along with Women's Lib." CT, 28 May 1972, sec. 1A, p. 5. col. 3.

4190. Stitt, Mrs. Raymond. "Wants No More 'Rights.'" CT, 4 June 1972, sec. 1A, p. 4, col. 3. (LE)

4191. Bobrinskoy, Betsey. "Mrs. Dyer Unconvincing." CT, 6 June 1972, p. 16, col. 5. (LE)

4192. Landis, Linda Lee. "Will the Women's Rights Proviso Work?" CT, 6 June 1972, sec. 2, p. 1, col. 5.

4193. "Women Set Anti-Equal Rights Trip." CT, 6 June 1972, sec. 2, p. 8, col. 3.

4194. Seslar, Thomas. "Rights Plan Wins Test in House." CT, 7 June
    1972, p. 3, col. 1.

4195. Hyde, Henry J. "Equal Rights Amendment: The Losses Can Outweigh
    the Gains." CT, 9 June 1972, p. 16, col. 3.

4196. Wolf, Edveta L. "Why the Hangup?" CT, 12 June 1972, p. 20,
    col. 3. (LE)

4197. Bailey, Ann A. "Hyde for Women." CT, 14 June 1972, p. 20,
    col. 4. (LE)

4198. Elmer, John. "Women's Rights Bid Fails." CT, 16 June 1972, p. 1,
    col. 8.

4199. "Kentucky Ratifies Rights Amendment." CT, 16 June 1972, p. 2,
    col. 2.

4200. "Another Blow to the E.R.A." CT, 18 June 1972, sec. 1A, p. 4,
    col. 1. (Ed)

4201. Mutka, Elizabeth. "Equal Rights Amendment." CT, 19 June 1972,
    p. 20, col. 4. (LE)

4202. Carey, Joanna A. "Angry Gal for E.R.A." CT, 27 June 1972,
    p. 12, col. 6. (LE)

4203. Newhouse, Kathie. "Analysis of E.R.A." CT, 3 July 1972, p. 12,
    col. 5. (LE)

4204. Goodyear, Sara Jane. "The Future of Equal Rights Amendment."
    CT, 12 November 1972, sec. 5, p. 2, col. 1.

4205. "Give the Ladies What They Want." CT, 16 December 1972, p. 8,
    col. 1. (Ed)

4206. "Equal Rights Plan Hits Snags." CT, 15 January 1973, sec. 1A,
    p. 2, col. 1.

4207. "Wyoming Ratifies." CT, 25 January 1973, p. 2, col. 7.

4208. Unger, Rudolph. "Women's Lib Fight Tougher." CT, 1 February
    1973, sec. 2, p. 5, col. 1.

4209. Kirkland, Vicki. "Illinois 'Right On' for Equal Rights?" CT,
    3 February 1973, p. 14, col. 1.

4210. Bangert, Lenora K. "Woman against Lib." CT, 7 February 1973,
    p. 12, col. 4. (LE)

4211. "Rights Amendment Wins Support." CT, 9 February 1973, p. 3, col. 1.

4212. "The Expanding Role of Women." CT, 9 February 1973, p. 16, col. 1.
    (Ed)

4213. Duggan, Mary Kathryn. "The ERA and Life." CT, 20 February 1973,
    p. 12, col. 6. (LE)

4214. Hutchinson, Louise. "N.O.W. Eyes Springfield Hot Line." CT, 21 February 1973, sec. 1A, p. 2, col. 1.

4215. Rede, Mrs. Wicklow. "Liberated Men." CT, 28 February 1973, p. 16, col. 6. (LE)

4216. Wolfe, Sheila. "Legislature Readies for Fight on Equal Rights." CT, 28 February 1973, sec. 2, p. 9, col. 5.

4217. "Maine Senate Turns Down Equal Rights." CT, 7 March 1973, p. 7, col. 1.

4218. "Rights Amendment Defeated in Maine." CT, 9 March 1973, p. 12, col. 1.

4219. Daniels, Mary. "'Sissy' Farenthold's Comments: Do Women Want Equal Rights?" CT, 10 March 1973, p. 17, col. 1.

4220. Hamm, Robert. "Snail's Pace of E.R.A." CT, 12 March 1973, p. 20, col. 6. (LE)

4221. Jurgens, Marylou. "Men Get Equality, Too." CT, 12 March 1973, p. 20, col. 6. (LE)

4222. Wolfe, Sheila. "Equal Rights Gets Housewives' Seal." CT, 13 March 1973, sec. 2, p. 3, col. 1.

4223. Wadington, Walter. "Women's Rights: Delay, Confusion." CT, 14 March 1973, p. 18, col. 5.

4224. Wolfe, Sheila. "E.R.A. Given Boost at State Breakfast." CT, 15 March 1973, sec. 2, p. 9, col. 1.

4225. "2 States Divide on Rights." CT, 16 March 1973, p. 3, col. 1.

4226. "Asserts States Can't Reverse Rights OK." CT, 17 March 1973, p. 3, col. 4.

4227. Schlafly, Phyllis. "ERA: Equal for Whom?" CT, 18 March 1973, sec. 5, p. 8, col. 6.

4228. "Evanston Asks Equal Rights Amendment OK." CT, 20 March 1973, sec. 2, p. 5, col. 1.

4229. Filezer, Lou. "Men for E.R.A." CT, 22 March 1973, p. 16, col. 6. (LE)

4230. Lewis, Mrs. C. "Against E.R.A." CT, 23 March 1973, p. 20, col. 6. (LE)

4231. Gilbert, David. "Equal Rights Wins Approval of House Committee." CT, 23 March 1973, sec. 1A, p. 4, col. 1.

4232. Miller, Thomas H. "ERA and the Constitution." CT, 31 March 1973, p. 10, col. 4. (LE)

4233. Wolfe, Sheila. "Only 24 Words in Equal Rights, But Millions of Words about It." CT, 1 April 1973, p. 33, col. 1.

4234. Gilbert, David. "Equal Rights Proposal Falls Twice in Assembly." CT, 5 April 1973, p. 1, col. 3.

4235. "Here's House Rollcall on Equal Rights Plan." CT, 5 April 1973, p. 8, col. 5.

4236. "For E.R.A.--But Legally." CT, 6 April 1973, p. 16, col. 1. (Ed)

4237. "Court Suit Eyed to Keep ERA Alive." CT, 6 April 1973, sec. 2, p. 14, col. 1.

4238. Gilbert, David. "Equal Rights Supporters Vow: 'We Have Only Begun to Fight.'" CT, 8 April 1973, p. 24, col. 1.

4239. Jensen, Richard. "Housewives May Divorce the ERA." CT, 8 April 1973, sec. 2, p. 3, col. 1.

4240. Levinstein, Janna. "Favors Equal Rights." CT, 10 April 1973, p. 10, col. 3. (LE)

4241. Thompson, Louis S. "Equality for All." CT, 10 April 1973, p. 10, col. 3. (LE)

4242. Leggett, Ann. "A Question of Chivalry." CT, 16 April 1973, p. 22, col. 3. (LE)

4243. Hamm, Joan M. "'ERA a Must.'" CT, 16 April 1973, p. 22, col. 6. (LE)

4244. "Florida Legislature Rejects Equal Rights." CT, 18 April 1973, p. 5, col. 2.

4245. "Claims 'Stop ERA' Victory; Florida Turns Down Equality for Women." CT, 18 April 1973, p. 12, col. 3.

4246. "Nixon Aide Sees ERA Dead in '73, But Wait . . ." CT, 19 April 1973, sec. 1A, p. 9, col. 3.

4247. "E.R.A. Loses in Senate." CT, 4 May 1973, sec. 1A, p. 3, col. 5.

4248. "4 Sue to Upset Defeat of Equal Rights." CT, 9 May 1973, sec. 1B, p. 10, col. 4.

4249. "Missouri Rejects Equal Rights 81 to 70." CT, 11 May 1973, p. 5, col. 4.

4250. Wittner, Dale. "'All Women's Liberationists Hate Men and Children.'" CT Magazine, 20 May 1973, pp. 12, 16, 21.

4251. "N.O.W. Reveals 20-State Drive to Ratify E.R.A." CT, 22 May 1973, p. 7, col. 1.

4252. Park, Virginia L. "'ERA Not Necessary.'" CT, 26 May 1973, p. 6, col. 6. (LE)

4253. Goodyear, Sara Jane. "Keeping an Eye on the ERA." CT,
      10 June 1973, sec. 5, p. 6, col. 1.

4254. "Schlafly Pro and Con." CT Magazine, 24 June 1973, p. 7. (LE)

4255. Thimmesch, Nick. "ERA's Chances Alive but Fragile." CT,
      28 June 1973, p. 26, col. 1.

4256. Terzino, Nancy R. "Phyllis Schlafly." CT Magazine, 22 July 1973,
      p. 8. (LE)

4257. "Equal Rights Backers Organize New Drive for Amendment." CT,
      26 August 1973, p. 21, col. 1.

4258. Merridew, Alan. "Feminists Urge ERA Approval in Illinois."
      CT, 7 October 1973, p. 45, col. 7.

4259. "All for Equal Rights." CT, 1 November 1973, sec. 2, p. 2, col. 1.

4260. Yabush, Donald. "Newsmakers: 3 Women's Targets." CT,
      9 November 1973, sec. 1A, p. 4, col. 1.

4261. "Equal Rights Approved by Maine; Seven to Go." CT, 19 January
      1974, p. 9, col. 5.

4262. Shanahan, Eileen. "Women's Equal Rights: How Amendment Fares."
      CT, 4 February 1974, sec. 3, p. 11, col. 1.

4263. Mize, Mable A. "Fight on ERA Urged." CT, 9 February 1974, p. 10.
      col. 4. (LE)

4264. LaVelle, Mike. "Labor Changes Its Mind on ERA." CT,
      14 February 1974, p. 18, col. 1.

4265. Gorman, Patrick E. "Denies 'ERA Connection.'" CT, 15 February
      1974, p. 12, col. 3. (LE)

4266. McDaniel, Naomi. "Assembly Line Sisters." CT, 16 February 1974,
      p. 10, col. 4. (LE)

4267. Budde, JoAnn. "'ERA to Aid Housewives.'" CT, 17 February 1974,
      sec. 2, p. 4, col. 4. (LE)

4268. Ryan, Shella. "ERA and Support Laws." CT, 21 February 1974,
      p. 16, col. 3. (LE)

4269. Elliott, Jean. "She Supports ERA." CT, 23 February 1974, p. 10,
      col. 3. (LE)

4270. "Pay Housewives?" CT, 1 March 1974, p. 10, col. 6. (LE)

4271. Thomson, Rosemary. "Drafting Women." CT, 11 March 1974, p. 20,
      col. 6. (LE)

4272. Turner, Suzanne. "Illinois Support Law." CT, 12 March 1974,
      p. 10, col. 5. (LE)

4273. Mulqueeny, Harriet. "ERA: 'Pandora's Box.'" CT, 14 March 1974,
    p. 20, col. 3. (LE)

4274. McClain, Leanita. "Women Told to Back ERA Candidates." CT,
    18 March 1974, sec. 1A, p. 2, col. 1.

4275. Hoch, Mary L. "ERA and Credit." CT, 23 March 1974, p. 12, col. 5.
    (LE)

4276. Witters, Cherie. "Drafting Women." CT, 25 March 1974, p. 18,
    col. 6. (LE)

4277. Dobbak (?), Paul. "Difficulties for ERA." CT, 31 March 1974,
    sec. 2, p. 4, col. 5. (LE)

4278. Sherry, Elizabeth G. "Absent Legal Protection." CT, 2 April
    1974, p. 12, col. 6. (LE)

4279. Barnes, Fred. "Approval of ERA Appears in Doubt." CT,
    12 April 1974, p. 9, col. 4.

4280. Brocker, Johanna. "'Pass the ERA!'" CT, 14 April 1974, sec. 2,
    p. 4, col. 4. (LE)

4281. Pratt, Steven. "Men Join Women on Equal Rights." CT,
    16 April 1974, p. 3, col. 5.

4282. Locin, Mitchell. "ERA Payola: Roses, Pie." CT, 17 April 1974,
    p. 7, col. 1.

4283. "D.A.R. Hits Satanism, Sex Equality." CT, 18 April 1974, sec. 2,
    p. 7, col. 1.

4284. "The Push for the E.R.A." CT, 19 April 1974, p. 14, col. 1. (Ed)

4285. Culhane, Anne. "'E.R.A. Discriminates.'" CT, 19 April 1974,
    p. 14, col. 6. (LE)

4286. Colander, Pat. "Alan Alda: Enm*a*s*hed: 'Hawking' the E.R.A."
    CT, 20 April 1974, p. 17, col. 1.

4287. "Sen. Keegan: Soft Words Showed Her Strength." CT, 21 April
    1974, p. 31, col. 1.

4288. Taylor, Lynn. "State Senate to Get 2d Look at E.R.A." CT,
    22 April 1974, p. 8, col. 1.

4289. "Chicago Jaycees Urge End to Sex Discrimination; Back ERA." CT,
    25 April 1974, p. 15, col. 1.

4290. "ERA Beaten by Tennessee." CT, 25 April 1974, p. 15, col. 4.

4291. Chrisman, Barbara. "'No Reason for E.R.A.'" CT, 25 April 1974,
    p. 20, col. 6. (LE)

4292. Rice, Carolyn. "Laws and Moods." CT, 26 April 1974, p. 16,
    col. 6. (LE)

4293. Moore, Elsie D. "'Gutless on E.R.A.'" CT, 29 April 1974, p. 20,
      col. 3. (LE)

4294. Zahour, Frank. "Approval of ERA Seen by 1975." CT, 5 May 1974,
      p. 7, col. 1.

4295. Beck, James L. "'Not for Women Only.'" CT, 7 May 1974, p. 16,
      col. 5. (LE)

4296. Meek, Joseph T. "'Yea or Nay Vote.'" CT, 13 May 1974, p. 14,
      col. 6. (LE)

4297. Brocker, Johanna. "Women Who Work." CT, 14 May 1974, p. 12,
      col. 6. (LE)

4298. "ERA Drive Lags in Legislature." CT, 15 May 1974, p. 6, col. 4.

4299. Elmer, John. "ERA Fails to Pass Senate." CT, 22 May 1974, p. 3,
      col. 1.

4300. "3 Senators Deny Voting against ERA." CT, 23 May 1974, sec. 1A,
      p. 2, col. 4.

4301. "New Suit Planned on ERA Ruling." CT, 24 May 1974, sec. 2,
      p. 13, col. 1.

4302. Zahour, Frank. "ERA Supporters to Take Vote Issue Back to Court."
      CT, 26 May 1974, p. 21, col. 1.

4303. "Suit Challenges ERA Vote." CT, 1 June 1974, sec. N1A, p. 20,
      col. 3.

4304. Jennings, Audrey. "Tradition of Discrimination." CT, 2 June
      1974, sec. 2, p. 4, col. 6. (LE)

4305. Brocker, Johanna; Misiolek, Carole; and Poag, Ann. "Republicans
      and E.R.A." CT, 5 June 1974, p. 12, col. 5. (LE)

4306. "ERA Suit against Blair Dropped." CT, 6 June 1974, sec. 1A,
      p. 9, col. 1.

4307. Zahour, Frank. "ERA Backers Maneuver for New Senate Vote." CT,
      7 June 1974, p. 7, col. 1.

4308. Schiller, Donna; McGraw, Bill; Fine, Sheila B.; and Budde, Jo Ann.
      "E.R.A. Rises Again." CT, 8 June 1974, p. 12, col. 6. (LE)

4309. Wohl, Marsha J. "Drafting Women." CT, 11 June 1974, p. 16,
      col. 3. (LE)

4310. Kleiman, Carol. "Day of Reckoning Nears for E.R.A.; Will
      Equality Rise Up from the Legislative Floor?" CT, 12 June 1974,
      sec. 2, p. 1, col. 1.

4311. "Dispelling the Myths Haunting E.R.A. Success." CT, 12 June
      1974, sec. 2, p. 1, col. 4.

4312. Elmer, John. "House Group OKs Resolution on ERA." CT,
13 June 1974, p. 10, col. 4.

4313. Newhouse, Kathie. "'E.R.A. Destroys Choices.'" CT, 18 June
1974, p. 10, col. 3. (LE)

4314. Zahour, Frank. "ERA Move Fails in Senate." CT, 19 June 1974,
p. 3, col. 5.

4315. "E.R.A. Loses (Or Wins) Again." CT, 20 June 1974, p. 24, col. 1.
(Ed)

4316. Zahour, Frank. "ERA Is Dead for This Session." CT, 22 June
1974, p. 9, col. 1.

4317. Shelton, Mary Ann. "E.R.A.'s Just Desserts." CT, 27 June 1974,
p. 16, col. 5. (LE)

4318. "'Wait Till Next Year,' Say E.R.A. Backers." CT, 4 July 1974,
sec. 1B, p. 4, col. 1.

4319. Tooley, Nadine H. "'E.R.A. Necessary.'" CT, 17 July 1974,
p. 16, col. 6. (LE)

4320. Becker, B. "Equal Rights and Illinois." CT, 29 July 1974,
p. 12, col. 3. (LE)

4321. Sneed, Michael. "Ms. Nemesis Hits Equal Rights Bill." CT,
19 August 1974, p. 5, col. 1.

4322. Lannin, Kay. "E.R.A. and Power." CT, 2 September 1974, p. 12,
col. 5. (LE)

4323. "Betty Ford Backs ERA, Hints Pro-Abortion Stand." CT,
5 September 1974, p. 2, col. 3.

4324. "Betty Ford Hopes to Work for ERA." CT, 7 September 1974, p. 3,
col. 1.

4325. "NOW Poll on ERA Contradicts Rep. Wolf." CT, 6 November 1974,
p. 4, col. 3.

4326. Elmer, John. "ERA Will Pass Easily, Partee Says." CT,
11 November 1974, p. 7, col. 5.

4327. "Elections Give E.R.A. Big Boost." CT, 18 November 1974, p. 9,
col. 4.

4328. Leon, John F. "Making ERA Consistent." CT, 2 December 1974,
sec. 2, p. 2, col. 6. (LE)

4329. Sfasciotti, Mary L. "G.O.P. and Equal Rights." CT,
3 December 1974, sec. 2, p. 2, col. 3. (LE)

4330. "ERA Sponsor Feeling Hopeful." CT, 14 January 1975, sec. 2, p. 6,
col. 3.

4331. McManus, Ed. "E.R.A. Gains Approval of Slate Panel." CT,
     5 February 1975, p. 3, col. 7.

4332. Jarrett, Vernon. "The Right to Earn an Unequal Income." CT,
     5 February 1975, sec. 2, p. 4, col. 1. (Ed)

4333. Kleiman, Carol. "A New Savvy Fuels the Drive for Equal Rights
     Passage." CT, 12 February 1975, sec. 3, p. 1, col. 2.

4334. ter Horst, Jerald. "Now's the Time for Men to Aid E.R.A." CT,
     16 February 1975, sec. 2, p. 6, col. 1. (Ed)

4335. Hemstock, Jack. "Emotions Heat Up in E.R.A. Battle." CT,
     17 February 1975, p. 5, col. 5.

4336. "Betty Rolls Up Her Sleeves." CT, 18 February 1975, p. 1, col. 5.

4337. Morrison, G. F. "Against E.R.A." CT, 21 February 1975, sec. 2,
     p. 2, col. 6. (LE)

4338. "Equal Rights Rejected by House in Arizona." CT, 27 February
     1975, p. 12, col. 1.

4339. Walch, L. J. "'Men Gain from E.R.A.'" CT, 28 February 1975,
     sec. 2, p. 2, col. 5. (LE)

4340. Salins, Barbara. "It's 3d Time Around for ERA in Senate." CT,
     3 March 1975, sec. 3, p. 1, col. 1.

4341. Mabley, Jack. "E.R.A. Has to Be OK, Considering Its Foes."
     CT, 4 March 1975, p. 4, col. 1. (Ed)

4342. "Time to Ratify E.R.A." CT, 4 March 1975, sec. 2, p. 2, col. 1.
     (Ed)

4343. Salins, Barbara. "Delay ERA Vote." CT, 5 March 1975, p. 1, col. 3.

4344. _____. "Senate Gives ERA Another Setback." CT, 6 March
     1975, p. 1, col. 7.

4345. "ERA Strategists May Go to House." CT, 7 March 1975, sec. 2,
     p. 1, col. 2.

4346. McManus, Ed. "Foes Give ERA Bandwagon a Flat Tire in Illinois."
     CT, 9 March 1975, p. 5, col. 2.

4347. "Indiana Beats Down ERA Action." CT, 11 March 1975, p. 6, col. 4.

4348. McClaughry, John. "E.R.A.'s Drawbacks." CT, 11 March 1975,
     sec. 2, p. 2, col. 4. (LE)

4349. "E.R.A. Vote under Fire in Iowa." CT, 13 March 1975, p. 12, col. 5.

4350. Mabley, Jack. "Illinois Has an ERA--With No Ill Effects." CT,
     14 March 1975, p. 4, col. 1. (Ed)

4351. Macdonald, Virginia B. "Urges Support for E.R.A." CT, 14 March 1975, sec. 2, p. 2, col. 4. (LE)

4352. Larsen, Betty 'Laine. "She Prefers a Pedestal." CT, 19 March 1975, sec. 2, p. 2, col. 5. (LE)

4353. Anderson, Bill. "Could E.R.A. Cost Us a Convention?" CT, 20 March 1975, sec. 2, p. 2, col. 3. (Ed)

4354. Margolis, Jon. "Women Use Convention as ERA Lever." CT, 21 March 1975, p. 7, col. 2.

4355. _____. "Dems Link Convention to E.R.A." CT, 22 March 1975, sec. N1, p. 6, col. 5.

4356. Mehler, Neil. "Tell Daley Pledge to Pass ERA." CT, 24 March 1975, p. 10, col. 6.

4357. McDaniels, Naomi. "'E.R.A. Makes Things Worse.'" CT, 25 March 1975, sec. 2, p. 2, col. 4. (LE)

4358. Wiedrich, Bob. "Ladies Flex Their Political Muscles." CT, 26 March 1975, sec. 2, p. 4, col. 1. (Ed)

4359. "Unfair Play for the E.R.A." CT, 28 March 1975, sec. 2, p. 2, col. 1. (Ed)

4360. Dixon, Christa K. "Religion and E.R.A." CT, 29 March 1975, sec. N1, p. 8, col. 5. (LE)

4361. "2d Setback Clouds Hope for ERA." CT, 30 March 1975, p. 7, col. 1.

4362. Dolehide, Robert A., M.D. "'E.R.A. Favors Singles.'" CT, 6 April 1975, sec. 2, p. 4, col. 5. (LE)

4363. Buchanan, Patrick. "ERA Could Force Social Revolution." CT, 6 April 1975, sec. 2, p. 6, col. 1. (Ed)

4364. "Key Vote Set in North Carolina on E.R.A." and "Pass E.R.A., Friedan Asks." CT, 13 April 1975, p. 20, col. 5.

4365. Schlafly, Phyllis. "Rights vs. Protection." CT, 13 April 1975, sec. 2, p. 4, col. 3. (LE)

4366. Jefko, Beryl Williams. "'Minority' Blocks E.R.A." CT, 16 April 1975, sec. 2, p. 2, col. 3. (LE)

4367. "House Panel OKs ERA." CT, 17 April 1975, sec. 2, p. 6, col. 6.

4368. "Hopes Raised for ERA Here." CT, 24 April 1975, sec. 2, p. 1, col. 3.

4369. "Marlo Thomas Urges ERA Here." CT, 26 April 1975, sec. N1, p. 2, col. 3.

4370. Burton, Nancy M. "Need for E.R.A." CT, 26 April 1975, sec. N1, p. 8, col. 4. (LE)

4371. Elmer, John. "House ERA Backers Are Confident." CT, 1 May 1975, sec. 2, p. 7, col. 3.

4372. _____, and Salins, Barbara. "ERA Passes House; Next Test in Senate." CT, 2 May 1975, p. 1, col. 6.

4373. Zahour, Frank. "NOW Holds Champagne Celebration." CT, 2 May 1975, p. 19, col. 1.

4374. "Words Are Simple; Its the Interpretation" and "How Illinois House Voted on ERA Amendment." CT, 2 May 1975, p. 19, col. 1.

4375. Beck, Joan. "E.R.A. Scores Illinois Gain, But Lags in U.S." CT, 2 May 1975, sec. 2, p. 2, col. 5. (Ed)

4376. Elmer, John. "ERA to Win in Senate: Partee." CT, 3 May 1975, sec. N1, p. 3, col. 3.

4377. _____. "ERA Nears Final, Decisive State Battle." CT, 4 May 1975, p. 22, col. 1.

4378. "Partee to Decide on ERA Strategy." CT, 7 May 1975, sec. 2, p. 1, col. 3.

4379. Salins, Barbara. "Partee Sidesteps Floor Fight; ERA Gets Full Hearing." CT, 8 May 1975, sec. 2, p. 6, col. 7.

4380. "City Council OKs ERA; 2 Women Vote against It." CT, 9 May 1975, sec. 4, p. 18, col. 1.

4381. Salins, Barbara. "ERA Bill Suffers Surprise Defeat." CT, 14 May 1975, p. 1, col. 2.

4382. "Move to Bring ERA to Senate Floor." CT, 15 May 1975, sec. 2, p. 1, col. 3.

4383. Becker, Bernice. "An E.R.A. 'Burocracy.'" CT, 15 May 1975, sec. 2, p. 2, col. 6. (LE)

4384. Butler, Margaret. "E.R.A. a 'Must.'" CT, 18 May 1975, sec. 2, p. 4, col. 4. (LE)

4385. Harris, Louis. "Majority Supports Women's Rights and the ERA." CT, 19 May 1975, sec. 2, p. 4, col. 3.

4386. Spaniol, Claire. "The Unequal Half." CT, 21 May 1975, sec. 3, p. 2, col. 3. (LE)

4387. "Assembly OKs New York ERA." CT, 23 May 1975, sec. 3, p. 19, col. 2.

4388. Merridew, Alan. "Jesse Jackson Backs ERA." CT, 25 May 1975, p. 8, col. 6.

4389. "Issue: Equal Rights Amendment." CT, 25 May 1975, sec. 2, p. 1, col. 3.

4390. Gage, Joyce. "'E.R.A. Hurts Women.'" CT, 28 May 1975, sec. 3, p. 2, col. 5. (LE)

4391. "Missouri Senate Kills E.R.A." CT, 3 June 1975, p. 7, col. 3.

4392. Schlafly, Phyllis. "E.R.A. Foes 'Smeared.'" CT, 10 June 1975, sec. 2, p. 2, col. 4. (LE)

4393. "Louisiana House Kills ERA." CT, 13 June 1975, p. 7, col. 4.

4394. "Daley Forces May Link ERA Vote to Remap." CT, 16 June 1975, p. 1, col. 3.

4395. McManus, Ed. "Netsch: ERA Is Hostage." CT, 18 June 1975, p. 5, col. 6.

4396. Miller, Sarah Bryan. "Anti-E.R.A. 'Hysteria.'" CT, 18 June 1975, sec. 3, p. 2, col. 3. (LE)

4397. Salins, Barbara. "ERA Fails to Pass Again in Sudden Senate Vote." CT, 21 June 1975, sec. N1, p. 1, col. 5.

4398. Lulkin, Sheli A. "Working Women and E.R.A." CT, 23 June 1975, sec. 2, p. 2, col. 3. (LE)

4399. McManus, Edward. "Daley Holds the Key to the E.R.A.'s Fate." CT, 23 June 1975, sec. 2, p. 2, col. 5. (Ed)

4400. _____. "ERA Dead until Fall: Partee." CT, 27 June 1975, p. 5, col. 1.

4401. Para, Mildred L., and Leonard, Charles S. "E.R.A.--Pro & Con." CT, 28 June 1975, sec. N1, p. 12, col. 3. (LE)

4402. Knudsen, Charles T. "Lysistrata and 'Scabs.'" CT, 4 July 1975, sec. 2, p. 2, col. 5. (LE)

4403. Hough, Joan. "New Snag for E.R.A." CT, 13 July 1975, sec. 2, p. 4, col. 4. (LE)

4405. Zanetello, Anthony. "'Ill-Founded' ERA." CT, 5 August 1975, sec. 2, p. 2, col. 6. (LE)

4406. Clarke, Elizabeth. "Against E.R.A." CT, 31 August 1975, sec. 2, p. 4, col. 5. (LE)

4407. Loveland, D.M. "'Losses' under E.R.A." CT, 4 September 1975, sec. 2, p. 2, col. 3. (LE)

4408. "Psychologists Go on the Record for Equal Rights." CT, 4 September 1975, sec. 2, p. 8, col. 1.

4409. Cross, Robert. "Dialog: Esther Saperstein." CT Magazine, 7 September 1975, p. 56.

4410. "Minority Efforts for ERA Sought." CT, 26 October 1975, p. 5, col. 2.

4411. Kleiman, Carol. "ERA Looks to Religion." CT, 30 October 1975, sec. 3, p. 4, col. 2.

4412. "New York, New Jersey Reject ERA." CT, 5 November 1975, p. 5, col. 2.

4413. "ERA Demonstration." CT, 6 November 1975, p. 19, col. 2.

4414. Cross, Robert. "Dialog: Phyllis Schlafly." CT Magazine, 9 November 1975, pp. 26-27.

4415. Kirk, Donald. "The ERA Battle Makes Strange Bedfellows." CT, 10 November 1975, p. 12, col. 1.

4416. Buchanan, Patrick. "The ERA: 'We Was Robbed.'" CT, 13 November 1975, sec. 2, p. 4, col. 3.

4417. Kroll, John J. "Buchanan and ERA." CT, 26 November 1975, sec. 2, p. 2, col. 3. (LE)

4418. Fielding, Joyce. "Cheers ERA Defeats." CT, 26 November 1975, sec. 2, p. 2, col. 3. (LE)

4419. "New ERA Drive Announced." CT, 1 December 1975, sec. 2, p. 1, col. 2.

4420. Beck, Joan. "Time to Try Anew for the ERA--In the Spirit of '76." CT, 5 December 1975, sec. 2, p. 2, col. 6. (Ed)

4421. Starshak, Barbara McGoorty; O'Connor, Jeannette; Stein, Rhonda; Miller, Sarah Bryan; Kahn, J. Kesner; and Milke, Elizabeth L. "ERA, Pro and Con." CT Magazine, 7 December 1975, p. 12. (LE)

4422. "ERA Stand Costs State a Convention." CT, 17 January 1976, p. 2, col. 4.

2.   *Christian Science Monitor*

[Unless otherwise noted, the citations are to the Eastern edition.]

4423. Lutz, Alma. "Women Citizens' Rights." CSM, 21 April 1935. Rep. in entry #2095a.

4424. Hornaday, Mary. "Showdown on Equal Rights: Amending the Constitution." CSM Magazine, 9 October 1943, p. 5.

4425. "Equal Rights for Women." CSM, 30 October 1943, p. 16, col. 2. (Ed) Rep. in entry #2380.

4426. Lutz, Alma. "Why Bar Equality?" CSM Magazine, 22 July 1944, p. 3.

4427. Norwood, Rose. "Why Bar Equality?" CSM Magazine, 19 August 1944, p. 10. (LE)

4428. Lutz, Alma. "Which Road, Women Workers?" CSM Magazine, 2 February 1946, p. 2. Rep. as a separate by the National Woman's Party.

4429. Anderson, Mary. "Which Road, Women Workers?" CSM Magazine, 13 April 1946, p. 14. (LE) Rep. in entry #19.

4430. Kitchelt, Florence L.C. "Which Road, Women Workers?" CSM Magazine, 11 May 1946, p. 21. (LE)

4431. Hornaday, Mary. "Another Way to Women's Equal Rights." CSM Magazine, 22 July 1946, p. E, col. 5. (Ed) Rep. in entry #224.

4432. Paul, Helen, and Bellamy, Ernestine Hale. "Equal Rights Amendment Backers See Influential Groups Lending Support." CSM, 7 July 1949, p. 12, col. 1. Rep. as a separate by National Woman's Party.

4433. Mayo, Betty D. "Women Record 'Rights' Gain." CSM, 27 July 1961, p. 4, col. 5.

4434. Mouat, Lucia. "Who's to Benefit from Equal Rights Amendment?" CSM, 12 May 1970, p. 10, col. 1. (WL)

4435. Levine, Jo Ann. "President's Appointee Takes Fresh Look." CSM, 21 July 1970, p. 12, col. 2. (WL)

4436. "A Call to Members." CSM, 21 July 1970, p. 12, col. 3. (WL)

4437. Lutz, Alma. "Women's Rights." CSM, 7 August 1970.(?) (WL)

4438. Mouat, Lucia. "Women Press for Action: Rights Amendment Reaches House." CSM, 10 August 1970, p. 1, col. 2.

4439. "Women's Rights Legislation Gains." CSM, 12 August 1970, p. 2, col. 2.

4440. "Gains for Women." CSM, 12 August 1970, p. E, col. 1. (Ed)

4441. "Two Amendments Rejected." CSM, 2 January 1971, p. E. (Western and Midwestern ed.)

4442. Drummond, Roscoe. "Rescuing Women's Lib." CSM, 9 October 1971, p. E, col. 3.

4443. "Equal Rights." CSM, 13 October 1971, p. E, col. 5. (Ed)

4444. "What Formula for Fair." CSM, 15 October 1971, p. E, col. 1. (Ed)

4445. "Higher Notch for Women's Rights." CSM, 26 November 1971, p. [B12], col. 1. (Ed) (WL; labelled 27 November 1971)

4446. Hey, Robert P. "New Gains for Woman's Rights?" CSM, 20 January 1972, p. 1, col. 2.

4447. Wilhelm, Marion Bell. "Equal-Rights Drive Stirs Anew." CSM, 14 February 1972, p. 10, col. 1.

4448. "Equal-Rights Amendment Gains." CSM, 1 March 1972, p. 2, col. 1.

4449. "Legislative Trespass?" CSM, 2 March 1972, p. E, col. 1. (Ed)

4450. "Sharing Rights . . . and Responsibilities." CSM, 24 March 1972, p. E, col. 1. (Ed)

4451. "A Volume of Rights." CSM, 24 May 1972, p. 11, col. 5.

4452. "Equal Rights Amendment Progresses." CSM, 20 September 1972, p. 12, col. 5.

4453. Leith, Lucia Johnson. "Equal Rights Ratification in '73?" CSM, 2 January 1973, p. 4, col. 3.

4454. "Equal Rights Amendment Fails in Utah Legislature." CSM, 30 January 1973, p. 3, col. 5. (Midwestern ed.)

4455. "Quote." CSM, 2 February 1973, p. 8, col. 4.

4456. Fallaci, Oriana. "Threat to Equal Rights Seen." CSM, 9 February 1973, p. 10, col. 4.

4457. Loercher, Diana. "Equality for Women Stalled?" CSM, 15 February 1973, p. 1, col. 2.

4458. "Vermont Ratifies ERA." CSM, 22 February 1973, p. 8, col. 4.

4459. "Nixon Backs Amendment." CSM, 23 February 1973, p. 8, col. 4.

4460. Drummond, Roscoe. "Are Men and Women Equal?" CSM, 24 February 1973, p. E, col. 3. (Ed)

4461. Mouckley, Florence. "Critics Boosters Collide in Women's Rights Debate." CSM, 13 March 1973, p. 1, col. 1.

4462. "Rights for Women." CSM, 19 March 1973, p. E, col. 1. (Ed)

4463. "Women's Rights and Women's Lib." CSM, 16 April 1973, p. E, col. 1. (Ed) Rep. in entry #347.

4464. "Eight States Reject Equal-Rights Proposal." CSM, 19 April 1973, p. 10, col. 5.

4465. Carroll, Betty. "Equal Rights." CSM, 24 April 1973, p. E, col. 5. (LE)

4466. "South Carolina Votes No." CSM, 27 April 1973, p. 8, col. 3. (LE)

4467. Robe, Elaine N. "Women's Rights." CSM, 24 May 1973, p. E, col. 4. (LE)

4468. "Equal Rights Drive Set to Go Again." CSM, 5 September 1973, p. 7, col. 1.

4469. "Fund to Aid Drive for Equal Rights." CSM, 24 September 1973, p. 8, col. 3.

4470. Kirp, David. "The Uneasy Case for ERA." CSM, 12 October 1973, p. E, col. 3. (Ed)

4471. "AFL-CIO to Fight Sex Discrimination." CSM, 24 October 1973, p. 5, col. 3.

4472. "AFL-CIO Withdraws Opposition to ERA." CSM, 24 October 1973, p. 6, col. 5.

4473. "Georgia Turns Down 'Rights' Amendment." CSM, 30 January 1974, p. 8, col. 1.

4474. "Ohio Ratifies ERA." CSM, 8 February 1974, p. 8, col. 3.

4475. Levine, Jo Ann. "The ERA: Where Is It?" CSM, 8 February 1974, p. F2, col. 1.

4476. "Tennessee Rescinds Equal-Rights Vote." CSM, 25 April 1974, p. 10, col. 1.

4477. Kirp, David L. "Sex-based Discrimination." CSM, 12 September 1974, p. E, col. 3. (Ed)

4478. "Equal Rights Amendment Gets Election Boost." CSM, 19 November 1974, p. 8, col. 5.

4479. "Equal-Rights Prospects Brighten." CSM, 4 December 1974, p. 3E, col. 4.

4480. "Ratification Drive Planned." CSM, 5 December 1974, p. 3D, col. 1. (Western ed.)

4481. "Rights Ratification." CSM, 5 February 1975, p. 4, col. 6.

4482. "Mrs. Ford Presses for Rights Amendment." CSM, 10 February 1975, p. 4, col. 1.

4483. "Georgians Reject ERA." CSM, 18 February 1975, p. 8, col. 1.

4484. Dillin, Gay Andrews. "U.S. Equal Rights Struggle." CSM, 20 February 1975, p. 3, col. 1.

4485. Rutledge, Henry. "'Vivent les femmes!'" CSM, 28 February 1975, p. E, col. 6. (LE)

4486. "Mrs. Ford's Mail Swings to Pro-ERA." CSM, 3 March 1975, p. 4, col. 1.

4487. "Equal Rights Vote Stalls." CSM, 6 March 1975, p. 4, col. 6.

4488. "Equal Rights Push Needed." CSM, 6 March 1975, p. E, col. 1. (Ed)

4489. "Indiana Votes No." CSM, 12 March 1975, p. 4, col. 6.

4490. "Equal-Rights Resistance Stiffens." CSM, 20 March 1975, p. 3A, col. 2.

4491. "S. Carolina Tables ERA." CSM, 28 March 1975, p. 4, col. 6.

4492. "ERA Sidetracked." CSM, 18 April 1975, p. 2, col. 5.

4493. "Women Say 1977 Is Earliest for ERA." CSM, 6 May 1975, p. 2, col. 4.

4494. "Fund-Raising Drive On for '76 Passage of ERA." CSM, 21 May 1975, p. 2, col. 2.

4495. "Equal Rights Delay." CSM, 18 June 1975, p. E, col. 4. (Ed) Rep. from Washington (D.C.) Star.

4496. Moneyhun, George. "Local Elections Bog Women's Rights Issue." CSM, 6 November 1975, p. 3, col. 1.

4497. "Some Answers on the ERA." CSM, 7 November 1975, p. E, col. 2. (Ed)

4498. Shipp, Nancy Dyson. "Equal Rights." CSM, 19 November 1975, p. 31, col. 4. (LE)

4499. Coquillette, William H. "ERA Answers." CSM, 1 December 1975, p. E, col. 4. (LE)

4500. Meyer, Howard N. "Don't Mourn the ERA--And Why." CSM, 20 January 1976, p. 27, col. 4. (Ed)

4501. Huntley, Dennis L. "ERA." CSM, 28 January 1976, p. 35, col. 3. (LE)

3.   *Honolulu Advertiser* and *Honolulu Star-Bulletin*

4502. "Equal Rights Bill Endorsed Jointly." HA, 8 February 1972, p. 10, col. 1.

4503. Engle, Murry. "A Note of Unity in Women's Lib." HSB, 8 February 1972, sec. C, p. 3, col. 1.

4504. "Women's Rights." HA, 14 February 1972, p. 10, col. 1. (Ed)

4505. "Equal Rights Bill Boosted in Senate." HSB, 16 February 1972, sec. B, p. 2, col. 1.

4506. Phillips, Kevin P. "Do Most Women Spurn Equality?" HA, 4 March 1972, p. 12, col. 3. (Ed)

4507. Krauss, Bob. "Isle Women's Rightists, Hail Amendment (Naturally)."
      HA, 23 March 1972, sec. B, p. 1, col. 1.

4508. "'You Are Crucifying Women on a Cross of Equality.'" HSB,
      23 March 1972, p. 2, col. 1.

4509. Taylor, Lois. "OK, Girls, Let's Hear It for the Legislature."
      HSB, 23 March 1972, sec. E, p. 1, col. 1.

4510. Cooke, Mary. "Equality Means G.I.(rl)." HA, 24 March 1972,
      sec. D, p. 3, col. 1.

4511. "'Women's Rights' Legislation Due for House Vote Today." HA,
      29 March 1972, p. 18, col. 3.

4512. "Women's Rights OK Expected." HSB, 29 March 1972, p. 1, col. 2.

4513. Arakaki, Joe. "Women's Rights Amendment Pushed." HSB,
      17 May 1972, p. 21, col. 1.

4.   *Los Angeles Times*

4514. "Women Invade Rights Hearing." LAT, 24 March 1932, p. 5, col. 1.
      Rep. in entry #1969.

4515. Mathews, Linda. "Equality-for-Women Bill, 47 Years Old, Approved
      by House." LAT, 11 August 1970, p. 1, col. 2. Rep. from entry #1073.

4516. Langway, Lynn. "Women's Equality Act Pushed." LAT, April 1971.
      (WL)

4517. "Victory for Women and for Justice." LAT, 24 November 1971,
      pt. 2, p. 6, col. 1. (Ed) (EOF)

4518. "Equal Rights for Women." LAT, 17 January 1972, pt. 2, p. 6,
      col. 1.

4519. Murphy, Jean. "Male VIPs under Equal Rights Banner." LAT,
      18 January 1972, pt. 4, p. 1, col. 2.

4520. "Women's Rights Bid Advances in Senate." LAT, 1 March 1972,
      p. 4, col. 4.

4521. "Time Limit Set on Equal Rights Debate." LAT, 3 March 1972,
      p. 11, col. 2.

4522. "Council Backs Equal Rights." LAT, 9 March 1972, pt. 4, p. 10,
      col. 1.

4523. "Women's Rights Get a Boost from Nixon." LAT, 19 March 1972,
      p. 15, col. 1.

4524. "Women Step Up Battle for Rights Amendment." LAT, 21 March 1972,
      p. 19, col. 1.

4525. Rich, Spencer. "Women's Rights Bill OKd, Sent to States." LAT, 23 March 1972, p. 1, col. 4.

4526. "Six States Ratify Women's Rights Act." LAT, 25 March 1972, p. 12, col. 1.

4527. Gillam, Jerry. "Legislature Hands Second Setback to Women's Lib Move." LAT, 7 April 1972, p. 3, col. 6.

4528. Kazickas, Jurate. "Equal Rights: Combat Role for Women?" LAT, 9 April 1972, p. 25, col. 1.

4529. Callandrillo, Linda, and Dunaway, James L. "Rights Amendment: A Victory for Women?" LAT, 15 April 1972, pt. 2, p. 4, col. 5. (LE)

4530. Murphy, Jean. "Crucial Test for Equal Rights Proposal." LAT, 17 April 1972, pt. 4, p. 1, col. 2.

4531. "Equal Rights for Women." LAT, 17 April 1972, pt. 2, p. 6, col. 1.

4532. Endicott, William. "Union Women, Liberationists Split on Rights." LAT, 19 April 1972, p. 3, col. 1.

4533. _____. "Women's Equality Amendment Clears Assembly, 56 to 11." LAT, 21 April 1972, p. 3, col. 6.

4534. "Amendment Ratified." LAT, 22 April 1972, p. 7, col. 1.

4535. Gandy, Winifred C.; Lloyd, Judy; and Waggoner, Laine. "Equal Rights for Women Amendment." LAT, 26 April 1972, pt. 2, p. 6, col. 3, 4. (LE)

4536. Endicott, William. "Senate Unit Blocks Women's Rights Issue." LAT, 27 April 1972, p. 3, col. 4.

4537. "Equal Rights for Women." LAT, 1 May 1972, pt. 2, p. 6, col. 1.

4538. Cimons, Marlene. "Feminists Hold ERA Strategy Talks." LAT, 16 May 1972, pt. 4, p. 3, col. 1. (WL)

4539. Gillam, Jerry. "Women's Rights Issue Blocked Again." LAT, 25 May 1972, p. 3, col. 1.

4540. Stumbo, Bella. "Fighters for Equal Rights Amendment." LAT, 26 June 1972, pt. 4, p. 1, col. 4. (WL)

4541. "Citizen Group Assails Senate Vote on Equal Rights Plan." LAT, 8 July 1972, pt. 2, p. 1, col. 5.

4542. Murphy, Jean Douglas. "A Last Ditch Effort to Free the ERA." LAT, 3 August 1972, pt. 4, p. 1, col. 2. (WL)

4543. _____. "ERA Panel Buoys Hopes of Feminists." LAT, 28 August 1972, pt. 4, p. 1, col. 4.

4544. Endicott, William. "Mills Gives Up Fight to Block Women's Equal Rights Measure." LAT, 9 September 1972, p. 1, col. 1.

4545. Kazickas, Jurate. "Equal Rights Amendment Gains Ground." LAT, 14 September 1972, pt. 1A, p. 6, col. 1.

4546. Gillam, Jerry. "State Senate Votes to Ratify Women's Rights Amendment." LAT, 10 November 1972, p. 3, col. 4.

4547. "Squeaks of Protest Greet Women's Rights Supporters." LAT, 11 November 1972, p. 1, col. 2.

4548. "Women's Rights." LAT, 12 November 1972, pt. J, p. 2, col. 2.

4549. Gillam, Jerry. "State Ratifies Women's Rights Amendment." LAT, 14 November 1972, p. 3, col. 1.

4550. Forsher, Trude. "The Blind Mice and the Equal Rights Amendment." LAT, 17 November 1972, pt. 2, p. 7, col. 3.

4551. Cornell, John; Kroeler, Betty; and St. John, Mary. "Equal Rights." LAT, 20 November 1972, pt. 2, p. 6, col. 4. (LE)

4552. "Libbers Donating Blood for the ERA." LAT, 4 January 1973, pt. 4, p. 11, col. 1.

4553. Murphy, Jean Douglas. "After ERA, What Course for Women?" LAT, 14 January 1973, pt. 9, p. 1, col. 2.

4554. "Rights Amendment Ratified by Wyoming." LAT, 25 January 1973, p. 4, col. 8.

4555. "Rights Amendment Rejected by Oklahoma." LAT, 1 February 1973, p. 12, col. 2.

4556. "Virginia Tables U.S. Amendment." LAT, 7 February 1973, p. 22, col. 3.

4557. "Survey Finds Rights Amendment in Trouble." LAT, 10 February 1973, p. 16, col. 3.

4558. "New Mexico OKs Rights Amendment." LAT, 13 February 1973, p. 6, col. 1.

4559. Cimons, Marlene. "ERA Top Priority for NOW." LAT, 19 February 1973, pt. 4, p. 1, col. 4.

4560. "Rights Amendment Ratified by Vermont." LAT, 22 February 1973, p. 8, col. 1.

4561. Furgurson, Ernest B. "The Harsh New Tactics of the Women's Push for Equal Rights." LAT, 26 February 1973, pt. 2, p. 7, col. 1.

4562. Forfreedom, Ann, and Gluck, Sherna. "Susan B. Anthony's Spirit Still Battles for Rights." LAT, 5 March 1973, pt. 2, p. 7, col. 1.

4563. "Maine Rejects Rights Measure." LAT, 7 March 1973, p. 21, col. 1.

4564. "Women's Rights Loses in Maine." LAT, 9 March 1973, p. 31, col. 3.

4565. "Two States Exercise Female Prerogative." LAT, 16 March 1973, p. 20, col. 1.

4566. "Dixie Prefers Southern Belle to Liberation." LAT, 17 March 1973, p. 21, col. 2.

4567. Cimons, Marlene. "Can States Rescind ERA Ratification?" LAT, 21 March 1973, pt. 4, p. 1, col. 2.

4568. "Women on Combat Patrols? The Raging Debate over ERA." LAT, 25 March 1973, pt. 6, p. 4, col. 1.

4569. Bremner, Donald. "Battle in the States: 'Equal Rights' 8 Short of Ratification." LAT, 25 March 1973, pt. 6, p. 5, col. 1.

4570. Mullin, Robert. "50 Years in Congress--Long Fight for No. 27." LAT, 25 March 1973, pt. 6, p. 5, col. 1.

4571. Penny, Elizabeth. "Woman on Pedestal?" LAT, 26 March 1973, pt. 2, p. 6, col. 5. (LE)

4572. Knowles, Loretta. "Rights Amendment." LAT, 30 March 1973, pt. 2, p. 6, col. 5. (LE)

4573. "Ohio Panel Kills Rights Proposal." LAT, 19 April 1973, p. 19, col. 2.

4574. "Missouri Rejects Rights Measure." LAT, 11 May 1973, p. 6, col. 4.

4575. "Women's Equality Day." LAT, 17 August 1973, pt. 2, p. 2, col. 3.

4576. "ERA Seen Ratified in 1975." LAT, 26 August 1973, pt. 10, p. 2, col. 3.

4577. "Betty Friedan Links Chauvinists, Scandal." LAT, 28 August 1973, p. 16, col. 1.

4578. "29 States In, 9 to Go for Rights Amendment." LAT, 10 October 1973, pt. 4, p. 13, col. 3.

4579. McManus, Elsie. "Equal Rights Measure." LAT, 6 November 1973, pt. 2, p. 6, col. 5. (LE)

4580. Pauley, Gay. "Fuel Crisis, ERA Top Concerns in '74." LAT, 6 January 1974, pt. 4, p. 13, col. 1.

4581. "Georgia Turns Down Equality for Women." LAT, 29 January 1974, p. 12, col. 5.

4582. "Ohio OKs Equal Rights Measure; 5 States to Go." LAT, 8 February 1974, p. 27, col. 2.

4583. Murphy, Jean Douglas. "$288,000 Awarded to Study Equal Rights
for Women." LAT, 1 March 1974, pt. 4, p. 1, col. 4.

4584. _____. "$288,000 Grant to Fund Rights Study." LAT,
7 March 1974, pt. 4, p. 24, col. 1.

4585. "Equal Rights Plan Loses 2nd Backer." LAT, 25 April 1974, p. 22,
col. 1.

4586. Frye, Roscoe J. "Destiny of the Human Race and Proper Role for
Women." LAT, 4 May 1974, pt. 2, p. 4, col. 3. (LE)

4587. Appleby, Jon H.; Bayley, Patricia A.; Davis, Mollie; Irwin, Beth;
Levin, Marili; Lindskoog, K.; McLaren, Betty; Newkirk, Madeleine;
Pelletier, Sandy; Tripi, Serena; and Wyatt, Gene A. "Destiny of the
Race and Proper Role for Women." LAT, 11 May 1974, pt. 2, p. 4,
cols. 3-5. (LE)

4588. "Women Visit Ford, Hear His Support for Equal Rights." LAT,
23 August 1974, p. 1, col. 3.

4589. "Equal Rights Backers Sure of Ratification." LAT, 29 November
1974, pt. 1A, p. 2, col. 1.

4590. "States Surveyed on Equal Rights Stand." LAT, 29 November 1974,
pt. 1A, p. 2, col. 1.

4591. Kilpatrick, James J. "Women's Rights: Uncertainties Surround
the New Amendment." LAT, 2 December 1974, pt. 2, p. 7, col. 4.

4592. Silverman, Sue, and Hoffner, Carol H. "'Women's Rights.'" LAT,
10 December 1974, pt. 2, p. 6, col. 4. (LE)

4593. Quinn, Sally. "Mrs. Schlafly: View from Pedestal." LAT,
10 December 1974, pt. 4, p. 10, col. 1.

4594. "Mormons Oppose Rights Amendment." LAT, 12 January 1975, pt. 1A,
p. 7, col. 3.

4595. "Opponents of Rights Proposal Question Mrs. Ford on Funds." LAT,
14 February 1975, p. 8, col. 5.

4596. "Equal Rights Rejected in Georgia." LAT, 18 February 1975, p. 4,
col. 1.

4597. Cimons, Marlene. "First Lady Sticks to Her Guns on ERA." LAT,
18 February 1975, pt. 4, p. 1, col. 2.

4598. "Utah House Votes Down Rights Plan." LAT, 19 February 1975,
p. 10, col. 1.

4599. "Rights Move Defeated." LAT, 20 February 1975, p. 5, col. 1.

4600. "Those Hypocritical Barriers." LAT, 27 February 1975, pt. 2,
p. 6, col. 1. (Ed)

4601. "Rights Measure Seems Dead for '75." LAT, 7 March 1975, p. 4, col. 1.

4602. "Sex Bias Measure Doomed for 1975." LAT, 27 March 1975, p. 4, col. 4.

4603. Isaacs, Stan. "'I Do What I Want to Do.'" LAT, 13 April 1975, pt. 5, p. 18, col. 1.

4604. "Florida Defeats Equal Rights Amendment." LAT, 26 April 1975, p. 2, col. 1.

4605. Cimons, Marlene. "ERA Backers Pool Hopes for Telethon." LAT, 19 May 1975, pt. 4, p. 1, col. 4.

4606. "Missouri Legislature Rejects Rights Amendment a 3rd Time." LAT, 3 June 1975, p. 12, col. 1.

4607. "The Era of ERA." LAT, 10 June 1975, pt. 2, p. 6, col. 2. (Ed)

4608. "Principal, Not Principle." LAT, 13 July 1975, pt. 4, p. 2, col. 2. (Ed)

4609. "BPW Votes to Push for Equal Rights Passage." LAT, 3 August 1975, pt. 9, p. 10, col. 1.

4610. Hendrix, Kathleen. "SMASHing Those Male Chauvinist Barriers." LAT, 5 September 1975, pt. 4, p. 1, col. 3.

4611. "A Challenge, Not an End, for ERA." LAT, 12 November 1975, pt. 2, p. 6, col. 1. (Ed)

4612. "Rights and the Spirit of '76." LAT, 8 January 1976, pt. 2, p. 6, col. 1. (Ed)

5.   *National Observer*

4613. Wanniski, Jude. "Liberating Women, or Harming Them?" NO, 17 August 1970, p. 2, col. 4.

4614. _____. "This Week in Washington." NO, 12 October 1970, p. 2, col. 4.

4615. Shah, Diane K. "Women's Amendment Passes House: Whimsical Debate Precedes First Big Victory." NO, 23 October 1971, p. 3, col. 1.

4616. _____. "Loss in the Senate: Women's Lib Wins in High Court." NO, 4 December 1971, p. 6, col. 5.

4617. "Rights--or Wrongs? Women's Amendment: Senate Debate." NO, 1 April 1972, p. 5, col. 1.

4618. Sorensen, Parry D. "Equal-Rights Proposal in Trouble: Mild-Sounding Amendment Evokes Some Impassioned Opposition." NO, 10 February 1973, p. 18, col. 1.

4619. "Speaking of People." <u>NO</u>, 9 February 1974, p. 6, col. 2.

4620. "A Faint Fanfare." <u>NO</u>, 2 March 1974, p. 18.

6. *New Orleans Times-Picayune*

4621. Benson, Miles. "Women's Libbers Pushing Amendment, Rights Bills." <u>NOT-P</u>, 29 January 1972, p. 13, col. 1.

4622. Chadwick, John. "Equal Rights Amendment Is Okayed by Committee." <u>NOT-P</u>, 1 March 1972, p. 1, col. 2.

4623. "Why Can't Women Be Draft Exempt?" <u>NOT-P</u>, 4 March 1972, p. 12, col. 1. (Ed)

4624. Lengel, John B. "Proposal Would Draft Women." <u>NOT-P</u>, 22 March 1972, p. 7, col. 3.

4625. Wilson, Richard. "24 Words Seen Potential Anti-Woman Time Bomb." <u>NOT-P</u>, 23 March 1972, p. 13, col. 1.

4626. "Women's Rights Measure Voted." <u>NOT-P</u>, 23 March 1972, sec. 5, p. 4, col. 3.

4627. "Lib Amendment--or Volstead Anew." <u>NOT-P</u>, 27 March 1972, p. 10, col. 1. (Ed)

4628. "Social Welfare Duty Next Draft Field?" <u>NOT-P</u>, 1 April 1972, p. 10, col. 1. (Ed)

4629. "Amendment Okayed by Tenth State." <u>NOT-P</u>, 6 April 1972, sec. 7, p. 2, col. 3.

4630. Bourgoyne, J.E. "Equal Rights Amendment Passage Urged by Panel." <u>NOT-P</u>, 18 May 1972, sec. 3, p. 6, col. 1.

4631. "Women's Rights Courses Differ." <u>NOT-P</u>, 19 May 1972, sec. 3, p. 10, col. 3.

4632. Gillis, James H. "Female Rights Move Opposed." <u>NOT-P</u>, 22 May 1972, p. 1, col. 2.

4633. "Equal Rights Issue Backed." <u>NOT-P</u>, 23 May 1972, p. 9, col. 7.

4634. "Clash in La. on Lib Amendment?" <u>NOT-P</u>, 24 May 1972, p. 10, col. 1. (Ed)

4635. "C of C Women Oppose Lib Bill." <u>NOT-P</u>, 24 May 1972, sec. 4, p. 3, col. 6.

4636. Yocum, Charlotte. "Rights Amendment." <u>NOT-P</u>, 25 May 1972, p. 12, col. 3. (LE)

4637. "League Endorses Rights Amendment." <u>NOT-P</u>, 27 May 1972, p. 8, col. 2.

4638. Milling, Mrs. R. King. "YWCA for ERA." NOT-P, 27 May 1972,
      p. 10, col. 7. (LE)

4639. "Coalition Gives Support to ERA." NOT-P, 28 May 1972, p. 30,
      col. 5.

4640. "Female Rights Move Offered." NOT-P, 29 May 1972, p. 19, col. 5.

4641. "Anti-Liberation Group Is Active." NOT-P, 31 May 1972, p. 11,
      col. 3.

4642. Massa, Joe. "'Liberation' Amendment Brief but Controversial."
      NOT-P, 1 June 1972, p. 4, col. 1.

4643. Roberts, John. "Rights Amendment Is Explosive Issue." NOT-P,
      4 June 1972, p. 4, col. 1.

4644. Hargroder, C.M. "Action Delayed on Rights Bill." NOT-P,
      6 June 1972, p. 1, col. 7.

4645. "Senate Vote Given on Returning Bill." NOT-P, 6 June 1972, p. 3,
      col. 4.

4646. "Louisiana Senate Okays Equal Rights for Women." NOT-P, 8 June
      1972, p. 1, col. 3.

4647. "Senate Votes Women's Rights." NOT-P, 8 June 1972, p. 5, col. 4.

4648. "Women Will Win If 13 States Nix ERA." NOT-P, 10 June 1972,
      p. 10, col. 1. (Ed)

4649. "Women's Rights Proposal Sent to Hostile House Unit." NOT-P,
      10 June 1972, p. 12, col. 4.

4650. Gaillard, Mrs. Dawson. "Supports ERA." NOT-P, 11 June 1972,
      sec. 2, p. 2, col. 3. (LE)

4651. "Women's Rights Move Rejected." NOT-P, 14 June 1972, p. 1, col. 6.

4652. Ashman, Heather. "ERA and the Draft." NOT-P, 14 June 1972,
      p. 12, col. 3. (LE)

4653. Pearson, Phyllis P., and Mathews, Lynne. "Readers Debate ERA."
      NOT-P, 16 June 1972, p. 16, col. 3. (LE)

4654. Trefny, Anita B. "Against ERA." NOT-P, 19 June 1972, p. 12,
      col. 3. (LE)

4655. Dantone, Jacqueline E. "WAF on ERA." NOT-P, 21 June 1972, p. 8,
      col. 3. (LE)

4656. "Women's Rights Bill Supported." NOT-P, 21 June 1972, p. 12,
      col. 2.

4657. Breaux, Janice. "Paper 'Biased.'" NOT-P, 26 June 1972, p. 8,
      col. 4. (LE)

4658. Salassi, Carmelite B. "'No' to ERA." NOT-P, 28 June 1972, p. 10, col. 3. (LE)

4659. Gillis, James H. "La. House Kills Measure on Women's Equal Rights." NOT-P, 30 June 1972, p. 1, col. 7.

4660. Kazickas, Jurate. "Equal Rights Amendment is Closer to Ratification." NOT-P, 13 September 1972, p. 6, col. 1.

4661. "Decision on ERA May Be Imminent." NOT-P, 13 January 1973, p. 12, col. 3. (Ed)

4662. "Women's Rights Issue Opposed." NOT-P, 18 January 1973, p. 17, col. 4.

4663. Minor, W.F. "It's Decision Time on Amendment." NOT-P, 4 February 1973, sec. 2, p. 2, col. 5.

4664. "Air Force Academy and the ERA." NOT-P, 5 February 1973, p. 10, col. 1. (Ed)

4665. "Georgians Blast Rights Measure." NOT-P, 8 February 1973, p. 18, col. 3.

4666. "ERA Proposal Dead in Mississippi." NOT-P, 9 February 1973, p. 21, col. 2.

4667. Latimer, Lucy F. "ERA Opposed." NOT-P, 16 February 1973, p. 8, col. 3. (LE)

4668. "Rights' Sponsors Withdraw Efforts." NOT-P, 22 February 1973, p. 18, col. 3.

4669. "Women's Rights Get B & PW Nod." NOT-P, 22 February 1973, sec. 6, p. 3, col. 5.

4670. "ERA Has Had It--But End It Well." NOT-P, 7 March 1973, p. 12, col. 2. (Ed)

4671. Ayres, Brown, and Pines, Lois. "Equal Rights Amendment Big Issue in Legislature." NOT-P, 11 March 1973, p. 18, cols. 1 and 2.

4672. Olson, Lynne. "YWCA Involved in Fight for Equality for Women." NOT-P, 15 March 1973, sec. 4, p. 4, col. 4.

4673. "Nebraska Reverses Self on Rights." NOT-P, 16 March 1973, p. 1, col. 4.

4674. "Connecticut OK's Rights Amendment." NOT-P, 16 March 1973, p. 4, col. 6.

4675. Gillis, James H. "Louisiana Constitutional Convention Approves Tentative Preamble." NOT-P, 18 March 1973, p. 10, col. 3.

4676. Fuoto, Ellen M., and Tillery, Frederick Y. "Questions Editorial." NOT-P, 19 March 1973, p. 8, col. 4. (LE)

4677. "Washington OKs Lib Amendment." NOT-P, 23 March 1973, p. 1, col. 3.

4678. Casey, Sarah. "The ERA Question." NOT-P, 26 March 1973, p. 14, col. 3. (LE)

4679. Simpson, Peggy. "Equal Right Amendment to Strengthen Family--East." NOT-P, 26 March 1973, p. 32, col. 1.

4680. "Nebraska ERA Vote Salutary Lesson." NOT-P, 30 March 1973, p. 10, col. 1. (Ed)

4681. "Women Voters Name Officers." NOT-P, 6 April 1973, p. 10, col. 4.

4682. Hargroder, C.M. "Equal Rights for Women CC-73 Committee Discussion Topic." NOT-P, 7 April 1973, p. 6, col. 1.

4683. Jory, Tom. "Edwards Still in Favor of ERA." NOT-P, 7 April 1973, p. 7, col. 1.

4684. Hargroder, C.M. "Lawyers Seek End to Review of Facts on Cases Decided on Trial Court Level." NOT-P, 8 April 1973, p. 14, col. 1.

4685. Kimbrough, Mary. "Phyllis Schlafly's Woman Power Beating Down ERA." NOT-P, 13 April 1973, p. 9, col. 1.

4686. "ERA Opponents Hear Edwards." NOT-P, 17 April 1973, sec. 2, p. 4, col. 3.

4687. "Florida Rejects ERA Proposal." NOT-P, 18 April 1973, p. 3, col. 6.

4688. "Anti-ERA Band Wagon Rolling." NOT-P, 21 April 1973, p. 10, col. 1. (Ed)

4689. Nelson, Marilyn. "ERA Advocate." NOT-P, 24 April 1973, p. 8, col. 3. (LE)

4690. Reboul, Mrs. Harvey. "ERA Foe." NOT-P, 25 April 1973, p. 10, col. 5. (LE)

4691. Treadway, Joan. "Sledgehammer to Slay a Fly?" NOT-P, 27 April 1973, sec. 3, p. 3, col. 1.

4692. Martin, Mrs. Elizabeth. "ERA Is Wrong." NOT-P, 28 April 1973, p. 10, col. 6. (LE)

4693. "Maryland State ERA Teaches Lesson." NOT-P, 2 May 1973, p. 10, col. 1. (Ed)

4694. Schuwerk, Robert P. "Backs ERA." NOT-P, 10 May 1973, p. 10, col. 3. (LE)

4695. "Wisconsin Voters Nix State ERA." NOT-P, 14 May 1973, p. 10, col. 2. (Ed)

4696. Breaux, Janice. "ERA 'Guarantee.'" NOT-P, 23 May 1973, p. 10, col. 4. (LE)

4697. "Women Voters." NOT-P, 11 October 1973, p. 26, col. 1.

4698. "Catholic Unit Vote Anti-ERA." NOT-P, 18 October 1973, p. 29, col. 2.

4699. Fawcett, Mrs. John R., Jr. "ERA Won't Help." NOT-P, 21 October 1973, p. 14, col. 6. (LE)

4700. "Disciples Unit Approves ERA." NOT-P, 1 November 1973, p. 30, col. 1.

4701. Schrodt, Anita. "ERA Will Pass, NOW Exec Says." NOT-P, 4 November 1973, p. 8, col. 1.

4702. "Equality Amendment." NOT-P, 10 December 1973, sec. 4, p. 5, col. 1.

4703. Granger, Bill. "She's for Equal Rights Amendment." NOT-P, 16 December 1973, sec. 4, p. 14, col. 3.

4704. "Equal Rights." NOT-P, 31 December 1973, p. 11, col. 8.

4705. Haynes, Valerie M. "Woman's Place in Home, House, Senate, Unit Told." NOT-P, 26 January 1974, p. 8, col. 7.

4706. DeNoux, Bonnie. "ERA Equality." NOT-P, 26 January 1974, p. 16, col. 7.

4707. Sanders, Mrs. J. Oran. "Opposes ERA." NOT-P, 6 February 1974, p. 10, col. 4. (LE)

4708. "Two Florida Nuns Fight against 'Oppression,' Campaign for ERA." NOT-P, 9 February 1974, p. 6, col. 5.

4709. Selva, Hilde Della. "Women for ERA." NOT-P, 10 February 1974, p. 14, col. 3. (LE)

4710. Milliner, Gladys. "Pro-ERA Response." NOT-P, 13 February 1974, p. 10, col. 3. (LE)

4711. Helwig, Jeanne. "ERA to Force It." NOT-P, 18 February 1974, p. 12, col. 4. (LE)

4712. "Backers of ERA Plan 'Big Push.'" NOT-P, 19 February 1974, p. 5, col. 1.

4713. Lagrange, Mrs. L. "'Equal Rights.'" NOT-P, 21 February 1974, p. 8, col. 5. (LE)

4714. Phillips, V.M. "Women on the Air." NOT-P, 7 April 1974, p. 12, col. 6. (LE)

4715. "LA. Units Seek Votes for ERA." NOT-P, 8 April 1974, p. 8, col. 3.

4716. "Liz Carpenter Addresses La. AFL-CIO Delegates." NOT-P, 10 April 1974, sec. 3, p. 5, col. 1.

4717. "Florida Rejects ER Amendment." NOT-P, 11 April 1974, sec. 5, p. 2, col. 2.

4718. "Windhorst: ERA Passage Would Shift Social Order." NOT-P, 18 April 1974, p. 16, col. 1.

4719. Poe, Edgar. "U.S. DAR Issues Censure of ERA." NOT-P, 19 April 1974, p. 21, col. 1.

4720. Osborne, Joan. "Windhorst on ERA." NOT-P, 23 April 1974, p. 10, col. 3. (LE)

4721. "ERA Rescinded by Tennessee." NOT-P, 25 April 1974, sec. 5, p. 24, col. 8.

4722. "Board Backing Lib Amendment." NOT-P, 26 April 1974, sec. 2, p. 15, col. 1.

4723. "With ERA in the Wings." NOT-P, 27 April 1974, p. 14, col. 1. (Ed)

4724. Thayer, Marilyn. "Wrongs Cited." NOT-P, 1 May 1974, p. 14, col. 4. (LE)

4725. "Equal Rights Amendment Backers Hear Mrs. Long." NOT-P, 5 May 1974, p. 3, col. 5.

4727. "Expert Says Amendment Will Not Benefit Women." NOT-P, 8 May 1974, p. 23, col. 7.

4728. "Women's Rights Backed by ERA Opposition Unit." NOT-P, 8 May 1974, sec. 5, p. 4, col. 3.

4729. "Catholic Group Backs Amendment." NOT-P, 9 May 1974, sec. 3, p. 11, col. 7.

4730. Ferry, Mrs. William J. "Pleased by Story." NOT-P, 10 May 1974, p. 10, col. 5. (LE)

4731. Turner, Nancy. "ERA Has Merit." NOT-P, 11 May 1974, p. 14, col. 3. (LE)

4732. Deem, Rev. Alvin J. "Opposes ERA." NOT-P, 11 May 1974, p. 14, col. 3. (LE)

4733. Kelleher, Barbara B. "Be Fair on ERA." NOT-P, 11 May 1974, p. 14, col. 4. (LE)

4734. Flower, Donna D. "ERA Foe." NOT-P, 11 May 1974, p. 14, col. 4. (LE)

4735. "Poll Indicates ERA Is Favored." NOT-P, 12 May 1974, p. 28, col. 2.

4736. Koerner, Peggy. "Women in Russia." NOT-P, 13 May 1974, p. 12, col. 3. (LE)

4737. Latimer, Clay. "Charges Bias." NOT-P, 14 May 1974, p. 10, col. 5. (LE)

4738. Marshall, George. "Scouts and ERA." NOT-P, 15 May 1974, p. 12, col. 3. (LE)

4739. "Alliance Unit Endorses ERA." NOT-P, 17 May 1974, p. 26, col. 1.

4740. "Metairie Club Opposes ERA." NOT-P, 17 May 1974, p. 29, col. 1.

4741. Salassi, Mrs. Raymond. "ERA Research." NOT-P, 18 May 1974, p. 12, col. 4. (LE)

4742. Ball, Millie. "Defeat of ERA Is Not Feared." NOT-P, 24 May 1974, p. 11, col. 1.

4743. Koerner, Francesca. "Can Get Credit." NOT-P, 26 May 1974, p. 10, col. 6. (LE)

4744. "ERA Opposition Being Restated." NOT-P, 26 May 1974, p. 33, col. 2.

4745. Estill, Jerry. "Senate Unit Defers Action on ERA, to Await House." NOT-P, 29 May 1974, p. 22, col. 1.

4746. "Husband Is Breadwinner." NOT-P, 1 June 1974, p. 14, col. 1. (Ed)

4747. Boynton, Bonnie F. "ERA Not 'Simple.'" NOT-P, 9 June 1974, p. 10, col. 6. (LE)

4748. Gibson, Frances. "Women Lack Rights." NOT-P, 16 June 1974, p. 10, col. 6. (LE)

4749. M'Daniel, Jonica. "House Panel Kills ERA Bill." NOT-P, 20 June 1974, p. 1, col. 4.

4750. "ERA Supporters Deflated after Amendment Defeat." NOT-P, 21 June 1974, p. 7, col. 1.

4751. Chiasson, Cheryl A. "Women, Stay Put." NOT-P, 23 June 1974, p. 10, col. 6. (LE)

4752. Armstrong, Anne. "Nixon and ERA." NOT-P, 25 June 1974, p. 14, col. 3. (LE)

4753. "More Harm Than Good in ERA, Opponents Say." NOT-P, 26 June 1974, p. 3, col. 3.

4754. Gum, Jane R. "'Local Lib.'" NOT-P, 28 June 1974, p. 16, col. 3. (LE)

4755. Seale, Carol. "Don't Scar ERA." NOT-P, 5 July 1974, p. 8, col. 3. (LE)

4756. "ERA Chances Said Bolstered." NOT-P, 11 November 1974, sec. 2, p. 2, col. 1.

4757. Kilpatrick, James J. "Both Libbers, Lawyers May Rejoice If ERA Okayed." NOT-P, 30 November 1974, p. 19, col. 1. (Ed)

4758. "American Woman Said Doing Just Fine." NOT-P, 30 November 1974, p. 22, col. 1.

4759. "ERA Opponents' Defeat 'Cheerful'--NOW Leader." NOT-P, 11 December 1974, p. 23, col. 1.

4760. Estill, Jerry. "Carter, PSC, Women's Lib on Agenda." NOT-P, 20 January 1975, p. 4, col. 4.

4761. Hargroder, C.M. "Era Clears Committee, Awaits Senate Action." NOT-P, 21 January 1975, p. 1, col. 8.

4762. "ERA May Have a Rough Time." NOT-P, 21 January 1975, p. 5, col. 1.

4763. "Women's Organization Quizzes 7 District 90 Candidates for House Seat." NOT-P, 21 January 1975, p. 9, col. 1.

4764. Hargroder, C.M. "Floor Debate on ERA Fails to Show." NOT-P, 22 January 1975, p. 8, col. 2.

4765. _____. "ERA Is Sidetracked in Louisiana Senate." NOT-P, 23 January 1975, p. 1, col. 1.

4766. "ERA Opposed by Mrs. Thayer." NOT-P, 24 January 1975, p. 3, col. 1.

4767. Hargroder, C.M. "Senate Dodging ERA Controversy." NOT-P, 26 January 1975, sec. 2, p. 6, col. 5.

4768. "Sen. De Blieux: 'Men Enough'?" NOT-P, 27 January 1975, p. 14, col. 1. (Ed)

4769. "ERA Ratified by 34th State." NOT-P, 4 February 1975, p. 3, col. 7.

4770. Lewine, Frances. "Betty Ford Pushing ERA in Nevada and Arizona." NOT-P, 13 February 1975, sec. 4, p. 9, col. 7.

4771. De Blieux, J.D. "Senator Replies." NOT-P, 14 February 1975, p. 12, col. 3. (LE)

4772. "Praise Given to Mrs. Ford." NOT-P, 18 February 1975, p. 3, col. 3.

4773. Moes, Garry J. "ERA Chance Is Poor in Utah." NOT-P, 19 February 1975, p. 16, col. 2.

4774. "ERA Lobbying with Taxes." NOT-P, 21 February 1975, p. 14, col. 1. (Ed)

4775. "Betty Ford Unperturbed Her Mail Is Running 3 to 1 against Her Support of ERA." NOT-P, 21 February 1975, sec. 3, p. 5, col. 1.

4776. "ERA Loses in Arizona." <u>NOT-P</u>, 27 February 1975, p. 14, col. 1.

4777. Hanson, Barry. "Illinois Vote on ERA Delayed." <u>NOT-P</u>, 5 March 1975, sec. 4, p. 4, col. 4.

4778. Cook, Louise. "Supporters: ERA by '79 'Inevitable.'" <u>NOT-P</u>, 13 March 1975, p. 12, col. 1.

4779. "Many U.S. Laws 'ERA-Inspired.'" <u>NOT-P</u>, 19 March 1975, p. 10, col. 2.

4780. Lofton, John D., Jr. "Back to Basics: ERA Unneeded." <u>NOT-P</u>, 31 March 1975, p. 24, col. 6. (Ed)

4781. "Era: Seven Years' Bad Luck?" <u>NOT-P</u>, 6 April 1975, p. 34, col. 1. (Ed)

4782. Buchanan, Patrick J. "ERA Still Four States in the Red." <u>NOT-P</u>, 7 April 1975, p. 16, col. 6.

4783. Gallup, George. "Majority Votes to Ban Sex Bias." <u>NOT-P</u>, 10 April 1975, sec. 5, p. 4, col. 1.

4784. "Florida Rejects ERA." <u>NOT-P</u>, 26 April 1975, p. 5. col. 5.

4785. Ewing, Martha. "Hits Ford on ERA." <u>NOT-P</u>, 28 April 1975, p. 12, col. 3. (LE)

4786. "ERA, School Funds in Bills." <u>NOT-P</u>, 2 May 1975, p. 7, col. 1.

4787. Sullivan, Marguerite. "Sex Equality Amendment." <u>NOT-P</u>, 4 May 1975, sec. 5, p. 16, col. 8.

4788. "Demo Conclave Lost to State?" <u>NOT-P</u>, 5 May 1975, sec. 2, p. 4, col. 1.

4789. Presley, Merikaye. "ERA Support Underrated." <u>NOT-P</u>, 6 May 1975, sec. 3, p. 3, col. 3.

4790. Riddle, Karen. "Time for ERA." <u>NOT-P</u>, 7 May 1975, p. 10, col. 6. (LE)

4791. Falgoust, Fernand J., and Falgoust, Joan S. "Defeat ERA." <u>NOT-P</u>, 11 May 1975, p. 10, col. 3. (LE)

4792. Hargroder, C.M. "Anti-ERA Debate Fogs Up Issue." <u>NOT-P</u>, 18 May 1975, p. 14, col. 6. (Ed)

4793. "New Group to Boost ERA." <u>NOT-P</u>, 20 May 1975, p. 5, col. 1.

4794. Landis, Mrs. Fred S. "LWV and ERA." <u>NOT-P</u>, 21 May 1975, p. 18, col. 2. (LE)

4795. Puneky, Claire. "ERA Adoption Is Group's Aim." <u>NOT-P</u>, 21 May 1975, sec. 3, p. 1, col. 1.

4796. "Group Opposes ERA, Backs Rights." <u>NOT-P</u>, 26 May 1975, p. 17, col. 5.

4797. "ERA Bill Is Defeated." <u>NOT-P</u>, 3 June 1975, p. 3, col. 5.

4798. "Governors Hit for Meeting in Louisiana." <u>NOT-P</u>, 9 June 1975, p. 8, col. 1.

4799. LaPlace, John. "No-Shows ERA Key." <u>NOT-P</u>, 11 June 1975, p. 14, col. 8.

4800. _____. "ERA Out Again." <u>NOT-P</u>, 12 June 1975, p. 1, col. 4.

4801. _____. "ERA Burial as Good as Dumped in Lake?" <u>NOT-P</u>, 13 June 1975, p. 8, col. 1.

4802. "Coalition Cites Lack of Action." <u>NOT-P</u>, 19 June 1975, p. 20, col. 1.

4803. "Era Criticized." <u>NOT-P</u>, 24 June 1975, p. 4, col. 4.

4804. Felt, Charlotte. "ERA Up to States." <u>NOT-P</u>, 1 July 1975, p. 12, col. 4. (LE)

4805. Ott, Dwight. "Boggs: ERA Out, Democracy Wins." <u>NOT-P</u>, 3 July 1975, p. 16, col. 2.

4806. Hodges, Louis N. "Jones Vows to Back ERA If He's Elected." <u>NOT-P</u>, 18 September 1975, sec. 3, p. 2, col. 4.

4807. Salassi, C.B. "ERA and Rescission." <u>NOT-P</u>, 21 September 1975, p. 10, col. 3. (LE)

4808. "N. J. and N. Y. Vote on ERA Tuesday." <u>NOT-P</u>, 2 November 1975, p. 8, col. 1.

4809. "ERA Is Defeated in New York, Jersey." <u>NOT-P</u>, 5 November 1975, p. 9, col. 2.

4810. Buchanan, James J. "ERA Elitists: 'We Are Robbed!'" <u>NOT-P</u>, 14 November 1975, p. 18, col. 3. (Ed)

7.   *New York Times*

4811. "Women Urge Amendment." <u>NYT</u>, 13 April 1914, p. 6, col. 8. Rep. in entry #491.

4812. "Call Woman's Party Council on Full Equality Amendment." <u>NYT</u>, 5 September 1921, p. 1, col. 4.

4813. "Women Lawyers Meet." <u>NYT</u>, 16 September 1921, p. 10, col. 2.

4814. "Equal Rights Drive Started on States." <u>NYT</u>, 26 September 1921, p. 15, col. 4. Rep. in entry #491.

4815. "Fixes Equal Rights Amendment Form." NYT, 12 December 1921, p. 17, col. 8.

4816. "Women to Demand All Rights of Men." NYT, 16 January 1922, p. 1, col. 7.

4817. "Women's Rights." NYT, 17 January 1922, p. 16, col. 2.   (Ed)

4818. Harrington, John Walker. "Woman's Rights Would Become Woman's Wrongs." NYT, 22 January 1922, sec. 7, p. 3, col. 1.

4819. C.M.W. "Are These Women Crazy?" NYT, 22 January 1922, sec. 7, p. 6, col. 3. (LE)

4820. Brannan, Eunice Dana, and Rogers, Elizabeth Selden. "Two Women Answer." NYT, 29 January 1922, sec. 7, p. 8, col. 4. (LE)

4821. "Women Rally to Equal Rights Bill." NYT, 10 February 1922, p. 2, col. 7.

4822. "Asks Blanket Law to Equalize Women." NYT, 12 April 1922, p. 5, col. 1.

4823. "Open Fund to Fight Woman's Equality." NYT, 16 May 1922, p. 19, col. 1.

4824. "Equal Rights." NYT, 17 May 1922, p. 18, col. 4. (Ed)

4825. Smith, Jane Norman. "The Equal Rights Amendment." NYT, 19 May 1922, p. 16, col. 6. (LE)

4826. "Women to Oppose 'Blanket Equality.'" NYT, 30 October 1922, p. 17, col. 7.

4827. "Women Give $85,000 for Equality Drive." NYT, 13 November 1922, p. 14, col. 8.

4828. Bent, Silas. "The Women's War." NYT Magazine, 14 January 1923, pp. 4, 15.

4829. "Women Open Fight for Equal Rights." NYT, 21 July 1923, p. 8, col. 8.

4830. "Women Adopt Form for Equal Rights." NYT, 22 July 1923, p. 1, col. 5.

4831. "News Condensed: Drive for Equal Rights." NYT, 25 September 1923, p. 3, col. 2.

4832. "Equal Rights Call Issued." NYT, 22 October 1923, p. 21, col. 6.

4833. Johnson, Rossiter. "Twentieth Amendment." NYT, 28 October 1923, sec. 2, p. 6, col. 7. (LE)

4834. "Plan Equal Rights Fight." NYT, 5 November 1923, p. 15, col. 2.

4835. "Coolidge Assures Women of Victory." NYT, 18 November 1923, p. 22, col. 1.

4836. "Equal Rights Meeting Held in Capitol Crypt." NYT, 19 November 1923, p. 3, col. 2. Rep. in entry #491.

4837. "Mills Turns Down Equal Rights Plea." NYT, 28 November 1923, p. 20, col. 3.

4838. "Mrs. Huck Says If Equal Rights Bill Fails, Women Will Pass It in the Next Congress." NYT, 10 December 1923, p. 1, col. 5.

4839. "Women See Coolidge on 'Blanket Equality.'" NYT, 13 December 1923, p. 3, col. 5.

4840. Smith, Ethel M. "Working Women's Case against Equal Rights." NYT, 20 January 1924, sec. 8, p. 12, col. 1. Rep. in entry #463 and as a separate by the National Women's Trade Union League of America.

4841. "Equal Rights Move Held Destructive." NYT, 21 January 1924, p. 17, col. 3.

4842. Morris, Paul Caruthers. "Equal Rights in Texas." NYT, 23 January 1924, p. 16, col. 7. (LE)

4843. "Women for Equal Rights." NYT, 29 January 1924, p. 3, col. 3.

4844. "Oppose 'Equal Rights.'" NYT, 17 March 1924, p. 15, col. 3.

4845. "Women Will Oppose Equal Rights Plan." NYT, 1 May 1924, p. 11, col. 5.

4846. "Strong Pleas for World Court before Committee: Women Offer Equal Plank." NYT, 11 June 1924, p. 3, col. 3.

4847. "Women Democrats Propose Dry Plank." NYT, 13 June 1924, p. 21, col. 7.

4848. "Woman's Party Asks Equal Rights Plank." NYT, 16 June 1924, p. 2, col. 2.

4849. "League Comes to Front for Democratic Action: Women Press for Equal Rights." NYT, 24 June 1924, p. 3, col. 5. (Article begins p. 1, col. 5)

4850. "Women Threaten a 'Bloc' in Congress." NYT, 26 June 1924, p. 5, col. 3.

4851. "Calls for Women's Bloc." NYT, 29 June 1924, p. 9, col. 2.

4852. "Women to Decide on Forming Bloc." NYT, 16 August 1924, p. 2, col. 8.

4853. "Wadsworth Deaf to Women's Party." NYT, 18 January 1925, p. 4, col. 1.

4854. "Discuss Equal Rights." NYT, 24 January 1925, p. 17, col. 7.

4855. "Advocate Equal Rights." NYT, 31 January 1925, p. 3, col. 6.

4856. "Equal Rights Amendment Hearings." NYT, 1 February 1925, p. 2,
col. 2.

4857. "100 Women Ask 'Rights.'" NYT, 5 February 1925, p. 4, col. 7.

4858. "Equal Rights Pleas Heard by Senators." NYT, 7 February 1925,
p. 17, col. 2.

4859. "Fight for Legal Equality." NYT, 6 March 1925, p. 2, col. 6.

4860. "Equality in Nation, Woman's Party Aim." NYT, 5 April 1925,
p. 14, col. 2.

4861. "Want Maiden Name Good on Passport." NYT, 1 May 1925, p. 12,
col. 1.

4862. "Working Women Ask Coolidge's Aid." NYT, 18 January 1926, p. 1,
col. 4.

4863. "Coolidge Sees Duty to Women Workers." NYT, 19 January 1926,
p. 1, col. 5.

4864. "'Equal Rights for Women.'" NYT, 19 January 1926, p. 26, col. 3.
(Ed)

4865. "Labor Women Carry Battle to Coolidge." NYT, 22 January 1926,
p. 2, col. 3.

4866. "Mrs. Catt Explains Ban on Woman's Party." NYT, 4 June 1926,
p. 24, col. 2.

4867. "Women Seek Coolidge Aid." NYT, 23 January 1927, p. 4, col. 4.

4868. "Women to See Coolidge." NYT, 13 February 1927, p. 18, col. 2.

4869. "Here for Women's Parley." NYT, 2 July 1927, p. 22, col. 3.

4870. "Women Will Carry Plea to Coolidge." NYT, 4 July 1927, p. 17,
col. 7.

4871. "Equal Rights Plea Finds Aid in West." NYT, 6 July 1927, p. 10,
col. 4.

4872. "Women to Visit Coolidge." NYT, 11 July 1927, p. 3, col. 3.

4873. "Woman Delegation Moves on Coolidge." NYT, 14 July 1927, p. 1,
col. 4.

4874. "Rapid City Hears Woman Delegation." NYT, 15 July 1927, p. 1,
col. 2.

4875. "Coolidge Receives Woman's Party Plea." NYT, 16 July 1927, p. 13,
col. 1.

4876. "Oppose Amendment for 'Women's Rights.'" NYT, 17 July 1927,
sec. 9, p. 12, col. 2.

4877. Laughlin, Gail. "Woman's Party Asks Equal Legal Rights." NYT,
11 September 1927, sec. 8, p. 10, col. 1.

4878. "Women Will Demand Equal-Rights Plank." NYT, 28 May 1928, p. 4,
col. 3.

4879. "Equal Rights Plan Heavily Attacked." NYT, 2 February 1929,
p. 10, col. 6.

4880. "Hails Walska's Victory." NYT, 18 January 1930, p. 8, col. 2.

4881. "Women Oppose Mrs. Pratt." NYT, 28 October 1930, p. 6, col. 3.

4882. "Broun Defends Views on Laws for Women." NYT, 1 November 1930,
p. 8, col. 3.

4883. "'Equal Rights' Plan Assailed as Futile." NYT, 23 November 1930,
p. 6, col. 1.

4884. "Equal Rights Argued by Women Leaders." NYT, 7 January 1931,
p. 10, col. 2.

4885. "Rights for Women Advocated by Ludlow." NYT, 24 March 1932. (?)
Rep. in entry #1970.

4886. "President Hears Plea for Women's Rights; Amelia Earhart Cites
Equality in the Air." NYT, 23 September 1932, p. 1, col. 6.

4887. "Seek Equality on Jobs." NYT, 14 January 1933, p. 10, col. 6.

4888. "Women Disagree on 'Equal Rights.'" NYT, 28 May 1933, sec. 2,
p. 1, col. 4.

4889. "Woman's Party Hit by Mrs. Roosevelt." NYT, 7 July 1933, p. 19,
col. 6.

4890. "Demands Equal Rights." NYT, 9 September 1933, p. 6, col. 7.

4891. "Clubwomen Insist on Anti-Pistol Bill." NYT, 25 May 1934, p. 8,
col. 4.

4892. "Woman's Party Convenes Today to Fight '1,000 Discriminations.'"
NYT, 17 November 1934, p. 17, col. 4.

4893. "Women See Rights Ignored in Europe." NYT, 18 November 1934,
sec. 2, p. 1, col. 3.

4894. "Jealousy Held Bar to Women's Rights." NYT, 19 November 1934,
p. 19, col. 7.

4895. "Plans Equal Rights Law." NYT, 1 December 1934, p. 16, col. 1.

4896. "Women Here Extol Susan B. Anthony." NYT, 16 February 1935,
p. 15, col. 7.

4897. "Meet on Campaign by Woman's Party." NYT, 30 November 1935,
p. 18, col. 4.

4898. Mallon, Winifred. "Women Pledged to Win Equality." NYT,
1 December 1935, p. 40, col. 1.

4899. _____. "Equality Is Made Major Polls Issue." NYT, 2 December
1935, p. 9, col. 1.

4900. _____. "Sees Victory Near for Equal Rights." NYT,
3 December 1935, p. 23, col. 1.

4901. "Women Renew War for Equal Rights." NYT, 3 January 1936, p. 21,
col. 6.

4902. "Constitution Held Unfair to Women." NYT, 14 February 1936,
p. 21, col. 8.

4903. Mallon, Winifred. "Slate Nominated by Women Voters." NYT,
30 April 1936, p. 21, col. 1.

4904. "Equal Rights Win Move in Congress." NYT, 31 May 1936, p. 1,
col. 5.

4905. "Platform Planks Sought by Women." NYT, 31 May 1936, sec. 2,
p. 7, col. 8.

4906. "Equal Rights Bill Fought by Women." NYT, 1 June 1936, p. 16,
col. 8.

4907. "Fight 'Equal Rights' Act." NYT, 2 June 1936, p. 14, col. 5.

4908. "Women in Dispute over Wage Plank." NYT, 24 June 1936, p. 18,
col. 4.

4909. "Women Are Heard in Platform Pleas." NYT, 25 June 1936, p. 15,
col. 2.

4910. "Women Join to Hail Susan B. Anthony." NYT, 27 August 1936,
p. 23, col. 1.

4911. Mallon, Winifred. "New Drive Begun for Equal Rights." NYT,
8 November 1936, sec. 6, p. 6, col. 8.

4912. "Triumph Is Seen for Equal Rights." NYT, 15 November 1936,
sec. 2, p. 1, col. 4.

4913. "Equal Rights Bill Up for 3 Debates." NYT, 21 March 1937, sec. 6,
p. 6, col. 2.

4914. "Women in Debate on Equal Rights." NYT, 23 March 1937, p. 25,
col. 5.

4915. "Debate Equal Rights Proposal." NYT, 2 May 1937, sec. 6, p. 4,
col. 3.

4916. "10,000,000 Women Held Underpaid." NYT, 6 June 1937, sec. 2,
p. 1, col. 1.

4917. "House Subcommittee Favors Equal Rights." NYT, 17 June 1937,
p. 6, col. 5.

4918. McLaughlin, Kathleen. "Democrats Hailed for Aid to Women." NYT,
17 June 1937, p. 8, col. 4.

4919. "Amendment for Equal Rights for Women Favorably Reported by Senate
Committee." NYT, 24 June 1937, p. 8, col. 2.

4920. Di Lorenzo, Anthonio. "Women; And Their Rights." NYT, 27 June
1937, sec. 4, p. 9, col. 8. (LE)

4921. McLaughlin, Kathleen. "Women Push Fight for Full Equality." NYT,
24 July 1937, p. 17, col. 1.

4922. Amamoto, R.K. "A Woman Discusses Women." NYT, 1 August 1937,
sec. 4, p. 8, col. 7. (LE)

4923. "Equal Rights' [sic] Held a Peril to Women." NYT, 8 August 1937,
sec. 2, p. 1, col. 4.

4924. La Hines, Elizabeth. "Prepare for Fight over Equal Rights." NYT,
3 October 1937, sec. 6, p. 8, col. 7.

4925. MacKenzie, Catherine. "Woman Strikes Again at This 'Man's
World.'" NYT Magazine, 14 November 1937, pp. 7, 22.

4926. "Jersey Unit Studies Equal Rights Issues." NYT, 28 November
1937, sec. 6, p. 6, col. 6.

4927. "Burke Backs Aims of Women's Party." NYT, 15 December 1937,
p. 6, col. 4.

4928. "Women Heartened in 'Equality' Drive." NYT, 16 December 1937,
p. 31, col. 4.

4929. "Union Women Back 'Equal Rights' Bills." NYT, 19 December 1937,
p. 8, col. 2.

4930. McLaughlin, Kathleen. "National Women's Groups Are Sharply
Divided over Proposals for Equal Rights Amendment." NYT, 19 December
1937, sec. 6, p. 5, col. 4.

4931. "Amelia Earhart Fund Is Set Up." NYT, 17 January 1938, p. 21,
col. 6.

4932. "Women Warned on Equal Rights." NYT, 3 February 1938, p. 25,
col. 1.

4933. "Club Women Ask Rights Bill Delay." NYT, 5 February 1938, p. 17,
col. 6.

4934. Petersen, Anne. "Lines Sharply Split on Eve of Equal Rights Amendment Hearing: 8 Women's Groups Fighting Proposal." NYT, 6 February 1938, sec. 6, p. 5, col. 1.

4935. McLaughlin, Kathleen. "Women Condemn Equal Rights Plan." NYT, 8 February 1938, p. 7, col. 1.

4936. _____. "Equal Rights Plea Attacked by Borah." NYT, 9 February 1938, p. 3, col. 1.

4937. _____. "Present Defense of Equal Rights." NYT, 10 February 1938, p. 5, col. 1.

4938. "Equal and Rugged." NYT, 10 February 1938, p. 20, col. 4. (Ed)

4939. McLaughlin, Kathleen. "Ask Equal Rights as National Logic." NYT, 11 February 1938, p. 5, col. 2.

4940. _____. "Equal Rights Move Called Dangerous." NYT, 13 February 1938, sec. 2, p. 2, col. 1.

4941. _____. "Women Argue 'Equal Rights.'" NYT, 13 February 1938, sec. 4, p. 7, col. 6.

4942. Ashurst Ignores Wires--Except from Home State." NYT, 14 February 1938, p. 6, col. 4.

4943. "'Equal Rights' Vote a Tie." NYT, 15 February 1938, p. 5, col. 6.

4944. "Arizona First." NYT, 20 February 1938, sec. 4, p. 2, col. 7.

4945. "Five Women Sponsor Equal Rights Fund." NYT, 25 February 1938, p. 11, col. 2.

4946. Petersen, Anne. "'Fight to the Last Ditch' Mapped against Equal Rights Proposal: Campaign Is Begun by 10 Women Here." NYT, 27 February 1938, sec. 6, p. 5, col. 1.

4947. "Reconsiders Rights Bill." NYT, 15 March 1938, p. 12, col. 4.

4948. "Equal Rights Bill Gets Senate Test." NYT, 22 March 1938, p. 3, col. 6.

4949. Petersen, Anne. "Leaders through Nation Join Fight on Equal Rights Proposal: Converts Sought by the Opposition." NYT, 27 March 1938, sec. 6, p. 5, col. 1.

4950. "Equal Rights Issue Off." NYT, 6 May 1938, p. 19, col. 8.

4951. "Labor Laws Held Unfair to Women." NYT, 6 June 1938, p. 19, col. 6.

4952. McLaughlin, Kathleen. "Women Will Fight for 'Equal Rights.'" NYT, 7 October 1938, p. 7, col. 1. Rep. in entry #491.

4953. _____. "Lady Liberty Stirs the Woman's Party." NYT 8 October 1938, p. 3, col. 4.

4954. _____ . "Equal Rights Veto by Collegians Hit." NYT,
9 October 1938, p. 32, col. 3.

4955. "Alice Paul Chosen World Party Head." NYT, 10 October 1938, p. 3,
col. 4.

4956. McLaughlin, Kathleen. "Women Voters Hit Snag over Power." NYT,
14 October 1938, p. 9, col. 1.

4957. "Opposes 'Equal Rights' Measure." NYT, 1 November 1938, p. 10,
col. 3.

4958. "Stamp Sale Would Spur Fight for Equal Rights." NYT, 6 November
1938, sec. 2, p. 5, col. 7.

4959. "Light Capitol Hill Urns to Burn for Equal Rights." NYT,
5 January 1939, p. 12, col. 6.

4960. "Mrs. Catt, 80, Bids Women Fight On." NYT, 10 January 1939,
p. 21, col. 1.

4961. Petersen, Anne. "Losses Feared in Equal Rights." NYT,
12 February 1939, sec. 2, p. 5, col. 1.

4962. "750 Join in Homage Here." NYT, 16 February 1939, p. 5, col. 1.

4963. Clark, Elizabeth Wallace. "Equality: Women's Goal." NYT,
19 March 1939, sec. 4, p. 9, col. 7. (LE)

4964. "Women's Rights Change Opposed by the City Bar Association
Group." NYT, 26 March 1939, sec. 3, p. 5, col. 6.

4965. "University Women Bar Equality Plan." NYT, 23 June 1939, p. 19,
col. 2.

4966. "University Women Unite on Social Aid." NYT, 24 June 1939, p. 15,
col. 4.

4967. "Demand Adoption of Equal Rights." NYT, 16 December 1939, p. 9,
col. 1.

4968. "Women Demand Equal-Rights Vote." NYT, 17 December 1939, p. 2,
col. 2.

4969. "Ask 'Equal Rights' Plank." NYT, 26 May 1940, p. 19, col. 1.

4970. "Text of the Platform Adopted by Republican Party at National
Convention: Equal Rights." NYT, 27 June 1940, p. 5, col. 6.

4971. McLaughlin, Kathleen. "Equal Job Rights for Women Backed." NYT,
27 June 1940, p. 1, col. 6.

4972. _____ . "Women Are Divided over Merits of Proposed Equal
Rights Plank in Platform: Praise, Criticism Sent on Proposal." NYT,
28 June 1940, p. 5, col. 1.

4973. _____. "Women Divided on Equal Rights." NYT, 14 July 1940,
   p. 3, col. 1.

4974. _____. "Attacks Proposal on Women's Plank." NYT, 15 July
   1940, p. 10, col. 2.

4975. _____. "Equal Rights Plea Hit by First Lady." NYT, 16 July
   1940, p. 5, col. 1.

4976. _____. "Women, Hastily Named to Resolutions Committee, Speak
   Minds Freely: Feminine Demands Change Platforms." NYT, 18 July
   1940, p. 5, col. 1.

4977. "Industry Assured of Draft Fairness." NYT, 9 September 1940,
   p. 8, col. 6.

4978. "Pearl Buck Calls for Full Equality." NYT, 8 December 1940,
   p. 57, col. 6.

4979. "Campaign Mapped for Equal Rights." NYT, 9 December 1940, p. 38,
   col. 1.

4980. "Equal Rights Amendment Will Be Offered Again." NYT, 2 January
   1941, p. 34, col. 3.

4981. "Clubwomen Urge Equal Rights Law." NYT, 9 July 1941, p. 17, col. 1.

4982. "Women Get Report on Equal Rights." NYT, 26 October 1941, p. 32,
   col. 6.

4983. "Asks I.L.O. to Aid Equal Rights Plea." NYT, 27 October 1941,
   p. 13, col. 6.

4984. "New Bill Put In for Equal Rights." NYT, 30 November 1941, sec.
   2, p. 5, col. 2.

4985. "War Work Is Put Ahead of Politics." NYT, 17 January 1942, p. 20,
   col. 8.

4986. "Delays Women's Rights Bill." NYT, 6 May 1942, p. 20, col. 4.

4987. "Equal Rights Bill Sent On to Senate." NYT, 12 May 1942, p. 22,
   col. 1.

4988. Handy, Adelaide. "Women in Fight on Equal Rights." NYT, 17 May
   1942, sec. 2, p. 4, col. 8.

4989. "Equal Pay, Rank Urged for Women." NYT, 8 June 1942, p. 12, col. 8.

4990. "Women Celebrate Seneca Falls Day." NYT, 20 July 1942, p. 9,
   col. 1.

4991. Lackman, Libby. "Links War Service with Equal Rights." NYT,
   25 October 1942, p. 25, col. 1.

4992. _____. "Miss Paul Elected by Woman's Party." NYT,
   26 October 1942, p. 11, col. 6.

4993. Mallon, Winifred. "Equal Rights Bill No. 1 in the House." NYT, 7 January 1943, p. 12, col. 7.

4994. _____. "Equal Rights Plan Up Again in Senate." NYT, 22 January 1943, p. 23, col. 5.

4995. "'Equality' Move Opposed." NYT, 1 February 1943, p. 8, col. 5.

4996. "Hits 'Equal Rights' Law." NYT, 8 February 1943, p. 21, col. 2.

4997. "House Urged to Pass Equal Rights Plan." NYT, 16 February 1943, p. 16, col. 7.

4998. "Senate Body Backs Equal Rights Move." NYT, 18 February 1943, p. 26, col. 8.

4999. "For Equal Rights Amendment." NYT, 22 February 1943, p. 14, col. 3.

5000. "Mrs. Luce Presses Equal Rights Bill." NYT, 23 February 1943, p. 16, col. 8.

5001. "Mrs. Catt Assails Equal Rights Move." NYT, 1 March 1943, p. 16, col. 8.

5002. "Backs Equal Rights Plan." NYT, 4 March 1943, p. 10, col. 3.

5003. "Oppose Amendment for Equal Rights." NYT, 7 March 1943, p. 5, col. 2.

5004. Barney, Nora Stanton. "Equal Rights Defended." NYT, 7 March 1943, sec. 4, p. 9, col. 2. (LE)

5005. "Fights Equal Rights Bill." NYT, 16 March 1943, p. 16, col. 4.

5006. "Equal Rights Foes Appeal to Congress." NYT, 27 March 1943, p. 10, col. 7.

5007. Buck, Pearl S., and Strauss, Anna Lord. "'Equal Rights' by Amendment?" NYT, 28 March 1943, sec. 2, p. 15, col. 1. Rep. in entries #491, 2335.

5008. Celler, Emanuel. "Equal Rights Plan Opposed." NYT, 9 April 1943, p. 20, col. 6. (LE)

5009. "Advances Equal Rights." NYT, 13 April 1943, p. 31, col. 4.

5010. Pollitzer, Anita. "Equal Rights Move Favored." NYT, 10 May 1943, p. 18, col. 6. (LE)

5011. "Group to Aid Fight for Equal Rights." NYT, 17 May 1943, p. 12, col. 4.

5012. "For Equal Rights Bill." NYT, 25 May 1943, p. 21, col. 7.

5013. "Celler Bids Women Back Equal Rights." NYT, 27 June 1943, p. 35, col. 1.

5014. "Celler Corrects Report." NYT, 29 June 1943, p. 17, col. 2.

5015. "For Equal Rights Law." NYT, 2 July 1943, p. 16, col. 1.

5016. "Asks Early Vote on Equal Rights." NYT, 10 July 1943, p. 16, col. 8.

5017. "Equal Rights Plea Voiced." NYT, 20 July 1943, p. 16, col. 1.

5018. "80 Sign to Oppose Rights Amendment." NYT, 19 August 1943, p. 16, col. 1.

5019. "Equal-Rights Move Praised, Attacked." NYT, 26 August 1943, p. 14, col. 7.

5020. "House Group Bars Equal Rights Vote." NYT, 6 October 1943, p. 26, col. 1.

5021. "Opposite Views Held on Equal Rights Bill." NYT, 8 October 1943, p. 16, col. 8.

5022. "Women's Rights Bill Is Pushed by Cannon." NYT, 14 December 1943, p. 22, col. 8.

5023. "Call Equal Rights a Vote Factor in '44." NYT, 3 January 1944, p. 18, col. 8.

5024. "Equal Rights Move Promised in House." NYT, 6 January 1944, p. 20, col. 1.

5025. Kitchelt, Florence L.C. "Women's Rights Are Upheld." NYT, 11 January 1944, p. 18, col. 6. (LE)

5026. "Urges Equality Proposal." NYT, 17 January 1944, p. 16, col. 8.

5027. Fishman, Nathaniel. "Anomalies in State Laws." NYT, 17 January 1944, p. 18, col. 7. (LE)

5028. Battle, George Gordon. "Equal Rights Favored." NYT, 18 January 1944, p. 18, col. 7. (LE)

5029. "Bids Industry Act to Retain Women." NYT, 24 January 1944, p. 14, col. 8.

5030. Blauvelt, Mary Taylor. "Argument for Equal Rights." NYT, 24 January 1944, p. 16, col. 7. (LE)

5031. Anderson, Mary. "Women's Measure Opposed." NYT, 25 January 1944, p. 18, col. 6. (LE)

5032. "Wallace Supports Equal Rights Bill." NYT, 27 January 1944, p. 22, col. 7.

5033. "Wallace Assailed on 'Equal Rights.'" NYT, 28 January 1944, p. 20, col. 1.

5034. "First Lady Fights Equal Rights Plan." NYT, 1 February 1944, p. 24, col. 4.

5035. Bowie, Jean L. "Against Equal Rights Amendment." NYT, 3 February 1944, p. 18, col. 6. (LE)

5036. "Friends, Foes of Equal Rights for Women Get Hearing in First Lady's Apartment." NYT, 10 February 1944, p. 20, col. 5.

5037. "CIO Head Opposes 'Equal Rights' Bill." NYT, 28 February 1944, p. 20, col. 1.

5038. "Federal School Fund Criticized by Women." NYT, 29 February 1944, p. 18, col. 3.

5039. "Asks President Back 'Equal Rights' Plan." NYT, 16 April 1944, p. 33, col. 2.

5040. "Equal Rights Drive Is Set for Election." NYT, 17 April 1944, p. 18, col. 7.

5041. "Pushes Equal Rights Bill." NYT, 25 April 1944, p. 21, col. 5.

5042. Stephenson, Dorothy. "Federation Poll Backs 'Equal Rights.'" NYT, 27 April 1944, p. 20, col. 1.

5043. Miller, Emma Guffey, and Kenyon, Dorothy. "Equal Rights: A Debate." NYT Magazine, 7 May 1944, pp. 14, 36-37.

5044. Nigrine, Nita N. "Equal Rights." NYT Magazine, 21 May 1944, p. 12. (LE)

5045. McLaughlin, Kathleen. "Platform Victory Is Won by Women." NYT, 27 June 1944, p. 15, col. 1.

5046. "Text of the Platform Adopted by Republican National Convention: Equal Rights." NYT, 28 June 1944, p. 14, col. 3.

5047. "Mary Anderson, at 71, Again Fights for Women." NYT, 30 June 1944, p. 18, col. 4.

5048. "Women Argue Equal Rights at Chicago, Then Hear Man Call It 'Lunatic Proposal.'" NYT, 18 July 1944, p. 9, col. 3.

5049. McLaughlin, Kathleen. "Contest Develops on 'Equal Rights.'" NYT, 19 July 1944, p. 13, col. 6.

5050. _____. "Democrats Yield on Equal Rights." NYT, 21 July 1944, p. 12, col. 6.

5051. "Women Urge Equal Rights." NYT, 17 August 1944, p. 14, col. 6.

5052. "Miss Miller Hits Equal Rights Plan." NYT, 18 August 1944, p. 10, col. 5.

5053. Anderson, Harriet. "Equality of Women Urged." NYT, 22 August 1944, p. 16, col. 7. (LE)

5054. "Push Equal Rights Bill." NYT, 26 August 1944, p. 14, col. 8.

5055. "Hails Equal-Pay Victory." NYT, 5 September 1944, p. 19, col. 2.

5056. "Delays 'Equal Rights' Action." NYT, 13 September 1944, p. 14, col. 3.

5057. "Denies CIO Delays Equal Rights Bill." NYT, 20 September 1944, p. 38, col. 6.

5058. "Women Rate Jobs, Miss Perkins Says." NYT, 14 October 1944, p. 16, col. 7.

5059. "Asks Equal Rights Action." NYT, 30 January 1945, p. 12, col. 4.

5060. "Asks Equal Rights Votes." NYT, 1 February 1945, p. 17, col. 5.

5061. "Women's Clubs Back Equal Rights Bill." NYT, 3 February 1945, p. 16, col. 4.

5062. Kitchelt, Florence L.C. "Equal Rights Are Debated." NYT, 19 February 1945, p. 16, col. 7. (LE)

5063. Wright, Quincy. "Amendment Not Considered." NYT, 10 March 1945, p. 16, col. 7. (LE)

5064. "Backs Equal Rights Amendment." NYT, 21 April 1945, p. 26, col. 5.

5065. "Best Progress Made by Equal Rights Bill." NYT, 25 April 1945, p. 20, col. 2.

5066. "Women's Rights Bill Introduced in Senate." NYT, 4 May 1945, p. 34, col. 3.

5067. Barney, Nora Stanton. "Women's Rights Upheld." NYT, 14 July 1945, p. 10, col. 6. (LE)

5068. "House Group Backs Equal Rights Bill." NYT, 17 July 1945, p. 11, col. 4.

5069. "Truman Reaffirms Equal Rights Backing." NYT, 22 September 1945, p. 14, col. 2.

5070. "Cardinal Favors Equal Rights Plan." NYT, 29 September 1945, p. 16, col. 7.

5071. "Push Equal Rights Amendment." NYT, 12 December 1945, p. 24, col. 8.

5072. Kitchelt, Florence L.C. "Mrs. Catt's Work Commended." NYT, 14 January 1946, p. 18, col. 6. (LE)

5073. Furman, Bess. "Senate to Vote on Equal Rights." NYT, 19 July 1946, p. 11, col. 1.

5074. _____. "Equal Rights Fails to Get Two-Thirds in Vote in Senate." NYT, 20 July 1946, p. 1, col. 5.

5075. "'Equal Rights' Amendment." <u>NYT</u>, 20 July 1946, p. 12, col. 1. (Ed)

5076. Kenney, Marion L. "Protective Laws and Equality." <u>NYT</u>,
      25 July 1946, p. 20, col. 6. (LE)

5077. Blackwell, Alice Stone. "Protective Legislation Endorsed."
      <u>NYT</u>, 29 July 1946, p. 20, col. 7. (LE)

5078. "Women's Clubs Press Rights." <u>NYT</u>, 20 October 1946, p. 29, col. 1.

5079. "Equal Rights Near, Women Are Told." <u>NYT</u>, 26 October 1946, p. 9,
      col. 5.

5080. Mallon, Winifred. "Equality Measure Offered in House." <u>NYT</u>,
      10 January 1947, p. 18, col. 5.

5081. "Women Protected in New Rights Bill." <u>NYT</u>, 18 February 1947,
      p. 28, col. 1.

5082. Kitchelt, Florence L.C. "Legal Status of Women." <u>NYT</u>, 21 February
      1947, p. 18, col. 7. (LE)

5083. "Equal Rights Drive Opens." <u>NYT</u>, 8 March 1947, p. 16, col. 1.

5084. "Capper and Robsion Honored by Women." <u>NYT</u>, 17 July 1947,
      p. 13, col. 1.

5085. "Equal Rights Urged for American Women." <u>NYT</u>, 11 March 1948,
      p. 25, col. 1.

5086. "CIO for Women's Rights." <u>NYT</u>, 12 March 1948, p. 26, col. 1.

5087. "Back Equal Rights Amendment." <u>NYT</u>, 30 April 1948, p. 24, col. 3.

5088. "Favor Equal Rights for Women." <u>NYT</u>, 13 May 1948, p. 29, col. 5.

5089. "Equal Rights Bill Is Approved." <u>NYT</u>, 2 June 1948, p. 34, col. 1.

5090. "Text of Tentative Draft of Platform for Republican Convention:
      Equal Rights for Women." <u>NYT</u>, 22 June 1948, p. 2, col. 6.

5091. "Women Clubs Vote Equal Rights Drive." <u>NYT</u>, 6 July 1948, p. 26,
      col. 1.

5092. "Planks in the Major Party Platforms Compared: Equal Rights."
      <u>NYT</u>, 15 July 1948, p. 10, col. 6.

5093. Kitchelt, Florence L.C. "To Insure Women's Rights." <u>NYT</u>,
      12 August 1948, p. 20, col. 6. (LE)

5094. "Layman Lectures Catholic Women." <u>NYT</u>, 14 September 1948, p. 33,
      col. 6.

5095. Furman, Bess. "Drive for Rights Pressed by Women." <u>NYT</u>,
      2 April 1949, p. 18, col. 7.

5096. _____. "U. N. Example Cited for Equal Rights." NYT,
3 April 1949, p. 76, col. 1.

5097. "Women's [sic] Party Fights On." NYT, 10 April 1949, sec. 4,
p. 12, col. 5.

5098. "Equal Rights Action Due." NYT, 21 December 1949, p. 6, col. 2.

5099. Furman, Bess. "Equal Rights Plea Put on War Basis." NYT,
24 January 1950, p. 20, col. 6.

5100. "U.S. 'Equal Rights' Opposed by Lehman." NYT, 25 January 1950,
p. 19, col. 3.

5101. Furman, Bess. "Senate Votes Equal Rights, but Retains Women's
Laws." NYT, 26 January 1950, p. 1, col. 6.

5102. "Roll-Call in the Senate on Women's Rights Vote." NYT,
26 January 1950, p. 19, col. 2.

5103. "Fight 'Feminist Ideology.'" NYT, 27 January 1950, p. 16, col. 6.

5104. "Equal Rights Fight in House Is Mapped." NYT, 27 January 1950,
p. 19, col. 4.

5105. "'Mott Amendment.'" NYT, 29 January 1950, sec. 4, p. 2, col. 3.

5106. "How Area Members Voted in the Week in Congress." NYT, 30 January
1950, p. 3, col. 5.

5107. "Clubs Back Equal Rights." NYT, 27 May 1950, p. 9, col. 8.

5108. "Nurses' Heads Oppose Equal Rights Change." NYT, 24 January 1951,
p. 30, col. 5.

5109. "Equal Rights Bill Urged." NYT, 3 February 1951, p. 13, col. 3.

5110. "Senate Committee Backs Equal Rights for Women." NYT, 22 May
1951, p. 11, col. 4.

5111. "'Good News' Reported for Equal Rights; Amendment Is Found in
'Friendly' Hands." NYT, 26 May 1951, p. 20, col. 6.

5112. "Bar Unit to Study Equal Rights Law." NYT, 21 September 1951,
p. 17, col. 4.

5113. Anderson, Mary. "To Grant Women Equality." NYT, 14 October
1951, sec. 4, p. 8, col. 5. (LE)

5114. "Nurses Reaffirm Stand on Equality." NYT, 23 January 1952,
p. 21, col. 5.

5115. Kitchelt, Florence L.C. "To Grant Women Equal Rights." NYT,
31 January 1952, p. 26, col. 6. (LE)

5116. Harrison, Emma. "Federation Seeks Equal Rights Data." NYT,
2 July 1952, p. 14, col. 6.

5117. "Text of the Republican Party's 1952 Campaign Platform Adopted by
National Convention: Equal Rights." <u>NYT</u>, 11 July 1952, p. 8, col. 7.

5118. "Text of Platform of the Democrats: Equal Rights Amendment."
<u>NYT</u>, 24 July 1952, p. 17, col. 7.

5119. "Equal Rights Bill in Congress Early." <u>NYT</u>, 3 January 1953, p. 13,
col. 4.

5120. "Equal Rights Hope Rises." <u>NYT</u>, 9 February 1953, p. 49, col. 2.

5121. "Senators Back Equal Rights." <u>NYT</u>, 26 February 1953, p. 13, col. 1.

5122. Kitchelt, Florence L.C. "Women and the Constitution." <u>NYT</u>,
14 April 1953, p. 26, col. 7. (LE)

5123. Upton, Marie T. "Women's Rights Questioned." <u>NYT</u>, 25 April
1953, p. 14, col. 6. (LE)

5124. "Committee Backs Equal Rights." <u>NYT</u>, 5 May 1953, p. 20, col. 7.

5125. "Men Lawyers Bid Women Be Good Citizens and Not Fret over Equal
Rights Amendment." <u>NYT</u>, 26 May 1953, p. 34, col. 1.

5126. Grant, Jane C. "Women's Rights as Citizens." <u>NYT</u>, 29 May 1953,
p. 24, col. 7. (LE)

5127. "Women Hopeful on Equal Rights." <u>NYT</u>, 13 June 1953, p. 12, col. 2.

5128. "All-Out Rights Drive Asked by Woman Leader." <u>NYT</u>, 14 June
1953, p. 24, col. 5.

5129. Furman, Bess. "Equal Rights Plan Nears Signal Gain." <u>NYT</u>,
20 June 1953, p. 15, col. 1.

5130. Asbury, Edith Evans. "University Women Bar Equal Rights." <u>NYT</u>,
25 June 1953, p. 17, col. 2.

5131. "Women Optimistic for Equal Rights." <u>NYT</u>, 2 July 1953, p. 26,
col. 2.

5132. "Equal Rights Plan Adopted by Senate." <u>NYT</u>, 17 July 1953, p. 10,
col. 4.

5133. "Women's Rights." <u>NYT</u>, 19 July 1953, sec. 4, p. 2, col. 3.
Rep. in entry #491.

5134. "Equal Rights Fight Is On." <u>NYT</u>, 19 July 1953, sec. 4, p. 9,
col. 5.

5135. Kitchelt, Florence L.C. "Equal Rights Amendment." <u>NYT</u>,
29 July 1953, p. 22, col. 7. (LE)

5136. "Business Women Get Equal Rights Appeal." <u>NYT</u>, 16 November 1953,
p. 18, col. 1.

5137. "Mrs. Leopold Defers Equal Rights Stand." NYT, 22 January 1954,
    p. 24, col. 6.

5138. Bellison, Lillian. "Nurses Bar Move for Equal Rights." NYT,
    29 April 1954, p. 39, col. 8.

5139. Harrison, Emma. "Business Women Oppose Inequities." NYT,
    2 July 1954, p. 16, col. 6.

5140. Kitchelt, Florence L.C. "Support for Equal Rights." NYT,
    10 November 1954, p. 32, col. 6. (LE)

5141. "Miss Anthony Honored." NYT, 21 February 1956, p. 26, col. 1.

5142. "Equality Bill Advanced." NYT, 15 May 1956, p. 23, col. 4.

5143. "Equal Rights for Women Stir a Distaff Argument." NYT, 12 August
    1956, p. 61, col. 1.

5144. "Civil Rights Proposal Omits Endorsing Court Ruling: Equal Rights
    Amendment." NYT, 16 August 1956, p. 14, col. 3.

5145. "Planks Pledge Aid to Veterans and Support of Supreme Courts
    Integration Decision: Equal Rights." NYT, 22 August 1956, p. 17,
    col. 2.

5146. "Equal Rights Mentioned in Message First Time." NYT, 17 January
    1957, p. 17, col. 7.

5147. "'Equal Rights' Bill Gains." NYT, 6 August 1957, p. 2, col. 3.

5148. "'Mere Man' Might Think Women Have Equality." NYT, 8 August
    1957, p. 6, col. 3.

5149. Grant, Jane. "Legal Equality of Women." NYT, 15 August 1957,
    p. 20, col. 7. (LE)

5150. "Equal Rights Backed." NYT, 23 August 1959, p. 62, col. 8.

5151. "Women Seek Equal Rights." NYT, 6 January 1960, p. 19, col. 5.

5152. "Backs Women's Rights." NYT, 3 September 1960, p. 18, col. 1.

5153. Shuster, Alvin. "President Names Panel on Women." NYT,
    15 December 1961. Rep. in entry #491.

5154. Grant, Jane. "Equal Rights for Women Urged." NYT, 17 January
    1962, p. 32, col. 5. (LE)

5155. "Senators Support Equal Rights Move." NYT, 31 August 1962,
    p. 45, col. 4.

5156. Hunter, Marjorie. "U.S. Panel Urges Women to Sue for Equal
    Rights." NYT, 12 October 1963, p. 1, col. 2.

5157. "Senators Back Amendment on Equal Rights for Women." NYT,
    12 September 1964, p. 10, col. 7.

5158. "May Hearings Set on Women's Rights." NYT, 27 February 1970, p. 40, col. 4.

5159. "Women Fill Hearing on Rights Equality." NYT, 6 May 1970, p. 38, col. 8. Rep. in entry #2926.

5160. "Congress Is Warned of Feminist Strike." NYT, 8 May 1970, p. 34, col. 2. Rep. in entry #2927.

5161. Shanahan, Eileen. "House Vote Expected Tomorrow on Amendment for Equal Rights for Women." NYT, 9 August 1970, p. 29, col. 1.

5162. _____. "Equal Rights Plan for Women Voted by House, 350-15." NYT, 11 August 1970, p. 1, col. 8.

5163. "Equal Rights Bill Pushed in Senate." NYT, 12 August 1970, p. 23, col. 1.

5164. "The Henpecked House." NYT, 12 August 1970, p. 40, col. 1. (Ed)

5165. Shanahan, Eileen. "Women's Rights Bill: A Boon or a Threat?" NYT, 16 August 1970, sec. 4, p. 2, col. 3.

5166. "Weeks Votes by Area's Congressmen." NYT, 17 August 1970, p. 14, col. 4.

5167. "Ervin Asks Measure on Women's Rights." NYT, 18 August 1970, p. 18, col. 3.

5168. "Substitute Bill Is Planned on Equal Rights for Women." NYT, 18 August 1970, p. 71, col. 4.

5169. "Ervin Provokes Women's Groups." NYT, 22 August 1970, p. 21, col. 4.

5170. "Lobby Campaign Begun in Capitol." NYT, 27 August 1970, p. 30, col. 6.

5171. "The Liberated Woman." NYT, 27 August 1970, p. 34, col. 1. (Ed)

5172. Di Leo, Ann Wallace. "Women's Rights." NYT, 28 August 1970, p. 30, col. 5. (LE)

5173. Shanahan, Eileen. "Woman Unionist Scores Equality Plan." NYT, 10 September 1970, p. 47, col. 1.

5174. _____. "'Reason' Is Urged on Sex Equality." NYT, 11 September 1970, p. 17, col. 1.

5175. _____. "Professor Shifts on Equal Rights." NYT, 12 September 1970, p. 6, col. 4. (WL)

5176. _____. "Equal Rights: Who Is against It and Why?" NYT, 13 September 1970, sec. 4, p. 6, col. 5. (WL) Rep. in entry #307.

5177. _____. "Women Unionists Back Equal Rights Plan; Doctor
Alleges Unnecessary Surgery by Men." NYT, 15 September 1970, p. 33,
col. 2.

5178. _____. "Women's Leader Says U.S. Suffers Because Sexes Have
Separate Roles." NYT, 16 September 1970, p. 9, col. 1.

5179. Sherrill, Robert. "That Equal-Rights Amendment: What, Exactly,
Does It Mean?" NYT Magazine, 20 September 1970, pp. 1, 25-27, 98-105.

5180. "Women's Rights Debate Set." NYT, 1 October 1970, p. 9, col. 1.

5181. Shanahan, Eileen. "Equal Rights Bid Runs into Trouble." NYT,
8 October 1970, p. 28, col. 1.

5182. "Riders Threaten Equal Rights Bid." NYT, 9 October 1970, p. 11,
col. 1.

5183. "Equal Rights." NYT, 10 October 1970, p. 24, col. 2. (Ed)

5184. "Free Choice Bid Loses in Senate." NYT, 13 October 1970, p. 26,
col. 4.

5185. Shanahan, Eileen. "Senators Amend Equal Rights Bill; It May Die
for '70." NYT, 14 October 1970, p. 1, col. 1.

5186. _____. "Bayh Substitutes Equal Rights Bid." NYT, 15 October
1970, p. 31, col. 1.

5187. "Legislating by Rider." NYT, 15 October 1970, p. 46, col. 1. (Ed)

5188. Shanahan, Eileen. "Women's Rights: Is It Not Yet Time?" NYT,
18 October 1970, sec. 4, p. 6, col. 7.

5189. Jones, Anne. "Stand on Drafting Women." NYT, 19 October 1970,
p. 38, col. 3. (LE)

5190. Jerard, Elise. "That Equal-Rights Amendment." NYT Magazine,
25 October 1970, p. 89. (LE)

5191. "Bayh Plans New Equality Bill." NYT, 3 November 1970, p. 19,
col. 5.

5192. Shanahan, Eileen. "Women's Rights Amendment Appears Dead for
1970." NYT, 12 November 1970, p. 19, col. 3.

5193. _____. "House Is Accused of Bias as Hearings on Women's
Rights Begins." NYT, 25 March 1971, p. 26, col. 4.

5194. "House Panel Votes Equal Rights Plan Decried by Women." NYT,
24 June 1971, p. 45, col. 4.

5195. "Death of Legislator's Wife Delays Equal-Rights Action." NYT,
21 September 1971, p. 34, col. 2.

5196. "Yale Lawyers Urge an End to Sex Bias." NYT, 26 September 1971,
p. 77, col. 6. (WL)

5197. "House Debates Amendment to End Sex Discrimination." NYT, 7 October 1971, p. 43, col. 3.

5198. "Congressman's Death Halt Action on Women's Rights." NYT, 8 October 1971, p. 71, col. 5.

5199. "Women's Rights Opposed." NYT, 12 October 1971, p. 33, col. 3.

5200. Shanahan, Eileen. "Equal Rights Amendment Passed by House, 354-23." NYT, 13 October 1971, p. 1, col. 2. Rep. in entry #491.

5201. "Rights Amendment Faces Delay in Busy Senate till '72 Session." NYT, 14 October 1971, p. 39, col. 2.

5202. "Week's Vote in Congress." NYT, 18 October 1971, p. 27, col. 1.

5203. Pincus, Jonathan H. "Rights Amendment: Is It Constructive?" NYT, 24 October 1971, sec. 4, p. 14, col. 3. (LE) Rep. in entry #126.

5204. Kelbley, Charles A. "Woman's Chains." NYT, 7 November 1971, sec. 4, p. 10, col. 5. (LE)

5205. Graham, Fred P. "Court, for First Time, Overrules a State Law That Favors Men." NYT, 23 November 1971, p. 1, col. 7.

5206. "Women and the Fourteenth." NYT, 23 November 1971, p. 40, col. 1. (Ed) (EOF)

5207. Schiff, Joseph L. "Equal Rights, Unlimited." NYT, 25 November 1971, p. 36, col. 3. (LE)

5208. Shanahan, Eileen. "Senate Panel Sets Vote on Women's Rights Move." NYT, 17 February 1972, p. 33, col. 2.

5209. "Sex Equality Bill Backed in Senate." NYT, 1 March 1972, p. 45, col. 1.

5210. Shanahan, Eileen. "Nixon Aid Sought on Equal Rights." NYT, 18 March 1972, p. 15, col. 3.

5211. _____. "Feminists Stress Lost Court Cases." NYT, 20 March 1972, p. 26, col. 1.

5212. "Senate Votes Today on Sex Rights Bill." NYT, 21 March 1972, p. 19, col. 1.

5213. Shanahan, Eileen. "Senators Bar Weakening of Equal Rights Proposal." NYT, 22 March 1972, p. 1, col. 5.

5214. _____. "Equal Rights Amendment Is Approved by Congress." NYT, 23 March 1972, p. 1, col. 6. Rep. in entry #491.

5215. "Two More States Ratify Amendment." NYT, 24 March 1972, p. 26, col. 5.

5216. "Call to Action." NYT, 24 March 1972, p. 40, col. 1. (Ed)

5217. "Votes in Congress." NYT, 25 March 1972, p. 20, col. 7.

5218. "Amendment on Equal Rights Now Approved by 6 States." NYT, 26 March 1972, p. 61, col. 3.

5219. Shanahan, Eileen. "A Vote for Equal Status--And Equal Burdens." NYT, 26 March 1972, sec. 4, p. 6, col. 1. Rep. in entry #491.

5220. "Kansas for Women's Rights." NYT, 29 March 1972, p. 46, col. 2.

5221. "Oklahoma House Rejects Equal Rights Amendment." NYT, 30 March 1972, p. 17, col. 5.

5222. Blau, Eleanor. "Rabbis See Women's Rights Measure as Threatening Orthodox Practices." NYT, 4 April 1972, p. 39, col. 3.

5223. _____. "Rabbis Assail Orthodox Stand against Equal-Rights Measure." NYT, 5 April 1972, p. 12, col. 4.

5224. "Tennessee Is 10th to Ratify Equal Rights Amendment." NYT, 5 April 1972, p. 42, col. 2.

5225. "Alaska Backs Equal Rights." NYT, 6 April 1972, p. 2, col. 5.

5226. Clarity, James F. "State Senate Votes to Ratify Women's Rights Amendment." NYT, 20 April 1972, p. 55, col. 4.

5227. "Rights Plan Set Aside." NYT, 27 April 1972, p. 17, col. 3.

5228. Bradsher, Nancy. "Women's Friend in the Assembly." NYT, 7 May 1974, p. 121, col. 1.

5229. "Excerpts from Proposed Democratic Platform Adopted by Convention Committee: Right of Women." NYT, 29 June 1972, p. 29, col. 1.

5230. "Equal-Rights Proposal Approved by 20 States." NYT, 21 August 1972, p. 47, col. 2.

5231. "Excerpts from Platform Approved by G.O.P. Resolutions Panel for the Convention: Equal Rights for Women." NYT, 22 August 1972, p. 35, col. 5.

5232. "Women Foresee Approval of Sex Amendment by May." NYT, 27 August 1972, p. 27, col. 6.

5233. "Pennsylvania Ratifies Rights." NYT, 21 September 1972, p. 50, col. 5.

5234. "21st State for Amendment." NYT, 22 September 1972, p. 45, col. 1.

5235. Shanahan, Eileen. "Opposition Rises to Amendment on Equal Rights." NYT, 15 January 1973, p. 1, col. 4. (WL)

5236. "House in Utah Rejects Equal Rights Measure." NYT, 26 January 1973, p. 38, col. 3.

5237. "Arkansas Senate Defeats Equal Rights Amendment." NYT, 2 February 1973, p. 32, col. 3.

5238. "Montana Senate Rejects Equal Rights Amendment." NYT, 3 February 1973, p. 14, col. 2.

5239. "Capital Women Sell Blood." NYT, 6 February 1973, p. 9, col. 8.

5240. "2 More States Back Rights Amendment." NYT, 9 February 1973, p. 15, col. 8.

5241. "New Mexico Becomes 27th to Back Equal Rights Plan." NYT, 14 February 1973, p. 20, col. 3.

5242. "Valentines for Legislators." NYT, 22 February 1973, p. 33, col. 8.

5243. "Vermont 28th to Ratify." NYT, 22 February 1973, p. 36, col. 1.

5244. "Shift on Rights Delayed." NYT, 24 February 1973, p. 60, col. 2.

5245. "An Amendment on Equal Rights in Jeopardy Despite Nixon Plea." NYT, 3 March 1973, p. 14, col. 4. (WL)

5246. "Connecticut House Backs Amendment on Women's Rights." NYT, 9 March 1973, p. 47, col. 5.

5247. Shanahan, Eileen. "Rights Plan Foes Called Devious." NYT, 15 March 1973, p. 21, col. 1.

5248. Fellows, Lawrence. "Women's Rights Amendment Wins Connecticut Ratification." NYT, 16 March 1973, p. 1, col. 4.

5249. Weaver, Warren, Jr. "Equal Rights Vote Now in Question." NYT, 17 March 1973, p. 13, col. 4.

5250. "Win One Lose One?" NYT, 18 March 1973, sec. 4, p. 3, col. 5.

5251. Kent, Mary Day. "Women and the Draft." NYT, 21 March 1973, p. 44, col. 5. (LE)

5252. "An Aide to Nixon Reaffirms Rights-Amendment Support." NYT, 22 March 1973, p. 21, col. 1.

5253. "Washington Is 29th State to Ratify Rights Measure." NYT, 23 March 1973, p. 5, col. 1.

5254. "Indiana Rejects Rights Bid." NYT, 3 April 1973, p. 34, col. 4.

5255. "Voters in Wisconsin Reject Women's Rights Amendment." NYT, 5 April 1973, p. 21, col. 6.

5256. Shanahan, Eileen. "Rights Strategy Voted by Women." NYT, 8 April 1973, p. 46, col. 1.

5257. "Florida Rejects Ratification of Equal Rights Amendment." NYT, 18 April 1973, p. 32, col. 3.

5258. "Ohio Panel Blocks Rights Amendment." NYT, 19 April 1973, p. 33, col. 1.

5259. "17th State Bar Rights Plan." NYT, 27 April 1973, p. 32, col. 3.

5260. Clarity, James F. "Notes on People." NYT, 3 May 1973, p. 49, col. 2.

5261. "Illinois Blocks Amendment." NYT, 5 May 1973, p. 13, col. 1.

5262. "Missouri Rejects Rights Bill." NYT, 11 May 1973, p. 55, col. 2.

5263. "The Price of Equality." NYT, 28 May 1973, p. 14, col. 1. (Ed)

5264. Shanahan, Eileen. "Rights Bloc Spurs Plan for Ratification." NYT, 29 May 1973, p. 28, col. 3.

5265. Zwerling, Sandra. "Women, Equal and Free." NYT, 8 June 1973, p. 38, col. 3. (LE)

5266. Griffiths, Martha W. "Equal Rights Amendment: A Time for Action." NYT, 19 June 1973, p. 38, col. 4. (LE)

5267. Thimmesch, Nick. "The Sexual Equality Amendment." NYT Magazine, 24 June 1973, pp. 8-9, 53.

5268. Cooper, Carolyn L.; East, Catherine; and Thimmesch, Nick. "Equal Protection." NYT Magazine, 15 July 1973, p. 21. (LE)

5269. "Optimistic on Equal Rights." NYT, 14 September 1973, p. 15, col. 1.

5270. Stetson, Damon. "T.W.U. Assails Nixon on Civil Rights." NYT, 10 October 1973, p. 29, col. 4.

5271. "League of Women Voters Starts Equal Rights Drive." NYT, 12 October 1973, p. 46, col. 1.

5272. "Foe of Rights Amendment Says the Tide Has Turned." NYT, 21 October 1973, p. 67, col. 5.

5273. "Women's Rights Supported." NYT, 1 November 1973, p. 36, col. 3.

5274. "Equal Rights Bracelet." NYT, 31 December 1973, p. 20, col. 1.

5275. "Equal Rights Amendment Passed by Maine House." NYT, 18 January 1974, p. 17, col. 2.

5276. "Maine 31st State to Ratify Equal Rights Amendment." NYT, 19 January 1974, p. 20, col. 8.

5277. Krebs, Albin. "Notes on People." NYT, 19 January 1974, p. 23, col. 2.

5278. Shanahan, Eileen. "Stiff Fight Looms over Ratification of Equal Rights Amendment." NYT, 29 January 1974, p. 15, col. 1. (WL)

5279. "104-70 Vote in Georgia." NYT, 29 January 1974, p. 15, col. 6.

5280. Klemesrud, Judy. "Bracelet with a Cause." NYT, 2 February 1974, p. 15, col. 1. (WL)

5281. "Nixon Reaffirms Support of Equal Rights Amendment." NYT, 3 February 1974, p. 32, col. 4.

5282. "Ohio Becomes 33d State to Pass Rights Amendment." NYT, 8 February 1974, p. 21, col. 3.

5283. "Equal Rights Amendment Rejected in Virginia House." NYT, 28 February 1974, p. 9, col. 1.

5284. "Tennessee Sets Back Vote on Amendment." NYT, 20 March 1974, p. 24, col. 4.

5285. Narvaez, Alfonso A. "Legislature Aims for Wider Power." NYT, 25 April 1974, p. 45, col. 3.

5286. "Tennessee Rescinds Equal Rights Support." NYT, 25 April 1974, p. 49, col. 3.

5287. "Wilson, Yielding to Legislature, Doubles College-Aid Allotment: Equal Rights." NYT, 7 May 1974, p. 11, col. 1.

5288. "Rights Amendment Fails." NYT, 23 May 1974, p. 35, col. 1.

5289. "Equal Rights Plan Rejected by Louisiana House Panel." NYT, 20 June 1974, p. 42, col. 2.

5290. "Minnesota G.O.P. Votes against Rights Proposal." NYT, 23 June 1974, p. 16, col. 5.

5291. Shanahan, Eileen. "Women See Delay on Equal Rights." NYT, 29 June 1974, p. 30, col. 1.

5292. Weaver, Warren, Jr. "Bar Association Endorses Amendment on Women's Rights and Promises to Help Seek Ratification." NYT, 17 August 1974, p. 20, col. 1.

5293. Shanahan, Eileen. "Ford Again Backs Rights Proposal." NYT, 23 August 1974, p. 34, col. 4.

5294. Greenhouse, Linda. "Women's Rights: Federal and State Amendments Face Trouble." NYT, 24 August 1974, p. 12, col. 4.

5295. Johnston, Laurie. "Women's Equality Day Marked Here by Bus Tour and Rally at Federal Hall." NYT, 27 August 1974, p. 37, col. 2.

5296. "Mrs. Ford Hints Aid for Rights Amendment." NYT, 7 September 1974, p. 15, col. 7.

5297. "Sex Bias Amendment Wins in Connecticut." NYT, 6 November 1974, p. 31, col. 5.

5298. "Backers of Equal Rights Amendment to Concentrate 1975 Drive in
10 States." NYT, 11 December 1974, p. 22, col. 1.

5299. "Amendment on Rights Defeated in Oklahoma." NYT, 22 January
1975, p. 10, col. 3.

5300. "Feminist Predicts April Ratification for Equal Rights." NYT,
31 January 1975, p. 23, col. 1.

5301. "North Dakota Is 34th State to Back Equal Rights Bid." NYT,
4 February 1975, p. 31, col. 3.

5302. Kneeland, Douglas E. "The Equal Rights Amendment: Missouri Is
the Target Now." NYT, 7 February 1975, p. 37, col. 1.

5303. "Rights Amendment Rejected in Arizona." NYT, 14 February 1975,
p. 9, col. 1.

5304. "Mrs. Ford to Continue Equal Rights Lobbying." NYT, 15 February
1975, p. 31, col. 1.

5305. "Rights Amendment Loses Georgia Vote." NYT, 18 February 1975,
p. 16, col. 3.

5306. "Nevada Senate Panel Backs Equal Rights Amendment." NYT,
19 February 1975, p. 30, col. 8.

5307. Reichel, Josephine. "Liabilities Amendment." NYT, 19 February
1975, p. 34, col. 5. (LE)

5308. Narvaez, Alfonso A. "Assembly Votes for Sex Equality." NYT,
19 February 1975, p. 39, col. 8.

5309. "Rights Amendment Defeated in Nevada." NYT, 20 February 1975,
p. 13, col. 1.

5310. Szefczek, Constance. "The First Lady's Campaign." NYT,
20 February 1975, p. 32, col. 3. (LE)

5311. "Mrs. Ford Scored on Equality Plan." NYT, 21 February 1975,
p. 32, col. 7.

5312. "Rights Repeal Bid Stirs in New Mexico." NYT, 23 February 1975,
p. 30, col. 4.

5313. "Approval on Rights Bid Held Dim in '75." NYT, 25 February 1975,
p. 15, col. 5.

5314. "Labor Vows Support." NYT, 25 February 1975, p. 15, col. 6.

5315. "Women in Arizona House Help Defeat Equality Bill." NYT,
27 February 1975, p. 25, col. 8.

5316. Shanahan, Eileen. "Equal Rights Test Is Near in Illinois." NYT,
2 March 1975, p. 1, col. 5.

5317. "Equal Rights Vote Delayed in Illinois." NYT, 5 March 1975,
p. 27, col. 4.

5318. "Equal Rights Proposal Is Hurt by Illinois Senate Ratifying Curb."
NYT, 6 March 1975, p. 42, col. 7.

5319. "Equal Rights Amendment Is Slipping." NYT, 9 March 1975, sec. 4,
p. 18, col. 2.

5320. "Rights Amendment Defeated in Indiana." NYT, 11 March 1975, p. 19,
col. 1.

5321. Maitland, Leslie. "U.S. Amendment: What It Will Do." NYT,
11 March 1975, p. 40, col. 1.

5322. Clines, Francis X. "State Equal Rights Amendment: Senate Opens
Hearings Today." NYT, 11 March 1975, p. 40, col. 3.

5323. "N.J., Connecticut: What They Did." NYT, 11 March 1975, p. 40,
col. 6.

5324. Clines, Francis X. "Women Clash in Albany on Equal-Rights
Proposal." NYT, 12 March 1975, p. 27, col. 5.

5325. Ayres, B. Drummond, Jr. "Ervin Folksiness Is Aimed at E.R.A."
NYT, 20 March 1975, p. 13, col. 1.

5326. Apple, R.W., Jr. "Democrats Avert Clash at Parley." NYT,
22 March 1975, p. 32, col. 1.

5327. Oelsner, Lesley. "Law Parley Finds Women Lagging in Rights."
NYT, 27 March 1975, p. 19, col. 1.

5328. "Rights Amendment Seems Dead for '75 after New Setback." NYT,
27 March 1975, p. 33, col. 1.

5329. Brozan, Nadine. "58% in Gallup Poll Favor Equal Rights." NYT,
10 April 1975, p. 45, col. 3.

5330. "Assembly Approves Women's-Rights Bill." NYT, 15 April 1975,
p. 75, col. 6.

5331. "Equal Rights Loses in North Carolina, Dooming It for '75."
NYT, 17 April 1975, p. 41, col. 1.

5332. Wicker, Tom. "One More Spring." NYT, 18 April 1975, p. 33,
col. 2. Rep. in entry #166.

5333. "Rights Amendment Rejected by Florida Senate 2d Time." NYT,
26 April 1975, p. 19, col. 5.

5334. Narvaez, Alfonso A. "Women's Rights Faces Snag in Albany." NYT,
1 May 1975, p. 45, col. 1.

5335. Johnston, Laurie. "Notes on People." NYT, 10 May 1975, p. 21,
col. 2.

5336. "Equal Rights Amendment Rejected by Illinois Panel." NYT, 14 May 1975, p. 5, col. 1.

5337. Hurwitz, Jacob S. "Of Male Chauvinists and the E.R.A." NYT, 14 May 1975, p. 44, col. 4.

5338. Clines, Francis X. "Equal-Rights Amendment Is Released for a Final Floor Vote in State Senate." NYT, 14 May 1975, p. 49, col. 1.

5339. "Coalition Planning Equal Rights Drive." NYT, 20 May 1975, p. 17, col. 1.

5340. "New York's E.R.A." NYT, 21 May 1975, p. 42, col. 1. (Ed)

5341. Clines, Francis X. "Equal-Rights Amendment Gets Final Albany Passage." NYT, 22 May 1975, p. 1, col. 5.

5342. "Equal Rights Plan Loses." NYT, 12 June 1975, p. 40, col. 2.

5343. Shanahan, Eileen. "Women's Caucus Plans Rights Drive." NYT, 30 June 1975, p. 12, col. 3.

5344. "Opposition Grows on Equal Rights." NYT, 7 July 1975, p. 53, col. 8.

5344a. "Senate Unit Vote on Rights Bill Due." NYT, 30 July 1975, p. 72, col. 8.

5345. Sullivan, Joseph F. "Senate Approves Malpractice Bill: Rights Amendment Passed." NYT, 1 August 1975, p. 60, col. 1.

5346. "G.O.P. Urged to Pick State Backing Rights Amendment." NYT, 3 August 1975, p. 21, col. 1.

5347. Churchill, Mary C. "Plan to Aid Byrne Scored." NYT, 3 August 1975, p. 62, col. 5.

5348. "State Unit Accused of Lobbying for a Bill." NYT, 8 August 1975, p. 60, col. 4.

5349. Ronan, Thomas P. "2 Sides Start Vote Campaign on Women's Equal Rights Bill." NYT, 10 August 1975, p. 20, col. 1.

5350. "Fiscal Crisis Deters Carey on Equal Rights." NYT, 26 August 1975, p. 35, col. 4.

5351. Cook, Joan. "Equal Rights Amendment Will Get Byrne's Support." NYT, 26 August 1975, p. 66, col. 1.

5352. Maitland, Leslie. "Byrne and Carey Ask Passage of Equal Rights Amendment." NYT, 27 August 1975, p. 37, col. 4.

5353. "Legislative Notes." NYT, 31 August 1975, p. 52, col. 4.

5354. "Women's Rights Amendment Backed." NYT, 5 September 1975, p. 33, col. 7.

5355. "Women Gird for Rights Fight." NYT, 7 September 1975, p. 70, col. 4.

5356. Klemesrud, Judy. "As New York Vote on Equal Rights Nears, Two Sides Speak Out." NYT, 18 September 1975, p. 46, col. 1.

5357. Robbins, Ruth. "In Support of the E.R.A." NYT, 26 September 1975, p. 36, col. 3. (LE)

5358. "Women's Suit Fails to Halt Equal Rights Referendum." NYT, 26 September 1975, p. 79, col. 7.

5359. Saxon, Wolfgang. "2 Women Debate E.R.A. Issue Here." NYT, 11 October 1975, p. 29, col. 3.

5360. Ronan, Thomas P. "Both Sides Predict Victory in Vote on E.R.A. Measure." NYT, 12 October 1975, p. 52, col. 3.

5361. Stern, Annette. "E.R.A. 'Pandora's Box.'" NYT, 21 October 1975, p. 36, col. 5. (LE)

5362. "House Rejects Bill on Women's Rights." NYT, 21 October 1975, p. 46, col. 5.

5363. Taylor, Angela. "Men Serve Women in Boost for E.R.A." NYT, 22 October 1975, p. 59, col. 1.

5364. "Court Bars State Unit's E.R.A. Aid." NYT, 23 October 1975, p. 43, col. 6.

5365. "New York's E.R.A." NYT, 24 October 1975, p. 36, col. 2. (Ed)

5366. "Misinformation on E.R.A. Charged." NYT, 24 October 1975, p. 41, col. 3.

5367. "Women Are Urged to Press for E.R.A." NYT, 25 October 1975, p. 15, col. 1.

5368. "Common Cause Urges Votes for Equal Rights Amendment." NYT, 25 October 1975, p. 63, col. 5.

5369. "Mrs. Ford Terms Rights Plan Vital." NYT, 26 October 1975, p. 18, col. 6.

5370. Churchill, Mary C. "Will a Vote for the E.R.A. Be a Vote for a New Era?" NYT, 26 October 1975, p. 69, col. 1.

5371. Ginsburg, Ruth Bader, and Gregory, A. de. "E.R.A.: A Vote 'For' and a Vote 'Against.'" NYT, 28 October 1975, p. 32, col. 3. (LE)

5372. "Women in Jersey Forgo Strike Today." NYT, 29 October 1975, p. 88, col. 3.

5373. Lynn, Frank. "State Equal Rights Vote Jeopardized by Public Apathy." NYT, 31 October 1975, p. 24, col. 1.

5374. "State E.R.A. Gains Support of Deans at 3 Law Schools." NYT, 31 October 1975, p. 71, col. 3.

5375. "Women Bid Voters Back Equal Rights." NYT, 2 November 1975, p. 75, col. 5.

5376. "Poll Shows Voters in Doubt on E.R.A." NYT, 2 November 1975, p. 82, col. 3.

5377. Carroll, Maurice. "Women's Rights and City Charter Dominate Ballot." NYT, 3 November 1975, p. 1, col. 3.

5378. "Statewide Referenda: No. 1--Equal Rights." NYT, 3 November 1975, p. 34, col. 1. (Ed)

5379. Carroll, Maurice. "Drive for Women's Rights Culminates at Polls Today." NYT, 4 November 1975, p. 1, col. 1.

5380. "Mother of U.S. Equal-Rights Measure Nearly Penniless in Nursing Home at 90." NYT, 4 November 1975, p. 21, col. 6.

5381. Hudson, Edward. "Mrs. Friedan Says 'Lies' Led to Amendments' Loss." NYT, 5 November 1975, p. 1, col. 6.

5382. Greenhouse, Linda. "Equal Rights Amendments Lose in New York and Jersey Voting; 6 City Charter Changes Backed." NYT, 5 November 1975, p. 1, col. 8.

5383. _____. "Defeat of Equal Rights Bills Traced to Women's Votes." NYT, 6 November 1975, p. 1, col. 7.

5384. "E.R.A.'s Setback." NYT, 6 November 1975, p. 40, col. 1. (Ed)

5385. Nemy, Enid. "Feminists Reappraise Direction and Image." NYT, 8 November 1975, p. 1, col. 6.

5386. "Save the Movement." NYT, 8 November 1975, p. 26, col. 2. (Ed)

5387. "Equal Rights Effort Lags." NYT, 9 November 1975, p. 37, col. 1.

5388. "Jersey E.R.A. Loss Laid to 4 Counties." NYT, 9 November 1975, p. 40, col. 1.

5389. "Foes Aim at Defeat of Federal E.R.A." NYT, 9 November 1975, p. 84, col. 4.

5390. Greenhouse, Linda. "What Happens to E.R.A. Now?" NYT, 9 November 1975, sec. 4, p. 7, col. 4.

5391. "Rescinding of E.R.A. Is Termed Illegal." NYT, 11 November 1975, p. 67, col. 1.

5392. Pitts, Cathy, and Ray, Eugenia P. "E.R.A.: After the Defeat." NYT, 12 November 1975, p. 42, col. 5. (LE)

5393. Waggoner, Walter H. "Vote Workers Err in Count for E.R.A." NYT, 16 November 1975, p. 99, col. 1.

5394. Cook, Constance E. "The E.R.A.'s Weaknesses." NYT,
18 November 1975, p. 36, col. 5. (LE)

5395. "Repeal of E.R.A. Ratification Asked." NYT, 21 November 1975,
p. 91, col. 1.

5396. Oelsner, Lesley. "Judge Stevens Questions Equal Rights Amendment."
NYT, 9 December 1975, p. 1, col. 1.

5397. _____. "Stevens Calls Court Pay Too Low; Puts His Net
Worth at $171,284." NYT, 10 December 1975, p. 32, col. 4.

5398. Klemesrud, Judy. "Opponent of E.R.A. Confident of Its Defeat."
NYT, 15 December 1975, p. 44, col. 1.

5399. Ginsburg, Ruth B., and Peratis, Kathleen W. "Equal Rights for
Women." NYT, 31 December 1975, p. 21, col. 1. (Ed)

8.   *Wall Street Journal*

5400. Falk, Carol H. "Suffragettes Live on, and They Might Win Another
Victory Soon." WSJ, 31 July 1970, p. 1, col. 4.

5401. Carlson, Elliot. "Proposal to Broaden the Rights of Women May
Bring Surprises." WSJ, 10 August 1970, p. 1, col. 4.

5402. "House Votes Women's Rights Amendment after Maneuver to Bypass
Celler Panel." WSJ, 11 August 1970, p. 3, col. 2.

5403. "The Ladies and the Constitution." WSJ, 13 August 1970, p. 6,
col. 1. (Ed) (EOF)

5404. Carlson, Elliot. "States Revising Labor Laws for Women, Even
without Equal Rights Amendment." WSJ, 3 September 1970, p. 7, col. 1.
(WL)

5405. "Protecting Women's Rights." WSJ, 25 September 1970, p. 6,
col. 1. (Ed)

5406. Large, Arlen J. "Fallen Women: An Amendment Fails." WSJ,
22 December 1970, p. 6, col. 3. (WL)

5407. "Women's Rights Gets a Push; or Is It a Kick?" WSJ, 23 June
1971, p. 12, col. 2.

5408. "Washington Wire: Women's Rights." WSJ, 25 February 1972, p. 1,
col. 5.

5409. "Women's Rights Constitutional Amendment Cleared by Senate Panel;
Floor Fight Seen." WSJ, 1 March 1972, p. 2, col. 3.

5410. "Women's Rights Amendment Moves Ahead in Senate; Final Passage
Possible Today." WSJ, 22 March 1972, p. 4, col. 2.

5411. "Amendment to Guarantee Women's Rights Cleared by Senate; 'Legal Chaos' Predicted." WSJ, 23 March 1972, p. 5, col. 3.

5412. "Labor Letter: Women's Rights Amendment Stirs Emotions as Ratification Battles Develop." WSJ, 26 December 1972, p. 1, col. 5.

5413. "Feminist Organization Is out for Blood--To Support Its Cause." WSJ, 2 February 1973, p. 30, col. 4.

5414. "Equality and the Equal Rights Amendment." WSJ, 26 March 1973, p. 12, col. 1. (Ed)

5415. "Labor Letter: Labor's Turnaround." WSJ, 23 October 1973, p. 1, col. 5.

5416. Lublin, Joann S. "Losing Momentum: Movement to Ratify Equal Rights Proposal Slowed by Opposition. WSJ, 26 July 1974, p. 1, col. 1.

5417. "Washington Wire: Women's-Rights Boosters Gear Up for a Victory in '75." WSJ, 13 December 1974, p. 1, col. 5.

5418. "What's News--Equal Rights Amendment." WSJ, 7 March 1975, p. 1, col. 3.

5419. "What's News--Equal Rights Amendment." WSJ, 27 March 1975, p. 1, col. 3.

5420. Sherman, Malcomb J. "Institutions and Equal Rights." WSJ, 7 May 1975, p. 20, col. 4. (Ed)

5421. Royster, Vermont. "The Era for ERA?" WSJ, 14 January 1976, p. 12, col. 3. (Ed)

9. *Washington Post*

5422. "Women in Industry." WP, 3 February 1929. Rep. in entry #1891.

5423. Miller, Hope Ridings. "Wanted: Equal Rights on Senate Floor While Calendar Carries Equal Rights Amendment." WP, 31 October 1943, sec. 4, p. 1, col. 7. Rep. in entry #10.

5424. "Illusory Women's Rights." WP, 19 July 1945, p. 10, col. 2. Rep. in entry #216.

5425. "Equal Rights." WP, 21 July 1946, sec. 2, p. 4B, col. 2. (Ed) Rep. in entry #26.

5426. Hepburn, Katharine; Kitchelt, Florence L.C.; Lutz, Alma; Weed, Helene Hill; and Wiley, Anna K. "Equality for Women." WP, 1 April 1949, p. 24, col. 4. (LE) Rep. in entry #228.

5427. Shelton, Elizabeth. "Women's Rights Recommendations." WP, 23 April 1970, sec. C, p. 3, col. 1. Rep. in entry #288.

5428. "Two for the People: Women and D.C." WP, 13 August 1970, p. 22, col. 1. (Ed)

5429. Crater, Flora. "'Women, Rights and Money.'" WP, 10 June 1971, p. 23, col. 2. (LE) (WL)

5430. "Women's Rights Vote Postponed." WP, 20 October 1971, p. 2, col. 4.

5431. Krause, Edward E. "Equality for Women." WP, 20 October 1971, p. 17, col. 3. (LE)

5432. Shelton, Isabelle. "Washington Scoop." WP, 20 October 1971. (?) Rep. in entry #3872.

5433. "Sex and the Single Administratrix." WP, 29 November 1971, p. 20, col. 1. (Ed) Rep. in entry #4007.

5434. Rich, Spencer. "Hill Tackles Sex Amendment." WP, 28 February 1972, p. 12, col. 1.

5435. "Senate Panel Clears Women's Amendment." WP, 1 March 1972, p. 1, col. 7. (WL)

5436. McCardle, Dorothy. "Bayh: Amendment 'Will Pass.'" WP, 3 March 1972, sec. B, p. 3, col. 6.

5437. "Rights Amendment Is Fought by Rabbis." WP, 4 April 1972, p. 3, col. 5.

5438. "W. Va. Ratifies 27th Amendment." WP, 23 April 1972, p. 10, col. 6.

5439. "Addenda." WP, 4 May 1972, p. 23, col. 7.

5440. Quinn, Sally. "A Big Day at the Jubilee." WP, 11 May 1972, sec. C, p. 1, col. 1.

5441. "Illinois Rejects 'Equal' Proposal." WP, 17 May 1972, p. 8, col. 7.

5442. "Women Lose Round." WP, 26 May 1972, p. 22, col. 4.

5443. "Women Veto Effort on Rights." WP, 8 September 1972, sec. C, p. 3, col. 3.

5444. Curley, Suzanne. "Equal Rights Amendment for Women--When?" WP Parade, 17 September 1972, p. 23. (WL)

5445. "Sexism in the Statutes." WP, 30 October 1972, p. 20, col. 1. (Ed)

5446. "Correction of October 30 Editorial on ERA." WP, 11 November 1972, p. 14, col. 3.

5447. "Women's Rights Become Law." WP, 6 December 1972, p. 6, col. 3.

5448. "Wyoming Ratifies Rights Amendment." WP, 25 January 1973, sec. D, p. 4, col. 4.

5449. McBee, Susanna. "Equal Rights Amendment Slows Down." WP, 28 January 1973, p. 2, col. 1.

5450. Dewar, Helen. "Women's Rights Measures in Trouble: Virginia: 1,000 Turn Out." WP, 2 February 1973, sec. C, p. 1, col. 1.

5451. Cohen, Richard M. "Women's Rights Measures in Trouble: Maryland: Thoughtful Look." WP, 2 February 1973, sec. C, p. 1, col. 1.

5452. Dewar, Helen. "Women's Rights Bid Dies in Va. Assembly." WP, 7 February 1973, p. 1, col. 4. Rep. in entry #345.

5453. "Rights Amendment." WP, 9 February 1973, p. 24, col. 1.

5454. Wexler, Henrietta. "'Pathetic Spectacle.'" WP, 12 February 1973, p. 21, col. 6. (LE)

5455. "Women's Rights." WP, 13 February 1973, sec. B, p. 3, col. 5.

5456. "N.M. Ratification." WP, 13 February 1973, sec. B, p. 4, col. 8.

5457. Berkowitz, Camille B. "'Equal Rights' Progress." WP, 14 February 1973, p. 15, col. 6. (LE)

5458. "A Sweet Note after Sour End." WP, 15 February 1973, sec. D, p. 2, col. 1.

5459. McFadden, Olivia. "One Who Testified." WP, 17 February 1973, p. 15, col. 6.

5460. McBee, Susanna. "Women's Group Has New Hope for Equal Rights Amendment." WP, 21 February 1973, p. 6, col. 1.

5461. "Addenda." WP, 22 February 1973, p. 15, col. 2.

5462. "President Pushes Rights Amendment." WP, 23 February 1973, p. 6, col. 2.

5463. Dewar, Helen. "Women's Rights Bill Loses in Va.: Confidential Memo Held to Blame." WP, 28 February 1974, sec. B, p. 1, col. 6. Rep. in entry #4037.

5464. "Rights Vote Loses." WP, 1 March 1973, p. 12, col. 2.

5465. McBee, Susanna. "Equal Rights Approval Seen as Unlikely in '73." WP, 7 March 1973, p. 2, col. 1.

5466. "Rights Measure Wins Backing." WP, 9 March 1973, p. 16, col. 4.

5467. McBee, Susanna. "Rights Amendment Explained." WP, 15 March 1973, p. 6, col. 1.

5468. Walsh, Edward. "Equal Rights Move Draws Mandel's Fire." WP, 16 March 1973, sec. C, p. 6, col. 4.

5469. "Rights Amendment." WP, 20 March 1973, p. 8, col. 2.

5470. "Equal Rights." <u>WP</u>, 23 March 1973, p. 8, col. 3.

5471. "Women's Rights." <u>WP</u>, 30 March 1973, p. 24, col. 2.

5472. "Addenda." <u>WP</u>, 4 April 1973, p. 6, col. 2.

5473. McBee, Susanna. "Rights Amendment Rejected in Indiana." <u>WP</u>, 7 April 1973, p. 3, col. 7.

5474. "Rejects Ratification." <u>WP</u>, 18 April 1973, sec. C, p. 6, col. 3.

5475. "Equal Rights Move Set Back by Ohio." <u>WP</u>, 19 April 1973, p. 2, col. 7.

5476. Smyth, Jeannette. "The DAR: Adopting Resolutions." <u>WP</u>, 19 April 1973, sec. B, p. 9, col. 1.

5477. "Addenda." <u>WP</u>, 9 May 1973, sec. B, p. 8, col. 1.

5478. "Equal Rights." <u>WP</u>, 12 May 1973, p. 7, col. 1.

5479. "Women's Rights." <u>WP</u>, 22 May 1973, sec. C, p. 5, col. 2.

5480. Beasley, Maurine. "Feminist Charges 'Sabotage.'" <u>WP</u>, 28 August 1973, p. 6, col. 1.

5481. Simpson, Peggy. "Women Push Rights Drive." <u>WP</u>, 28 August 1973, p. 10, col. 6.

5482. "Approval Seen for Rights Move." <u>WP</u>, 14 September 1973, p. 13, col. 4.

5483. "New Symbol." <u>WP Parade</u>, 30 September 1973, p. 20.

5484. "AFL-CIO Now Backs Rights Amendment." <u>WP</u>, 23 October 1973, p. 4, col. 5.

5485. "Maine to Act on Rights Law." <u>WP</u>, 3 January 1974, p. 3, col. 1.

5486. "Maine Votes Equal Rights Amendment." <u>WP</u>, 19 January 1974, p. 4, col. 1.

5487. "Mont. Is 32d State to Vote for ERA." <u>WP</u>, 22 January 1974, p. 2, col. 8.

5488. "Rights Amendment Rejected by Georgia." <u>WP</u>, 29 January 1974, p. 6, col. 3.

5489. Bredemeier, Kenneth. "Va. Hears Report on Rights Bill." <u>WP</u>, 31 January 1974, sec. C, p. 20, col. 1.

5490. "Ohio Ratifies Equal Rights Amendment." <u>WP</u>, 8 February 1974, p. 14, col. 1.

5491. Omang, Joanne. "Va. Proponents Rally for Equal Rights Bill." <u>WP</u>, 13 February 1974, sec. C, p. 6, col. 3.

5492. Dewar, Helen. "Women's Rights Bill Loses in Va." WP,
28 February 1974, sec. B, p. 1, col. 5.

5493. "Calif. Panel Given Grant on ERA Study." WP, 1 March 1974,
p. 24, col. 1.

5494. Dewar, Helen. "ERA Ratification 'Dead' in Virginia." WP,
1 March 1974, sec. B, p. 4, col. 1.

5495. _____, and Bredemeier, Kenneth. "Thomson Attacks Equal
Rights Memo Critics." WP, 2 March 1974, p. 15, col. 5.

5496. "Secret Memos and Equal Rights." WP, 5 March 1974, p. 22, col. 1.
(Ed)

5497. Kristula, Michelle A., and Morrison, Joyce. "'Shoddy Reasoning.'"
WP, 13 March 1974, p. 27, col. 2. (LE)

5498. "Tennessee Rescinds Ratification." WP, 25 April 1974, p. 7, col. 1.

5499. Quinn, Sally. "Phyllis Schlafly: Sweetheart of the Silent
Majority." WP, 11 July 1974, sec. D, p. 1, col. 6.

5500. "Group Stand on the ERA Reaffirmed." WP, 13 September 1974,
sec. D, p. 15, col. 2.

5501. Dewar, Helen. "Va. ERA Measure Advances." WP, 18 January 1975,
p. 8, col. 5.

5502. "Women's Rights." WP, 22 January 1975, p. 3, col. 3.

5503. Johnson, Janis. "ERA Bill Goes Back to Va. Panel." WP,
22 January 1975, sec. C, p. 8, col. 4.

5504. "Playing Games with Equal Rights." WP, 24 January 1975, p. 26,
col. 1. (Ed)

5505. Dewar, Helen. "Equal Rights Amendment Killed in Va." WP,
25 January 1975, p. 16, col. 1.

5506. Stratton, Pamela M. "Smothered Abilities." WP, 28 January 1975,
p. 19, col. 5. (LE)

5507. Rayburn, Carole A. "ERA in Virginia." WP, 4 February 1975,
p. 19, col. 4. (LE)

5508. "ERA Approval Gains." WP, 5 February 1975, p. 17, col. 1.

5509. Mayer, Hermine Herta. "Women's Rights." WP, 6 February 1975,
p. 19, col. 5. (LE)

5510. Witcover, Jules. "Women on Both Sides of Equal Rights Amendment
Argument." WP, 8 February 1975, p. 7, col. 1.

5511. "Betty Ford vs. Goldwater on the ERA." WP, 13 February 1975,
sec. B, p. 3, col. 1.

5512. "Betty Ford Fails to Sway Ariz. on ERA." <u>WP</u>, 14 February 1975, p. 13, col. 8.

5513. Hyde, Nina S. "Phoning for ERA Passage." <u>WP</u>, 15 February 1975, sec. C, p. 3, col. 5.

5514. Cotterell, William. "ERA Rejected by Georgia Senate." <u>WP</u>, 18 February 1975, p. 2, col. 5.

5515. Evans, DeAnn. "Utah Rejects Equal Rights Amendment." <u>WP</u>, 19 February 1975, sec. D, p. 4, col. 3.

5516. "Nevada Rejects ERA." <u>WP</u>, 20 February 1975, p. 4, col. 7.

5517. "Equal Rights Amendment Adoption Doubtful in '75." <u>WP</u>, 25 February 1975, p. 4, col. 5.

5518. "ERA Amendment." <u>WP</u>, 6 March 1975, p. 28, col. 1.

5519. Weisman, Joel D. "Proponents Pessimistic about ERA." <u>WP</u>, 7 March 1975, p. 19, col. 5.

5520. "ERA Link Sought to '76 Convention." <u>WP</u>, 11 March 1975, p. 2, col. 4.

5521. "ERA Defeated in Indiana." <u>WP</u>, 11 March 1975, p. 7, col. 2.

5522. "S.C. House Kills ERA for 1975." <u>WP</u>, 27 March 1975, p. 26, col. 1.

5523. Fordham, James, and Fordham, Andrea. "The Unknowns of Equal Rights." <u>WP</u>, 31 March 1975, p. 19, col. 1. (Ed)

5524. Ginsburg, Ruth Bader. "The Fear of the Equal Rights Amendment." <u>WP</u>, 7 April 1975, p. 21, col. 1. (Ed)

5525. "ERA Gains in Florida." <u>WP</u>, 12 April 1975, p. 4, col. 3.

5526. Bayh, Birch; Warrick, Ronni; Bender, Susan; Glennon, Ann E.; Cowles, Elizabeth S.; and Kruse, Ann. "The Equal Rights Amendment." <u>WP</u>, 12 April 1975, p. 11, col. 4. (LE)

5527. "N.C. House Rejects Rights Amendment." <u>WP</u>, 17 April 1975, p. 22, col. 1.

5528. Witcover, Jules. "Strong Opposition in Marginal States Scuttles ERA for 1975." <u>WP</u>, 21 April 1975, p. 3, col. 1.

5529. "ERA Rejected." <u>WP</u>, 26 April 1975, p. 4, col. 3.

5530. Fordham, James, and Fordham, Andrea. "Replying to Senator Bayh on ERA." <u>WP</u>, 27 April 1975, sec. C, p. 7, col. 5. (LE)

5531. "Illinois House Votes for ERA." <u>WP</u>, 2 May 1975, p. 4, col. 2.

5532. MacKenzie, John P. "The Battle for Equal Rights." <u>WP</u>, 11 May 1975, p. 3, col. 1.

5533. Zelenko, Benjamin L. "Questioning the Constitutional Amendment
   Process." WP, 24 May 1975, p. 11, col. 4. (LE)

5534. Proctor, Pam. "Phyllis Schlafly: She Thinks Women Are Better
   Off Than Men." WP Parade, 25 May 1975, p. 12.

5535. Gorney, Cynthia. "ERA Tops Agenda for '75 Tribunal." WP,
   20 June 1975, p. 17, col. 2.

5536. "Democrats Defend Statement on ERA." WP, 5 August 1975, sec. C,
   p. 5, col. 2.

5537. Will, George F. "Equal Rights: Politics of Gesture." WP,
   10 November 1975, p. 27, col. 4. (Ed)

5538. Goodman, Ellen. "Fear of the ERA." WP, 18 November 1975, p. 27,
   col. 5. (Ed)

10.   Editorials on File

5539. Arizona Republic, 12 August 1970.

5540. Baltimore Sun, 12 August 1970.

5541. Burlington (Vermont) Free Press, 12 August 1970.

5542. Chicago Sun-Times, 12 August 1970.

5543. Dallas Morning News, 12 August 1970.

5544. Dallas Times Herald, 12 August 1970.

5545. Denver Post, 12 August 1970.

5546. Portland (Maine) Evening Express, 12 August 1970.

5547. Buffalo Evening News, 13 August 1970.

5548. Long Island Press, 13 August 1970.

5549. Wall Street Journal, 13 August 1970.

5550. Wisconsin State Journal, 13 August 1970.

5551. Detroit Free Press, 14 August 1970.

5552. Pittsburgh Post-Gazette, 14 August 1970.

5553. Toledo (Ohio) Blade, 14 August 1970.

5554. Chicago Sun-Times, 26 August 1970.

5555. Cincinnati Post, 26 August 1970.

5556. Pittsburgh Post-Gazette, 28 August 1970.

5557. New York Times, 23 November 1971.

5558. San Juan (Puerto Rico) Star, 23 November 1971.

5559. Boston Globe, 24 November 1971.

5560. Chicago Today American, 24 November 1971.

5561. Los Angeles Times, 24 November 1971.

5562. St. Louis Globe-Democrat, 24 November 1971.

5563. Boston Herald Traveler, 25 November 1971.

5564. Chicago Sun-Times, 25 November 1971.

5565. Pittsburgh Post-Gazette, 25 November 1971.

5566. Hartford Courant, 26 November 1971.

5567. Oregonian, 27 November 1971.

5568. Atlanta Constitution, 29 November 1971.

5569. Greenville News, 30 November 1971.

5570. Milwaukee Journal, 30 November 1971.

5571. Minneapolis Tribune, 30 November 1971.

5572. Akron Beacon Journal, 23 March 1972.

5573. Buffalo Evening News, 23 March 1972.

5574. Pittsburgh Post-Gazette, 24 March 1972.

5575. Rock Hill (South Carolina) Evening Herald, 24 March 1972.

5576. St. Louis Globe-Democrat, 24 March 1972.

5577. Norfolk (Virginia) Ledger-Star, 25 March 1972.

5578. Oregon Journal, 25 March 1972.

5579. Tulsa Daily World, 25 March 1972.

5580. Memphis Commercial Appeal, 26 March 1972.

5581. The Philadelphia Inquirer, 26 March 1972.

5582. Arkansas Democrat, 28 March 1972.

5583. The Des Moines Register, 28 March 1972.

5584. Ann Arbor News, 31 March 1972.

5585. Norfolk (Virginia) Ledger-Star, 1 February 1973.

5586. St. Louis Review, 2 February 1973.

5587. Rock Hill (South Carolina) Evening Herald, 5 February 1973.

5588. Daily Oklahoman, 6 February 1973.

5589. Memphis Commercial Appeal, 6 February 1973.

5590. Atlanta Constitution, 9 February 1973.

5591. Kansas City Times, 9 February 1973.

5592. Boston Herald American, 10 February 1973.

5593. Norfolk (Virginia) Ledger-Star, 10 February 1973.

5594. Cleveland Plain Dealer, 11 February 1973.

5595. Biloxi (Mississippi) Daily Herald, 12 February 1973.

5596. Portland Press Herald, 13 February 1973.

5597. Louisville Times, 16 February 1973.

5598. Worcester Telegram, 16 February 1973.

5599. Cincinnati Enquirer, 20 February 1973.

5600. Philadelphia Evening Bulletin, 22 February 1973.

5601. Arizona Republic, 25 February 1973.

5602. St. Louis Globe-Democrat, 15 February 1975.

5603. Arizona Republic, 17 February 1975.

5604. Atlanta Constitution, 18 February 1975.

5605. Salt Lake Deseret News, 19 February 1975.

5606. San Jose Mercury, 19 February 1975.

5607. Orlando (Florida) Sentinel Star, 20 February 1975.

5608. Toledo (Ohio) Blade, 22 February 1975.

5609. Springfield (Massachusetts) Union, 23 February 1975.

5610. Columbia (South Carolina) State, 25 February 1975.

5611. Denver Post, 27 February 1975.

5612. Detroit Free Press, 27 February 1975.

5613. St. Louis Review, 28 February 1975.

5614. Chicago Daily News, 1 March 1975.

5615. Chicago Sun-Times, 2 March 1975.

5616. Rocky Mountain News, 2 March 1975.

5617. St. Louis Post-Dispatch, 3 March 1975.

5618. Pittsburgh Press, 4 March 1975.

5619. Albuquerque Journal, 12 March 1975.

5620. Rochester Democrat Chronicle, 12 March 1975.

5621. Kansas City Star, 13 March 1975.

5622. Winston-Salem Sentinel, 14 March 1975.

5623. Oklahoma City Times, 15 March 1975.

5624. Orlando (Florida) Sentinel Star, 23 March 1975.

5625. Columbia (South Carolina) State, 28 October 1975.

5626. Buffalo Evening News, 6 November 1975.

5627. Garden City (New York) Newsday, 6 November 1975.

5628. Memphis Commercial Appeal, 7 November 1975.

5629. Oklahoma City Times, 7 November 1975.

5630. St. Louis Globe-Democrat, 7 November 1975.

5631. Chicago Sun-Times, 8 November 1975.

5632. Philadelphia Evening Bulletin, 8 November 1975.

5633. Pittsburgh Post-Gazette, 8 November 1975.

5634. Boston Globe, 9 November 1975.

5635. Baltimore News American, 10 November 1975.

5636. Des Moines Tribune, 10 November 1975.

5637. Hartford Courant, 10 November 1975.

5638. Cincinnati Enquirer, 11 November 1975.

5639. Fort Worth Star-Telegram, 13 November 1975.

11. Miscellaneous

[The following citations consist of the primary source cross-
references taken from other sections of this bibliography and
of the miscellaneous material on Herstory and Women and the
Law microfilm collections not cited elsewhere. Often it has
been impossible to check out these citations because of the
unavailability of the newspapers; thus, page numbers are often
omitted. Moreover, the references from these primary sources
and microfilm collections are often inaccurate. A question mark
at the end of the citation indicates that the editor could not
locate the article from the information given. They are left
in so that the material can be identified and read on the
microfilm if not the primary source.

Only cross-references which have a specific date are listed
here; any reference which does not have enough information for
the researcher to find with relative ease is given with the
secondary source citation.

Arrangement is alphabetical by author and title.]

5640. "All Men Are Created Equal." Guardian, 8 August 1970, p. 10.
(Ed) (WL)

5641. "Amendments on Women, Voting OKd." San Francisco Chronicle,
29 July 1970, p. 9, col. 3. (WL)

5642. Amick, Donna. "Campaign for Women's Equal Rights Arrives in
Trenton." Trenton Evening Times, 5 May 1970. Rep. in entry #2925.

5643. Anderson, Judith. "Equal Rights--An Amendment to Change the
U.S." San Francisco Chronicle, 17 August 1972, p. 22, col. 1. (WL)

5644. _____. "Equality or Protection?" San Francisco Chronicle,
7 May 1970, p. 27, col. 1. (WL)

5645. "Annul Anti-Rape Laws?" San Francisco Chronicle, 31 March 1972,
p. 18, col. 3. (WL)

5646. "Another Go Round for Women's Rights?" Oakland Tribune,
2 March 1971, p. 21, col. 4. (WL)

5647. "Author of Women's Rights Amendment Claims Victory." San Pedro
(California) News, 23 September 1972. (WL)

5648. Banowsky, Bill. "What's Right with 'Equal Rights.'" Los Angeles
Herald Examiner, 6 August 1972, p. 19, col. 2. (Ed) (WL) Rep. in
entry #3719.

5649. Behrens, Earl C. "Equal Rights Bill Blocked in Senate." San
Francisco Chronicle, 27 April 1972, p. 1, col. 3. (WL)

5650. _____. "Labor's Fight on Equal Rights Bill." San Francisco
Chronicle, 24 April 1972, p. 4, col. 2. (WL)

5651. _____. "Second Look at Women's Amendment." San Francisco Chronicle, 12 April 1972, p. 8, col. 4. (WL)

5652. _____. "Women Act to Get Their Amendment." San Francisco Chronicle, 14 April 1972, p. 8, col. 4. (WL)

5653. Blakkan, Renee. "Women Build for Mass Action." Guardian, 15 August 1970, p. 7. (WL)

5654. _____. "Women's Rights Fight in Congress." Guardian, 18 July 1970, p. 3. (WL)

5655. Boyd, L.M. "Why Do Women Want Equal Rights?" San Francisco Chronicle, 29 April 1972, p. 33, col. 1. (WL)

5656. "California: Another State for Women's Rights." San Francisco Examiner and Chronicle, This World, 19 November 1972, p. 6. (WL)

5657. "The Case against the ERA." Guardian, 12 April 1972, p. 7. (WL)

5658. Celler, Emanuel. "Amendment Represents neither Sound Law nor Sound Behavior." Daily Compass, 17 March 1950. Rep. in entry #232.

5659. Columbia Women's Liberation Group. "Equal Rights Amendment Attracts Growing Support." Militant, 2 October 1970, pp. 8-9. (WL)

5660. Cook, Louise. "Equal Rights Move in Jeopardy." San Francisco Examiner, 9 March 1973, p. 24, col. 1. (WL)

5661. Count Marco. "Are Women Created Equal, Too?" San Francisco Chronicle, 19 April 1972, p. 20, col. 1. (WL)

5662. _____. "That Idiotic Equal Rights Amendment." San Francisco Chronicle, 17 August 1970, p. 19, col. 7. (Ed) (WL)

5663. Crawford, Clare. "Sens. McCarthy, Tower Sponsor Ladies." Washington (D.C.) Daily News, 7 February 1969. Rep. in entry #3434.

5664. Draper, Anne. "Change Women's Rights Amendment, Unionist Urges." San Jose Union Gazette, 21 January 1972, p. 6. (WL)

5665. _____. "Radical Forum." Guardian, 12 April 1972, p. 7. (WL) Also "Against 'Pure' ERA." Guardian, 10 May 1972, p. 8. (LE)

5666. "Equality before the Law." New York Herald Tribune, 20 September 1943. (Ed) Rep. in entry #202.

5667. "Equality Bill in Trouble." Berkeley Daily Gazette, 28 August 1970, p. 2, col. 7. (WL)

5668. "Equality Measure Opposed." San Francisco Progress, 21 March 1973. (WL)

5669. "'Equal Right' Ratification Measure." Berkeley Daily Gazette, 1 March 1972, p. 26, col. 1. (WL)

5670. "Equal Rights—A Long Way to Go." Oakland Tribune, 18 August
1972, p. 31, col. 7. (WL)

5671. "Equal Rights Amendment." Berkeley Daily Gazette, 13 November
1970, p. 6, col. 4. (WL)

5672. "Equal Rights Amendment Endorsed by U.S. Commission on Civil
Rights." Atlanta Journal, 31 July 1973. (HU, S2, R3)

5673. "Equal Rights Amendment Sidetracked." San Francisco Chronicle,
7 April 1972, p. 8, col. 1. (WL)

5674. "Equal Rights for Women: They May Be Drafted." Berkeley Daily
Gazette, 11 August 1970, p. 2, col. 1. (WL)

5675. "Equal Rights Gets Semi-Public Hearing." Atlanta Journal,
7 September 1973. (HU, S2, R3)

5676. "Equal Rights Law Set Back." San Francisco Examiner, 7 March
1973, p. 2, col. 3. (WL)

5677. "ERA." The Dallas Morning News, 16 July 1973. Rep. in entry
#4075.

5678. "ERA Delayed in Illinois." Milwaukee Journal, 5 April 1973.
Rep. in entry #3704.

5679. "ERA in Jeopardy." Guardian, 24 October 1970, p. 7. (WL)

5680. "ERA—Is It 'Brink of Hill'?" San Francisco Examiner, 8 February
1973, p. 14, col. 1. (WL)

5681. "ERA Ratified by Vermont." San Francisco Examiner, 21 February
1973, p. 2, col. 7. (WL)

5682. "The Feminist Amendment." Chicago Journal of Commerce and La
Salle Street Journal, 17 January 1925, p. 392. Rep. in entry #1726.

5683. Fernstrom, H. "Woman's Rights." Pioneer, 4 March 1971. (LE) (WL)

5684. "Full Citizenship for Women." Militant, 10 December 1971, p. 6.
(Ed) (WL)

5685. "Gains for Women." College of San Mateo (California), 12 August
1970. (WL)

5686. "GFWC Urges Women to Support Equal Rights." Berkeley Daily
Gazette, 3 February 1973, p. 4, col. 1. (WL)

5687. Gillette, Jay. "The Equal Rights Amendment." D.C. Gazette
(Washington), 17 May 1972. (WL)

5688. "House Panel Approves Sex Bias Amendment." Washington (D.C.)
Evening Star, 30 April 1971. (WL)

5689. Hutton, Ginger. "Equal Rights Proposal Affects Men, Children, Too."
Arizona Republic, 26 January 1973, p. 45. (WL)

5690. Jaquith, Cindy. "Women: The Insurgent Majority--Communications Workers Support ERA." Militant, 19 May 1972, p. 7. (WL)

5691. _____. "Women: The Insurgent Majority--The Equal Rights Amendment." Militant, 16 June 1972, p. 7. (WL)

5692. Kantor, Seth. "UNM Prof Changes Equal Rights Views." Albuquerque Tribune, 13 September 1970. (WL)

5693. Kay, Jane. "Attorney, Ph.D. Collaborate on Study of How ERA Will Affect State Laws." Arizona Daily Star, 18 January 1973, sec. C, p. 1. (WL)

5694. "Kentucky OKs Sex Amendment." San Francisco Chronicle, 16 June 1972, p. 24, col. 7. (WL)

5695. Kilpatrick, James. "Do Women Really Want Equality?" Sacramento Bee, 27 October 1971. (?) (Ed) (WL)

5696. Krueger, Jeannine. "The Long Struggle for Equal Rights." Berkeley Freedom News, October 1971, pp. 28-29. (WL)

5697. Lawrence, David. "The Supreme Court and Women--Ruling for Segregation of Men or Women Is Compared to Integration Decision." Washington (D.C.) Evening Star, 8 April 1959. Rep. in entry #54.

5698. "Lib Shrillness Turns Off Many Women; Some Opposed to Equal Rights Amendment." Minneapolis Star, 26 August 1970, sec. C, p. 10. (WL)

5699. Lincoln, Gould. "Rights Laws by the Dozen, But--." Washington (D.C.) Star, 22 May 1965. Rep. in entry #65.

5700. Lovell, Sarah. "Open Letter to Myra Wolfgang: For Equal Rights and Shorter Hours." Militant, 2 October 1970, p. 8. (WL)

5700a. Lund, Caroline. "Women: The Insurgent Majority." Militant, 22 October 1971, p. 17.

5700b. _____. "Women: The Insurgent Majority." Militant, 29 October 1971, p. 7. Rep. in entry #3079.

5701. Lutz, Alma. "Equal Rights and the Hayden Rider." New York Herald Tribune, 1 August 1953. Rep. in entry #242.

5702. _____. "Hits AFL-CIO Opposition to Equal Rights." Boston Sunday Herald, 13 July 1958. Rep. in entry #53.

5703. Martin, Tybie. "Equal Rights Amendment Defeated in California." Guardian, 26 April 1972. (?) (WL)

5704. Mellenkoff, Abe. "Morning Report." San Francisco Chronicle, 13 August 1970, p. 44, col. 5. (WL)

5705. "Mills Bows to NOW on Equal Rights." San Francisco Chronicle, 9 September 1972, p. 12, col. 5. (WL)

5706. "Misleading Amendment Dies." Cleveland Plain Dealer, 22 July 1946. Rep. in entry #222.

5707. "Montana 'No' on Equality." San Francisco Examiner, 2 February 1973, p. 19, col. 7. (WL)

5708. Moseley, Ray. "Fem Lib Movement Reaches Congress." Oakland Tribune, 22 July 1970, p. 16, col. 5. (WL)

5709. "Myths about ERA." Minneapolis Star, 15 January 1973. Rep. in entry #3704.

5710. "Nevada Again Rejects Equal Rights Proposal." San Francisco Examiner, 8 March 1973, p. 16, col. 3. (WL)

5711. "New Law for Women." San Francisco Examiner and Chronicle, This World, 26 March 1972, p. 8, col. 4. (WL)

5712. "New Round for ERA Fight." Milwaukee Journal, 29 May 1973. Rep. in entry #3704.

5713. "New York for Equal Rights." New York Herald Tribune, 29 March 1945. (Ed) Rep. in entry #208.

5714. "New Women's Rights Plan." San Francisco Examiner, 18 August 1970, p. 2, col. 7. (WL)

5715. "Nixon Backs Equal Rights for Women." Oakland Tribune, 19 March 1972, p. 30, col. 7. (WL)

5716. "Nixon Endorses Amendment to Aid Women." San Diego Union, 19 March 1972, p. 8, col. 8. (WL) Rep. in entry #3709.

5717. "Nixon Endorses Equal Rights Amendment." San Francisco Examiner, 22 February 1973, p. 13. (?) (WL)

5718. "An OK for Rights Bill." San Francisco Chronicle, 21 September 1972, p. 13, col. 1. (WL)

5718a. "On the Line." People's World, 19 August 1972. (WL)

5719. "On with Women's Rights Amendment." Palo Alto Times, 15 October 1971. Rep. in entry #336.

5720. Ostrowdizki, Vic. "Women's Present Rights: Impact of Amendment." San Francisco Examiner and Chronicle, 16 August 1970, p. 23, col. 8. (WL)

5721. Paynter, Susan. "The Fight for Equal Rights: A Fifty-Year Struggle for Change." Seattle Post-Intelligencer, August 1972, pp. 1-19 (series of articles; entire issue). (WL)

5722. "Prayer Rider to Women's Rights." San Francisco Chronicle, 14 October 1970, p. 12, col. 1. (WL)

5723. "Professor Says Women's Rights Is No Cure-All." Albuquerque Journal, 12 September 1970. (WL)

5724. "Public Hearing to Be Held on Equal Rights." University of Washington Daily, 6 February 1973. (WL)

5725. "Reaction to Women's Amendment." San Francisco Chronicle, 25 March 1972, p. 13, col. 6. (WL)

5726. Reed, Elaine. "Women Debate Ways to Right the Wrongs." Oakland Tribune, 8 May 1970, p. 33, col. 1. (WL)

5727. "Rights Amendment 'Sick.'" San Francisco Examiner, 7 February 1973. (?) (WL)

5728. "Rights and Reservations." College of San Mateo (California), 24 July 1970. (WL)

5729. "Rights Drive Offshoot." San Francisco Chronicle, 14 April 1972, p. 8, col. 2. (WL)

5730. "Rights Vote Reversals." San Francisco Examiner, 16 March 1973, p. 2, col. 6. (WL)

5731. Robbins, Daniel. "ERA." Guardian, 19 April 1972, p. 8. (LE) (WL)

5732. Scherf, Margaret. "Club Women Are Mobilizing for Passage of Amendment." Albuquerque Journal, 4 August 1971. (WL)

5733. "Senate Roadblock for Women's Bill." Guardian, 27 October 1971, p. 4. (WL)

5734. "Sen. Mills Clears Way for Women's Rights Amendment." Berkeley Daily Gazette, 9 September 1972, p. 3, col. 1. (WL)

5735. "Sexual Equality: Mischief Potential." Berkeley Daily Gazette, 20 August 1970. (Ed) (WL)

5736. "S.F. Board Resolution on Women." San Francisco Chronicle, 29 June 1971, p. 2, col. 1. (WL)

5737. Shelton, Elizabeth. "Rights Hearing Irks Women Lawyers." Denver Post, 18 September 1970. (WL)

5738. Shelton, Isabelle. "How Equal Rights Passed Senate." Washington (D.C.) Sunday Star, 26 March 1972, p. G-3. Rep. in entries #3355, 4018.

5739. Sims, Patsy. "Stumping for Women against Labor's Objections." San Francisco Chronicle, 18 April 1972, p. 18, col. 1. (WL)

5740. Smith, Julie. "The Plight of the Equal Rights Amendment: How the Congressmen Line Up." San Francisco Chronicle, 2 January 1970, p. 16, col. 1. (WL)

5741. "So Near, & Yet . . ." Washington (D.C.) Star-News, 4 March 1974, p. A-14. Rep. in entry #4033.

5742. Stammer, Larry. "State Okays Equal Rights for Women." San Jose Mercury, 14 November 1972, p. 1. (?) (WL)

5743. "State Senate Moves on Equal Rights Measures." San Francisco Chronicle, 9 November 1972, p. 7, col. 5. (WL)

5744. "State Senate Ratifies Women's Amendment." San Francisco Chronicle, 10 November 1972, p. 1, col. 5. (WL)

5745. Suelzle, Marijean. "Accepting the Challenge of Equal Rights (Sex) Amendment." Berkeley Daily Gazette, 31 December 1970, p. 6, col. 4. (Ed) (WL) Rep. in entry #487.

5746. "Support for Equal Rights Amendment." Berkeley Daily Gazette, 25 August 1970, p. 5, col. 7. (WL)

5747. "Support the ERA." Guardian, 12 April 1972, p. 8. (Ed) (WL)

5748. "Surprise Move to Release Women's Rights Bill Fails." Oakland Tribune, 8 July 1972, p. 2, col. 6. (WL)

5749. "SWP Candidates Urge Congress Adopt Equal Rights Amendment." Militant, 26 June 1970, p. 9. (WL)

5750. "Taking Sides on Sex Bill." San Francisco Chronicle, 25 September 1970, p. 20, col. 1. (WL)

5751. "Telling It to the Sisters: Women's Liberation Turns Its Back on the Senate." Liberation News Service, 3 June 1970. Rep. from Off Our Backs. (WL)

5752. Thompson, Lil. "Equal Rights? Women Not Completely Sold." North Carolina Journal and Sentinel, 16 August 1970. Rep. in entry #84.

5753. "Tiptoein' through the Tulips: Women on Equality." Daily Californian, 2 November 1970. (WL)

5754. "Trouble for Equal Rights Measure." San Francisco Chronicle, 10 February 1973, p. 12, col. 7. (WL)

5755. Tully, Andrew. "Going Overboard with Women's Lib." Berkeley Daily Gazette, 14 February 1973, p. 14, col. 3. (Ed) (WL)

5756. _____. "Knock Off the ERA Jazz." Berkeley Daily Gazette, 14 March 1973, p. 10, col. 5. (Ed) (WL)

5757. _____. "Proposed Amendment Questioned." Wyoming Caspar Star Tribune, 22 September 1970. (WL)

5758. "2 States OK Equal Rights Amendment." San Francisco Chronicle, 9 February 1973, p. 15, col. 8. (WL)

5759. "Unfinished Business." New York Herald Tribune, 20 July 1946.
(Ed) Rep. in entry #223.

5760. "Vigil at Capitol." Militant, 10 October 1970. (?) (WL)

5761, Weisser, Peter. "Assembly Votes for Rights for Women." San
Francisco Chronicle, 21 April 1972, p. 1, col. 3. (WL)

5762. _____. "NOW Threatens 'Purge.'" San Francisco Chronicle,
16 May 1972, p. 18, col. 2. (WL)

5763. _____. "A Setback for Women's Amendment." San Francisco
Chronicle, 6 April 1972, p. 11, col. 1. (WL)

5764. "Why Bay Congressmen Opposed Women's Bill." Oakland Tribune,
11 August 1970, p. 1, col. 2. (WL; labelled "A 'No' Vote on Women")

5765. "Why Can't Missouri Be Counted on Equal Rights?" Kansas City Star,
19 March 1974. Rep. in entry #3141.

5766. Wilson, Richard. "Women's Rights Amendment May End Protection."
Washington (D.C.) Evening Star, 14 August 1970. Rep. in entries
#79, 305.

5766a. Wolfgang, Myra. "'Don't Talk Theory to Me, Tell Me the Practice.'"
People's World, 5 December 1970, p. M-11. (WL)

5767. "Woman Denies She's Equal." San Francisco Examiner, 1 March 1973.
(?) (WL)

5768. "Women." San Francisco Examiner and Chronicle, Sunday Punch,
16 August 1970, p. 1, col. 2. (WL)

5769. "Women." San Francisco Chronicle, 9 August 1972. (?) (WL)

5770. "Women." San Francisco Chronicle, 20 August 1972. (?) (WL)

5771. "Women and Equal Rights." Oakland Tribune, 5 May 1970, p. 18,
col. 1. (Ed) (WL)

5772. "Women Draft Lib Amendment Fight." Oakland Tribune, 26 August
1971, p. 3, col. 1.

5773. "Women Expose 'Rights' Law: Unionists Fear Loss of Labor
Protection Laws." People's World, 24 July 1971, p. 4. (WL)

5774. "Women Forfeit Anti-Bias Law." San Francisco Chronicle,
19 November 1970, p. 13, col. 1. (WL)

5775. "Women Go to Washington." Waterloo (Iowa) Daily Courier,
5 October 1945. Rep. in entry #220.

5776. "Women in Struggle: Equal Rights Amendment." Guardian,
19 July 1972, p. 15. (WL)

5777. "Women Move In for Senate Plea." San Francisco Chronicle, 6 May
1970, p. 12, col. 4. (WL)

5778. "Women Now Happy with Mills." <u>Oakland Tribune</u>, 14 September 1972, p. 6, col. 1. (WL)

5779. "Women Oppose Diluted Equal Rights Amendment." <u>San Francisco Chronicle</u>, 23 June 1971, p. 6, col. 3. (WL)

5780. "Women See Hope for Equal Rights." <u>Washington (D.C.) Daily News</u>, 3 September 1971. (WL)

5781. "Women's Equality Fight." <u>Des Moines Register</u>, 6 March 1975. (Ed) Rep. in entry #165.

5782. "Women's Equal Rights Bill Cooled." <u>San Diego Union</u>, 14 October 1971, p. 4, col. 3. Rep. in entry #3707.

5783. "Women's Rights Amendment OKd." <u>San Francisco Chronicle</u>, 23 March 1972, p. 1, col. 5. (WL)

5784. "Women's Rights at a Rest Room Door." <u>San Francisco Chronicle</u>, 11 September 1970, p. 17, col. 1.

5785. "Women's Rights Changes Killed." <u>San Francisco Chronicle</u>, 22 March 1972, p. 12, col. 1. (WL)

5786. "Women's Rights Foe's Plea." <u>San Francisco Chronicle</u>, 3 February 1973, p. 8, col. 1. (WL)

5787. "Women's Rights Petition in House." <u>San Francisco Chronicle</u>, 21 July 1970, p. 8, col. 1. (WL)

5788. "Women's Rights Vote Postponed." <u>Washington (D.C.) Sunday Star</u>, 17 October 1971. Rep. in entry #3872.

5789. "Women's Rights Win House Vote." <u>San Francisco Chronicle</u>, 11 August 1970, p. 1, col. 3. (WL)

5790. "Women's Rights Year?" <u>College of San Mateo</u> (California), 4 April 1970. (WL)

5791. "Women to Keep House in Order." <u>Washington (D.C.) Evening Star</u>, 26 August 1971. (WL)

5791a. Woodhouse, Chase Going. "Equal Rights Amendment." <u>New Haven (Connecticut) Union Times</u>, 21 July 1945. Rep. in entry #218.

5792. Yeargin, Bob. "Legislature's Reaction to ERA--Uncertain." <u>Las Vegas Sun</u>, 29 December 1972. Rep. from entry #344.

5793. _____. "Like Women--They Do Not Agree." <u>Las Vegas Sun</u>, 28 December 1972. Rep. from entry #344. (4 more articles of this series appear in the <u>Las Vegas Sun</u> during December of 1972; they are reprinted in the <u>Congressional Record</u>, see entries #342 and 343, but the specific dates are not cited.)

[The following articles on Women and the Law are cited incompletely.]

5794. Brower, Millicent. "Women Are 'Persons.'" San Francisco
     Examiner, April 1970. (WL)

5795. "Equal Rights Amendment."

5796. "Labor Bill Approved."

5797. "Senate Oks Equal Rights for Women." n.t., 23 March 1972.

5798. "Sex Bias under the Gun." San Francisco Examiner and Chronicle,
     n.d.

5799. Untitled. San Francisco Chronicle, 17 October 1972. (?)

5800. "Women's Rights."

Addenda to Periodicals

925a. Brady, David W., and Tedin, Kent L. "Ladies in Pink: Religion and Political Ideology in the Anti-ERA Movement." Social Science Quarterly 56 (1976): 564-75.

973a. Cross, Robert. "Dialog: Phyllis Schlafly." Chicago Tribune Magazine, 9 November 1975, pp. 26-27. (N)

1134a. Farr, Louise. "The Anti-ERA Hustle." Ms., April 1976, p. 19.

1238a. Komar, Gregory M. "Who's Foggy?" Advocate, 21 April 1976, p. 25. (LE) (N)

1245a. Langer, Elinor. "Why Big Business Is Trying to Defeat the ERA: The Economic Implications of Equality." Ms., May 1976, pp. 64-66, 100, 102, 104, 106, 108.

1254a. Letter to the Editor. Ms., April 1976, p. 8.

1272a. "A Marketing Blitz to Sell Equal Rights." Business Week, 19 April 1976, p. 146.

1354a. Paulson, Ralph. "Can the ERA Become a Reality before Our Species Goes the Way of the Dinosaur?" Ms., May 1976, pp. 7-8. (LE)

1446a. Starshak, Barbara McGoorty; O'Connor, Jeannette; Stein, Rhonda; Miller, Sarah Bryan; Kahn, J. Kesner; and Milke, Elizabeth L. "ERA, Pro and Con." Chicago Tribune Magazine, 7 December 1975, p. 12. (LE) (N)

Author Index

In the list below, the numbers after each name

refer to item numbers in the Bibliography.

A

Abbott, Elizabeth, 860
Abernethy, Thomas G., 963
Abzug, Bella, 358, 861-62
Ackley, Fannie, 2550
Ackroyd, Margaret F., 863
Adams, James Truslow, 607, 616
Ahern, Virginia H., 3183
Albert, Carl (Representative), 295
Albert, Marilyn, 871-72
Alda, Alan, 1393
Alexander, Dolores, 1311
Algeo, Sara M., 1753
Allan, Virginia R., 299
Allen, Ella Vollstedt, 2361
Alpern, Harriet, 2817
Alvarez, Edna R.S., 686
Amamoto, R.K., 4922
Amick, Donna, 2925, 5642
Anderson, Bill, 4353
Anderson, Harriet, 5053
Anderson, Jannell, 442
Anderson, Judith, 5643-44
Anderson, Lee Berger, 687
Anderson, Mary, 19, 888, 943, 1022, 1247, 1371, 4429, 5031, 5113
Anthony, Daniel (Representative), 192, 977, 1022
Anthony, Susan B., II, 688, 891
Antieau, Chester James, 434
Apple, R.W., Jr., 5326
Appleby, Jon H., 4587
Arakaki, Joe, 4513
Arbogast, Kate A., 894
Aries, 2805-806
Armstrong, Anne, 4752
Armstrong, Florence A., 35, 236, 237, 2404, 2603
Asbury, Edith Evans, 5130

Ash, Marian, 3777-805
Ashman, Heather, 4652
Avery, Edwina Austin, 896, 2210
Avery, Nina Horton, 972, 996, 2508, 2595
Avery, Patricia, 897
Ayres, B. Drummond, Jr., 5325
Ayres, Brown, 4671

B

Babcock, Barbara Allen, 777
Babcock, Caroline Lexow, 1351, 1371, 2268, 2325, 2462, 2470
Bailey, Ann A., 4197
Baker, Elizabeth Faulkner, 898, 1357
Baker, Jayne, 2970
Baldwin, J.W., 899
Ball, Millie, 4742
Bang, Mrs. Charles, 211
Bangert, Lenora K., 4210
Banning, Margaret Culkin, 607, 1188, 1351, 1371
Banowsky, Bill, 3719, 5648
Barbour, W. Warren, 1351, 1371
Barclay, Robert W., 900-904
Barham, Mack E., 692
Barnes, Fred, 4279
Barney, Nora Stanton, 215, 2403, 2474, 5004, 5067
Bassette, Linna E., 943, 1371
Battle, George Gordon, 44, 221, 2273, 5028
Bayh, Birch, 693-94, 905, 962, 5526
Bayley, Patricia A., 4587
Beard, Charles A., 435
Beard, Mary R., 435
Beasley, Maurine, 5480
Beck, James L., 4295
Beck, Joan, 4375, 4420

Organization Index

[Organization addresses are impossible to provide with complete
accuracy due to both their somewhat rapid birth and demise and
their peripatetic nature. This list is at least a beginning.

The organizations are listed alphabetically by title the way
they appear in the actual citation. Local chapters of a
national group are listed under that group's national heading
(e.g., the League of Women Voters of Washington will be found
under the League).

The addresses are as up-to-date as it was possible to find.
When there was a choice of addresses, the one most seemingly
connected with an office or P.O. Box number was chosen; the
citation to an officer of the group usually indicates the home
address of that person, although the sources often do not make
that clear.

Differences between the locations of the organizations as
listed in the index and the newsletters may be accounted for
by the facts that the address may have changed or the only
listing for the group is the home address of an officer.

NOW chapters are often very difficult to track down because
there are so many local chapters even within the same city.
The title given here is taken from the publication itself and
offers another way of getting to their newsletters, which were
listed by title in the newsletter section.

In the list below, the numbers after each organization refer
to item numbers in the Bibliography.]

AAUW. See American Association of University Women

AFL-CIO (815 16th St., N.W., Washington, D.C. 20006), 133, 352,
864-66; magazine, 997, 1177, 1209, 1320

Albuquerque Women's Center (University of New Mexico, 1824 Las Lomas,
N.E., N.M. 87106), 3182-84

Alliance Link (Equal Rights Alliance, 2140 N. Magnolia Ave., Chicago,
Ill. 60614; 5256 Fairmont Ave., Downers Grove, Ill. 60515), 3236-38

Alliance of Media Women (12310 Chandler Blvd., Suite 8, North Hollywood,
Ca. 91607; Inter-Studio Feminist Alliance, Box 2268, Hollywood, Ca.
90028), 3282-83

American Association of University Women (2401 Virginia Ave., N.W.,
   Washington, D.C. 20037), 493-501, 858, 943, 1371; magazine, 1052,
   1381, 1443, 1456, 1475-76, 1496; newspaper, 917, 974, 983, 1091, 1093,
   1115-16, 1185, 1259, 1277, 1290, 1303, 1338-39, 1341, 1350a, 1361,
   1370, 1384, 1449, 1451, 1523; 3224-25

   AAUW, California Division (Marilyn Poluzzi, Pres., 3229 S. Bonita St.,
      Spring Valley 92007), 496; newsletter, 2758-60

   AAUW, Illinois Division (Mary Carlson, Pres., 207 East School La,
      Prospect Hgts. 60070), 497

   AAUW, North Carolina Division (Gloria Blanton, Pres., 1322 Dogwood La,
      Raleigh 27607), 498

   AAUW, North Dakota Division (Lila Nelson, Pres., 1314 Cherry St.,
      Grand Forks 58201), 499

   AAUW, Texas Division (Polly Orcutt, Pres., 10015 Lakedale Dr., Dallas
      75218), 500

   AAUW, Utah Division (Helen Camp, Pres., 4187 Shanna St., Salt Lake
      City 84117), 501

American Bar Association (1155 E. 60th St., Chicago, Ill. 60637), 137,
   747

American Business Women's Association (9100 Ward Parkway, Kansas City,
   Mo. 64114), 969, 1001, 1004, 1044, 1533, 1535

American Civil Liberties Union, Women's Rights Project (22 E. 40th St.,
   New York, N.Y. 10016), 502-508; newsletter, 2684, 2963

American Federation of Labor (815 16th St., N.W., Washington, D.C.
   20006), 21, 867, 875-87. See AFL-CIO.

American Federation of State, County and Municipal Employees (1155
   15th St., N.W., Washington, D.C. 20005), 509

American Home Economics Association (2010 Massachusetts Ave., N.W.,
   Washington, D.C. 20036), 869, 900-904, 1003, 1019, 1087, 1243, 1549

American Library Association, Social Responsibilities Round Table,
   Task Force on Women (50 E. Huron St., Chicago, Ill. 60611), 2746-47

Anchorage Women's Liberation (7801 Peck Ave., Alaska 99504), 3534-47

Arizona Legislative Council (324 State Capitol, Phoenix 85007), 396

Arkansas Governor's Commission on the Status of Women (Rm. 08, State
   Capitol, Little Rock 72201), 121

Arkansas Legislative Council, Committee on Judiciary (Rm. 315, State
   Capitol, Little Rock 72201), 397

Association of American Colleges, Project on the Status and Education of
   Women (1818 R St., N.W., Washington, D.C. 20009), 2804

Tacoma NOW (Janice Stonestreet, Pres., 5903 Lagoon La. N.W., Gig
   Harbor, Wash. 98335), 3499-500

Temple Hills NOW (Box 31296, Md. 20031), 3424

Thurston County NOW (Carroll B. Dick, Pres., 406 Stillwell, Olympia,
   Wash. 98506), 3408-409

Tippecanoe NOW (Rona Ginsburg, Pres., 112 Knox Dr., West Lafayette,
   Ind. 47906), 3877

Tucson NOW (Box 4770, Ariz. 85715), 3899-914

Twin Cities NOW (Box 1348, Minnetonka, Minn. 55434), 3915

Union County NOW (Gloria Deodata, Pres., 521 Boulevard, Westfield,
   N.J. 07090), 3916-23

Ventura NOW (Box 3017, Ca.93003), 3931

Virginia Beach NOW (Betsy L. Bretz, Pres., 4325 Cambria Circle, Va.
   23455), 3682-88

Virginia NOW (Barbara Leerskov, State Coor., 39 Nash St., Herndon
   22070), 603-604

Washington, D.C. NOW (1424 16th St., N.W., Suite 104, 20036),
   3934-44

Western Connecticut NOW (Barbara Levine, Pres., 204 Ridgeview Ave.,
   Fairfield 06430), 3957-64

Willamette Valley NOW (Carolyn Hutton, Pres., 920 Tamarak, N.E.,
   Salem, Ore. 97303), 3333-34

Witchita NOW (Liz Clark, Contact, 5101 E. 3rd St., Kan. 67208),
   3979-82

National Trade Union League of America (Defunct), 619

National Woman's Party (144 Constitution Ave., N.E., Washington, D.C.
   20002), 256, 605-18; Equal Rights, 1558-2683

National Women's Commission of the C.P.U.S.A. (Communist Party, U.S.A.,
   23 W. 26th St., New York, N.Y. 10010), 648

National Women's Political Caucus (1921 Pennsylvania Ave., Wash. D.C.
   20006), 3300-307

   Alameda County (Northern California) WPC (Sybil Galazin, Coor., 1470
      Creekside Dr., Walnut Creek 94598), 3308-10

   Arizona WPC (Joyce Hunter, Chair, 5519 N. Marion Way, Phoenix
      85018), 2791-99

Seattle Women's Liberation (YWCA, 3rd and Seneca, Wash. 98101),   2762

Slippery Rock Women's Liberation (Re: The Hand That Rocks the Rock,
   c/o Ronny Howard, Dept. of English, Slippery Rock State College,
   Slippery Rock, Pa. 16057),   3116-18

Society of American Archivists, Women's Caucus (National Archives and
   Records, Pennsylvania Ave. at 8th St., N.W., Washington, D.C.
   20408),   3281

South Carolina Coalition for the Equal Rights Amendment (311 Springlake
   Rd., Columbia 29206),   421, 642-47

South Carolina Office of the Attorney General (300 Wade Hampton State
   Office Bldg., Columbia 29201),   421

Stop ERA (Box 618, Alton, Ill. 62002),   649; state chapters, 650-51

Storrs Women's Center (Box 18, Conn. 06268),   4085-86

Susan B. Anthony Memorial, Inc.,   265

Tennessee Commission on the Status of Women (921 Andrew Jackson Bldg.,
   Nashville 37219),   422

Texans for Equal Rights Amendment (603 W. 13th St., No. 203, Austin
   78701),   653

Texas Stop ERA,   651. See Stop ERA; Women Who Want to Be Women

Texas Subcommittee on H.C.R. 57 of House Committee on Constitutional
   Revision (State Capitol, Austin 78711),   423

Twin Cities Female Liberation (2953 Bloomington Ave. South,
   Minneapolis, Minn. 55407) 3083

Union W.A.G.E. (2137 Oregon St., Berkeley, Ca.94705),   993-95,
   1329-31, 1342, 1401, 1478

Unitarian Universalist Women's Federation (25 Beacon St., Boston, Mass.
   02108),   1043, 1053, 1065, 2838-43

United Auto Workers--CIO, Women's Dept. (8000 E. Jefferson, Detroit,
   Mich. 48214),   207, 329

United Church of Christ, Task Force on Women in Church and Society
   (297 Park Ave., S., New York, N.Y. 10010),   144

United Methodist ERA Support Project (100 Maryland Ave., N.E.,
   Washington, D.C. 20002),   655-56. See Board of Church and Society;
   Church and Society Task Force

United Methodist Women's Caucus (2121 N. Sheridan Rd., Evanston, Ill.
   60201),   4166

United Presbyterian Church of U.S.A., Council on Women and the Church
(475 Riverside Dr., New York, N.Y. 10027), 1489; newsletter 2989

United Sisters (Box 5984, Tampa, Fla. 33675), 3924-27

United Sisters (Re: Puce Mongoose, Box 41, Garwood, N.J. 07027),
3636

[Some United States agencies are listed with the rest of their title,
e.g., President's Commission on the Status of Women, President's Task
Force on Women's Rights and Responsibilities, Citizens' Advisory
Council on the Status of Women, Women's Bureau, Equal Employment
Opportunity Commission.]

United States Commission on Civil Rights, Women's Rights Program Unit
(1121 Vermont Ave., N.W., Washington, D.C. 20425), 383-84

United States Department of Labor (Washington, D.C. 20210), 142, 4053.
See Women's Bureau

United States Department of Justice (10th and Pennsylvania Ave., N.W.,
Rm. 1614, Washington, D.C. 20530), 382

United States National Women's Agenda (Women's Action Alliance
Information Center, 370 Lexington Ave., New York, N.Y. 10017), 1493

University of New Mexico Law Students (Albuquerque 87106), 624

University of Virginia, Continuing Education for Women (4210 Roberts
Rd., Fairfax 22030), 3928

Urban Research Corporation (5464 S. Shore Dr., Chicago, Ill. 60615),
3823-51

Utah Governor's Committee on the Status of Women (210 State Capitol,
Salt Lake City 84114), 424

Utah Office of Legislative Research (326 State Capitol, Salt Lake City
84114), 425

Vermont Legislative Council (State House, Montpelier 05602), 426

Vocational Center for Women. See Nassau County Dept. of General
Services

Washington Forum (915 19th St., N.W., Washington, D.C. 20006), 666

Washington Legislative Council, Judiciary Committee (Rm. 147 North,
State Capitol, Madison 53702), 427

Waterbury Women's Center (25 Grand St., Conn. 06702), 3533

Wayne County CIO Council (2310 Cass St., Detroit, Mich. 48201), 201

Wisconsin Equal Rights Coalition (713 E. Johnson St., Madison 53703),
657-59

Young Americans for Freedom (Woodland Rd., Sterling, Va. 22170), 1309, 1404

YWCA News of Atlanta (Midtown Atlanta YWCA, 45 11th St., N.E., Georgia 30309), 4168-68a

YWCA Women's Center (395 Main St., Orange, N.J. 07052), 3098-99

Zero Population Growth (1346 Connecticut Ave., N.W., Washington, D.C. 20036), 4169